The Fall
of Hong Kong

The Fall of Hong Kong

China's Triumph
and Britain's Betrayal

MARK ROBERTI

John Wiley & Sons, Inc.

New York · Chichester · Brisbane · Toronto · Singapore

Copyright © 1994 by Mark Roberti
Published by John Wiley & Sons, Inc.

Library of Congress Cataloging-in-Publication Data:

Roberti, Mark. 1961–
    The fall of Hong Kong : China's triumph and Britain's betrayal /
Mark Roberti.
        p.   cm.
    Includes index.
    ISBN 0-471-02621-2
    1. Hong Kong—Politics and government.   2. Great Britain—Foreign
relations—China.   3. China—Foreign relations—Great Britain.
I.   Title.
DS796.H757R628   1994
951.2505—dc20   94-9891

Printed in the United States of America

10 9 8 7 6 5 4 3 2 1

For my mother and father

Acknowledgments

T HERE ARE several people without whom I would never have been able to write this book. I am forever indebted to my wife Lydia, who supported me emotionally and financially during the two years it took to complete the manuscript; to my agent Diane Cleaver, who helped to get the project off the ground and then saw it through to completion; and to my friend and mentor Sam Toperoff, who read the manuscript at a critical juncture and offered invaluable suggestions for improving it.

I am especially grateful to Winnie Lee, who provided the invaluable and difficult service of translating documents and articles from Chinese to English; to Hana Lane, my editor, who made important suggestions and helped to get the manuscript ready for publication; to Maria denBoer, who copy edited the manuscript with intelligence and care; to Julia Markus, who got the whole thing started by introducing me to Diane Cleaver and who encouraged me throughout the period I worked on the book; to John Hull, who read numerous drafts of the manuscript and was extraordinarily generous with his ideas, support, and brandy; and to Seymour Kurtz, whose contribution was not in vain.

An investigative project like this would never be possible if the researcher did not have access to secondary source material. I would especially like to thank Jan Bradley and Roger Tam at the *Far Eastern Economic Review* library; Judy Young and her amiable staff at the *South China Morning Post* library; and the staffs at the American Library and the Hong Kong University Library.

I am indebted to all of the daily newspaper journalists who covered the situation in Hong Kong under very difficult circumstances. Their work provided the foundation on which I was able to build. I am particularly grateful to journalists Chris Yeung, Stanley Leung, Willy Lam, and Cheng Takshing, who covered firsthand many of the events I wrote about and shared their insights.

I would also like to thank the following individuals in Hong Kong for their help and support: Steve and Irene Knipp, Tom Boesberg, Thomas

Chan, Albert Chen, Amitabha Chowdhury, Nihal Jayawichrama, Kevin Lau, Lau Siu-kai, Richard Margolis, Margaret Ng, Shui Sin-por, John Walden, B.Y. Wong, Kenneth Wong, and Patrick Wong.

I am grateful to Ken Vance and the staff at Southwell House, who put me up for a month while I conducted my research in London. I would like to thank the following people in London: Greg and Margaret Ketteridge, whose warm friendship made the trip enjoyable as well as productive; historian Peter Hennessy, who shared his infinite knowledge of Whitehall with me; members of the Omelco Office; John Yaxley and the staff at the Hong Kong Government Office, who helped me dig up whatever information I needed; and Robert Archer and Steve Tsang.

My deepest thanks go to all of those who, despite the sensitive nature of the subject matter and the rules prohibiting disclosure, gave their cooperation, time, and support to this project. You know who you are.

Contents

Preface

A T MIDNIGHT on June 30, 1997, British officials will pull down the
Union Jack from the flagpole outside Government House for the last
time. Cadres from Beijing will run up the Chinese five-starred red flag. With
that simple act, Britain will erase a legacy of injustice—and create a new one.
For London is not just handing back the tiny outcropping of land on the
South China Coast that she took during the last century. She is also handing
over her six million Chinese subjects living there.

Britain is stripping the people of Hong Kong of the protection of British
democracy and forcing them to live under a communist dictatorship. Britain
and China have told them they will be allowed to maintain their way of life,
capitalist economy, and legal system for fifty years after 1997. The two
governments have promised them that they will manage their own affairs,
enjoy a high degree of autonomy, and exercise the same rights and freedoms
they had under British rule.

But these promises already seem hollow. Beijing has ensured that it will
control every facet of Hong Kong's affairs through a hand-picked governor. It
will be able to interfere in court cases because China's rubber stamp
legislature—not local judges—will interpret the post-1997 constitution. The
legislature will be only partially elected and will have little power to check
abuses by the executive branch of government. Moreover, the people of
Hong Kong do not know who will be running China in 1997, what his
policies will be, if he will uphold the right of private ownership in Hong
Kong, and whether he will respect human rights and the rule of law or will
resort to the gun to implement his will. They await the transfer of sovereignty in dread.

Britain did not want to return the last jewel in her imperial crown, but
was forced to sign away her last important colony because of an accident of
history. In the mid-1800s, she fought two wars with China. Opium was the
excuse, but trade was the real issue. At the time, China considered herself to
be superior to all nations. She refused to establish relations with any European nation and restricted trade to the southern port of Guangzhou (Canton). British merchants deemed it their god-given right to do business in

China. They wanted the whole country opened to trade and encouraged London to use the Royal Navy to do it.

Despite the Celestial Emperor's delusions of superiority, China was an empire in decline. The mandarin bureaucracy had become bloated, inefficient, and corrupt. Scientific advancement had fallen behind the West and most of the population lived in appalling poverty. Britain, on the other hand, was a rising power. Her armed frigates easily defeated China's sluggish junks, and she forced Beijing to sign two humiliating treaties under which Hong Kong Island and the tip of the Kowloon Peninsula across the harbor were ceded to Britain "in perpetuity."

China's defeat showed how weak and vulnerable she really was. In 1895, Japan routed China in the first Sino-Japanese war and grabbed the Liaotung Peninsula, which controlled the strategic opening to Beijing. That sent the European powers scrambling for China's territory: Germany seized Kiaochow across from the Korean Peninsula; Russia occupied Lushun in northern China and renamed it Port Arthur; and France grabbed Kwangchow Wan, 210 miles southwest of Hong Kong. Officials in the British colony feared that the French might also try to seize Hong Kong. Moreover, if the Chinese ever summoned the courage to take back the ceded territories by force, they controlled both entrances to Hong Kong Harbor and could shell the heart of the city from their own territory. London was encouraged to secure the land between the Kowloon hills and the Shenzhen River to provide some protection.

The decrepit Manchu dynasty was powerless to stop the Europeans from taking what they wanted, but tried to avoid losing land permanently. It agreed to lease to Britain the area south of the Shenzhen River and 235 islands scattered off the coast for ninety-nine years. It must have seemed like virtual annexation to the British negotiators who accepted the deal, but in leasing the New Territories, as the new land was called, they destroyed Hong Kong's territorial integrity and assured that China would one day recover the whole colony.

Hong Kong became a borrowed land living on borrowed time. No one seemed to mind as long as 1997 was far in the future. After World War II, businesspeople invested heavily in plants and machinery, and the colony's economy took off. By the late 1970s, Hong Kong had been transformed from a barren rock into a major commercial center and economic powerhouse. Though just 412 square miles—about one-third the size of Rhode Island—it exported more toys, watches, and radios than any country in the world. It was the second largest exporter of clothing and ranked twenty-first in world trade (by 1993, it would be tenth). But the New Territories accounted for over ninety percent of Hong Kong's land area. Much of its manufacturing, a third of its population, and all of its local water supply was situated there. The colony could not survive without it.

In 1978, it became clear to the governor of Hong Kong that something had to be done to resolve the question of Hong Kong's future or business confidence would gradually erode as 1997 grew closer. Britain wanted to maintain control of her colony, and in September 1982, Prime Minister Margaret Thatcher went to Beijing to initiate negotiations with that aim. Beijing refused to accept any form of British presence in Hong Kong after 1997. China experts in the British Foreign Office wanted to negotiate a deal and be done with Hong Kong, but an adviser to the governor named S.Y. Chung, and his colleagues in Hong Kong's Executive Council, pushed the diplomats relentlessly to get the best agreement for the colony, one that would guarantee that local residents could continue to live as they always had.

Under the Joint Declaration, an agreement signed by the British and Chinese in 1984, Britain agreed to return Hong Kong to China, and China spelled out the liberal promises of freedom and autonomy. The accord was widely hailed the world over as a shining example of how two countries can work out their differences peacefully. The Hong Kong people, however, were given a stark choice: to be returned to China under an internationally binding agreement with liberal provisions—which Britain conceded it could not enforce—or to be returned without any guarantees.

They accepted the agreement reluctantly. Many doubted China's willingness to stick to the terms. Britain encouraged the people of Hong Kong to believe that they would run their own government after 1997, which would protect them from interference and abuses by Beijing. But when the Hong Kong government took steps to replace the colonial system (under which the governor was a virtual dictator) with a more democratic system, Beijing opposed the changes. It said it would determine the future political structure of Hong Kong through a hand-picked committee codifying the terms of the Joint Declaration into the Basic Law, a mini-constitution under which the colony would exist after 1997.

The Basic Law Drafting Committee was made up of Hong Kong and mainland drafters. The Hong Kong contingent was stacked with conservative businesspeople who were opposed to democratic reforms. They arrogantly asserted that they had made Hong Kong successful and therefore should be allowed to run the colony after 1997. Beijing, eager to ensure its control over Hong Kong and to keep the tycoons from emigrating, agreed.

The "unholy alliance" of capitalists and Communists would have had its way without fuss had it not been for one man: Martin Lee, a British-educated lawyer who was appointed to the Basic Law Drafting Committee. Lee felt that an independent judiciary and an elected government that could stand up to meddling by Beijing was vital for Hong Kong's future. He took to the streets and enlisted the support of butchers and bus drivers, seamstresses and students to force two faraway governments to stick to their word.

In the end, Britain's resolve to do right by her colony wavered, and Lee and his followers did not have enough leverage to influence Beijing. When the Basic Law was promulgated in April 1990, it called for only a third of the legislators to be elected in 1997 and only half by 2003. Many people now fear Hong Kong will never have a democratic government or guaranteed human rights. They are leaving in record numbers to live in freedom elsewhere.

I ARRIVED IN Hong Kong in 1984, eager to study Asia. As a journalist for *The Executive*, a regional business magazine, I watched the confidence created by the Joint Declaration slowly erode as China reneged on her promises and Britain caved in to maintain cordial relations with Beijing. In the summer of 1987, while covering the fierce debate over democratic elections for *Asiaweek* (a weekly news magazine owned by Time Inc.) I first considered writing a book on the secret history of the transfer of Hong Kong's sovereignty. There were many questions central to the debate and critical to Hong Kong's future that could not be answered by someone working with a weekly deadline. What did China mean when she said in the Joint Declaration that the Hong Kong legislature would be "constituted by elections" and that the executive would be "accountable" to it? Why weren't these terms spelled out? What secret agreements, if any, did Britain make about democracy? No one knew. The negotiations between Britain and China were strictly confidential. Even the British Parliament was not privy to the details of the talks. Under Britain's Official Secrets Act, records are not released for at least thirty years.

The drafting of the Basic Law was conducted more openly than the Sino-British negotiations. Reporters were briefed on the progress of each meeting. But the sessions were conducted behind closed doors, and all members agreed not to discuss the positions of individual drafters, which, in the case of the mainland members, meant the Chinese government.

Academics trying to analyze what happened and why had to guess at what went on behind the scenes. But how the political and economic framework was constructed was as important as what it was made of: If China negotiated the Joint Declaration and the Basic Law openly, democratically, and with the best interests of Hong Kong at heart, people would have faith in them and make them work; if Beijing bullied Britain and Hong Kong, gave concessions reluctantly, and reinterpreted the provisions in a way that served its own interests, people would consider them worthless scraps of paper, no matter what they contained. Therefore, it was important to get behind the official statements, the disinformation, and the contradictory press reports to uncover the real story of Hong Kong's transition to Chinese rule.

I took as my starting point articles published in the two daily English newspapers in Hong Kong (the *South China Morning Post* and the *Hong Kong Standard*), and then referred extensively to the two regional weekly news magazines (the *Far Eastern Economic Review* and *Asiaweek*) and other local magazines (e.g., *Hong Kong, Inc.*). Background information on the major players, dates, and economic data contained in this book come primarily from these sources. Based on the published reports, I drew up a list of over 200 people to interview: all of the British, Hong Kong, and Chinese officials involved with the Sino-British negotiations; all of the Hong Kong Basic Law drafters; foreign diplomats; pro-China journalists and business people; members of Parliament; and members of Hong Kong's Executive and Legislative Councils.

Penetrating the veil of secrecy surrounding the negotiations was a daunting task. All of those on the British side, including the Executive Councilors in Hong Kong, signed an oath of secrecy. Basic Law drafters agreed not to reveal the positions of their colleagues during the closed-door meetings. Anyone who did so could be the target of reprisals by the Chinese government after 1997. The only way to shed light on the subject was to conduct the interviews "on background"—that is, use the information, but not identify the source.

I worked full time for more than two years, interviewing 142 people in Hong Kong, London, and Beijing. I saw almost all of the major players, including former British Foreign Secretary Geoffrey Howe and Shao Tianren, a legal adviser to the Chinese Foreign Ministry, both of whom dealt with Hong Kong at the highest level. About a third of my sources were interviewed more than once and some as many as eight times. I would like to publish a list of the people interviewed, but many requested that their name not be connected with the book in any way. It would be misleading to publish a partial list.

There has been a great deal of misinformation and disinformation about the exchange of sovereignty over Hong Kong. Press reports attributed to anonymous sources that could not be confirmed have not been used. In most cases where private conversations are quoted, two or more people present were interviewed and only the corroborated portions used. Where exact words could not be recalled, quotes have been omitted. Thoughts, beliefs, and attitudes attributed to the participants were either told to me directly by the person involved, or related by someone close to that person.

In addition to the interviews, I filed over a hundred Freedom of Information Act requests with the United States government. The State Department was briefed by the British and Chinese governments during Hong Kong's transition to Chinese rule. All of the documents obtained under the act, as well as those passed to me by sources in the Hong Kong government and on the Basic Law Drafting Committee, have been donated to the Hoover Institution at Stanford University and will be made available to other researchers.

What emerged from my research was not just startling information that disproves some of the most commonly believed information about the handover (such as that Mrs. Thatcher went to Beijing in 1982 and insisted the nineteenth-century treaties were valid), but a human drama. This book is the story of a handful of people who fought doggedly for Hong Kong's interests: of S.Y. Chung and the Executive Councilors battling Foreign Office diplomats who put Britain's interests ahead of those of her colony; of Martin Lee and his supporters campaigning tirelessly to convince Britain and China to give Hong Kong the vote at the risk of their careers and their future in the colony.

This book is not a history of Hong Kong. It does not deal with its colonial beginnings or its development into an economic powerhouse. Other books have done that well. This book is the story of a diplomatic takeover. It covers the first half of the transition back to Chinese rule from 1978—when the Hong Kong and British governments first confronted the problem of the expiration of the New Territories lease—to 1990—when China promulgated the Basic Law for Hong Kong. During this critical period, the legal, constitutional, and economic framework for post-1997 Hong Kong was completed. For better or worse, Hong Kong will have to live with this charter until 2047.

A Note about Style

I have used the pinyin version of mainland Chinese names and places, except in historical contexts, where the reader will be more familiar with the Wade Giles rendition. It may seem awkward to refer to Beijing and Guangzhou in the nineteenth century instead of Peking and Canton. But the pinyin spellings have been accepted by most newspapers as the standard.

I have used English given names whenever possible for Hong Kong Chinese. These will be easier to remember for English readers unfamiliar with the people in this book. Chinese names consist of a surname followed by two characters that make one given name. For example: Chung Sze-yuen. In many cases Hong Kong Chinese without given English names use the initials of their given Chinese name. Thus, Chung Sze-yuen is known as S.Y. Chung. I have used this rendition for those who have adopted it themselves. For all other Chinese I have adopted a uniform style. Hong Kong given names are hyphenated, while mainland Chinese names are not. Not all people write their names this way, but it is a useful practice to avoid confusion.

All figures are in U.S. dollars unless otherwise stated.

PART ONE

PART ONE

Chapter 1

An Ingenious Proposal

I N JANUARY 1978, as the United States Senate was deliberating on the Panama Canal treaty, a Eurasian lawyer named T.S. Lo was considering the future of another disputed piece of territory on the other side of the world: Hong Kong. Lo was a Legislative Councilor and a rising political star in the colony. He was worried about Britain's lease on the large tract of land north of the Kowloon hills, which was due to expire in 1997. If the question were not settled, all of Hong Kong would have to be handed back to China at that time.

Lo had begun considering the lease question in 1977 after he was appointed by the governor to the Advisory Committee on Diversification, a sixteen-member body set up to suggest ways of reducing Hong Kong's dependency on textiles, cheap electronics, and plastic products that accounted for more than two-thirds of exports. Members of the committee quickly realized that if the government were to make long-range plans for economic diversification, the issue of the New Territories lease would have to be resolved. Commercial leases issued by the Hong Kong government were due to expire three days before the termination of the New Territories lease. The length of new commercial leases would shorten as the deadline neared; businesspeople would be unable to recoup their investments before their leases expired. Confidence in Hong Kong would deteriorate.

Lo took it upon himself to find a solution. Though he had no experience in dealing with the Chinese government, he was a shrewd politician, and he very much wanted the British to stay in Hong Kong. His family was one of the oldest and most influential in the colony. Its fortune, like the fortunes of Hong Kong, depended on the British.

When the Royal Navy had landed in Hong Kong in 1841, the island had only a few fishing villages with a total population of a few thousand. The arrival of British merchants attracted Chinese from Guangdong (Canton), mostly men who could get jobs loading and unloading ships, working as personal servants, or doing other menial jobs. The British despised the Chinese, who lived in flimsy sheds and squatter huts, seemed oblivious to the idea of personal hygiene, often visited opium dens, and sometimes resorted to stealing to provide for their families back in their villages. (Perhaps most offensive of all, even the lowest among them was convinced that he was superior to any European.) The British carried firearms for protection and hired guards to protect their goods. Eventually, Indians were brought in to serve as police.

The Chinese equally despised the British, whose habits were strange, who were snobbish and aloof, and who rarely bothered to learn Chinese. In 1857, the most respected baker in the colony tried to kill the principal British residents by putting arsenic in their bread. (He was unsuccessful because he used too much, causing them to vomit.) The Chinese did not understand the Europeans and this gave rise to wild stories, which were widely believed. As late as 1921, there was a rumor that the British planned to build a bridge across the harbor resting on ninety-nine piers, and that a Chinese child would be sacrificed at the base of each one. The census that year recorded an abnormally low number of children, reportedly because Chinese mothers hid their children from the census takers.

As the colony developed, relations did not improve. The Chinese were almost completely excluded from social and political institutions in those early years. In 1918, the government passed a law that effectively barred Chinese from living on the Peak, an area favored by the British because the temperature was a few degrees lower and the view of the harbor was spectacular. It remained in effect until World War II. By this time, however, the vast majority of the population was Chinese, and they were no longer just coolies. They controlled most of the major companies and accounted for over ninety percent of the government's revenue. Wealthy Chinese wanted representation in the Legislative Council, the colony's largely advisory legislature, so they would be consulted on government policies that affected their lives and businesses.

As in other colonies, the British-appointed governor was the queen's representative, the head of the civil service, the president of the legislature, and the commander-in-chief of the British armed forces. He ruled by the Letters Patent and Royal Instructions and enjoyed powers, according to one academic, that "may be compared to those once possessed by a King of England before the coming of democracy." The governor, however, had to court the local elite to ensure the cooperation of the rest of the population. In the early days of the settlement, the Legislative Council was comprised of a handful of *taipans*, the heads of big British companies in the colony. In 1880, the first Chinese was appointed to the Council, and by 1929, there were three Chinese out of the eight non-civil servant, or "unofficial," members on it. They acted as go-betweens with the Chinese population, the way the compradors did between the British bosses and Chinese workers in private companies.

Chinese were also appointed to the Executive Council, which was sometimes described as Hong Kong's cabinet. In reality, it had no administrative functions. It simply advised the governor on all administrative decisions, but he could ignore their advice. Having Chinese on the Council, however, gave the administration insight into how the Chinese population would react to new policies and provided the colonial government some legitimacy by giving locals, however unrepresentative, a say in decision making.

The British felt most comfortable with Chinese who spoke English and understood English customs. They relied mainly on graduates from missionary schools to work as interpreters, assistants, and compradors. The Central School—later renamed Queen's College—was founded in 1862 to turn out Anglicized Chinese. Both British and Chinese youngsters attended, and they formed friendships (and sometimes intermarried, though it was frowned upon by both groups), which served them well as adults. Those Chinese who attended were in the best position to profit from the alliance with the British, and they created a Cantonese aristocracy. The founders of three of the most prominent and influential Chinese families in the colony were alumni of the school: Lee Hysan, Robert Ho Tung, and T.S. Lo's grandfather, Lo Cheung-shiu.

Lo Cheung-shui established a close friendship with the Ho Tung family. He worked as an assistant comprador with Robert Ho Tung's brother at Jardine Matheson and married one of his nieces. Lo Cheung-shui had four sons, the eldest of which was M.K. Lo, T.S. Lo's father. He was born in Hong Kong in 1893 and was sent to England to study when he was thirteen. He reportedly received the highest mark in England on his solicitor's exam and was among the first Chinese from Hong Kong to qualify as a lawyer in England. After graduation, he returned to Hong Kong and set up his own law firm. That year, he married Robert Ho Tung's eldest daughter. Hong Kong's governor, Sir Henry May, attended the ceremony.

M.K. Lo was appointed to the Legislative Council in 1935. One of the few Chinese willing to adopt a confrontational role in public, he was said to have questioned government policy more often than the rest of the Council combined. He fought against discrimination, opened new opportunities for Chinese (he persuaded the government to allow them to be nurses in public hospitals), and campaigned against the censorship of Chinese newspapers that had been imposed in 1925 after the Nationalists organized a boycott of British goods and instigated labor strikes in Hong Kong. He was eventually appointed to the Executive Council and became its most influential non-civil servant member.

The Japanese attacked Hong Kong on the same day that they bombed Pearl Harbor. The British surrendered on Christmas day, 1941, and the new imperialists wanted to use M.K. Lo to give credibility to their administration. He was kept in solitary confinement until he agreed to join the Japanese Imperial Army Legislature. When he did attend its meetings, he refused to speak as a protest. After the war, he retained his seat on the Legislative Council.

Upon his return to power, the British governor wanted to introduce a democratically elected municipal council to boost Britain's reputation, which had suffered serious damage in Asia during the war. M.K. Lo was instrumental in blocking the proposal by recommending limited franchise elections to the Legislative Council to protect his influential position and those of his colleagues. (In the end, meaningful reform was abandoned because of the civil war in China.)

M.K. Lo was knighted for his contribution to Hong Kong in 1948 and retired from the Executive and Legislative Councils in 1958 at the age of 66. He died of a heart attack a year later, a day after attending a reception for Prince Philip.

T.S. Lo was over six feet tall and close to 200 pounds. His imposing physique, family background, and reputation for ruthlessly cutting down opponents intimidated many people. He was born in Hong Kong in 1935, the youngest of M.K. Lo's six children. His only brother and his oldest sister died in childhood. After the Japanese invaded Hong Kong, T.S. was sent to Guangzhou to study at a prestigious school. A month later he contracted malaria and had to return to Hong Kong. During the four years of Japanese occupation, he was taught at home by a private tutor, who, he says, imbued him with a love for and understanding of Chinese culture. After the war, while tens of thousands of refugees lived in appalling poverty, Lo lived in splendor on his family's estate on the south side of Hong Kong Island (site of the present-day American Club). He was a big boy, very athletic, and crazy about tennis. He earned a three-inch scar over his right eye when, in his haste to get to the court one day, he banged his head on a pole.

He was sent to Britain and attended a British preparatory school before studying law at Oxford. After graduation in 1960, he returned to Hong Kong and began practicing law. He married a European woman in 1965, divorced twice, and married a third time in 1979, which raised some eyebrows in conservative Hong Kong. He was a member of the Hong Kong Country Club, the Royal Yacht Club, and the Jockey Club and like his father before him, served on the board of several major companies. He was awarded the Order of the British Empire in 1976.

His huge size made him slow around the tennis court, so he threw himself into something more intellectual: bridge. He was a member of the winning pair at the Far East Bridge Championships in 1975. He was extremely quick witted, could spot an opponent's weakness, and was always several moves ahead of everyone else. It was the same in politics. Governor MacLehose appointed him to the Legislative Council in 1974 at the age of 39. T.S. felt a great deal of pressure to live up to the achievements and larger-than-life reputation of his father. He was blatantly ambitious, extraordinarily arrogant, and strutted with the natural confidence of someone born to the aristocracy. He did not care about being popular and despised his colleagues who did. He was outspoken like his father and was said to be the one unofficial who could put the fear of God into senior civil servants. He would be promoted to the Executive Council in 1980.

Lo was eager to see the British remain in Hong Kong after 1997. He knew it would be tricky. The Chinese saw the Opium Wars as one of the darkest periods in China's history, and being forced to give up Hong Kong, part of the sovereign territory, was an unprecedented disgrace. The period of foreign domination that followed was still fresh in the minds of older Chinese. Any request by Britain to renew the lease of the New Territories, even for a substantial sum of money, would be seen as an attempt to perpetuate British colonial rule over Chinese territory and would be rejected.

After the Communist Revolution in 1949, China could have demanded Hong Kong back at any time. Militarily, the colony was indefensible, and it depended on the mainland for most of its food and water. Beijing did not demand the colony's return because it was useful to have a major trading port on the coast. China earned foreign exchange from Hong Kong and used it as a base for dealing with countries with which China had no formal relations.

The Communists' position, like that of the Nationalists before them, was that the three nineteenth-century treaties with Britain were signed under duress and were therefore invalid. Hong Kong was Chinese territory and must one day revert to Chinese rule. Lo reasoned that if the Chinese government considered the Second Convention of Beijing, under which Britain had leased the New Territories for ninety-nine years, to be invalid, then 1997 was a meaningless date in a meaningless agreement. The problem was Britain. When the lease expired, it would have no legitimate claim to the New Territories. Lo believed that if London could find some way to unilaterally extend its authority over the area beyond 1997, the deadline might disappear.

The issue was complicated. The treaties did not provide the legal foundation for the British government to rule the colony. Under British law, the monarch issued an Order in Council before Britain could formally take possession of a territory. The 1898 Order incorporating the New Territories into Hong Kong stated that the area would be part of the colony "within the limits and for the term described in the said convention." The queen could issue a new Order in Council extending British rule beyond 1997. A year after Britain obtained the New Territories, the Crown had issued an Order extending British jurisdiction over the Walled City of Kowloon. That was possible when China was weak and docile. If Britain tried it now, Beijing might object and accuse her of trying to extend her imperial rule beyond 1997. A diplomatic wrangle would damage confidence in Hong Kong and bring the question of its future into the open prematurely.

Lo believed something much more subtle was needed. He came up with a plan to test China's attitude towards continued British rule in Hong Kong after 1997. The idea was deceptively simple. When businesses in the New Territories applied to extend their commercial leases, the Hong Kong government would give twenty-five-year extensions backdated to 1970, then 1971, 1972, and 1973 to show the Chinese government the pattern. If China did not object to a lease being issued beyond 1997, the Hong Kong government would issue a lease expiring after the deadline to a company controlled by the Chinese government to make sure it understood what was happening. Further silence would be clear evidence that Beijing wanted to maintain the status quo indefinitely. The British Crown could then quietly issue a new Order in Council without risking the wrath of the communists.

In late 1977, Lo took his idea to London and approached a well-respected lawyer, who later became a High Court judge. He advised Lo that the scheme was legally faultless. Under British law at the time, a tenant (the British in Hong Kong) could grant a sublease beyond his own tenure, and the sub-tenant (businesspeople in the New Territories) would enjoy legal protection.

When he returned from London, Lo showed his plan to a number of businesspeople, including the *taipan* of Jardine Matheson. They suggested he present it quietly to the Hong Kong government. There was good reason to believe that it might work. China earned at least a third of its foreign exchange from Hong Kong. It could have taken Hong Kong back at any time and never did, even during the tumultuous years of the Cultural Revolution in the mid-1960s. All the evidence indicated that Beijing did not want, as colonial officials often put it, "to kill the goose that lays the golden eggs." But it would be forced to recover Hong Kong unless the lease question could be avoided.

On January 9, 1978, T.S. Lo wrote to Philip Haddon-Cave, Hong Kong's financial secretary and the chairman of the Advisory Committee on Diversification. In the letter, he outlined his proposal for solving the question of the New Territories lease and explained the benefits of approaching the problem indirectly. Haddon-Cave, a brilliant and dedicated public servant, liked the scheme and suggested that Lo take it up directly with the governor.

A meeting was arranged for later that month at Government House. The governor's official residence was built in the 1880s on a hill overlooking the harbor. A modest house (compared with the palaces built in India) in the neoclassical style, with pillars and arches all around, it was renovated by the Japanese, who joined the main house and the annex by building a tall, eaved tower between them. Lo drove through the huge iron gates, which bore the government crest, around the circular drive, and pulled up under the stately porte cochere. The building was quiet, like a hospital. He was led down a long corridor to the right of the foyer, which was lined with large oil paintings of important British historical figures, to the governor's study, a large room at the back of the house. The window behind the desk once offered a commanding view of the harbor. It was now partially obscured by the skyscrapers going up in Central District, the business and financial heart of Hong Kong.

It was unusual for the governor to discuss the question of the New Territories lease with a Legislative Councilor. The Hong Kong government had an unwritten policy of not raising the issue internally. It was absolutely never broached with Chinese officials, and when nosy foreign correspondents asked about it, their questions were sidestepped. But Lo had a proposal, which he felt was ingenious, and he wanted to share it. During the hour-long meeting, he explained his proposal in detail, stressing the importance of not raising the issue of the lease with the Chinese government directly. When he finished, Governor MacLehose said the plan had some merit. He agreed to pass it on to the Foreign Office in London for consideration.

UNKNOWN TO Lo, or anyone else in Hong Kong, MacLehose had raised the issue of the New Territories lease with officials in London the previous year, and the Foreign Office had begun to study the lease issue even before that. When Edward Heath was elected prime minister in 1970, he appointed an extremely capable Conservative Member of Parliament (MP) named Anthony Royle to the Foreign Office. Royle was given responsibility for Asia, including Hong Kong.* He had visited the colony for the first time in 1961 and was impressed with the Hong Kong government's massive housing program. He believed more needed to be done to educate people in the United Kingdom about what was going on in the colony. In 1964, he set up an all-

* Under the Westminster system, elected representatives are put in charge of ministries, while professional civil servants carry out their orders. Usually three or four MPs are posted to the Foreign Office.

party Parliamentary group for other MPs interested in keeping abreast of developments in Hong Kong.

Royle felt that it was time to look at the question of the New Territories lease and what would happen after its expiration. The issue was not urgent, but it would be irresponsible of the British government to wait until there was a crisis in Hong Kong. Royle got Heath's permission to set up a committee consisting of officials from the Foreign Office and members of the Cabinet to examine the problem. Should Britain raise it, or wait for China to do so? When was the right time to broach it? What would happen if the question were not settled? When would confidence begin to deteriorate?

The existence of the committee has never before been revealed, and its findings are still classified secret. The committee believed that China gained significant benefits from Hong Kong and might want to maintain the status quo indefinitely. The question of the New Territories lease would have to be raised. The timing would be crucial. Since the issue was not pressing, it was placed on the back burner.

At the same time, Britain's relations with China were improving. The upheaval of the Cultural Revolution gave way to more pragmatic policies in Beijing, and in October 1971, the People's Republic of China was voted into the United Nations. One of the first acts of its permanent representative, Huang Hua, was to request that Hong Kong and Macao be removed from the list of colonies that were to be granted independence. In a letter to the Special Committee on Colonialism, Huang said that the question of their future was "entirely within China's sovereign right," and they should not be included in the list of colonial territories to be granted independence. The Chinese government would settle the issue "in an appropriate way when conditions are ripe."

The statement prompted the British government to reassess at the highest level its relationship with Hong Kong. The colony was no longer considered to be important. Heath's government resolved that Britain would stay there as long as she could, but the days of colonialism were over. (The Colonial Office was gone, and the Commonwealth Office had been merged with the Foreign Office.) There were prospects for trade with China. London knew, too, that China would never permit Hong Kong to become independent. Prime Minister Heath's government did not object to China's proposal, although it meant that the people of Hong Kong would lose their right to self-determination. It decided that Hong Kong would be returned when Beijing asked for it, and an arrangement worked out at that time.

The Foreign Office saw China's statement as positive and recommended that every attempt be made to improve Sino-British relations. Contacts between Hong Kong and neighboring Guangdong increased throughout the

1970s. When Mao Zedong died in 1976, Governor MacLehose attended a memorial service in the colony. Two years later, relations between Hong Kong and the mainland were almost friendly. There was every indication that China wanted to see the status quo maintained indefinitely.

MACLEHOSE WAS was the one person in Hong Kong aware of the existence of Royle's committee. It is likely he also knew of the Heath government's decision in 1971. Still, he felt an effort should be made to keep Hong Kong under British rule, with China's approval.

Murray Crawford MacLehose was a formidable character—tough, intellectually sharp, and above all, demanding. At six-foot-four, he was physically impressive. He carried himself with dignity and came across publicly as a confident and charismatic leader. In private he was fastidious, reserved, and chose his words carefully. A British minister once referred to him as "this gloomy Scot."

MacLehose was born into the Scottish aristocracy in 1917. After graduating from Oxford, he joined Britain's war effort and rose to become a lieutenant in the Royal Navy Volunteer Reserve. He joined the Foreign Service in 1947 and was posted to Hangkow, China, as Acting Consul General. He served as ambassador to South Vietnam during the height of the Vietnam War and to Denmark from 1969 to 1971. When Prime Minister Heath appointed him to be Hong Kong's twenty-fifth governor, MacLehose was the first to be chosen from the ranks of the Foreign rather than Colonial Service, a sign of the changing times. (Hong Kong was no longer a colony to be held and managed, but a diplomatic issue to be resolved.) MacLehose had no experience running anything bigger than a mid-size British embassy and had to be given a few months of special training in big city administration. However, he turned out to be the right man for the times.

Big Mac, as he quickly became known, was an imperious headmaster. The civil servants were his students. He was firm and autocratic. He used to type his comments on official papers in red ink so they stood out from those of his underlings. He did not sign his name, or even his initials. Instead, he scrawled a huge "M" at the foot of his memos. He was contemptuous of bureaucrats. As political adviser in Hong Kong in the early 1960s, his job was to counsel the governor on foreign relations, particularly those with China. But he saw many things wrong with the way the colony was run. During walks through the New Territories with a young District Officer named John Walden, he spoke of the administration as a mickey mouse operation and would say of local civil servants: "I've never met a better bunch of people for doing nothing."

At the time, MacLehose was exactly what Hong Kong needed. The colony had become a sweatshop. Prior to the Chinese Revolution in 1949, Hong Kong was a transhipment center. It made its money by bringing goods in from China, storing them, and then selling them to the West. After the Communists came to power, they cut off trade with the West and the flow of goods to Hong Kong dried up. Denied its principal source of income, the colony turned to manufacturing. It benefitted from a fortuitous mixture of immigrants. Hundreds of wealthy Shanghainese and foreign businesspeople fled to Hong Kong before the communist takeover. They brought with them capital and business experience. They soon bought looms from Japan and the United States and set up textile factories. Joining them in their thousands were peasants from neighboring Guangdong Province, who provided cheap labor. Soon the colony would be exporting so much clothing that Britain would have to put quotas on imports to protect British industry.

Like the United States government in the nineteenth century, the colonial administration maintained a strict laissez-faire economic policy. It kept taxes low, bureaucratic red tape to a minimum, and often one eye closed to counterfeiting of foreign products and other unscrupulous practices. It provided only the most basic social services and emphasized job creation. Land was provided and infrastructure built to enable private enterprise to expand. The policy worked because standards of living rose steadily and because the predominantly Chinese population relied on family, rather than government, for support.

Then in 1967 Hong Kong was rocked by communist-inspired riots as the Cultural Revolution spilled across the border. The Communists tried to exploit the poor working and living conditions in the colony with some success. The Hong Kong government survived the ordeal but was shaken out of its complacency. In April 1969 it drew up a paper, still classified as secret, which stressed that the Communists would continue to expand their base unless the government improved social conditions.

There was resistance from the businesspeople who dominated the Executive and Legislative Councils and from some rank-and-file civil servants who preferred the status quo. MacLehose, with his never-say-can't style, pushed major changes through the bureaucratic barricades. (Civil servants dubbed him "Murray in a Hurry" and some other less flattering names.) He manipulated the Executive Council with great flair. He would give each member a chance to air his views and when one said something that he liked, he would say: "Now, that's an interesting point. Can you develop that further? Agreed, gentlemen? Good."

In 1972, MacLehose announced an ambitious plan to rehouse 1.8 million people in ten years and eliminate the squatter huts that clung to the hillsides.

He extended free education from six to nine years and got the Legislative Council to approve funds to build swimming pools, running tracks, sports stadiums, auditoriums, concert halls, cultural centers, and a planetarium. He targeted more money for social services, medical and health services, crime prevention, family planning, and pollution control. During the first eight years of his administration, spending on social welfare increased nearly twenty-fold.

At the time T.S. Lo came to see him, MacLehose was recovering from the worst debacle of his governorship. In 1974, the government had set up the Independent Commission Against Corruption (ICAC) to tackle graft in the government and police force. It was very successful—too successful. Hundreds of police officers (mainly Chinese in the rank and file) had been tried since its inception. In October 1977 alone, 174 were arrested. Later that month, over 2,000 policemen met in Central District and marched to the office of the police commissioner. They demanded the right to form a junior police association, which was immediately granted. The policemen really wanted the ICAC to stop its work, and an estimated one hundred of them stormed its headquarters and attempted to destroy evidence.

MacLehose had to act before the government was held hostage by its police force—or worse, before there was a total breakdown of law and order. On November 5, he announced a partial amnesty. The ICAC would not prosecute police officers for offenses committed before January 1, 1977, except in cases where the person involved had already been dismissed or fled the colony. It was a major blow, not just to the ICAC, but to the credibility of the government itself. MacLehose took it hard. According to a maid who worked in Government House at the time, he spent hours sitting in the garden, motionless, his head resting in his enormous hands. Any other governor would have been sacked. He was allowed to stay on because his record was otherwise exemplary and perhaps because no obvious replacement was available.

Like T.S. Lo, MacLehose saw that the ever-shortening commercial leases in the New Territories would erode confidence in the colony's economic future. He raised the question in telegrams to the Foreign Office in 1977, a year before Lo came to him. There was no urgency about the issue. Some businesspeople and civil servants speculated over lunch at the Hong Kong Club as to how it would be resolved. But most people did not look that far ahead; companies usually made a return on their investments after just three to five years, since Hong Kong had no heavy industry that required long pay-back periods.

MacLehose felt the issue should be cleared up before it became a matter of concern. If it were left unresolved too long, Hong Kong's dynamic economy might collapse. In November 1977, he went to London with his political adviser, Alan Donald, for what was described as "routine discussions" with ministers. In reality, he wanted to raise this issue with Foreign Secretary David Owen and Lord Goronwy-Roberts, Royle's successor when Labour won the general election in 1974. Owen was temperamental, but highly respected. Goronwy-Roberts was, according to one magazine, "a dour Welsh schoolteacher whose devotion to socialism was matched by his penchant for sermonizing." The two ministers listened carefully to MacLehose's arguments. Owen was more interested in reforming the Hong Kong civil service than perpetuating colonial rule. He did not think the issue was pressing and did not raise it in the Cabinet.

When MacLehose passed T.S. Lo's suggestion to the Foreign Office in London, it still seemed too early to broach it with China. No firm leadership had replaced the Gang of Four, the hard-line group that tried but failed to seize power after Mao's death. But events on the mainland during the year convinced MacLehose that the time might soon be right.

Chapter 2

"Put Your Hearts at Ease"

B Y EARLY 1978, it was becoming increasingly clear that Deng Xiao-ping was in control of China. A short, intense man with a well-known habit of chain-smoking cigarettes and a fondness for bridge, Deng was seen as a pragmatist. He had been purged twice for his opposition to Mao's radical policies. MacLehose and the China experts within the Foreign Office felt he would be more receptive to extending the lease of the New Territories than some of the more ideologically minded communist leaders.

Deng was born in 1904 in the backwater of Guangan County, Sichuan Province. During his childhood China was still under Western influence and was divided by warlords, who fought among themselves for land and power. At sixteen, Deng left with a group of students to join a work-study program in France. The students believed the only way for China to cast off the yoke of foreign domination was to modernize its industry and compete with the West on equal terms. During his five-year stay in France, Deng developed his love of bridge and his revolutionary ideas. He joined the Chinese Communist Party in 1924, studied briefly in the Soviet Union, and then returned to China in 1927 to join the Sun Yat-sen Military and Political Academy in Xian. He became a representative of the party's Central Committee and was sent to southern Guangxi Province, where he led uprisings in 1929 and 1930.

Deng was one of the old guard. He took part in the Long March and was at the Zunyi Conference in northern China, which established Mao Zedong as the undisputed leader of the Communist Party. During the Sino-Japanese war, Deng served as a political commissar with the Eighth Route Army. He continued to make his reputation as a leader during the civil war. In April 1949, he led, along with Liu Bocheng and Marshal Chen Yi, an army of one million across the Yangtze River to capture Nanjing, the Nationalist capital. After the communist victory in 1949, he returned to his native Sichuan and was involved in the "liberation" of Tibet in 1951. Five years later, he was elected general secretary of the party's powerful Central Committee, a position he held for seven years.

During the Cultural Revolution, Deng was branded "China's Khrushchev" and a "capitalist-roader" and was removed from his party posts and exiled to the countryside. He was rehabilitated in 1973 but purged again by Mao after Zhou Enlai's death sparked riots in Tiananmen Square on April 5, 1976. He began his final comeback after the Gang of Four was arrested for allegedly organizing an assassination attempt against Premier Hua Guofeng. In July 1977, he was reinstated to the posts he had held before being purged.

MacLehose and other observers of the situation in China were surprised when Hua Guofeng was confirmed as premier by the National People's Congress, China's rubber-stamp legislature, which met in Beijing in early 1978. They had expected Hua to resign and to be replaced by Deng, but Deng was biding his time and solidifying his position within the leadership. He installed many of his closest allies in key positions in the party and government. At the end of the conclave, delegates approved a new constitution that stressed economic advancement over revolutionary ideology. This marked the start of China's steady movement towards more open and pragmatic policies. Western technology would be used to modernize China's economy, enabling China to take her place among the great nations of the world—Deng's dream as a teenager.

During 1978, Deng's position as China's paramount leader in fact, if not in title, was confirmed. He was cleared of any complicity in the 1976 Tiananmen Square riots. In June, over 100,000 right-wing dissidents detained by Mao were released. China revised the rules on its citizens traveling abroad and planned to encourage patriotic Chinese living overseas to visit their homeland. Then, at the third plenum of the eleventh Central Committee in December, the leadership adopted in principle the policy of opening China's doors to the outside world. During this session, Deng put forward three national goals: to modernize the economy, to reunify the country, and to oppose hegemony in Asia.

People in Hong Kong were not alarmed by the statement about reunification. Chinese leaders, including Mao, had long said that Hong Kong and Macao would be recovered after Taiwan was. The prospects for reunification with Taiwan any time soon were remote. Deng, in fact, hoped to achieve a political settlement with Taiwan by the end of the century, and the party was already at work on a plan to do so. To ensure peaceful reunification, Taiwan would be allowed to maintain its capitalist system; this would also help to boost China's economy. When the standard of living on the mainland reached that of Taiwan, a smooth integration would be possible. This policy would eventually become known as "one country, two systems."

Unknown to anyone in the colony, in 1978 China reorganized the bureaucracy which handled Hong Kong and Macao affairs. When the People's

Republic had been founded in 1949, the constitution named the National People's Congress as the highest organ of power. In reality, the party's Central Committee formulated policy, which was then carried out by the State Council. A "leading group" under the Central Committee determined China's policies regarding Hong Kong and Macao. These were executed by the External Affairs Office under the State Council, which handled matters that were not officially considered foreign affairs. After the Cultural Revolution, the new leadership ordered a total reorganization of China's bureaucracy, separating the party from the government. A Hong Kong and Macao Affairs Office was set up under a new State Council.

The new department was headed by Liao Chengzhi, a seventy-year-old, friendly, easy-going man. His father, Liao Zhongkai, had been born to a rich Chinese family in California and was assassinated in 1925 for urging the Nationalists to compromise with the newly founded Communist Party. Liao Chengzhi had contacts with and was influenced by close family friends in Hong Kong. Under his leadership, the Hong Kong and Macao Affairs Office began reexamining Beijing's policies towards Hong Kong, with the hope of using the colony to promote economic development. Pro-China businesspeople in Hong Kong were given the green light to trade with Taiwan, and mainland-owned companies made high-profile purchases of prime real estate in the British colony. The Chinese government planned to create special economic zones adjacent to Hong Kong and Macao that would run on a semi-capitalist system, offer special investment incentives to attract foreign businesspeople, and be allowed to retain earnings from exports to promote rapid growth. Eventually, these zones would act as a bridge between the two colonies and the mainland.

The Hong Kong and Macao Affairs Office concluded that to take maximum advantage of Hong Kong, the Chinese government would have to improve relations with the colonial administration. It had never officially recognized the Hong Kong government; to do so would have given British rule legitimacy. Instead, Beijing referred to the Hong Kong Government in official statements as "the local authorities." The Hong Kong and Macao Affairs Office decided that the Chinese government would maintain its position that the three nineteenth-century treaties with Britain were invalid and that Hong Kong was Chinese territory. It would be recovered under the policies being developed for reunification with Taiwan. But in the meantime, to improve relations, the colonial administration could be given "face," if not formal recognition.

Behind the scenes, the Xinhua News Agency, China's unofficial consulate in the colony, increased contacts with the Hong Kong government and gave broad hints that Governor MacLehose would be welcome to visit China.

Then, in December 1978, China's vice-minister of foreign trade, Li Qiang, made a brief stop in Hong Kong on his way home from an overseas visit. As a courtesy, the governor invited Li to lunch at Flagstaff House, the oldest Western-style building in Hong Kong (the wooden roof of Government House was being repaired). Li told MacLehose that Hong Kong had a major role to play in China's modernization program and said that the Chinese government would like to invite him to visit China. This was followed early in the new year by a formal letter.

THE INVITATION WAS a breakthrough, a clear sign that China wanted Hong Kong to play a catalytic role in the country's modernization. MacLehose felt the visit presented an excellent opportunity to resolve the question of the New Territories lease. The Foreign Office suddenly gave it high priority. Robin McLaren, a prickly and overly serious diplomat, headed the General Department (later, the Hong Kong and General Department), which looked after Hong Kong. He examined the options available, including T.S. Lo's proposal. Some diplomats were opposed to raising the question at all. MacLehose was keen. Deng was seventy-four years old. He could be dead in a year or two, and the opportunity would be lost forever.

MacLehose consulted only three people in Hong Kong: David Wilson, his political adviser; Chief Secretary Jack Cater, the most senior civil servant in the colony; and Y.K. Kan, the senior Executive Councilor. Wilson was one of the China experts within the Foreign Office and thus was naturally involved in discussions that related to China. Cater was MacLehose's most senior aide, and had to be kept abreast of important developments. The decision to consult Y.K. Kan and not the other Executive Councilors was highly unusual—and questionable.

Kan was a member of the Cantonese aristocracy. His father was a banker and used to play tennis with T.S. Lo's father. He was born in Hong Kong in 1913 and obtained a Bachelor of Arts degree from Hong Kong University. He wanted to be a doctor or a writer but his father convinced him to go into law. (Much later in life, he took some correspondence courses in short story writing and his younger brother went on to become an esteemed medical professor at the University of California.) He went to England in 1935, where he worked as a clerk during the day and studied law at the University of London in the evenings. On the eve of his final exams, World War II broke out in Europe. He returned to Hong Kong via the United States and took a job with his father's Bank of East Asia as secretary to the board (he became chairman in 1963). After the war, he joined Lo and Lo, M.K. Lo's law firm.

One journalist described Kan as "a solicitor by training, a banker by inheritance, and a public figure by coincidence." He was appointed to the

Legislative Council in 1961 and the Executive Council five years later. During the riots in 1967, he strongly supported the colonial administration and was on the leftists' assassination list because of it. He was given a bodyguard, and Cater offered him tips, such as taking a different route to and from work every day. Kan would say years later: "I earned my double knighthood."

After he became senior Executive Councilor in 1974, Kan became Mac-Lehose's most trusted adviser. Their relationship was much closer than that of any previous senior unofficial with his governor. MacLehose often called Kan in the middle of the day to Government House to give advice on some issue. In one or two cases, when an important matter was pressing and there was no time to convene the entire Executive Council, MacLehose consulted only Kan, which annoyed his colleagues tremendously. According to one Executive Councilor, if Kan opposed something MacLehose was particularly keen on, the governor would call Kan into his office a half hour before the council met to discuss it. Having failed to sway MacLehose in private, Kan would remain silent during the session.

Kan opposed raising the issue of the New Territories lease with Deng. He believed Britain should approach a low-level cadre in Beijing, someone familiar with Hong Kong who could broach the issue at a higher level in a way that would find favor. If China was angered by the proposal, senior British officials could smooth things over by saying that the person acted without authority.

MacLehose would not listen. He was determined to go ahead. In early February, he held a meeting with David Wilson, Jack Cater, and British Ambassador Percy Cradock in the secure chambers of the Executive Council on the first floor of the government secretariat. Sitting at the conference table in the long, rectangular, and dimly lit room, the governor said that he planned to ask Chinese officials if the Hong Kong government could extend commercial leases in the New Territories beyond 1997. That would solve the problem of confidence; the issue of renewing Britain's lease of the whole area could be discussed later.

How will you raise the question of commercial leases without mentioning the lease of the New Territories itself? Cater asked.

It can be done, MacLehose said.

Like Kan, Cater opposed raising the question at such a high level.

"For heaven's sake," he said, "whatever you do, don't get a rebuff."

While serving briefly as acting governor, Cater wrote to the Foreign Office to say that MacLehose's plan to raise the subject of the commercial leases in the New Territories should be put before the Executive Council, in accordance with the Royal Instructions, part of Hong Kong's colonial constitution. He never received a reply.

Discussions continued in London with British Foreign Secretary David

Owen, who was scheduled to visit China in April. Owen suggested that it might be better for him to raise the issue. The China advisers in the Foreign Office were aghast. Owen was a politician who knew little about China. They were sure he would blow it. After lengthy discussions, they came up with a plan. If conditions seemed appropriate, MacLehose would ask Chinese officials if the Hong Kong government could extend commercial leases in the New Territories beyond 1997. If the officials agreed, it would be a strong indication that Beijing intended to be flexible on the question of the New Territories lease. Owen would then follow up with a proposal that Britain formally recognize Chinese sovereignty over all of Hong Kong. In return, Beijing would allow the British to continue administering the enclave beyond 1997. This would make Hong Kong's status similar to that of Macao.*

The Foreign Office diplomats did consider T.S. Lo's proposal, and while they thought it quite clever on the surface, they did not believe that it would be taken seriously. It would leave Britain open to charges of abrogating the 1898 Convention of Beijing. The experts in international law were divided over whether the plan was even legal. The diplomats decided that it was better to simply ask Beijing to allow the Hong Kong government to extend leases beyond 1997. Owen raised the matter with Prime Minister James Callaghan, who approved this decision. An Order in Council was drawn up. If Beijing's response was positive, the Order would be issued by the queen.

ON MARCH 6, 1979, the Hong Kong government announced that Governor MacLehose would visit Guangzhou and Beijing later that month. He would be accompanied by his senior Executive Councilor Y.K. Kan, and his political adviser David Wilson. Senior Hong Kong officials leaked word to the press that the lease of the New Territories would not be brought up. Instead, the main topics on the agenda would be mundane items such as economic cooperation, illegal immigration from China, and the problem of certificates of origin for Hong Kong goods made of raw materials from China. The public should not expect any major revelations from the governor's meetings with Chinese officials. No one, not even the other Executive Councilors, was told that MacLehose planned to make an attempt to resolve the problem of commercial leases in the New Territories.

The delegation arrived in Beijing on the evening of Monday, March 27, a day after Israel and Egypt signed the historic Camp David peace accord in Washington, D.C. It was the outstanding achievement of the Carter adminis-

---

* In 1974, Portugal and China came to an understanding that Macao was Chinese territory under Portuguese administration. This was put in a formal agreement in February 1979.

tration, and its significance could not have escaped Murray MacLehose. At least one person he consulted believed that the governor was hoping that the successful resolution of Hong Kong's future would be the crowning achievement of his governorship.

It was cool and windy when their plane touched down at the airport. The three men were brought directly to the former American embassy, a group of somewhat dilapidated European-style buildings in the old legation quarter east of Tiananmen Square. The governor was given the main building. Wilson and Kan and their wives were brought to smaller dwellings in the compound.

MacLehose had been told before he left Hong Kong that he would be seeing "a Chinese leader" in Beijing. The next morning, during a meeting with the director of the Bureau of Travel, he was informed that he would be given an audience with Deng Xiaoping the next day. It was an unusual honor and was evidence of the importance Beijing attached to Hong Kong. After a performance of *Swan Lake* that evening, MacLehose and Wilson went to the British embassy, a ponderous-looking stone building in the diplomatic quarter, to meet Ambassador Cradock. The three decided that the meeting with Deng would be the best time to raise the question of the commercial leases in the New Territories. Cradock may have cabled London for final approval from Owen.

The next day, MacLehose and Kan had breakfast together. Wilson woke late and did not join them. MacLehose was excited about the meeting with Deng. When they had finished eating, the governor jumped up and asked Kan to join him for a walk in the garden of the compound. As they strolled around the grounds, MacLehose rehearsed the best way of bringing up the subject of commercial leases. Kan made a last, vain attempt to dissuade him from raising it.

When the delegation arrived at the meeting room in the spacious Great Hall of the People, Deng was seated in a large sofa chair. He got up and strode to the door to greet his guests. He wore a gray Mao suit and looked fit and alert. MacLehose, nattily dressed in a dark pinstriped suit, seemed almost twice Deng's height. They shook hands and went inside where there were several large sofa chairs with a name card on each. Deng took his seat. MacLehose sat to his right, then Cradock, Kan, and Wilson. Despite the formal surroundings, the absence of hordes of journalists and a battery of television lights made one member of the delegation feel as though they were calling on a prominent Chinese citizen in the privacy of his home. (China was just beginning to allow Western journalists to be based in Beijing.)

A Chinese interpreter sat behind a small table between Deng and MacLehose. (The British did not bring their own interpreter because this was only a courtesy call and because MacLehose, Wilson, and Cradock spoke fluent Mandarin. Only Kan, the lone Chinese on the British side, needed an interpreter because he spoke Cantonese.) After a brief photo call, Deng opened the hour-long meeting by saying that he hoped Hong Kong would play a role in China's modernization. He asked the governor to encourage businesses to invest in Guangdong Province and the rest of China. Mac-Lehose responded positively and said that there was room for closer cooperation between Hong Kong and China in many areas. The discussion was amiable.

MacLehose raised the question of illegal immigration. Hong Kong had been inundated during the past months since China relaxed restrictions on movement. Deng said that China had been trying to stop the exodus, but Hong Kong's superior standard of living was a magnet attracting poor peasants from the southern regions. China would take additional measures to solve the problem.

"This has been said to us before," MacLehose responded. "I do hope some vigorous action will be taken."

"I know we have done things in the past, and they may not have been very marvelous," Deng responded. "I'm sure you will understand that governing one billion people is more difficult than governing five million."

The Chinese leader broke into a broad smile.

As the meeting drew to a close, MacLehose decided the time was right to broach the subject of the leases. He explained that the Hong Kong government could not issue commercial leases beyond 1997 and that businesspeople would not be willing to invest without an assurance that they could hold the land beyond 1997. Confidence in the colony would deteriorate, hurting China as well as Britain. If China allowed the Hong Kong government to issue commercial leases beyond 1997, investors would have faith in the future of the colony.

Deng had not been briefed that MacLehose would raise this question, in accordance with normal diplomatic protocol. MacLehose made the final decision to raise it only the previous evening. There was hope that if he put it to Deng directly, without a team of low-level bureaucrats poring over it, the leader might be made to see the obvious practical benefits and accept it. Deng did not have a good grasp of the issue and did not catch the subtlety of the proposal. He thought MacLehose was asking him to extend Britain's lease of the New Territories. Not having a prepared response, he explained, in a rambling monologue, China's vague formulas for reunification with Taiwan, indicating that these would apply to Hong Kong and Macao as well.

"Hong Kong has its own special status," he said, according to notes written during the meeting by one member of the delegation. "People are worried what will happen in 1997. There are still eighteen years to go before

1997. Eighteen years is not a long time. We may have to have a special discussion . . . to solve this question."

Deng said that Hong Kong was part of China and would be recovered, but he insisted that Beijing would respect Hong Kong's special status. The new policies would not hurt investments. "We will also respect the special status of Taiwan," he continued. "We will not affect the social system [there]. Taiwan can even have its own army. But there can be no two Chinas, or one-and-a-half Chinas. This is not just our policy now. It has been our policy for a long time. Why? Because we need them for our Four Modernizations. We are thinking of passing legislation to protect profits of foreign investments. I ask you to tell investors to put their hearts at ease. China's policy towards Hong Kong is guaranteed. Not only for this century, but for the next century. Hong Kong can go on being capitalist. We will continue with our socialist system. In 1997, if we take over Hong Kong it will not affect investments."

The meeting ended shortly thereafter. Deng had not accepted or rejected the governor's proposal. He had merely restated China's formal position on the Hong Kong question and left his options open.

Later that day MacLehose, Cradock, and Wilson met Foreign Minister Huang Hua, China's former ambassador to the United Nations. Huang said that it was inappropriate for MacLehose to have raised the issue of the New Territories lease with Deng. The governor insisted that the problem would not go away.

Worried that Deng had not grasped what he had proposed, MacLehose requested a meeting with Liao Chengzhi, head of the still secret Hong Kong and Macao Affairs Office. Liao said he was busy and could give the governor only a quarter of an hour of his time. The meeting was held at five o'clock that evening. MacLehose explained that he was not attempting to extend British rule in Hong Kong beyond 1997. If China would allow the Hong Kong government to extend commercial leases beyond 1997 it would boost confidence in the colony. This would not compromise China's position on sovereignty. The leases would be issued "on behalf of whatever government was administering Hong Kong at the time."

"I'm sorry," Liao said. "I cannot say anything more than what Chairman Deng has told you."

MACLEHOSE RETURNED to Hong Kong aboard the first through train from Guangzhou since 1949. It rolled into the No. 6 platform of the Kowloon railway station at 11:26, cutting through a ribbon across the track. The governor's party was greeted by Chief Secretary Cater. As he stepped off the train, MacLehose said one word to his deputy: "Rebuff."

At a crowded press conference in the government's official briefing room the next day, the governor stressed the great importance mainland officials put on Hong Kong and the great contribution it could make to China's modernization program. Deng Xiaoping himself, he said, has "formally requested me to ask investors in Hong Kong to put their hearts at ease."

When he briefed the Executive Council on the visit, MacLehose said little more than what he had released to the press. He gave no indication that he had raised the question of the commercial leases in the New Territories. Although the Royal Instructions, one of the colonial charters under which Hong Kong was governed, stipulated that the governor had to discuss all matters of importance with the Council, he was exempted from raising "cases which may be of such a nature that Our Service would sustain material prejudice by consulting the Council thereupon." MacLehose felt that it was understood within the Foreign Office that this was a delicate matter between the British and Chinese governments, which should not be raised in the Council. If news was leaked that China had rejected an initiative to extend leases beyond 1997, confidence would plummet. (MacLehose may have been worried that the Executive Councilors would sell off their assets in Hong Kong, which would be a clear sign that something was wrong. Much later, there were unsubstantiated rumors that Kan had sold some of his holdings.)

Some unofficial members of the Executive Council pushed Kan to give a full and frank account of the meeting with Deng. Kan refused, saying that it was up to the governor to brief them. He did not speak publicly about the visit until years later, though upon his return, he did tell one close friend, who was also a signatory to the Official Secrets Act: "It's all over."

ON THE SAME DAY that MacLehose met Deng, the Labour government of James Callaghan lost a no-confidence vote in the British Parliament. Foreign Secretary David Owen's trip to China in April was canceled. (He was unlikely to ask China to extend Britain's rule beyond 1997 after what MacLehose had been told.) A general election was held on May 3, and the Conservative Party, headed by a grocer's daughter named Margaret Thatcher, romped to victory.

The Foreign Office followed up on MacLehose's initiative. Ambassador Cradock went to the Foreign Ministry in July to explain at a lower level the need to resolve the issue of the commercial leases in the New Territories. During a series of meetings with Chinese Vice-Foreign Minister Zhang Wenjin, Cradock explained MacLehose's proposal again. After examining it, the minister told Cradock that China would not allow the Hong Kong administration to issue leases beyond 1997. The question of the New Territories lease would have to be resolved through formal means.

"This is a bilateral issue," Zhang said. "It must be solved through bilateral negotiations."

Chapter 3

"Another Nail in Our Coffin"

THE GOVERNOR's account of his visit, particularly the meeting with Deng, created tremendous optimism in Hong Kong. Many businesspeople—Chinese and expatriate alike—believed that Deng's "put your hearts at ease" comment meant that China would maintain the status quo in Hong Kong beyond 1997. There was a touch of arrogance to this belief, which bordered on self-delusion. Hong Kong is too important to China, people said. The Communists need us.

Hong Kong was already in the midst of the biggest property boom in her history (compared with the United Kingdom, which was suffering through the worst recession since the 1930s). There was a feeling that with the question of 1997 out of the way and China embarking on the path to economic modernization, Hong Kong was entering a golden age. The sense of euphoria was enhanced by China's unprecedented and enormously successful campaign to woo the world. Suddenly, Deng was the cuddly Communist. China was no longer a dragon to be feared, but a gentle one hungry only for foreign investment and technology. Delegations of smiling diplomats were dispatched to every corner of the globe to court international recognition and respectability. (The favorable image of China was brought into sharp focus by the aggressiveness of the Soviet Union, which invaded Afghanistan in December 1979.)

Businesspeople from around the world were invited to China, given elaborate banquets, taken on tours of ancient landmarks, and encouraged to sign contracts. Many set up offices in Hong Kong, which was an effective and comfortable base for doing business in China. Demand for office space and residential accommodation soared. Hong Kong tycoons were among those most actively courted. At first, many were reluctant to visit the mainland; many had fled before liberation and left behind large fortunes. Before long, however, dozens of companies were setting up factories in the Pearl River Delta, where land was plentiful and labor was cheap.

China accommodated working-class residents as well. Travel was made easier. Many young Hong Kong Chinese toured the open areas of the country and were stared at because of their strange clothes, expensive cameras, and unusual habits. Many elderly people returned to their ancestral villages for the first time in decades. They brought radios, televisions, video recorders and motorcycles for their relatives, whetting the locals' appetite for consumer goods. When China announced that it would sell land at a discount to those who had property seized after the Revolution, many Hong Kong Chinese accepted the offer. Eager to impress relatives and old friends, they built monstrous concrete homes, which looked like giant refrigerator boxes that had dropped out of the sky and landed haphazardly in the lush, green rice paddies of Guangdong.

The investment was not all one way. Mainland companies speculated in the property market, invested in manufacturing, and established wholesale and retail outlets in Hong Kong. Provinces set up their own trade and investment offices to establish contacts and learn about foreign markets. National investment companies established branch offices and were given special deals by Hong Kong businesspeople who were eager to make friends with Beijing and win contracts for development projects on the mainland. Some people worried about the effects China's investment might have on Hong Kong. Most saw it as another sign that Beijing wanted to maintain the status quo after 1997.

Hong Kong was riding high, and few ordinary people gave much thought to 1997. But now that Britain had raised the question of the New Territories lease and been rebuffed, MacLehose and the Foreign Office diplomats wanted to move the issue to the front burner. They believed that Deng's reforms would face problems and they wanted to force the Chinese to address the issue while Deng was still in power and while China was still stable. When Hong Kong's financial secretary, Philip Haddon-Cave, was invited to China in May 1980 by the Ministry of Foreign Trade, MacLehose instructed him to "smoke the Chinese out" on their plans for Hong Kong after 1997. The Chinese still did not think the matter urgent and told Haddon-Cave little more than what Deng had said to the governor a year earlier.

BRITAIN HAD closed her door to the people of Hong Kong through a series of immigration laws enacted since 1962. When the Thatcher administration submitted a new Nationality Bill to Parliament in January 1981, S.Y. Chung knew Britain was just double-locking the door.

A short pugnacious-looking man with a square jaw, close-cropped hair, and thick black-framed glasses, Chung was a throwback to the 1950s. He had taken over as senior Executive Councilor after Y.K. Kan retired. He was not as brilliant or as sophisticated as Kan. His bluntness sometimes came across as crudeness. But he did not care about his image, in public or in private; he cared about getting things done. He never had a self-doubt, and when he argued, he came at you like a freight train. Although his honesty put some people off, his integrity was above reproach.

Chung was no great lover of the British. Unlike Kan, he was not a member of the Cantonese aristocracy. He was one of the new breed, a self-made man, and thus he did not owe his success to the British or to anyone else. His father came to Hong Kong at the turn of the century from Foshan, a small city in the Pearl River Delta, and eked out a living as a merchant. S.Y. was born in the colony in 1917 and went to Shanghai to study civil engineering at St. John's University, China's Harvard. He returned to Hong Kong in 1937 and studied mechanical engineering at the Hong Kong University. Always industrious, he and three classmates set up a small shop close to the school where they designed and built machine parts. Despite working while studying, he managed to obtain a first-class honors degree.

Chung was working as a foreman on the Kowloon docks when the Japanese invaded. He fled to Macao, then China, and found a job as chief engineer in Jiangxi Province. When he realized that he needed some of his engineering books, he slipped back into the occupied colony disguised as a fisherman, packed a trunk full of books, and then left with the Japanese none the wiser. He stayed in China briefly after the war and worked for an electric and waterworks company. He was reportedly offered a vice-ministerial rank in Manchuria, but returned home instead.

Chung realized it was a propitious time. Hong Kong was entering a period of tremendous economic growth. From 600,000 at the end of World War II, the population surged to 2.5 million by 1951. Even after the Communists sealed China's border, many refugees risked their lives to come to Hong Kong in the leaky hulls of old fishing boats. Many wound up in tin and cardboard shacks on public land. The lucky ones shared cramped apartments that were poorly ventilated and had no indoor plumbing with several other families. Thankful for an opportunity to get ahead and to keep what they made, they worked hard, stressed education, and made something of their lives.

Manufacturers used the cheap and efficient work force to switch nimbly from one popular product in the West to the next—from plastic flowers to wigs to transistor radios. Usually these were designed and engineered overseas, or were cheap copies of North American and European products. Often the factories were nothing more than tiny rooms in tiny apartments, where parents and children worked late into the night assembling toys for export. Savvy businesspeople invested their profits in real estate, where Hong Kong's chronic shortage of land guaranteed that prices, sooner or later, would always go up. Many of the early Shanghainese immigrants quickly amassed fortunes that dwarfed the ones they had lost to the Communists in 1949. In the 1960s and 1970s, foreign businesses were attracted to the colony by the cheap labor, the government's economic policy, and an independent legal system. British administration provided a stable base in a region that was going through the trauma of decolonization and numerous communist insurgencies.

Hong Kong became a dynamic international city-state by the late 1970s. Skyscrapers clung desperately to the foothills of the picturesque mountains of Hong Kong Island. The forty-eight-story headquarters of Jardine Matheson dominated the harborfront. Earthmoving machines were constantly tearing away the hillsides and filling in the harbor to make room for taller and more sophisticated structures, which jostled for position below the Peak. Across the natural, deep-water harbor, which first attracted the British to this corner of China, twelve-story apartment buildings were packed neatly in rows like microchips on a circuit board. It was said to be the most densely populated area of the world. The city now sprawled beyond the hills of Kowloon northward towards the border with China. Farmland in the New Territories was being paved to make room for entire towns that would house tens of thousands of young, upwardly mobile families. Industrial estates were being built on land reclaimed from the sea to provide space for the colony's expanding industry.

Chung caught the crest of the wave. In the 1950s, he won a scholarship to conduct research at the University of Sheffield in England. After returning to Hong Kong with a doctorate he joined Sonca Industries. He developed and patented new production methods and built the company into the world's largest flashlight producer. (By 1990, it was producing 35 million annually.) He rose to managing director in 1966 and chairman of the board in 1977.

Instead of pursuing a commercial empire, Chung put his energy and creativity into public service. He considered himself to be a Hong Konger. He loved the city and its people. He was rich enough already, and he wanted to give something back. When he was appointed to the Legislative Council in 1965, he quickly earned a reputation for being a nonconformist. After his maiden speech, he shocked the conservative Council by abstaining from a vote on a plan to build a tunnel under the harbor (he was not satisfied with the design). He gave speeches in Cantonese, forcing the government to provide translation services.

In his first speech as senior Legislative Councilor in late 1974, he called on the governor to appoint to the Council people from the grass roots and suggested that they be paid. His suggestions were eventually accepted. He also advocated a form of social security. Hong Kong's population was getting older; people needed to be looked after. Some of the Shanghainese industrialists were shocked. It sounded too much like socialism and would erode Hong Kong's competitiveness. This idea was still being debated in the early 1990s. After he was appointed to the Executive Council in 1972, he spent every Sunday studying papers for its meeting the following Tuesday. No one was more dedicated to serving the interests of the colony.

Chung wanted to fight the new Nationality Bill. He knew it would be difficult, probably even futile. The British government worried about a massive influx of refugees from the colony. Hong Kong's five million people were equivalent to about ten percent of Britain's total population, and over three million of these were British subjects by virtue of being born in Hong Kong. If they all took up residency in the United Kingdom, the size of the country's minority population would triple. London's concern became more acute after 1972 when Heath's administration decided that Hong Kong would eventually be returned to China.

The purpose of the bill, according to the Thatcher government, was to tidy up Britain's nationality laws. At the time, they were a mess. There was only one category of citizenship: Citizens of the United Kingdom and Colonies. But some passport holders had the right to live in the U.K., and some did not. Prior to 1962, anyone who was a citizen of the British Empire had the right to live in Britain. A flood of immigrants from the Caribbean and the Indian subcontinent prompted Parliament to pass the Commonwealth Immigration Act that year, which denied subjects of existing and former colonies, including Hong Kong, the automatic right to live in Britain. This did not entirely curtail immigration; subsequent legislation closed some of the loopholes.

When the Labour Party won the election in 1974, it no doubt became aware of the previous administration's thinking on Hong Kong. An influx of Chinese workers was a direct threat to its constituency. In 1977 the party published a Green Paper (a consultative document) on nationality, which proposed streamlining nationality laws by creating two categories of citizenship: British Citizens with the right to live in the U.K., and British Overseas Citizens for citizens of existing or former colonies who did not have the right to enter freely and live in Britain.

The unofficial members of the Executive and Legislative Councils—known collectively as Umelco—in Hong Kong wrote to the British government to propose a third category of citizenship for British subjects in existing colonies and dependent territories. Y.K. Kan and S.Y. Chung flew to London to lobby for the proposal. On the airplane, Kan, a lawyer, explained to

Chung that Britain did not have the legal authority to strip its subjects of their nationality and rights. The two had "a very unpleasant meeting" with Lord Goronwy-Roberts over the issue. "Umelco will fight you all the way on this one," Kan said.

When Labour lost the general election in May 1979, the Conservatives took responsibility for drafting the nationality legislation. Part of Thatcher's platform had been to curtail immigration from the Third World. With the economy stagnating and many immigrants receiving government aid, the policy won wide support in Britain. In July 1980, the Conservatives published a White Paper (a policy document) entitled "British Nationality Law: Outline of Proposed Legislation." The document created a third category of citizenship, Citizens of British Dependent Territories, for existing colonies such as Hong Kong. Holders would not have the right to live in the U.K. They would be given citizenship of their country when it became independent from Britain.

The new law was blatantly racist and discriminatory. While non-whites would be kept out of Britain, the government allowed whites of British descent in the colonies to retain their citizenship. This was done by enabling those with patrial status—that is, one parent or grandparent born in the U.K.—to apply for full citizenship. Thus, a person born in South Africa, for example, who had never lived in Britain and whose parents had never lived in Britain, was considered more British than someone born on British territory in Hong Kong, who had grown up under a British administration, attended British schools, pledged their loyalty to the queen, and possibly even served in the British military.

Though tens of thousands of people around the world still claimed some connection to Britain, the law was clearly aimed at Hong Kong. It was by far the most populous colony. The combined population of Gibraltar, the Falkland Islands and a clutch of other tiny islands scattered in faraway seas like pebbles in a lake did not equal that of Kowloon. The government knew that Hong Kong could never become independent because China would not allow it, but this was not explained to Members of Parliament.

The people of Hong Kong had no representatives in Parliament and thus no say in the nationality issue. Despite the Hong Kong government's avowed policy of consultation, London's White Paper was not made available in the colony. The Hong Kong government had requested advance copies, but none were received. Umelco was given only four days' notice of the debate on the Nationality Bill, not enough time to effectively lobby Members of Parliament. Unaware of the true nature of MacLehose's visit to Beijing, or the follow-up by Cradock, Chung did not make a strong stand against the bill. He and his colleagues in Umelco requested only that the words "British national" be retained in the new passport.

The Hong Kong people felt the bill was another move by Britain to keep them out of the country, and most did not expect anything more from London. They did not really want to go to the U.K. anyway, and the possibility of the Communists taking over Hong Kong seemed remote. There was one group of Hong Kong Chinese, however, that was genuinely concerned about the bill: administrative officers, the senior grade of civil servants. Some had served during the communist-inspired riots in 1967 and had been branded "running dogs of the imperialists." They had been promised special consideration by a visiting Labour minister at that time. Some members and former members of the Executive and Legislative Councils were in a similar position. In February 1981, a group of administrative officers went to see MacLehose privately to express their concerns. He said he would look into the problem.

That month, the Nationality Bill went to the committee stage, where amendments could be made. MacLehose flew to London on March 9 to press home Hong Kong's concerns before the bill was ready for its final reading in Parliament. The British government agreed to insert a clause giving the home secretary the discretion to grant, in exceptional individual cases, automatic British citizenship. It also addressed Umelco's concerns by allowing Citizens of a British Dependent Territory to apply for British citizenship after living in the U.K. for five years, without having to satisfy other residency requirements.

Following the governor's visit, senior civil servants were informed that they would each be given a secret number, which would be registered with the Home Office in London. In the event of a crisis, they could quote the number to the immigration official in Britain and be admitted into the country. The senior civil servants pressed for a written assurance, but this was never given. Members of the Executive and Legislative Councils were informed that they would be included under the "special cases" amendment. Thus, the people in a position to fight for the rights of Hong Kong residents had no further incentive to do so.

RELATIONS BETWEEN Britain and China continued to improve. In April 1981, a few days after President Reagan narrowly escaped an assassination attempt by John Hinckley, Jr. in Washington, British Foreign Secretary Lord Carrington went to Beijing to establish ministerial contacts. Senior British officials told reporters that Carrington would not be raising the question of the New Territories lease. In reality, the Foreign Office wanted to get the Hong Kong question settled, and Carrington planned to use the opportunity to draw the Chinese out on their policy towards the colony.

After the usual friendly banquets, toasts of *mao tai* (a strong rice wine), speeches about mutual cooperation, and talks with Chinese Foreign Minister

Huang Hua, Carrington met Deng Xiaoping at the Great Hall of the People on April 3. China was more open now, and journalists were allowed to take photographs and ask questions before the meetings started. When they were ushered out and the doors closed, Carrington explained Hong Kong's growing concern about the 1997 question. If something was not done soon, confidence would erode, investment would dry up, and Hong Kong's economy would stagnate.

Deng still felt that the issue was not pressing. He understood little of leases, mortgages, or long-term investments. He told Carrington that China's intention was to offer Taiwan a high degree of autonomy. The Taiwan people could maintain their own economic system, their way of life, even their own army. A detailed formula would be announced shortly. He said he hoped Britain would study China's solution for the Taiwan problem. The message was clear: China intended to recover Hong Kong under the same guidelines used for reunification with Taiwan. Deng also told Carrington that Prime Minister Thatcher would be welcome in China.

Carrington remained tight-lipped about what he had been told. At a press conference in Beijing, he said Deng had repeated with "even greater emphasis" that investors in Hong Kong should not worry about the future. Deng added his own reassurances, wrapped in a blanket of vagueness.

"Even if there is some change in Hong Kong's status in sixteen years' time," he told British television reporters, "the interests of investors will not be harmed."

The next day, the front-page headline in the *South China Morning Post*, Hong Kong's leading English-language newspaper, said: DON'T WORRY ABOUT THE FUTURE.

THE NATIONALITY BILL continued to make its way through Parliament. In June 1981, the House of Commons approved the bill, with amendments, in a vote of 287 to 234. During the committee stage in the House of Lords, an amendment was introduced to give the people of Gibraltar the right to enter the U.K. and settle without fulfilling any residency requirement. Proponents argued that Gibraltar was a member of the European Economic Community, loyalty to Britain had been demonstrated during World War II, and the future of British subjects there was uncertain because of Spain's claim to the enclave.

Lord Geddes argued that Hong Kong was also in a sensitive position and that residents there could not look forward to becoming citizens of an independent country. Residents felt that the change of wording in their passports indicated that Britain was down-grading her commitment to the colony and they feared that the change would create problems for them when traveling abroad. The Lords passed the Gibraltar amendment but rejected Geddes's arguments. (The people of the Falkland Islands were later given the right to settle in Britain without fulfilling the residency requirement, leaving Hong Kong the only major colony without it.)

ON SEPTEMBER 30, 1981, the eve of China's National Day, Marshal Ye Jianying unveiled the nine-point plan for reunification with Taiwan that Carrington had been told about. In an official statement, Ye said that Chinese from Taiwan would be able to participate in running the unified country. The island's current way of life, economic system, and cultural relations with other countries would be allowed to continue.

"After the country is unified, Taiwan can enjoy a high degree of autonomy as a special administrative region and it can retain its armed forces. The central government will not interfere in local affairs on Taiwan."

Ye specifically mentioned in his statement that Chinese in Hong Kong and Macao should "continue to act as a bridge and contribute their share to reunification of the motherland."

A spokesperson for the Nationalist government in Taiwan dismissed the offer as a "continuation of [the Communists'] United Front propaganda" and said that it contained nothing new.

THE DEBATE on the Nationality Bill was scheduled to resume in the House of Lords on October 9, 1981. Umelco was considering sending a delegation to London to push for better assurances for Hong Kong people. Sir Paul Bryan, a Conservative MP who was chairman of the All Party Hong Kong Parliamentary Group in Britain, happened to be in town. Umelco invited him to attend a private, in-house meeting on October 7.

Bryan, a stout man with thin streaks of silver hair, had been chairman of the Hong Kong Parliamentary group since 1974 and had spoken on Hong Kong in Parliament often. But like most MPs, he put Britain's interests above those of Hong Kong.

"I understand that you are intending to send a delegation to London to lobby for Hong Kong," Bryan said. "I wouldn't if I were you."

He explained that there was no hope of getting special status similar to that of Gibraltar. Even if Umelco could convince the Lords, the Commons would never accept it. "There is nothing hanging in the balance. Do you want at this juncture to do something that is obviously hopeless and could irritate Mrs. Thatcher as well? You have everything to lose and nothing to gain."

After about half an hour, Bryan left. The Councilors then debated among themselves. T.S. Lo felt that Bryan had flown out to Hong Kong specifically to dissuade them from sending a delegation and therefore, there *was* something hanging in the balance. Some of his colleagues thought he was too suspicious. No decision was made.

Three days later Umelco learned that Lord Geddes had proposed an amendment to make it clear that Citizens of British Dependent Territories were British nationals. This was one of the concessions Umelco had been pushing for. This time, members decided to send a delegation to London to lobby for the amendment. S.Y. Chung, as senior Executive Councilor and leader of Umelco, went up to Government House to inform MacLehose of the group's decision. The governor said that he had raised the issue with Humphrey Atkins, a junior minister handling the Nationality Bill, who said that under no circumstances would the government let the Geddes amendment pass because it was flawed.

"Even if it is passed by the Lords it will be voted down in the House of Commons because it is defective," MacLehose said. "If this is so, it would be a pity that you go on a hopeless mission."

Chung said Umelco understood that there was no guarantee of success but still wanted to do everything possible to look after the interests of Hong Kong people.

"I do not want to carry your message to my colleagues," he said. "I think it is better that you advise them yourself."

That afternoon, Chung convened a meeting at the Umelco office on the eleventh floor of Swire House in the heart of the business district. Mac-Lehose sat at the head of the elliptical conference table and repeated that the effort would be in vain. The Councilors backed Chung. They said that if they did not go, they would feel they had not done their job properly.

According to several councilors present, MacLehose indicated that if they went against his advice, he would not do anything more for them on this issue. That put them in a difficult position. The governor, as a member of the Foreign Office, had good connections in London. He could probably achieve more for Hong Kong than they could. If they sent the delegation, it could harm Hong Kong's interests rather than serve them. Members decided against going, and instead, conveyed their "strong support" for the Geddes amendment. It was defeated in the Lords 105 to 102. Chung and other Umelco members felt they had been deceived by Bryan and MacLehose.

When the bill returned to the House of Commons on October 27, Bryan requested an assurance that should Hong Kong cease to be a British Dependent Territory, British subjects there would remain British. In a written reply, the home secretary stated they would remain British nationals "in the sense that the U.K. will afford consular protection and represent their interests internationally." He refused to say that they would remain British if there were a change in Hong Kong's status. That would be for Parliament to decide.

Three days later, the Nationality Bill, which would come into force on January 1, 1983, was passed. It would later be seen as a direct result of MacLehose's visit to China. No doubt, it would have been introduced even if MacLehose had not gone to China. However, if the governor had given a frank account of his discussion with Deng and the follow-up by Percy Cradock, the Executive Council might have fought harder for Hong Kong's interests. Y.K. Kan, the one Executive Councilor who knew what had transpired at the MacLehose-Deng meeting, told reporters that the Nationality Act was "another nail in our coffin."

Chapter 4

Deng's Solution:
One Country, Two Systems

T HE MASSIVE stone building on the corner of Whitehall and King
Charles Street in London, which protects admirably the prime minister's residence at No. 10 Downing Street and is just a few minutes walk from the Houses of Parliament, was designed by the distinguished Victorian architect Sir George Gilbert Scott in classical Roman style. It boasts a square courtyard, elaborate windows and balconies, and elegant statues hiding in tiny niches—a masterpiece in a city full of architectural masterpieces. The building is home to the Foreign and Commonwealth Office, and if it is anachronistic and forbidding, it accurately reflects the organization that occupies it.

Unlike the United States, where government bureaucrats are often seen as people who could not cut it in the private sector, Britain respects, even reveres, her civil servants. After attending Britain's leading universities, many of the kingdom's best and brightest—often members of aristocratic families—choose a career in the Foreign Service, something considered far more noble than going into business. Those who make it in the diplomatic corps are tough, smart, and dedicated. They form a secret society which is much admired and little understood.

Technically, these diplomats are functionaries who serve elected politicians (who are often from the middle class). But most MPs are not interested in foreign affairs, and the diplomats are given freer rein than domestic civil servants. The diplomats see Parliament as a nuisance that stands in the way of what they want to achieve. They try to sell their policies to MPs, and since the diplomats are the experts and control information, they usually succeed. They flatter ministers assigned to the Foreign Office, share confidences with them, show them secret files, make them feel that they are now part of the secret society. Even after a minister has left the Foreign Office, he continues to be briefed for as long as he sits in Parliament. He, in turn, usually remains loyal to the Foreign Office, defending its policies among his colleagues.

Within the Foreign Office, the China experts—the Old China Hands—are a select breed. China is a unique, complex, and enigmatic country, and while the China experts in the U.S. State Department were vilified after China went Communist, those in the Foreign Office saw their position enhanced. They dealt with a country that was hard to understand and incredibly obstinate. The Old China Hands were given a little extra respect because their work was so demanding.

The job of negotiating with China over Hong Kong's future would fall to this select group of individuals. With Murray MacLehose scheduled to retire in April 1982 after ten years as governor and the negotiations over the colony's future just around the corner, the Old China Hands wanted to make sure his replacement was one of their own. The man they proposed, and who Thatcher accepted, was Sir Edward Youde, chief clerk at the Foreign Office (an ancient and misleading title for the chief administrator of Britain's entire Foreign Service) and a skilled negotiator with more than thirty years of experience in dealing with the Chinese. Although he had had a triple bypass operation in August, his doctors pronounced him fit enough to handle the rigorous duties of the governorship.

Youde was, in many ways, the antithesis of MacLehose. He was pink-skinned, bald except for a few wisps of silver hair around the ears, a little pudgy around the middle, quiet, and imperturbable. As a young diplomat, he had a reputation as a hot-head. He developed heart problems in his mid-forties, when he was private secretary to Harold Wilson, and that forced him to keep his emotions under control. One British newspaper described him as being "so self-effacing that when he leaves a room, it seems as if someone has come in." He was reserved and serious—not an easy man to get to know. In private he was only slightly more relaxed than in public.

He gave the impression of being a very sincere man. During the coming negotiations, the press would beseige him at every official function to find out the latest on the talks. Youde could not breach the confidentiality of the negotiations, but he still gave the journalists the feeling that he was glad to see them and managed to say something that revealed nothing. They always went away happy.

Unlike MacLehose, Youde was not from the aristocracy. He was born into what he described as "an ordinary family" in the small Welsh town of Penarth in 1924. His father was a company secretary for a timber firm. In high school, Edward—Teddy to his friends—was captain of the rugby team and liked history and languages. He won a scholarship to London University's School of Oriental and African Studies, and he decided to study Chinese because the Sino-Japanese war was getting a lot of attention in the U.K. A career in the Foreign Service seemed a natural choice for a bright young man with his interests. He joined in 1947 and did a brief stint in the China Department before being posted to the British mission in Nanjing, the capital of Nationalist China at that time. There, he fell in love with a young linguist in the embassy whom he later married. He learned to speak Mandarin fluently. After being appointed governor to Hong Kong, he studied Cantonese, the local dialect.

As a twenty-four-year-old junior attaché, he displayed extraordinary courage in April 1949 when a British ship was attacked by Communist troops. As Mao's forces were about to cross the Yangtze River, the *HMS Amethyst* was sent to get supplies for the British embassy in Nanjing. When it was about 160 miles upriver, it was fired on and crippled. Twenty-three men were killed and thirty-one were wounded. After two attempts by the Royal Navy to rescue the ship, Youde was dispatched to the Communists' military headquarters to negotiate the ship's release. He trekked through Communist-controlled territory for a day and a half. By the time he reached the command, the ship had made a daring nighttime escape past Chinese artillery along the riverbank. Nevertheless, he was made a Member of the British Empire. (Years later, while serving as ambassador to Beijing, Youde was summoned to the Chinese Ministry of Defense to discuss a request by the Royal College of Defense Studies to tour China. The man who summoned him turned out to be the Red Army commander he had met during the *Amethyst* incident.)

In addition to his knowledge of China, Youde brought with him a reputation for maintaining the highest personal standards of conduct. The British press made much of the fact that one of his first decisions after being appointed Britain's second ambassador to Communist China in 1974 was to reduce the maximum stake at the bimonthly Monte Carlo Night from twenty-five pence to one penny. He feared a young diplomat might be compromised if he ran up a huge debt. Friendly gambling had been popular with staff at the embassy because there was little else to do in the Chinese capital. Many were unhappy when he later banned gambling altogether. Translators in the Hong Kong government gave him the Chinese name Yau Tak (Greater Virtue). Sometimes described as a workaholic, Youde was known for immersing himself in details and for being unwilling to delegate. These were qualities that would serve him well during negotiations with China.

It was clear to Youde and the other Old China Hands that China had some very general policies towards the future of Hong Kong. They wanted to press ahead and enter negotiations. In January 1982, Humphrey Atkins, now the deputy foreign minister, was dispatched to Beijing to lay the groundwork for Prime Minister Thatcher's state visit to China in September. The general purpose would be to strengthen Sino-British ties. The main item on the agenda would be to open negotiations aimed at settling the future of Hong Kong.

While in China, Atkins was told of China's policies towards Hong Kong. In addition to what Lord Carrington had been told six months earlier, there were new points, such as China maintaining Hong Kong's status as a free port and international financial center.

The Chinese government wanted to put off negotiations until after the Twelfth Party Congress. The Communist Party had begun educating grass-roots members on its Hong Kong policy. The population on the mainland had to be convinced that it was in the best interests of the motherland to allow Hong Kong to have special status above the rest of the country. The Congress would give senior leaders the opportunity to consult party members and explain the official position.

BY THE SPRING of 1982, the colony's economic boom had reached its peak. In February, Hong Kong Land, one of the colony's biggest property companies, had paid $775 million for a plot of reclaimed land on the waterfront. At the time, it was the highest price paid for real estate anywhere in the world. But it was the last major deal. As new buildings were opened, supply exceeded demand and prices began to slide. The economic outlook was becoming increasingly bleak. The United States, Hong Kong's largest export market, was mired in a recession. The colony was approaching the date when no more fifteen-year property leases could be granted in the New Territories, and businesspeople were growing skeptical about China's willingness to accept the status quo indefinitely.

On April 2 anxiety increased when Argentina invaded the Falkland Islands, a tiny colony with a population of only 1,800 people, most of which were sheep farmers. Britain and Argentina had been discussing the future of the Falklands on and off for sixteen years. The Argentine government, exasperated and looking for something to boost its standing at home, launched an invasion. Thatcher was furious with the Foreign Office which had insisted that Buenos Aires was bluffing. Three days after the attack, Foreign Secretary Carrington resigned, along with Humphrey Atkins and the junior minister in charge of the Americas, Richard Luce. Thatcher tried to persuade Carrington to stay on, but his sense of honor and growing criticism in Parliament prevented him from doing so.

Carrington was replaced by the defense secretary, Francis Pym, a dour man whom Thatcher found depressing. During the war, he acted like a dove in the Cabinet and a hawk in Parliament, which annoyed the prime minister. Their relationship would be troubled and his stay at the Foreign Office, short.

On the day Carrington resigned, a naval task force sailed for the South Atlantic to recapture the Falklands. The war was intensively covered in Hong Kong, with special bulletins interrupting local television shows and wide coverage in local Chinese newspapers. Some expatriates were surprised that the people of Hong Kong were interested in the war in the South Atlantic. Perhaps with the question of Hong Kong's future on everyone's mind, local residents were heartened by Thatcher's willingness to go to war for one of her colonies.

Though Beijing stressed that the two sides should resolve the dispute through peaceful negotiations, China's sympathies clearly lay with the Argentineans. A *People's Daily* editorial said that "it has always been China's consistent stance to oppose hegemonism and colonialism." All official Chinese reports referred to the Malvinas, the Argentine name for the Falklands.

THE *Lady Maurine* pulled up to Queen's Pier about ten minutes late on a clear afternoon in May. Rough seas forced her to make a second approach, while throngs of spectators waited anxiously. Edward Youde stepped from the launch wearing a white tropical uniform with gold epaulets and a cocked hat with red and white plumes. The royal honors pinned proudly to his chest and the ceremonial sword at his side completed the anachronistic outfit. He was greeted by a seventeen-gun salute. The skies were festooned with brightly colored smoke streamers dropped from Royal Navy helicopters, and the fireboat *Alexander Grantham* spurted jets of water into the air.

Youde arrived in Hong Kong in grand style. A military band struck up the national anthem as he stood at the dais to accept the first royal salute. Then, he inspected a Gurkha honor guard before proceeding into the City Hall theater, where a semicircular table was set up on stage. Members of the Executive Council dressed in formal black attire took their seats. The chief justice, Sir Denys Roberts, wearing his traditional bright red robe and white wig, administered the three oaths: the Oath of Allegiance to the Queen; the Official Oath of the Governor; and the Judicial Oath, in which the governor pledged to "do right to all manner of people after the laws and usages of this Colony, without fear or favor, affection or ill will."

It was a day for pomp and circumstance, but S.Y. Chung wanted to make it more than that. He was unaware that Britain intended to use Prime Minister Thatcher's visit in September to open negotiations and he wanted to put the issue of Hong Kong's future on the governor's agenda. Chung and his colleagues had been considering the problem informally for more than a year.

Committees were set up to research the issues involved, to consider what role Umelco should play, and to discuss how the question of the New Territories lease should be solved. He felt Britain's Conservative Party was more engaged in international affairs than the Labour Party and would get a better deal for Hong Kong. An election would have to be held before 1984. It would be best to get the talks going while Thatcher was in power and before she got too involved with a general election. He and his colleagues decided that Youde's arrival would be the appropriate time to go public and put pressure on the British government and the new governor.

When it was Chung's turn to speak, he stood at his seat, adjusted the microphone in front of him, and welcomed the new governor on behalf of the Executive and Legislative Councils. Then he got to the point: "Your Excellency will have many preoccupations in the administration of Hong Kong, but I hope you, Sir, will agree with me that the first priority must be the question of the future of Hong Kong, which is of such concern to us all. . . . To maintain confidence, it is necessary that the future of Hong Kong be satisfactorily resolved as soon as possible."

Youde was well prepared. He had been given an advance copy of Chung's speech as a matter of courtesy. He stood, put on his glasses, and read from a prepared text. The British government remained committed to Hong Kong, he said, and its relationship with China has never been better. "If there is an issue to be addressed, there is also, in addressing it, a common recognition of the vital importance of the continued prosperity and stability of this territory and a common wish to preserve them. . . . I see good reason why confidence should remain high."

The next day, British troops launched their main assault on the Falklands. An official spokesperson for the Chinese government said it regretted London's actions. Despite some embarrassing setbacks, British troops recaptured Port Stanley, the capital of the Falklands, on June 14, 1982. Thousands of Argentinean troops gave themselves up, and the terms of surrender were announced at nine o'clock that evening. It was a tremendous victory for Thatcher and boosted her popularity at home and her standing abroad.

BY MID-1982, the Chinese government had spelled out its policy for Hong Kong in four sentences, each consisting of four Chinese characters. Roughly translated, they said:

> Recover sovereignty
> No change in social systems
> Hong Kong people ruling Hong Kong
> Preserve stability

This "sixteen character solution," as it later became known, was supposed to guarantee the smooth integration of one of the world's most successful and dynamic capitalist cities with the world's largest communist nation. After it had been explained to party members, China geared up its United Front to win support for it in Hong Kong.

In June, the Hong Kong and Macao Affairs Office, whose existence had finally been revealed by a Taiwan newspaper, arranged for prominent Hong Kong residents to visit Beijing to meet "the leadership." It started with a delegation of leading leftists, then independent businesspeople, academics, and journalists. Some saw Deng Xiaoping, others Zhao Ziyang, China's premier. Among those invited was Legislative Councilor Rayson Huang. As vice-chancellor of one of the colony's two universities, he was an important ally because he could influence thousands of students who would one day take over the administration of Hong Kong.

Huang was flown to Beijing, put up in the Beijing Hotel, and brought to the massive Great Hall of the People, where MacLehose had met Deng three years earlier. As Huang entered the room, he nearly stumbled over the tiny Chinese leader, who was standing behind the door. They sat in two large sofa chairs. A spittoon sat on the floor to the right of the Chinese leader.

Deng explained that China had to reclaim Hong Kong; the Chinese leadership was accountable to future generations. The "unequal treaties" were "a black mark" in Chinese history. Suddenly, flush with emotion, he stood up. "If we don't answer that then we are as bad as those who signed the unequal treaties. I will not go down in history as another Li Hung-chang," he said referring to the mandarin who had signed the lease on the New Territories.

He explained that China would resume exercising sovereignty over Hong Kong. The colony would be allowed to maintain its capitalist system. China would continue to practice socialism. He called this policy, for the first time, "one country, two systems."

"We will not send people down to run Hong Kong," Deng said. "Hong Kong people will gradually take over. Your way of life, your capitalist system, your education will all remain unchanged. You can print your own banknotes. Everything will remain as it is."

Huang was not asked for his opinion, and he did not offer it. The meeting lasted exactly one hour. When Huang returned to Hong Kong, he did not tell anyone about what Deng had said.

In early July 1982, Peng Zhen, China's chief spokesperson on legal and constitutional affairs, called for a debate on the future of Hong Kong and

Macao within the framework of China's constitution. He explicitly included Hong Kong with Macao and Taiwan as territories that would eventually be designated "special administrative regions" within the People's Republic. By initiating a debate, Deng was forging a consensus to prevent his opponents within the Communist Party from using his liberal policies towards Hong Kong against him.

It was becoming increasingly clear to some China-watchers that Beijing's position had changed. The colony would not be reclaimed after reunification with Taiwan; it would be used as a bridge to the island. By showing that capitalist Hong Kong could survive under communist rule, Deng would pave the way for eventual reunification with Taiwan and seal his place in history. The realization made the colony increasingly jittery. When the Hong Kong government announced in August that it would sell the last large, undeveloped property in the business district to the Bank of China, Beijing's central bank, at a friendship price, the Hang Seng Index—the main stock market index and the best barometer of business confidence—plunged eighty points. The Hong Kong dollar fell 1.5 percent against the U.S. dollar. The sale was seen as a sign of weakness, a hopeless attempt to appease China. The *Far Eastern Economic Review* described it as "a kind of danegeld," the tribute paid by the English in the ninth century to buy off the Viking invaders.

The Hang Seng Index shed another 180 points over the following two weeks, as political uncertainties exacerbated economic problems.

THE HEAD OF the Hong Kong and General Department, which looked after the remaining scraps of the British Empire for the Foreign Office, was now Dick Clift, a short, scruffy man who did not fit in with the usual aristocratic Foreign Office types. His predecessor, Robin McLaren, left notes in some of the files. In what turned out to be a drastic understatement, one said: "Things have been bubbling up on the question of Hong Kong's future. They may get interesting."

Clift had to formulate a policy on Hong Kong's future to recommend to Prime Minister Thatcher. The Old China Hands were well aware that China was intent on taking back Hong Kong. They had been given a consistent, though vague, picture since MacLehose went to Beijing in 1979. They knew that China's pride and confidence had been badly damaged by foreign domination in the nineteenth and early twentieth centuries. She was particularly sensitive to any issue dealing with her sovereignty and wanted to right the wrongs of the past.

The Old China Hands knew, too, that China held all the cards. Legally, the lease of the New Territories would expire in 1997, and Britain would have no claim to over ninety percent of the colony. Militarily, the colony was indefensible. China could simply stop supplying food and water and starve the British out. Britain had only two bargaining chips: The first was that Hong Kong Island and the tip of the Kowloon Peninsula had been ceded to Britain "in perpetuity." The second was that China wanted to maintain the economic advantages she derived from Hong Kong and Britain knew more about running the colony than she did.

The diplomats were divided. Some advocated a "withdrawal with honor." The colonial era was over, Britain had no leverage, and China was too important to risk damaging relations over Hong Kong. Others believed that Hong Kong was a source of prestige and gave Britain standing in Asia. If we could hold on to it with Beijing's consent, they said, we should. Governor Youde and others who shared this view, however, felt that if the colony were retained then Britain would have to continue administering it as it saw fit; there could be no joint administration. An attempt had to be made. China could be bluffing. Even if she were not, Britain had to try. All were agreed that Hong Kong should not become an obstacle to better Sino-British relations.

Clift and his team examined every possible way of approaching the problem and every possible solution. Ideas were put up and knocked down. The Foreign Office's legal experts were brought in to look at the feasibility of different proposals. Most commentators in Hong Kong were urging the British government to offer to recognize Chinese sovereignty over Hong Kong in exchange for the right to continue administering the colony—the so-called Macao Solution. The Old China Hands knew that the Chinese government already did not recognize Britain's sovereignty over Hong Kong, and therefore, they had nothing to exchange. They concluded, instead, that the prime minister should offer to recognize China's sovereignty over Hong Kong and then stress that it would be in her interest, as well as Britain's, for the status quo to continue in Hong Kong for the foreseeable future.

MOST PEOPLE in Hong Kong felt that Britain had taken the colony illegally. However, they did not want to see her leave. The iniquities of colonial rule were preferable to the brutality of Communism. Few residents were willing to speak up for fear of seeming antipatriotic and perhaps for fear of retaliation from China. The Hong Kong government made no attempt to rally public support as it had during the communist-inspired riots in 1967 because Youde felt doing so would only inflame the Chinese government.

S.Y. Chung well understood local sentiments because he shared them. He also understood how the Old China Hands saw the issue, and he feared that they would give up the colony without a fight. He stressed to Youde that officials in London should not underestimate their bargaining position. Beijing was deriving enormous benefits from Hong Kong. The colony bought about a quarter of China's exports and accounted for about forty percent of its foreign exchange earnings. China was getting investment from the colony and obtaining technology and management expertise. Beijing was eager to maintain these benefits.

Chung had a profound sense of duty to the people of Hong Kong. While others saw a seat on the Executive Council as a personal privilege and a reward for their public service, Chung realized it came with responsibilities. If the Executive Council did not fight for the people of Hong Kong, no one would. The Chinese and British governments would quietly wrap up a deal, and the people of Hong Kong would be forced to live with it.

Chung also had a profound sense of history. He was senior Executive Councilor, and if he did not fight for Hong Kong, history would judge him badly. During the height of the negotiations, when Chung was working feverishly to keep up with his personal commitments, the routine decisions of the Executive Council, as well as the negotiations, a friend felt sorry for Chung because his term as senior member had come at such a difficult time. "Don't feel sorry for me," Chung responded. "I am lucky. Great men are remembered by history only because they lived in difficult times." He was concerned that history remember him accurately. When the negotiations were finally concluded, the Hong Kong government had two civil servants write a history of Hong Kong's role in them. It was placed in the Executive Council's safe and members were told that they could look it over to ensure that it was accurate. S.Y. Chung was the only one who did.

Chung wanted Umelco involved from the start. During the steamy days of August, it met secretly and drew up a paper outlining five possible solutions to the lease question. Britain could recognize Chinese sovereignty over the enclave and renew the New Territories lease for a sum of money; work out an arrangement for joint Sino-British administration; return the leased territory and retain the ceded areas with Chinese approval and cooperation; move Hong Kong's industry and people to another place; or return the entire colony to China with some guarantees of autonomy and a residual British presence. Chung asked the governor to present the paper to the British government. Instead, Youde arranged for a small delegation of Executive Councilors to go to London in early September to present it themselves. Chung and his colleagues were very pleased with the new governor. Unlike MacLehose, he did not try to censor their views.

The five-member delegation, led by Chung and Youde, boarded a British Airways 747 bound for London on September 4, 1982. After separate meetings with Foreign Secretary Pym and Dick Clift at the Foreign Office, the group met Prime Minister Thatcher at 10 Downing Street on September 8. Of the five, only Chung had been inside the prime minister's official residence before. There was a brief photo call in front of the large marble fireplace in the foyer. Then Thatcher led them down the long corridor lined with nineteenth-century British oil paintings borrowed from local museums and into a small study on the ground floor. One member commented that the house was much larger than it appeared from the outside. (It is actually two Georgian houses combined. The interior is a maze of rambling staircases, hallways, and rooms.)

Chung did not try to dictate what Thatcher's position should be. Instead, he spelled out the five options in Umelco's paper. Thatcher listened patiently and asked questions. What would be China's reaction? What would be the consequences of success? Of failure? Chung made it clear that if China was intent on recovering sovereignty and administration over Hong Kong, the people of Hong Kong would expect the British government to make every effort to maintain administrative control over the colony. They would accept nothing less. It was an argument that appealed to the Iron Lady—and horrified the Foreign Office.

After the meeting, she hosted a lunch for the delegation in the smaller of the two wood-paneled state dining rooms. Thatcher did not reveal what she was thinking, or how she would handle the situation when she went to China.

AN AIR OF confusion surrounded last minute preparations for Thatcher's trip. The press reported that the prime minister had appointed former Governor MacLehose to be her personal adviser on Hong Kong affairs. Journalists assumed that MacLehose would accompany her to Beijing. After Umelco met Thatcher, Youde told reporters that he would be going to Beijing with the prime minister. MacLehose's appointment was withdrawn without a public explanation. Youde had politely told Thatcher that it would be counterproductive to have "two governors of Hong Kong" advising her.

A last-minute briefing by Jack Cater, the chief secretary who had become Hong Kong's commissioner in London, was also canceled without explanation. As she left for Asia, even the prime minister's closest advisers were not sure which tack she would take. The Old China Hands feared that she was overconfident because of her victory in the Falklands War and might take a high-handed approach with Chinese leaders. This, they felt, would be disastrous. They dispatched Ambassador Percy Cradock from Beijing to meet her in Tokyo. The press was told that Cradock wanted to brief her on the results of China's recent National People's Congress. His real mission was to impress upon his prime minister the need for subtle diplomacy.

She arrived in Beijing on Wednesday, September 22, at 1:30 P.M. It was unseasonably warm as she stepped off the plane and was greeted by Chinese Vice-Foreign Minister Zhang Wenjin and his wife. Her motorcade drove directly to the Diaoyutai State Guest House in a western suburb of Beijing. After a brief rest and a change of clothes, she was taken to Tiananmen Square for a welcoming ceremony outside the eastern entrance of the Great Hall of the People. There, she was met by Chinese Prime Minister Zhao Ziyang, who accompanied her on an inspection of a military Honor Guard. They strode past hundreds of colorfully dressed school children performing a song and dance.

That evening, Zhao hosted a banquet in Thatcher's honor. She was suffering from a head cold, but pushed gamely through the formalities. She said she looked forward to discussing Hong Kong's future with Zhao the following day. At times, she showed little sensitivity for China's feelings about the past. She described a century of British exploitation of China as one in which "cultural and scientific contact went from strength to strength." But for the most part, she stuck to issues the two countries agreed upon: opposing Soviet hegemonism and increasing bilateral trade.

The following morning, Zhao arrived a few minutes early for their meeting at the Great Hall of the People. A large group of reporters was cordoned off at the back of the room. Flashes popped and photographers jostled for position to get a picture of the Chinese leader. Noticing the commotion, Zhao casually walked over and chatted with the reporters. One journalist asked if Hong Kong people should be concerned about their future.

"I don't think that Hong Kong needs to be concerned about the future," Zhao responded. "What do they have to be concerned about?"

Does China intend to recover sovereignty? another reporter asked.

"Of course China must regain sovereignty. But I don't think the question of sovereignty will affect Hong Kong's prosperity."

Why not?

"Because if China regains sovereignty, it will certainly take a series of measures to guarantee Hong Kong's prosperity and stability."

By stating the Chinese government's position publicly, Zhao was making it clear that there could be no compromise on the issue of sovereignty. To reverse this position would mean a loss of face.

Thatcher's arrival interrupted the discussion. After a brief photo call, the journalists left, and the two leaders got down to business. Although her instincts said take a strong stand, Thatcher was persuaded against this by Cradock. Following the script drafted by the Old China Hands, she commented on the current healthy state of Sino-British relations. After a brief mention of international matters, she went on to explain how Hong Kong was administered and why it was so successful. She said that China, like Britain, enjoyed the advantages of a productive Hong Kong. The best way to maintain these advantages would be for China to allow Britain to continue administering the colony after the lease of the New Territories expired in 1997. If the two sides could work out a mutually satisfactory arrangement, she was confident that Parliament would formally recognize China's sovereignty over all of Hong Kong.

Zhao acknowledged the success of Hong Kong under British administration. However, sovereignty and administration were inseparable. China had to reclaim both as a matter of national pride. If it were a choice between sovereignty and prosperity, he said, China would choose sovereignty every time. He explained that China would take steps to maintain the colony's stability and prosperity after it reverted to Chinese rule. China had amended its constitution to allow the National People's Congress to create "special administrative regions," which could operate under different economic and legal systems from the mainland. China would not send cadres down to run Hong Kong. Local people would administer it. The colony would remain a free port and international financial center. He hinted that if Britain cooperated in the transformation process, her interests would be looked after.

The meeting lasted two and a half hours. Each side came away with a better understanding of the other's position, which were far apart indeed.

THE IMPORTANT meeting was the next morning. Thatcher and Youde met Deng Xiaoping in the Fujian Room of the Great Hall at ten o'clock. As they chatted in front of reporters, the subject turned to food. Deng had just returned from his native Sichuan Province. He said the food of Sichuan and Guangdong were famous throughout China.

"I suppose Sichuan cuisine is even better than Guangdong cuisine," he said to Youde. "What do you think?"

The governor replied that Sichuan was the first place he had visited in China.

"That's a very diplomatic reply," Thatcher quipped.

When the reporters were ushered out and the doors closed, Thatcher began the same way she had with Zhao the day before, emphasizing the need to maintain confidence in Hong Kong. She said if China announced that it was going to recover the colony, it would have "disastrous effects."

Deng said there were three issues involving Hong Kong's future: the question of sovereignty, how China would maintain Hong Kong's prosperity after 1997, and how Britain and China would cooperate "to avoid major disturbances" during the transition period. On the question of sovereignty, China's position was not negotiable. Sovereignty and administration over all of Hong Kong would be recovered in 1997. It was the first time the Chinese had explicitly stated a date for taking back Hong Kong. Deng said China would announce intentions to recover Hong Kong and explain policies towards the colony "within one or two years." He said it would take that long for China to consult people and formulate policies. He was sure the policies would maintain confidence in Hong Kong, but he was worried about unrest there during the transition period. He said the aim of consultations between Britain and China should be to avoid this. He agreed that diplomatic talks should begin, but with "the understanding that China will take over Hong Kong in 1997." He hinted that if the British created trouble during the transition, China was prepared to move in early.

Thatcher did not like Deng's inflexible stance and toughened her own. She insisted that Britain had two treaties ceding Hong Kong and Kowloon in perpetuity. These were valid until the two governments came to another arrangement.

The session, described by one British diplomat as "courteous but tough," lasted two hours and twenty minutes. When it was over, the two sides issued a communiqué, which said:

> Today, the two leaders of the two countries held far-reaching talks in a friendly atmosphere on the future of Hong Kong. Both leaders made clear their respective positions on the subject. They agreed to enter talks through diplomatic channels following the visit with the common aim of maintaining the stability and prosperity of Hong Kong.

When the Xinhua News Agency in Beijing released the communiqué, it added "the Chinese government's position on the recovery of the whole region of Hong Kong is unequivocal and known to all."

On her way out of the Great Hall, Thatcher slipped and fell on her hands and knees. To one writer, it looked like she was making "a crude kowtow in the direction of Mao's mausoleum." The superstitious in Hong Kong saw it as a bad omen.

That afternoon, she gave a press conference in the Great Hall. Journalists repeatedly asked her to expand on the joint statement. Time after time she refused. She would not say whether China would take Hong Kong back, or whether Britain could continue to administer Hong Kong after 1997. "I think the people of Hong Kong will recognize that to maintain confidence, you must also maintain confidentiality," she said.

How do you expect Hong Kong people to remain confident about the future without knowing what Beijing and London have in store for them? one reporter asked.

"I think they will read the statement, every word of it, and see that we are both committed to maintaining the stability and prosperity of Hong Kong."

Thatcher had tried it the Foreign Office's way and got nowhere. Now she tore up the prepared script and went with her instincts. "There are treaties in existence," she declared. "We stick by our treaties unless we decide on something else."

AFTER BRIEF stops in Shanghai and Guangzhou, Thatcher arrived in Hong Kong on Sunday, September 26, looking fatigued. She was whisked directly to Government House in a black Rolls-Royce. A small group of college students protested outside the airport gates against "the British claim to Hong Kong through three unfair treaties signed with China." Their posters were seized by plainclothes police officers.

Many people, particularly the business community, greeted the prime minister's tough stand with delight. An editorial in the *South China Morning Post* said her remarks about the validity of the treaties "should be pondered by all who spent the weekend cleaning the dust off their share script and composing 'flat for sale' advertisements. For what they amount to are assurance . . . that in Britain's eyes treaties are something that should be honored as long as they remain in existence."

The following day, Thatcher met members of the Executive and Legislative Council at their Swire House office. She gave a brief account of her trip and promised to keep in close touch with Umelco during the negotiations. Members of the Executive and Legislative Councils were concerned about the nationality question, which seemed more grave now. S.Y. Chung said that Hong Kong people were eager to maintain some link with Britain and that it would comfort them to have the term "British national" in their passports. Thatcher said she would look into it. His request was eventually granted.

Later that day, the prime minister told a luncheon audience: "I am the first to understand the importance of these talks [with China]. Given our common objective, it should be possible to reconcile our differences of approach with the Chinese government. Above all, I give you this assurance: In conducting these talks, I shall speak not only for Britain, but for Britain's moral responsibility and duty to the people of Hong Kong."

As she arrived for a press conference that afternoon, Thatcher was jeered by a small group of protestors who had put up banners saying: Down with the unequal treaties; Never forget the agony of our ancestors; and The treaties forced upon China should never be recognized. Inside she restated her commitment to the people of Hong Kong to a room packed with local and international reporters: "I have been at pains to stress that the British government has a clear responsibility for the people of Hong Kong. As leader of that government, what matters to me is that we discharge our moral duty to them."

The press conference was televised live in Hong Kong. People shopping or on their way home from work watched on televisions in store windows.

"Britain has three treaties," Thatcher said. "Two of those refer to sovereignty in perpetuity, one of them refers to a lease which ends in 1997. You've got to take all of those things into account, and when you do, you'll see why we had to enter into talks, not only to reconcile the differences between China and Britain, but to discuss the future of Hong Kong."

She repeated that "Britain keeps her treaties" and declared pugnaciously: "If a country will not stand by one treaty, it will not stand by another."

Chapter 5

Deadlock in Beijing

W HOEVER TODAY tries to cling to these unequal treaties will only awaken the memories of the British imperialist invasion of China in the minds of the people in China, Britain, and the whole world."

So warned the Xinhua News Agency in a bulletin released on October 1, 1982, China's National Day. The agency, controlled by China's Communist Party, condemned Margaret Thatcher's comments in Hong Kong and said that the Chinese people had always held that the treaties under which the colony had been ceded to the British were "illegal and therefore null and void." It also attacked Thatcher's claim to have a moral responsibility for and duty to the people of Hong Kong, saying that as the government of a sovereign country, Beijing alone "has a responsibility [for] and duty to the Chinese residents in Hong Kong."

A political and diplomatic storm was brewing, the likes of which Hong Kong had never seen. Many businesspeople who initially were delighted with Thatcher's tough stand on the treaties realized after Xinhua's verbal attack that it meant there would be a long and bitter confrontation over the colony's future.

Investors dumped their stocks. Share prices fell twenty-five percent in one six-day period. On October 5, the Hong Kong dollar fell to 6.50 against the U.S. dollar, beginning a year-long slide against most major currencies. Slumping real estate prices were pushed even lower by the political uncertainty. A sense of doom invaded a colony that could only be described as cocky a year earlier.

SHORTLY AFTER Thatcher left Beijing, Ambassador Cradock called on Vice-Foreign Minister Zhang Wenjin to work out an agenda for the negotiations on Hong Kong. They discussed how many members each negotiating team would have, who they would be, how often they would meet, and various other details.

Cradock was the Foreign Office's most experienced and brilliant China expert, the doyen of the Old China Hands. Tall and lanky with a high forehead, he was always dressed impeccably in a pinstriped suit and looked like an accountant or corporate lawyer. Like all good diplomats, he avoided the limelight assiduously. British historian Peter Hennessy described him as "very detached, very precise and very discreet" and said he was "a relative rarity" in the British government because he was "highly prized by both his ministers and his fellow bureaucrats."

Cradock was born into the British establishment in 1923, went to Cambridge, and joined the Foreign Service in 1954. He was intelligent and tough, and he knew it. In 1967, he was head of the chancery at the British embassy in Beijing. When the Hong Kong government arrested left-wing journalists for inciting riots and then refused to release them, Red Guards stormed the embassy and set fire to it. They seized Cradock and held him for hours. They tried to force him to *kowtow*, and when he refused, they threw things at his feet so they could get a picture of him as he bent down to pick them up. He would not move. The Red Guards gave up before he did.

As a diplomat, he naturally felt that Britain's relationship with China was paramount. A great supporter of the Cold War, he saw the world in terms of strategic alliances. (After the collapse of Eastern Europe, he was said to be the last among Thatcher's inner circle to believe the Cold War was really over.) When he took over from Sir Edward Youde as Britain's ambassador to Beijing in 1978, his job was to foster relations with China and encourage her integration into the free world economy. His determination not to alienate her would be perceived, at times, as softness, but he was anything but soft. He was the one diplomat that Thatcher respected because he was perfectly prepared to stand up to Beijing if necessary.

He knew little about Hong Kong, having spent only a year there in the early 1960s studying Mandarin before being posted to Beijing. He saw the question of the colony's future not in terms of the six million lives who would be affected by the outcome, but as a touchy diplomatic issue to be resolved pragmatically. Deng Xiaoping had rejected Thatcher's offer to formally recognize Chinese sovereignty over Hong Kong and refused to allow Britain to continue administering Hong Kong after 1997. Cradock believed that this position was unlikely to change and that Britain should negotiate the most favorable terms for Hong Kong.

Thatcher saw things differently. She was contemptuous of the Foreign Office "wets," as she called them. They had advised her that Argentina was bluffing over the Falklands. When they proved wrong, only her steadfast leadership and determination had kept the islands British. They had advised her to use subtle diplomacy with Beijing and that also failed. She felt confident after her Falklands victory and believed that her forthright style might carry the day with the Chinese. The Executive Council, which ostensibly represented the people of Hong Kong, was advising her to stand tough, to fight for continued British administration after 1997, and that is what she was going to do.

When Cradock approached the Chinese Foreign Ministry, he ran into a stone wall. Zhang Wenjin insisted that talks could not start until Britain agreed to hand over Hong Kong. "You must agree to concede sovereignty over all of Hong Kong," he said. "On the basis that you concede sovereignty, we can agree to talk."

Returning to the original Foreign Office line, Cradock said Britain was prepared to accept China's claim to sovereignty over all of Hong Kong, but it was in China's interests to allow Britain to continue administering the colony. Negotiations should be held to find a mutually satisfactory arrangement.

Zhang countered that Hong Kong was part of Chinese territory. China did not have to negotiate with a foreign power at all and was merely doing so in the interest of maintaining stability in Hong Kong. As far as Beijing was concerned, the two sides would not be negotiating *whether* Hong Kong would be returned, but *on what terms* it would be returned. He told Cradock that China would rather "recover Hong Kong as a barren rock than allow Britain to continue administering it."

It was a typical Chinese negotiating ploy to erect a principle and say that it had to be met before negotiations began. Since the principle was usually the main point of contention, the other party was asked to concede the game before walking onto the field. Cradock stood firm. At one point Zhang claimed that the joint communiqué issued during Thatcher's visit stated that the talks would be held on the condition that Britain agreed to hand over Hong Kong. "Nonsense!" Cradock replied.

The discussions went nowhere.

WITH THE TWO governments at loggerheads, Governor Youde feared that Beijing might pressure Britain by cutting off food and water supplies to Hong Kong. This had always been a worry. With six million people in such a small area, food shortages could quickly create panic. The Hong Kong government had elaborate contingency plans. Rice importers, for example, were required by law to keep a minimum sixty-day supply on hand at all times. Youde wanted to ensure that these measures were adequate and up-to-date.

Youde also anticipated that the British team would need current information when the negotiations got underway. Cradock and his staff in Beijing had no first-hand knowledge of the colony. They would need documents to support their arguments. Youde wanted to create a government branch to act as secretariat for the negotiations.

At that time, Lewis Davies, the secretary for security, was about to retire. Soft-spoken, amiable, and given to self-deprecating humor, Davies could not have found controversy if he were looking for it. He was an able administrator, popular with superiors and subordinates alike. He joined the Colonial Service in 1948. After rising to deputy governor of the Bahamas, he was transferred to Hong Kong in 1973. During his nine years as secretary for security he had dealt with the colony's contingency plans and could be trusted to be discreet with sensitive information. Youde asked him if he would like to help out with the negotiations. His job would be to assist Youde and Chief Secretary Haddon-Cave in all work related to the discussions in Beijing and to make sure the contingency plans were adequate.

Davies did not think he was the right choice. He could not speak Cantonese or read Chinese, and he did not know Hong Kong as intimately as some of the other civil servants. He had never been to China and did not keep up on the intricacies of her domestic politics. But Youde convinced him to take the job. He was given an office on the fifth floor of the government secretariat between those of the political adviser and the chief secretary. Davies enjoyed a warm friendship with Haddon-Cave. Their wit and comraderie would provide welcome relief for the few civil servants in Hong Kong who carried the weight of the negotiations on their shoulders. In November 1982, the Hong Kong government announced the creation of the General Duties Branch. Davies, the only staff member, became known as "Mr. 1997."

Because Beijing was refusing to begin the formal negotiations, there was little for Davies to do after he had reviewed the contingency plans. He set about collecting public opinion on the future of Hong Kong, interviewing members of the Executive and Legislative Councils, local businesspeople and academics, and gathering reports of professional surveys conducted locally. These were digested and passed on to Cradock in Beijing.

The British and Chinese governments had agreed that, in accordance with normal diplomatic protocol, all formal and informal exchanges regarding Hong Kong would be kept confidential. The Foreign Office was particularly keen to keep the talks secret because it felt that information leaks or public pronouncements would limit Cradock's room to maneuver and could cause panic in Hong Kong's financial markets. Initially, Davies was one of only four people in the Hong Kong government privy to the discussions in Beijing. The others were Governor Youde, Chief Secretary Haddon-Cave, and Robin McLaren, the former head of the Hong Kong department who had become political adviser. Even Executive Councilors were kept in the dark.

WHEN Y.K. Kan retired from the Executive Council, Governor MacLehose convinced him to chair the Trade Development Council. Kan was told that his primary objective was to improve economic relations with China. As part of that effort, he was supposed to lead a trade delegation to China in October—a trip that had been in the planning stages for six months. But Youde apparently did not share his predecessor's belief that trade relations with China needed to be enhanced, or perhaps China's stubbornness had changed the Foreign Office's thinking. Two weeks before the delegation was to leave, a Hong Kong trade official told Kan that he could not go to China. A few days later, Youde summoned Kan to Government House. Youde said that McLaren, who was supposed to accompany Kan, would not be able to go.

The trip went ahead (though Youde's deliberate attempt to sabotage the trade mission led Kan to resign his position shortly thereafter). While in Beijing, Kan was invited to meet Xi Zhongxun, the vice-chairman of the Standing Committee of China's National People's Congress, at the exclusive Zhongnanhai compound. (Liao Chengzhi's health was failing and Xi took over his responsibilities temporarily.) The Chinese considered Kan an old friend because he had been a member of the MacLehose delegation in 1979. They did not realize that as a former Executive Councilor he was completely cut off from the government. Kan himself was unsure why he had been invited. He went to the British embassy and asked Cradock what he thought. Cradock said he did not know, but that it would not hurt to go and find out.

The meeting was held at 5:30 P.M. on November 1 in a large greeting hall within the compound. Xi delivered a long spiel covering everything from agriculture in China to the upcoming National People's Congress. Kan's neck was starting to hurt when, after almost an hour, Xi finally got to the point. He said that Hong Kong was a special place that required special policies and special arrangements. Sovereignty was not negotiable. Management and administration were. "Kissinger-like shuttle diplomacy" would be used to solve the problem. Xi said Beijing would maintain Hong Kong's prosperity, stability, and confidence up to and beyond 1997. It was guaranteed that there would be no changes to Hong Kong's existing political, economic, and legal systems after China regained sovereignty over the colony. Xi did not say when that would be, but added that a solution should be worked out "within one or two years."

Two days later in Shanghai, Kan was invited to meet Mayor Wang

Daohan at the Jinjiang Club, an old European-style building not far from where President Nixon and Zhou Enlai signed the Shanghai Communiqué in 1972. Wang said that what Xi had told Kan were China's official policies. The Chinese government would not reveal details of the discussions with Britain. However, it felt free to disclose its plans for Hong Kong. China considered all Chinese in Hong Kong to be citizens of the People's Republic, and the government had the right to explain its policies to its own citizens. Xi's comments to Kan were the start of a well-planned propaganda campaign aimed at undermining Britain's case for continued administration after 1997. It had an immediate effect. When Kan briefed reporters on what he had been told, the Hang Seng Index rose fifty points.

THE FIFTH session of the National People's Congress (NPC) opened in Beijing in November, two weeks after the death of Soviet leader Leonid Brezhnev. The Chinese legislature adopted a new constitution which had been in the works since late 1978. The most striking feature, as far as Hong Kong was concerned, was Article Thirty-one which stated that the NPC "may establish special administrative regions [SARs] when necessary. The systems to be instituted in the SARs shall be prescribed by law enacted by the NPC in light of specific conditions." According to a prominent left-wing journalist, this article was drafted in 1978 with Hong Kong in mind.

As the colony slid deeper into recession, local businesspeople became more convinced that something had to be done to resolve the political uncertainty surrounding the colony's future. They pored over statements from China, searching for good or bad signs. Like a child alone in an old house at night, they envisioned with each creak or squeak out of China, some impending disaster, the end of Hong Kong as they knew it. Sensing the anxiety, the Hong Kong and Shanghai Banking Corporation, the colony's largest bank, announced in December that it would extend the period for repaying housing loans to twenty years, well beyond 1997. Beijing saw it as an attempt to make it appear that Hong Kong's problems were due to China's policies and that the British were taking steps to rectify the situation. In response, the Hong Kong branch of the Bank of China announced that it would offer cut-rate loans to local industrialists to help boost the economy.

Businesspeople were not the only ones concerned. Everyone from doctors to dock workers began thinking about their future. People belatedly realized the importance of the British Nationality Act of 1981. They had no delusions about Britain's willingness to take responsibility for her subjects. Many looked for their own ways out. Other Asian countries were keen to attract Hong Kong capital and offered residency to lure investors. The Singapore government sent a team to attract Hong Kong industrialists. The price for a safe haven: $465,000.

The sense of despondency in the colony was exacerbated by an unusually cold winter and a series of financial scandals, resulting from wild property speculation between 1979 and early 1982. Derek Davies, editor of the *Far Eastern Economic Review*, captured the mood in his weekly column with a version of "Santa Claus Is Coming to Town:"

> *He's making a list; he's checking it twice*
> *Gotta find out who's naughty or nice,*
> *Deng Xiaoping is coming to town.*
>
> *He knows when you are sleeping,*
> *He knows when you're awake,*
> *He knows if you've been bad or good,*
> *So be good for goodness sake . . .*
>
> *You better not shout, you better not cry*
> *You better not pout, I'm telling you why,*
> *Deng Xiaoping is coming to town.*

THE PREPARATORY talks in Beijing were suspended briefly in December when Zhang Wenjin was appointed China's ambassador to the United States. Cradock flew to Hong Kong to meet Governor Youde and Lord Belstead, the new Foreign Office minister responsible for Hong Kong. One item on the agenda was determining the role Hong Kong would play in the talks. Beijing was staunchly opposed to giving Hong Kong residents any say. This would be tantamount to having its own citizens sitting across the negotiating table. The Foreign Office did not want to complicate the difficult negotiations further. S.Y. Chung had other ideas. He had flown to London several times on business since September. Each time, he went to the Foreign Office and tried to confirm press reports about the discussions in Beijing. Each time, Dick Clift rebuffed him. Chung was adamant that the Executive Council should be consulted. He knew that the Foreign Office would put Britain's interests above those of her colony. Someone had to fight for Hong Kong's interests.

"When it comes time for us to vote on the agreement, we will not be able to face the people of Hong Kong," he told his colleagues in the Executive Council. "If we do not know the background and process of the negotiations, we cannot know if Britain got the best deal. History will judge us badly."

Chung was prepared to resign. The others agreed that if the British government was going to keep them in the dark, it should find another group of unofficials. The message was conveyed to the British foreign secretary by

Belstead when he returned to London, and in January, Thatcher agreed that the Executive Council would be kept informed of developments at the negotiating table and asked for advice.

BEFORE leaving for London, Lord Belstead held a press conference. This was standard practice; the local press was appeased with bland quotes and nothing of substance was ever revealed. Belstead avoided questions regarding the negotiations in Beijing. He casually mentioned that any arrangement for Hong Kong's future had to have the support of the British and Chinese governments and the people of Hong Kong, like a table with three legs. "All three legs are important because if one gives way, the table will give way as well."

In January, while Thatcher was in the Falklands basking in the glow of victory, the pro-China *Ta Kung Pao* newspaper published a stinging attack on what it called "the three-legged stool concept." It said that when "a senior British official" spoke about the collapse of one of the three legs, he wanted to give the impression that once China took back Hong Kong, the colony's economy would collapse. "This is blatant blackmail," the paper said, "an attempt to convince people that one cannot have both sovereignty and prosperity."

Beijing kept up a furious propaganda barrage throughout the early months of 1983. The pro-China papers argued that Hong Kong's success had nothing to do with the British, that it was, in fact, due to the "arduous struggle by our Hong Kong compatriots and to help from the interior"—meaning China. This help was in the form of cheap imports, which made Hong Kong products more competitive on world markets.

The pro-communist papers attacked Britain's claim that sovereignty and administration could be separated. One *Ta Kung Pao* commentary stated that an extension of British rule in Hong Kong beyond 1997 would be "a travesty of sovereignty" and that "maintaining alien rule on Chinese territory is unacceptable and unthinkable." Another asked: "How could China account for itself to its ancestors and future generations if, by 1997, it has still not recovered Hong Kong?"

Hong Kong read these editorials and trembled.

IN THIS TENSE atmosphere, the talks about talks continued. Cradock called on, or was summoned to, the Chinese Foreign Ministry about twice a month. There was little progress. He continued to argue that China benefitted far more from Hong Kong than Britain. This was becoming more true every day. The value of China's trade through Hong Kong in 1982 was $3.5 billion, more than twelve percent of her total foreign trade. Re-exports of goods from China tripled between 1978 and 1981, and the value of China's re-imports through Hong Kong grew more than six-fold. Cradock insisted that China would lose the benefits of this dynamic port if Britain withdrew from Hong Kong because the colony's economic system was fundamentally incompatible with socialism. Moreover, the people of Hong Kong and foreign investors had no confidence in China's ability to run a sophisticated financial, commercial, and industrial city like Hong Kong.

The Chinese government still refused to start the negotiations until Britain agreed to hand over the colony. It did, however, respond to Cradock's claim that China could not run Hong Kong by expanding on its original four points (the sixteen character solution). Over the next few months, Vice-Foreign Minister Yao Guang, Zhang Wenjin's replacement, informed Cradock that Hong Kong would be run by local residents and given a high degree of autonomy in all areas except foreign affairs and defense, which would be handled by Beijing. It would have the power to enact laws locally, and its legal system would be maintained. The lifestyle of local residents would remain basically unchanged. They would enjoy freedom of press, speech, and assembly. The local police would maintain internal security.

Hong Kong's capitalist system, free port, and status as a financial center would all be retained. The colony could continue to issue its own currency, which would be freely convertible (the design of the notes and coins, which featured the head of Queen Elizabeth, would have to be changed).* Although Beijing would handle most foreign affairs, Hong Kong would be free to deal independently with other countries on a wide range of economic and cultural matters. Local residents would help to draft a charter for the future Hong Kong Special Administrative Region, which would be set up under Article Thirty-one of the Chinese constitution. The charter would spell out in detail how the colony would be run after 1997. After an open debate in Hong Kong, it would be enacted by the National People's Congress.

These policies were hopelessly vague and would do little to maintain confidence in Hong Kong. The talks were deadlocked.

THERE was a growing feeling among the Old China Hands and among some of Thatcher's closest advisers that the British position was hopeless. The

---

* In July 1983, the Legislative Council voted to delete from its standing orders all references to Hong Kong as a colony. The two local note-issuing institutions followed quickly with announcements that they would remove the word "colony" from new banknotes. Officials began to refer to Hong Kong as "a territory."

Chinese government was not going to give in, even if it meant Hong Kong's economy would collapse. Britain had few cards to play. World opinion, or at least Third World opinion, was siding with Beijing. China was offering Hong Kong residents self-rule, something Britain had never done in 140 years. Some diplomats and Cabinet ministers felt there was no alternative but to negotiate on the basis that the colony would be returned to China in 1997. Thatcher (and the Executive Council) did not see it that way. She believed concessions could be won, and she was not going to let the "wets" in the Foreign Office talk her into giving up without a fight.

The Chinese government was given a hint of this split in British thinking in March 1983. Beijing had announced that its ambassador to Britain, Ke Hua, would be recalled at the end of the month. Field Marshal Edwin Bramall, the chief of Britain's Defense Staffs, knew Ke well and invited him to a farewell lunch.

Bramall was a stubby, white-haired soldier and one of the few in Britain with a flair for politics. He had served as Commander of British Forces in Hong Kong from 1973 to 1976 and was closely following the situation in the colony. To the lunch he invited Lord Chalfont, a former defense minister*; Alan Donald, an Old China Hand and former political adviser to Mac-Lehose; and Jack Cater, the Hong Kong government's commissioner in London. It was an informal gathering held at Bramall's apartment near the Albert Hall on March 5. The men brought their wives. Ambassador Ke was also accompanied by the military attaché from the Chinese embassy.

At the end of the meal, the ladies were asked to leave the room. Port was poured, and Bramall brought up the subject of Hong Kong. He said that he liked "the package" that China had put forward for the future of Hong Kong and asked Ambassador Ke to explain it to the other guests.

Ke was slightly nonplussed.

"I don't know what you mean," he said.

"The proposal you put forward for Hong Kong," Bramall said. "Why don't you tell everyone again."

"Field Marshal Bramall," Ke said in English, "you are familiar with China's position. Why don't you brief the others?"

Bramall explained that under China's plan, Hong Kong would not become socialist after 1997. He recounted some of the promises Chinese leaders had made to delegations visiting Beijing. "I think it's a rather good package," he said. "It should reassure the people of Hong Kong."

"Your prime minister obviously doesn't think so," Ke said.

---

* Chalfont did not recall the lunch and threatened legal action if his name was used in connection with this event. Bramall and another person present confirm that he was there.

According to one person present, Bramall and Donald indicated that the prime minister would soon change her mind. Both deny they made such comments. Nevertheless, Cater, an old colonialist who had spent his whole career serving the interests of Hong Kong, came away believing that two senior British civil servants were undermining their government's official policy. Though his interpretation was disputed, the lunch would have an impact on later events.

TWO DAYS AFTER the lunch, Governor Youde and Ambassador Cradock flew to London to discuss with the prime minister and foreign secretary how to get the talks going. Cradock was convinced that Britain had to agree to sever all links with Hong Kong and negotiate the terms on which it would be returned to China. S.Y. Chung and his fellow unofficial Executive Councilors were adamantly opposed. They believed it was much too early to concede the game.

Cradock, hoping to get the talks going, came up with a subtle compromise. Britain would suggest putting aside the issue of sovereignty and begin examining arrangements that would maintain Hong Kong's stability and prosperity after 1997. It was a slight shift towards China's position. But then Cradock would argue that the only way to maintain stability and prosperity would be to allow Britain to continue running Hong Kong. Thatcher accepted the plan and a letter to Premier Zhao Ziyang was drawn up. It read, provided an agreement can be reached between the two sides on "administrative arrangements for Hong Kong, which would guarantee the future prosperity and stability of Hong Kong, would be acceptable to the British Parliament and to the people of Hong Kong as well as to the Chinese government, I would be prepared to recommend to Parliament that sovereignty over the whole of Hong Kong would revert to China." It was to be delivered by Cradock through the Chinese Foreign Ministry.

When they arrived in Hong Kong, Cradock and Youde briefed the Executive Council on the letter. The Councilors had no choice but to accept it. The prime minister had made her decision. Chung knew China would never compromise on British administration now. He would push the British government as hard as he could to get the best possible deal for Hong Kong.

JACK CATER AND Alan Donald had accompanied Cradock and Youde to the airport for their flight back to Hong Kong. In the VIP lounge at Heathrow, Cater asked Cradock and Youde if they had heard about the extraordinary lunch hosted by Bramall. They had not. Cater recounted his version of what had transpired. Neither Cradock nor Youde seemed alarmed by the story.

S.Y. Chung heard about the Bramall lunch indirectly. He was very concerned about it and discussed it during an Executive Council meeting. He asked the governor to investigate Cater's claims. Several weeks went by without a response. Chung raised the issue again. Youde said he was looking into it. When Chung broached the subject a third time, Youde said: "There's nothing in it. It never happened."

Throughout the negotiations, Chung and his colleagues relied on Youde to present their views to the British government and to represent them at the negotiating table. He never put words in their mouths and never hinted that they should not raise a point with Her Majesty's Government. They respected him for that and trusted him. "He was our man and we never doubted him," one of them says. When Youde said there was nothing in it, most believed him.

DESPITE THE REBOUND of Hong Kong's exports and an improvement in the trade deficit, the local currency continued to fall against the U.S. dollar, closing at a record low of 7.10 on May 28, 1983. The decline was hurting Beijing because the money it earned from selling food, vegetables, and water to Hong Kong was converted into other currencies to purchase technology for her modernization drive. By Beijing's estimate, about $1 billion had been lost in 1982 because of the fall of the Hong Kong dollar. Beijing suspected that Britain and powerful businesses in Hong Kong were manipulating the currency markets to pressure China into maintaining the status quo. This strategy would not work. Zhao Ziyang was quoted as saying: "No nation can sacrifice sovereignty for prosperity."

The general manager of the Hong Kong branch of the Bank of China demanded publicly that the Hong Kong authorities stabilize the local currency and abolish a ten percent tax on Hong Kong dollar deposits. There was no tax on foreign currency deposits, which encouraged people to switch.

Chinese leaders realized that Hong Kong's economic woes were due mainly to China's insistence on reclaiming the colony and stepped up their United Front effort. Beijing appointed more Hong Kong residents to mainland political bodies, including the National People's Congress. (Like Britain's royal honors, the appointments gave face in exchange for loyalty.) More Hong Kong delegations were invited to China and advised of the policies that the leadership had worked out for Hong Kong under mainland rule. The presentations were very convincing. "All of us in this room have been victims of extreme leftist policies," one delegation was told. "We all suffered during the Cultural Revolution. Those days are over. It can never happen again."

The Chinese expected the delegations to spread the word in Hong Kong through the left-wing and independent press. London did not state its position publicly, or propose any solutions to counter the Chinese propaganda. Cradock stuck quietly and tenaciously to Britain's original line.

ON JUNE 9, 1983, Thatcher's Conservative Party won a landslide victory. The Tories took 397 of the 650 seats in the House of Commons, giving the prime minister an overwhelming majority and tremendous political clout. Two days later, she replaced Foreign Secretary Francis Pym with Geoffrey Howe, and Foreign Office Minister Lord Belstead with Richard Luce. Luce was a tall, savvy politician who had resigned along with Lord Carrington over the Falklands debacle.

Chubby and owlish, Howe was renowned for his reserve. One Labour MP said being attacked by him was like "being savaged by a dead sheep." Thatcher considered him to be a bore, but he had a reputation as a man of integrity and someone who could master enormous amounts of detail. He was taking over at a crucial time, as far as Hong Kong was concerned. The talks were about to enter a new phase, and Howe would be the minister with overall responsibility. Hong Kong generally welcomed his appointment and that of Luce, who, as a member of the Commons, had more political clout than Lord Belstead.

The news from Beijing was less encouraging. Liao Chengzhi died on June 10. He had been China's main spokesperson on national reunification and the individual most closely associated with Hong Kong policies.

During the sixth National People's Congress being held in Beijing that month, Deng Xiaoping himself joined the propaganda war, waving a stick at Britain and offering Hong Kong a carrot. He told delegates from the colony that for the sake of the colony's well-being, the question of its future should be resolved with Britain by September 1984, or "we will have our own ideas." He added that there would be "no changes" in Hong Kong for fifty years after China recovered the colony. It was the first time a Chinese leader had mentioned the deadline given to Thatcher in public, or spelled out how long the one country, two systems arrangement would last. Deng was clearly growing impatient.

Chapter 6

Britain Concedes the Game

I T WAS A HOT subtropical summer day. The temperature was over ninety degrees and the humidity was stifling when the short, elderly Chinese man with close-cropped, iron-gray hair stepped off the train from Guangzhou. He wore, outside his baggy trousers, a white, button-down shirt with the collar open. Tinted glasses, which were popular in China, hid his tiny eyes. As he emerged from customs, a group of journalists surged towards him, thrusting microphones in his face. He was not alarmed, though such a scene would never have been allowed in China. He smiled broadly and declared: "I am here to strive with the compatriots of Hong Kong for the unification of the motherland."

It was June 30, 1983, exactly fourteen years before Britain's lease of the New Territories was to expire. Xu Jiatun was arriving to take up his post as the new director of the Xinhua News Agency in Hong Kong. As China's chief representative in the colony—in effect, its consul general—he would play an important role in China's recovery of the colony.

The Xinhua News Agency was, like Hong Kong itself, a historical anomaly. It was set up in 1947 as a propaganda organ, like Moscow's Tass. After the 1949 Revolution, China wanted to set up a diplomatic commissioner's office in the colony. The Hong Kong government cleverly insisted that Beijing establish a full consulate. This would have been tantamount to recognizing Britain's sovereignty over Hong Kong, so the Chinese government refused. Xinhua thus became the unofficial consulate. Because China considered Hong Kong to be part of Guangdong, Xinhua was run by the Hong Kong and Macao Work Committee, which was based in Guangzhou and was part of the provincial arm of the Communist Party. It took orders directly from the External Affairs Office in Beijing.

Xu (pronounced *Shu*) was the most senior Communist ever to head Xinhua. He was a surprise choice because he had almost no experience in international affairs and he did not speak Cantonese. Deng Xiaoping apparently wanted someone in Hong Kong during the negotiations who could be trusted and who was answerable directly to the party leadership. He reportedly handpicked Xu for the job.

Xu was born in 1916 to a peasant family in the fertile farmland region north of the Yangtze River in Jiangsu Province. He married in 1937 and joined the Communist Party and Red Army in 1938 to fight the Japanese. He was a guerilla and rose within a few years to become a secretary to Communist Party committees in counties near his birthplace. After the Japanese were defeated in World War II, the communist guerilla forces were combined with larger units of the Third Field Army under Marshal Chen Yi. Xu saw action during the civil war as political commissar to the Twenty-ninth Army, which marched into Fujian Province, just north of Guangdong on the coast, at the end of the war. Xu stayed there and became deputy secretary of the Fuzhou party committee after liberation.

Five years later, Xu returned to his native Jiangsu and joined the Nanjing branch of the Communist Party. In 1956, he was promoted to the provincial party committee, where he enjoyed a brilliant career. Under his leadership, the cities of Wuxi, Changzhou, Suzhou, and Nantong grew so quickly that they became known collectively as "the Four Little Tigers." At the start of the Cultural Revolution, he was vice-governor of Jiangsu and first secretary to the provincial party committee. Because of his emphasis on economic advancement, he was branded a "capitalist roader" and disgraced. He was rehabilitated in 1976 and elected the following year to the party's Central Committee. He eventually became governor of the province.

As a member of the Central Committee, Xu enjoyed direct access to the party leadership. His personal rapport with Deng Xiaoping and Zhao Ziyang gave him tremendous freedom to pursue China's policies as he saw fit. His job at Xinhua was to report directly to Beijing on events in Hong Kong, to deal with the colonial administration on a consular level, to oversee China's rapidly expanding economic interests in the colony, and most important during the coming negotiations, to win support for China's policies through the United Front. He would use all the forces at his disposal: pro-China newspapers, trade unions, companies, and grass-roots organizations in the New Territories.

Shortly after arriving, Xu toured the Walled City in Kowloon. The area had originally been excluded from British rule under the lease of the New Territories, but the queen had issued an Order in Council in 1899, which brought it under British jurisdiction. The wall was disassembled by the Japanese army and used to extend the airport runway during the occupation. The rural village was replaced by a jumble of buildings with multiple illegal additions, which became a haven for illegal immigrants from China, criminals, drug addicts, prostitutes, and other fugitives from the law. Clad in an open-neck shirt and his tinted glasses, Xu strode about the slum as though he were taking possession of Chinese territory. When he was told that the Walled City was managed by elected members of a neighborhood committee, he commended the residents for their "self-administration."

The walk and this comment in particular drew a torrent of derision from many independent newspapers. In a play on China's policy of Hong Kong people ruling Hong Kong, an editorial in the *Economic Journal* was headlined: WALLED CITY PEOPLE RULING THE WALLED CITY: ONE BIG MESS! This set off a furious war of words in the press. Pro-communist papers defended Xu's "familiarization tour" and condemned the *Journal* writer as a "henchman" of the British.

Xu quickly switched to a more subtle approach in the propaganda war. Every night he dined with local bankers and businesspeople. Their support was crucial. If they all fled when China reclaimed Hong Kong, the economy would collapse. Xu seduced them with promises that Beijing would respect private property, free enterprise, and the current capitalist system. Everything would be the same after 1997; everything would be fine. Whenever someone mentioned that a continued British presence in Hong Kong after 1997 would help preserve confidence, Xu politely responded in the negative.

Hong Kong boasted the freest press in Asia, and many journalists were skeptical of China's apparent willingness to give Hong Kong a high degree of autonomy. Xu used dinner diplomacy on publishers and senior editors of independent newspapers. Reporters and columnists were invited to China and feted by officials. Xinhua sent them fresh lychees and sweet hami melons from Xinjiang Province when these were in season. The gifts were often accompanied by a hand-written note from Xu Jiatun or one of his deputies. Political commentators noticed a subtle shift in many newspapers. Criticism of Beijing was toned down and positive news about China was played up.

CRADOCK'S LETTER proved to be a breakthrough, and just before Xu Jiatun's arrival, the British and Chinese governments agreed on the terms of the negotiations. They would be held in Beijing. The teams would be headed by Percy Cradock and Vice-Foreign Minister Yao Guang. The agenda was broken into three broad topics: the question of sovereignty and administration, issues affecting Hong Kong before 1997, and issues affecting Hong Kong after 1997. On July 1, Britain and China announced that the "second phase" of the talks on Hong Kong's future would begin on July 12. The Hang Seng Index rose ninety-five points.

Now that the formal talks were about to start, S.Y. Chung was concerned that Britain would quickly bow to China's demands to hand over

Hong Kong and negotiate the terms. Governor Youde understood Chung's position and arranged for all nine unofficial members of the Executive Council to go to London in July to express their concerns directly to Foreign Secretary Howe.

During the trip, the Foreign Office revealed that Youde would be a member of Britain's negotiating team. He would represent Hong Kong's interests and provide expertise on how the colony worked. The Chinese government had agreed to his participation, but had very different ideas about the role he would play.

When Youde arrived back in Hong Kong with the delegation, he gave a brief press conference at the airport. When one reporter asked whom he would be representing at the talks, he replied: "I am the governor of Hong Kong. Indeed, I represent the people of Hong Kong. Who else would I represent?"

Beijing was determined not to give the people of Hong Kong any say in the negotiations. The next day, the Chinese Foreign Ministry issued a statement saying that Youde was part of the British team. "Therefore, he can only represent the British government in the talks." China also prevented a senior Chinese Hong Kong civil servant from accompanying Youde to Beijing as his press aide by refusing to give the official a visa.

THE NEGOTIATIONS were expected to be long and difficult. The British team consisted of three arms, one each in Beijing, London, and Hong Kong. In addition to Cradock and Youde, the negotiators in Beijing included Political Adviser Robin McLaren and three secretaries from the British embassy. In London, Dick Clift was assisted by some of the Foreign Office's best diplomats and legal experts. There was a sense of history being made, and many of those involved said later they would not have missed it for the world. The number of staff in the department went from three before Thatcher's trip to Beijing to twenty-three at the height of the negotiations. Clift's team was supported by the Cabinet Office, the Treasury, the Ministry of Defense, the Home Office, and the Department of Transport. The Cabinet also set up a committee chaired by the prime minister herself. Though not involved in the day to day negotiations, this committee approved all major decisions made throughout the negotiations.

The Hong Kong arm comprised the Executive Council and the General Duties Branch. The Council would be consulted on all important matters, but would not enjoy unlimited access to all information relating to the talks. In addition to its usual Tuesday morning meetings, it would hold special sessions every Wednesday to discuss developments at the negotiating table.

Extraordinary meetings were called by the governor or chief secretary when-ever important matters arose.

While S.Y. Chung and his fellow Councilors would be under tremen-dous political pressure to ensure that the agreement would be acceptable to the people of Hong Kong, most of the workload and the deadline pressure would be on the staff of the General Duties Branch. They would supply all the critical information about how the colony was run. They had to provide briefing papers for the Executive Council and seek the Council's endorsement for speaking notes to be used in the talks. Though they were headquartered in the government secretariat, all confidential cables from Beijing would be received in the basement of Government House. Towards the end of the negotiations, a British expatriate civil servant who had been appointed to assist Lewis Davies moved into the governor's official residence to monitor the telex machines. Two Chinese civil servants were also assigned to the General Duties Branch.

Youde and the Foreign Office had long realized that the talks would have to enter a more detailed stage. In early 1983, Davies and his assistant began talking to the heads of government departments who would have to supply critical information. They wanted to ensure that the British negotiators would have access to everything they might need. After the deadlock was broken, the General Duties Branch drafted four papers to be presented at the first few rounds. These covered the four pillars of Hong Kong's success: her legal system, economy, financial system, and administration. They were meant to show that Hong Kong's success depended on the maintenance of confidence. The underlying message was that confidence could only be sus-tained by continuing British administration.

GOVERNOR YOUDE flew to Beijing on July 11, 1983, with Political Adviser McLaren and interpreter Y.P. Cheng. When the three emerged from the airport VIP lounge, accompanied by Percy Cradock, Youde was besieged by some forty Hong Kong journalists jabbing microphones in his face. There was a tremendous sense of anticipation. Hong Kong's future was about to be decided, and the press was hungry for any scrap of information. Beijing had never seen anything like it. One foreign correspondent said it was like "the *paparazzi* hunting an Italian movie queen." Youde appeased the horde with a noncommital quote, and the four sped off in Cradock's waiting limousine, which, coincidentally, sported the license plate number 31-1996.

Journalists were not informed when and where the negotiations would take place. The next morning, they gathered outside the British embassy. By 8:30 A.M. there were a dozen cars lining the street. Suddenly, the gates opened and a dusty white compact dashed out. Reporters jumped into their cars and gave chase. The compact pulled into a gas station three blocks away. Bob Pierce, a first secretary, got out, filled up his tank, and returned to the embassy, followed by several carloads of embarrassed reporters.

A few minutes later, a limousine carrying Cradock, Youde, and McLaren left the embassy, followed by two other cars carrying the three secretaries and the team's interpreter. Once again the journalists gave chase, jumping traffic lights and switching lanes along spacious Changan Avenue. The motorcade turned left into the old legation quarter east of Tiananmen Square and through the rusty gates of the old Austro-Hungarian embassy.

Taichichang, as it was renamed, was an old, European-style building with high ceilings and a long, curved stairway leading to the second floor. Except for a few Chinese paintings in the reception area, the decor was plain and shabby. The negotiations were held in a large room on the ground floor, perhaps the former dining room. A long table was set up with seven chairs on each side. Cradock sat in the center with Youde and McLaren to his right, the interpreter to his left.

The Chinese team leader, Yao Guang, was a "Chinese Chinese," as one member of the British team put it. Though he had been ambassador to several countries, including Canada and France, he was quiet and conservative, rarely ever saying more than hello to the press. He did not like Western food and was very reserved during the informal dinners which were hosted by the two teams alternately after each round of talks. He was supported by three representatives from the Foreign Ministry and one each from the Hong Kong and Macao Affairs Office and the Xinhua News Agency in Hong Kong. The Chinese team had little firsthand knowledge of Hong Kong, so Xinhua recruited "patriotic" Chinese, who provided background information on the intricacies and complexities of the capitalist system.

Under the agreed format, each round of negotiations would last two days. There would be one session each day lasting from 9:00 A.M. until noon, with a short break about 10:30. During the first two-day session, Cradock presented the paper on Hong Kong's economy and asked Youde to explain the complexities involved, particularly those regarding trade. Youde emphasized the importance of the international agreements Hong Kong was party to under Britain, such as the General Agreement on Tariffs and Trade (GATT). Yao Guang listened carefully. At the end of the presentation, he asked questions about specific points in the paper. Because the two sides had agreed to put it aside, there was no discussion of who had sovereignty over Hong Kong. At the end of the round, the British requested that a brief statement be issued describing the talks as "useful and constructive." The purpose was to avoid creating too much optimism in Hong Kong when things were going well, or to create concern when there were problems.

Round two proceeded the same way. Cradock presented a paper that explained Hong Kong's financial system, especially how trade was financed. Again, Youde explained everything from letters of credit to the need for a freely convertible currency, stressing those areas where the British link was crucial. Yao Guang was not a brilliant man, nor China's most gifted negotiator, but he realized that Cradock and Youde were still arguing for continued British administration. Yao vented his anger on Youde, who, he said, was speaking for the people of Hong Kong. From the third round onward Cradock did all the talking for the British side. The joint statement at the end of the round said only that the talks were "useful."

During the third round, Yao said casually that "troops stationed in Hong Kong [after 1997] would be paid for by China," not Hong Kong. The British were alarmed. Nothing would kill confidence faster than having Chinese troops pouring into the colony. Cradock argued that the role of the British military could be taken over by the Hong Kong police. He pointed out that Britain had to station troops in Hong Kong because it was 7,000 miles away. China, on the other hand, could garrison troops across the border in Shenzhen and move them to Hong Kong when it was faced with an external threat. (This argument formed the basis of a paper presented during the later rounds.) The Chinese continued to insist that their soldiers would be based in Hong Kong.

Yao's patience ran out, and he refused to include any adjectives in the joint statement. This, along with the constant propaganda from the pro-China press in Hong Kong, was ample evidence that the talks were not going well.

THERE WAS A seven-week break in the talks between rounds three and four. The Chinese government stepped up the pressure on Britain. On August 15, Hu Yaobang, the general secretary of the Communist Party and the second in command in China, told reporters from Japan's *Mainichi* newspaper that China would respect history and take back Hong Kong when the New Territories lease expired on July 1, 1997. It was the first time a Chinese leader had mentioned the date of recovery publicly. He said China had "a set of systematic policies for maintaining Hong Kong's prosperity."

In Hong Kong, Xu Jiatun used China's propaganda machine to undermine Britain's financial and moral arguments for maintaining administrative control over the colony. A left-wing trade union released a statement saying: "Everybody knows that the sovereignty of a country is expressed by the right to govern. Without the right to govern, such sovereignty is empty sovereignty." The union claimed that such suggestions as exchanging administration rights for sovereignty, delaying the resumption of sovereignty, and joint administration of Hong Kong were equivalent to "prolonging the colonial rule of Hong Kong." Another pro-China union announced that its members unanimously supported Beijing's plan to recover Hong Kong, and that China's policy "is completely in line with the wish of Hong Kong's numerous labor compatriots." The left-wing *Ta Kung Pao* said: "Theirs is the true public opinion."

Investors were growing increasingly nervous. It was apparent that China was fully intent on taking back the colony. They unloaded their stocks, and foreign exchange dealers dumped Hong Kong dollars. The colony's woes were compounded when Typhoon Ellen scored a direct hit on September 9, packing winds of 120 knots. Angry seas crashed over the waterfront. Heavy rains caused mud slides and destroyed farmlands on the outlying islands. Eight people were killed and thousands made homeless. More than twenty ships ran aground, and over one hundred pleasure crafts were sunk or severely damaged.

AS THE STORM was raging in Hong Kong, former British Prime Minister Edward Heath arrived in Beijing for a private visit. Heath had been ousted as Conservative Party chairperson by Margaret Thatcher in 1975. He retained a bitter animosity towards her and at every turn attacked her policies and leadership of the party. The deadlock in the talks with China and the financial crisis in Hong Kong gave him plenty of ammunition. He argued that she was only antagonizing Beijing and driving it away from the West. Britain should concede sovereignty over Hong Kong and use the remaining time before September 1984 to work out the best solution for the colony's future under Chinese rule.

Heath enjoyed cordial relations with the Chinese leadership. He had been in power when Beijing was admitted to the United Nations, and the Chinese never forgot a friend. When he arrived in Beijing, he was treated like a visiting head of state and given a forty-five-minute audience with Deng Xiaoping. The Chinese leader spelled out China's policies towards Hong Kong in detail. When Heath spoke to reporters in Beijing, he expressed every confidence that China could maintain Hong Kong's stability and prosperity.

Heath arrived in the colony a few days after Typhoon Ellen left. He was invited to brief Umelco on his trip. S.Y. Chung would then host a dinner for him, a standard practice with visiting MPs. Chung was well aware that Heath's position on Hong Kong was diametrically opposed to his own. Although Heath held no ministerial post, he was an influential member of the Conservative Party and his views would carry great weight in Parliament when it debated any agreement reached with China. Before the briefing,

Chung called a meeting of the unofficial members of the Executive and Legislative Councilors to discuss strategy. How should they handle Heath? Could they convince him that his position was wrong? The members decided that they would grill him and expose the flaws in his reasoning.

On the evening of Monday, September 12, Heath met Umelco members in their Swire House office. Sitting at the head of the conference table, he recounted what he had been told in Beijing and said that, contrary to the common belief in Hong Kong, he believed that China's current leadership understood fully how Hong Kong operated.

Umelco members knew Hong Kong was on the ropes. Britain was close to conceding sovereignty. They were suffering because of China's propaganda campaign. They had nothing to lose, so they fired off pointed questions, one after the other. How can China guarantee stability in Hong Kong when it has no formal mechanism to facilitate a smooth change of leadership? How can China guarantee human rights in Hong Kong when China is not a signatory to the U.N. covenants? Why should investors trust China when they can go to Singapore, Taiwan, or Korea? Heath parried these questions with the skill of a seasoned politician.

"Thank you, Mr. Heath, you have done an excellent job," Chung said when the briefing was over.

"What do you mean?" Heath asked.

"You are an excellent salesman."

"If you are saying that I have come here to sell you China's policies, you are mistaken."

"I'm sorry if I have used the wrong word," Chung said. "I didn't mean to offend you. But I cannot change what I think."

"I'm sorry, I cannot accept your position," Heath said, his puffy, white face turning noticeably red. "I will not be staying for dinner."

When the former prime minister stormed out of the building, Chung called the governor.

"Excuse me, sir. Have you eaten?"

"No," said Youde. "Why?"

"Mr. Heath will be joining you. He refused to be our guest tonight."

THE BRITISH government reassessed its position during the break in the talks. Cradock and Youde flew to London for talks with senior officials. The question was: Should the British negotiators accept China's position and agree to sever all links with Hong Kong after 1997? Or should they continue to stick to their original position? Youde was strongly urged by Chung and the Executive Council not to give in. Cradock feared that Beijing might break off the negotiations. Thatcher instructed him to hold out for one more round.

When word leaked that the British team would stick to its guns, foreign exchange dealers unloaded Hong Kong dollars as fast as they could. On September 16, the currency fell below the 8.00 mark for the first time in its history. Pro-China newspapers accused Britain of manipulating the currency markets in an effort to convince Beijing that the only way they could maintain the benefits of Hong Kong was to allow Britain to continue running it after 1997.

The British and Hong Kong authorities made no attempt to shore up the currency. John Bremridge, Hong Kong's brilliant and irascible financial secretary, told reporters: "It is not possible to fix the exchange rate of the Hong Kong dollar to any particular level. This must depend upon the forces of the marketplace." Foreign exchange dealers took the comment as a sign that the Hong Kong government would not intervene to boost the currency and continued to unload Hong Kong dollars. The financial secretary also refused to abolish a ten percent withholding tax on Hong Kong dollar deposits. The tax was not the main reason that depositors were switching to foreign currencies, but Bremridge's refusal to scrap it was another sign that the Hong Kong government would not take steps to support the local currency.

China hit back with hostile editorials that showed she would never bow to economic pressure. On the day before round four was to begin, the *People's Daily*, the official organ of the Chinese Communist Party, published an editorial accusing Britain of trying to impose "a new unequal treaty" on China in an effort "to continue its colonialist domination of Hong Kong even after 1997." The paper spelled out Beijing's position: "When China talks of regaining sovereignty over Hong Kong, it means reviving the enactment of sovereignty, including reviving administrative powers." It did not mean regaining sovereignty in name only and renouncing administrative power. "This is self-evident."

ON THE FLIGHT to Beijing, Youde was reading a book on China, *The Gate of Heavenly Peace* by Jonathan Spence. He was expecting anything but a peaceful round of negotiations.

The session got off to a tense start when Yao Guang accused the British government of engineering the currency crisis to pressure China into accepting a British presence in Hong Kong after 1997. He said London was fully capable of resolving the problem. Cradock denied that Britain had anything to do with it, and then went through the motion of presenting the final paper on the administration of Hong Kong, stressing everything from the apolitical civil service to Britain's role in applying international standards in the colony. As expected, Yao stuck to China's position that there could be no constitutional link between Britain and Hong Kong after 1997. He would be willing to discuss arrangements for Hong Kong after 1997 only when Britain had accepted this position. During six hours of face-to-face discussions, no progress was made.

On the day the round concluded, the Hang Seng Index fell sixty-three points to 785, down from 1,100 just ten weeks earlier, and the Hong Kong currency slipped to 8.83 during trading.

The people of Hong Kong had been kept in the dark about their future for almost a year now. Nervous and browbeaten by Beijing's constant propaganda, they were ready to snap. When banks opened on Saturday, September 24, customers lined up at foreign exchange counters to switch their life savings out of Hong Kong dollars. Reports said that the exchange rate was dropping so quickly that at one bank, the U.S. dollar rate for the first person in line was 9.15, for the second 9.20, and for the third 9.30. By the time the foreign exchange markets closed shortly after noon, the Hong Kong dollar had fallen to an all-time low of 9.50 against the U.S. dollar, compared with 5.90 less than a year earlier.

The following day, housewives rushed to the markets to stock up on rice, cooking oil, toilet paper, and other household items before prices could be adjusted to the sharp fall of the local currency. Supermarket shelves were cleaned out. Fearing food riots, the police went on alert.

YOUDE'S FLIGHT back to Hong Kong was two hours late. During the delay at Beijing airport, he sat in the virtually empty VIP room and read a paper by a local economist on the value of and a method for pegging Hong Kong's currency to the U.S. dollar. When he returned to the colony, Youde discussed the idea with senior civil servants. Chief Secretary Haddon-Cave and others did not believe the mechanism would work, but were eventually convinced. On Sunday evening, the Hong Kong government announced that it was planning to peg the Hong Kong dollar.

On Tuesday, September 27, while all the world was talking about Australia's stunning victory in the America's Cup, breaking the United States' 132-year hold on yachting's most prestigious trophy, Hong Kong's financial system was teetering on the brink of collapse. At 6 P.M. Governor Youde called an emergency meeting of the Legislative Council to pass a bill enabling the government to buy out the Hang Lung Bank, which was about to go under. It was the first time in Hong Kong's history that the government had intervened to rescue an ailing bank. Financial Secretary Bremridge said that the bank's problems had nothing to do with the currency crisis. But the lack of confidence in Hong Kong's financial markets, no doubt, made it essential to rescue Hang Lung.

Two weeks later, after consultations with the Bank of England and the United States government, Bremridge announced in a televised speech that the Hong Kong currency would be pegged to the U.S. dollar at a rate of 7.80 to 1. He also abolished the ten percent withholding tax on Hong Kong dollar deposits. The currency quickly stabilized. This supported China's claim that the Hong Kong authorities had always had the means to resolve the crisis but held out for political reasons.

IN MID-OCTOBER, an article was published in the *South China Morning Post* which quoted "senior sources" in London as saying that "Mrs. Thatcher is now looking to Hong Kong to give her, and her party, a much needed boost to morale. She sees the future of the territory as another Falklands and is hoping to pull off a personal diplomatic coup." It was a classic piece of disinformation, probably put out by what American politicians call spin doctors.

After round four, the talks were clearly at a critical stage. The Executive Councilors flew to London for what would turn out to be the most important meeting of the negotiations. They gathered in the Cabinet Room of No. 10 Downing Street on October 7 with Prime Minister Thatcher, Foreign Secretary Howe, Ambassador Cradock, and Foreign Office Minister Luce. Thatcher sat at her usual seat near the fireplace. (It was distinguished by her chair, which was the only one with armrests.)

Chung, the most hawkish Executive Councilor, believed that it was too early to cave in to China's demands. He was not afraid that the talks would be broken off. There were still fourteen years to go before 1997. Hong Kong could withstand a crisis now. It had withstood many in the past. He believed that no agreement was preferable to a bad agreement. Though proud to be Chinese, he felt no shame at pushing for continued British administration. He believed this was best for Hong Kong and what most residents wanted. During the ninety-minute meeting, he argued forcefully that it would be a mistake to concede administration.

"You are experts in Chinese affairs," he told the British diplomats, "not Chinese culture. Chinese people have a different attitude towards bargaining." He explained that even if a Chinese thinks the price of an item is fair, he will bargain. If the seller does not compromise, the buyer will walk out of the shop. If the seller calls him back, only then will he know he got the best deal.

"Confidence in Hong Kong has been badly shaken. If the Chinese government breaks off the talks, then we will know that we did everything we could."

Cradock was sometimes impatient and dismissive with those who could not grasp his arguments quickly. The Executive Councilors felt, at times, as though he was a country lawyer treating them like yokels. He insisted to the mainly Chinese Councilors that the Chinese leadership was not bluffing. It was no good pushing them to the brink because if they broke off talks, they would announce a unilateral solution, which they could not go back on. This would spark a real crisis in Hong Kong. He proposed that the talks should proceed on the basis of examining the Chinese government's proposals to see if a suitable arrangement could be found for maintaining Hong Kong's stability and prosperity without British administration.

Howe saw things very much the way Cradock did and did not have to be convinced that it was time to change tack. Thatcher had believed that her forthright style and determination would produce concessions from Beijing, but it seemed clear now that the stubborn Chinese leadership would never give in. Another letter to Zhao Ziyang was drawn up. This time, Thatcher suggested that the negotiations focus on the Chinese government's proposals for Hong Kong. If the two sides could agree on arrangements that would provide for Hong Kong's continued stability and prosperity under Chinese rule, "the British government would be prepared to recommend to Parliament a treaty enshrining them."

One British *taipan* on the Executive Council felt that the Foreign Office made the right decision. Some British businesspeople with large investments in Hong Kong were "peeing in their pants." If they had been more resolute, he believed, perhaps the British government could have pushed Beijing harder. Chung had a different view. He told friends that if the Foreign Office had not "cracked," Britain would have gotten a better deal for the colony. Some Foreign Office diplomats agreed with Chung. Others felt that the bruising battle during the first four rounds left the Chinese with profound suspicions of Britain's intentions, making the rest of the negotiations more difficult.

ROUND FIVE marked the start of the real negotiations. Cradock began drawing out the Chinese team on how Beijing intended to administer the colony. He wanted to give substance to China's vague policies, which had evolved from four points to ten and now to twelve. The General Duties Branch prepared papers of four to six pages covering roughly the topics touched on in China's twelve points. The purpose was to spell out in detail how Hong Kong worked, so that when the Chinese team said that existing systems would remain unchanged, Cradock could pin them down. (The papers often involved a massive amount of work. When researching a paper on Hong Kong's external relations, Lewis Davies found that there was no list of international organizations, conventions, and treaties that applied to Hong Kong under Britain's auspices. It took three lawyers more than five months to come up with an exhaustive list.)

When the round ended, the words "useful and constructive" reappeared in the joint statement. The talks, in fact, had not gone as well as the British team had expected. Beijing still suspected that London would cling to some special link to enable it to continue running Hong Kong after 1997. It was not until Thatcher conveyed through Cradock during the next round in November that Britain was prepared to sever all links with Hong Kong that the Chinese team started spelling out Beijing's position in detail.

Chapter 7

"After the Rain, the Sky Is Clear"

W HEN ROUND eight opened in January 1984, both sides had new
team leaders. Percy Cradock had turned sixty years old in October,
the normal retirement age for British diplomats. S.Y. Chung and his colleagues knew Cradock was the toughest negotiator among the Old China
Hands and asked him to stay on. He agreed to stay but only until December
because his wife was ill and he wanted to return to England. Thatcher also
wanted him to continue running the negotiations. She made him deputy
under secretary of state at the Foreign Office with special responsibility for
overseeing the negotiations. She also appointed him to be her personal adviser on foreign affairs. (He remained in the latter post even after she resigned as prime minister in November 1990. A secret cable in 1989 from the
U.S. embassy in London to the State Department in Washington described
Cradock as "one of the most powerful and least understood men" in the
British government.)

The front-runner to replace Cradock had been Alan Donald, the bald,
portly diplomat in attendance at Field Marshall Bramall's lunch for the Chinese ambassador in March. Donald was popular with his colleagues and had
extensive knowledge of China. But Executive Councilors were adamantly
opposed to his appointment. Although they accepted Youde's explanation
that nothing had happened during the Bramall lunch, they considered Donald to be one of the Old China Hands who advocated a graceful withdrawal
from Hong Kong.

Richard Evans, a fifty-five-year-old diplomat with extensive experience in
China, was chosen to replace Cradock. Although he had done two stints in
China in 1955 and 1962, and had been a Fellow at Harvard's Center for
International Affairs, Evans had been considered a long-shot. He was not
popular with some of his colleagues, and most important, he was not regarded
as a tough or experienced negotiator, which was vital as the talks entered the
crucial stage. Some Executive Councilors thought he was "a ninny."

Evans was selected by process of elimination. Cradock recognized that

Evans was not an aggressive negotiator, but did not believe this to be a major problem. Cradock planned to give Evans explicit instructions from London, keeping him on a very short leash.*

That Evans would take over from Cradock as Britain's representative at the negotiating table had been known since September. There was some surprise, however, when the Chinese government replaced Yao Guang with his assistant, Zhou Nan. Senior Chinese officials were not happy with Yao's performance (he was not particularly tough and had difficulty grasping the complexities of Hong Kong) and used Britain's replacement as an opportunity to change their own representative.

Zhou was Yao's opposite. Where Yao was uncomfortable outside of a traditional Chinese setting, Zhou was witty and urbane and liked to charm people by quoting classical Chinese poems. Although he wore old-fashioned glasses and drab Chinese-made suits, he spoke fluent English and was regarded as a sophisticated international diplomat. He was said to be a descendant of one of Confucius's seventy-two disciples. Where Yao was soft and unsure of himself at the negotiating table, Zhou was tough, aggressive, even brutish. He was a ferocious negotiator who carried out instructions ruthlessly. "He's a shit," said one British diplomat, "a real nasty piece of work."

Born in 1927, Zhou was too young to be a member of the old guard. His real name was Gao Qingzong, and he hailed from Changchun in northern Jilin Province. Shortly before the Japanese invaded Manchuria, his family moved south to Tianjin, known as "the Shanghai of the north" for its industrial output. He studied philosophy at Beijing University, then economics at Beijing's Yenching University and finally foreign literature at the same school. Like most university students at the time, he had to choose sides in the civil war. He joined the Communist Party in 1946 and organized anti-Nationalist activities. He adopted the name Zhou Nan at that time.

After the 1949 Revolution, he taught English at the Institute of Foreign Languages. He was sent to North Korea in 1950 to interrogate American prisoners of war, which helped to hone his language skills. He joined the Foreign Service in 1951 and was posted to the newly created Chinese embassy in Pakistan. In the early 1960s, he served in Tanganyika (later Tanzania). During the Cultural Revolution, he was disgraced (for unknown reasons) and assigned to serve tea at a college for young Communists. That, it was said, was where he developed his love for the classics. When the People's Republic joined the United Nations in 1971, Zhou was posted to New York as a first

---

* Alan Donald was made ambassador to Indonesia and did not get the Beijing post until Evans retired in 1988. Years later, he was still bitter about what he saw as a misunderstanding over the Bramall lunch.

secretary. He stayed ten years and spent much of his free time during that period visiting museums in the city. When he returned to Beijing, he was assigned to the Western European Department and dealt mainly with Britain, particularly regarding issues related to Hong Kong.

Right from the start of round eight, Zhou made his position clear: The Chinese government would make arrangements for post-1997 Hong Kong as it saw fit. "He made quite a show of his lack of enthusiasm [for our papers]," according to one member of the British team. Still, he read them and commented on them extensively, making it clear that the Chinese side took them seriously.

During the remaining formal rounds, there would be very little give and take across the green felt-covered negotiating table. Evans was not an aggressive negotiator and preferred to stick to the formal routine of presenting papers that explained in detail how Hong Kong worked. He did not want to make any concessions that would prejudice the British side. Zhou accepted the information, asked questions, requested more information, and refused to commit his government to anything more than the policies it had already spelled out.

MEMBERS OF Hong Kong's Legislative Council had endured the sixteen months of secret negotiations in impotent silence. Those who were not also members of the Executive Council knew little more than the man on the street. Although Parliament alone would approve any agreement reached with China, most members felt that they owed it to the people of Hong Kong to hold a formal debate on it. On February 24, the senior member of the Legislative Council, Roger Lobo, informed the Hong Kong government that he would introduce a motion, which said: "This Council deems it essential that any proposals for the future of Hong Kong should be debated in this Council before any agreement is reached."

This seemingly benign and natural act by Hong Kong's appointed legislature touched off a furious controversy. The Chinese government saw it as an attempt to revive "the three-legged stool" and give Hong Kong a voice in the negotiations. Pro-China newspapers attacked the motion and Lobo personally. The *New Evening Post* said the motion breached the confidentiality of the talks because Lobo was an Executive Councilor and was privy to the diplomatic exchanges. The paper said London "should be held responsible for all acts of the Legislative Council and the consequences" of the Lobo motion. The motion had actually been drafted in January by Dr. Harry Fang, the second most senior Legislative Councilor, while Lobo was in London with a delegation of Executive Councilors. Lobo introduced it because he was the senior member.

Governor Youde was consulted before the motion was filed. Though he probably anticipated China's reaction, he did not object. The motion was debated on March 14, amid tight security. It attracted an unusual amount of interest. Over 200 local and overseas journalists crammed into the galleries, and many local residents listened to a live radio broadcast. None of the twenty-one Councilors who spoke during the four-and-a-half hour session disputed China's claim to sovereignty over all of Hong Kong. Five made strong appeals for the British and Chinese governments to lift the veil of secrecy over the talks.

"If the proposals are beyond question acceptable [to the people of Hong Kong], what has anyone got to lose by letting us examine them before it is too late?" asked businessman Alex Wu. "We are a modern people who cannot relish the prospect of an arranged marriage."

John Swaine, a Eurasian lawyer, criticized Britain's handling of the nationality issue. He called on London to maintain some link with the three million people in Hong Kong who were British either by birth or by naturalization, but who did not have the right to live in the U.K. "It would be the gravest injustice and an abdication of responsibility," he said, "if Her Majesty's Government were to write off these people by the signing of a treaty."

Youde, presiding as president of the Council, sat straight-faced throughout the debate. Chief Secretary Haddon-Cave, responding for the government, made it clear that Parliament alone would have the final say on the agreement.

The Lobo Motion was passed unanimously.

Zhou Nan was a suspicious man, who saw a conspiracy behind everything. Whenever a British diplomat asked him at an informal gathering about some recent event in the Soviet Union or the United States, he always saw some devious plot behind it. Therefore, when the British negotiators sat down for another round two days later, Zhou Nan accused the British of orchestrating the debate to pressure the Chinese side. "There are only two parties to these talks," he insisted, "Britain and China."

Evans patiently explained that the British and Hong Kong governments had nothing to do with the motion, that Legislative Councilors felt it was their duty to debate any agreement reached. Zhou insisted that Britain could have discouraged them from introducing the motion.

"We don't work like that," Evans said. "We don't lean on Legislative Councilors."

JUST AS THE controversy over the debate was fading, Hong Kong was rocked by the news that Jardine Matheson, a major British trading house, was moving its domicile to Bermuda. Jardines was "the Princely *Hong*," the oldest and most influential company in the colony. William Jardine had been instrumental in the birth of the colony.

Simon Keswick, the company's debonair *taipan*, was a descendent of a nephew of the company's founder. His family was the largest shareholder, and he wanted to protect the company from instability in Hong Kong, "to ensure in future that our holding company is able to operate under English law and to have access to the Privy Council in Britain." At a press conference on March 28, he said that the company was not pulling out of Hong Kong, but simply creating a new holding company in Bermuda. Its operations and seventy-two percent of its investments were in Hong Kong and would not be withdrawn. At the same time, he admitted that it was not desirable to have "all one's eggs in one basket." (During the following years, Jardine expanded aggressively overseas to reduce its exposure to Hong Kong.)

Left-wing newspapers saw the move as yet another British-inspired plot to show the Chinese government that a British administrative presence was necessary. The Hong Kong government was informed about the move only a few days before it was announced. It could not and would not prevent the company from making a sound business decision. Keswick himself had told Xinhua Director Xu Jiatun that specific guarantees for Hong Kong's future spelled out in a legally binding and internationally recognized agreement were needed to maintain confidence, not simply assurances from Beijing that everything would be okay. At the start of the following round of negotiations, Zhou Nan insisted that Britain had encouraged Jardines to make the move to undermine China's negotiating position. He could not believe that Britain did not even know about it. Evans tried to convince him that there was no plot, but made no headway.

DESPITE PERIODIC hiccups, the talks were progressing. In March, they were moved to the Diaoyutai State Guest House, where Margaret Thatcher had stayed during her visit in September. Diaoyutai (Fishing Terrace) was an 800-year-old retreat where Emperor Zhang Zong had built a platform for fishing. The Communist regime sealed off the park and constructed fifteen villas, each in a different style, decorated with Chinese antiques. The larger ones, used to house visiting heads of state, had living quarters, kitchens, conference rooms, and banquet halls. Linking the villas was a meticulously maintained garden, where brooks flowed under stone bridges, peacocks roamed, and wild birds nested. Anthony Galsworthy, a member of the British team, was a keen bird-watcher and often brought a pair of binoculars to the meetings to catch a glimpse of the local wildlife during breaks.

The official reason for the change of venue was that the old Austro-Hungarian embassy was due to undergo renovation. The Hong Kong press believed that it was because Britain was being more cooperative. It was certainly a step up from Taichichang. The negotiators were served succulent peaches the size of softballs, which could not be found anywhere else in China, instead of dry Chinese biscuits.

That month, the British team presented its last paper on how Hong Kong functioned. Cradock, who had taken up his posts in London, wanted to take the negotiations to the next level. He believed that if the two sides were to reach an agreement by September, there would have to be contacts at the ministerial level. Chung felt the British team should not be held to Deng Xiaoping's arbitrary deadline. He was supported by his colleagues, several of whom believed that Cradock was being too soft on the deadline issue because he did not want to damage good relations with Beijing. Cradock argued that they should try to complete an agreement before September 1984 because he believed Beijing could and would enforce the deadline. He also believed that the British negotiators could use the deadline to their advantage; the Chinese side would be bound by it as well and would be forced to make concessions to reach an accord on time.

Cradock prevailed, and in early March, Ambassador Evans went to the Chinese Foreign Ministry with a message for Zhou Nan: "My minister thinks it would be helpful if he held face-to-face talks with your minister." Zhou passed the message to Wu Xueqian, who had taken over from Huang Hua as Chinese foreign minister, and a trip was arranged for the following month.

APRIL WAS A hectic month for Youde. He led a delegation of Executive Councilors to London to press for a detailed, legally binding treaty. Beijing was insisting that it could not enter a treaty with Britain over Hong Kong because Hong Kong was Chinese territory. It would simply issue a unilateral declaration of its policies towards the colony after 1997. Chung and his colleagues wanted to impress the importance of having an agreement that was binding on China in international law upon the prime minister and the Foreign Office.

After the visit to London, Youde flew to Beijing for round twelve, during which the two sides moved to the third part of the agenda: arrangements for Hong Kong during the transition period. Three days later, he returned to Beijing to join Howe's entourage, which included Cradock, Wilson, the former political adviser who had been brought over from the Southern European Department, and Fred Burrows, a legal expert from the Foreign Office who resembled Fred Astaire. Burrows's presence attracted a great deal of attention in the press. It was assumed that because Howe brought a legal expert, an agreement was being drafted. In fact, the foreign secretary always traveled with someone who could provide legal advice.

Two days after his arrival, Howe held a meeting in the Great Hall of the People with Ji Pengfei, who had replaced the late Liao Chengzhi as head of the Hong Kong and Macao Affairs Office. Small, frail, and wrinkled, seventy-three-year-old Ji was long past the age when he could fight aggressively for China's interests. He was chosen, apparently, because he was the one expert in international affairs that the old guard trusted. As foreign minister from 1970 to 1974, he had played an important role in China's opening to the West. He took part in the negotiations with the United States when President Nixon visited China in 1972 to begin normalizing relations. After retiring from the Foreign Service, he continued to rise within the party ranks. He was made vice-premier in 1979 and a State Councilor in June 1983. Although the negotiations were being conducted by the Chinese Foreign Ministry, he was already working behind the scenes to help to establish the policies that China would use to keep Hong Kong prosperous after 1997.

Howe had three major items on his agenda. He wanted a commitment from the Chinese government that the agreement reached would spell out in detail China's policies towards Hong Kong after 1997 and be legally binding. Cradock had realized that it would not be possible to draft such an agreement holding two-day rounds every two weeks. Howe wanted to set up a working group which would meet every day to draft an accord. Deng had decreed that the agreement should be completed by the end of September (probably in time for China's National Day on October 1). Howe wanted to convince the Chinese that it would not be possible constitutionally to have the agreement come into force by October. Howe said he hoped the two sides would reach an agreement that could be initialled by then. But it would have to be debated by Parliament before being signed, and then there would have to be a waiting period before it could be ratified.

Deng had instructed the Chinese team that the agreement with Britain should not be too long or too detailed, but Ji was willing to give some ground in this area. He said that China's policies could be included in an annex to the main agreement, however, under no circumstances could the agreement be a treaty. This would bring up the question of whether the new treaty was replacing the ones from the nineteenth century, which China had never recognized. Moreover, Beijing could not agree to include future policies towards a part of its own territory in a formal treaty with a foreign country. Ji wanted the accord to be a joint communiqué similar to the Shanghai Communiqué under which China and the United States established relations without resolving points of contention. Each side would simply state its position.

Howe accepted that the accord would be called a "joint declaration" and that each side would spell out its own policies. Fred Burrows, the Foreign Office's legal expert, advised him that it did not matter what it was called as long as it included a clause that said both sides were bound by the terms of the accord. Ji refused to include such a clause.

Ji readily agreed to set up a working group, but he cross-examined Howe on why the agreement could not come into force by the end of September. Why does Parliament have to approve the accord? Why can't a debate be held before the end of September? How long is the ratification period? Eventually, he was satisfied. The accord would be initialed by September, signed by the end of the year, and come into force in mid-1985.

Howe held a round of talks with Premier Zhao that afternoon and was scheduled to see Deng the next morning in the Fujian Room of the Great Hall. Before the meeting with Deng, a member of the Chinese team advised Howe not to use the word "detail." It was a concept the Chinese leader did not like. Instead, Howe focused on the need to include assurances on the technical issues to give people in Hong Kong, particularly investors, confidence in the accord. During the meeting, Deng supported all the points reached with Ji and Zhao.

The trip set a routine for future visits. Howe would start with lengthy discussions with Foreign Minister Wu on broad issues, then hold detailed talks with Ji and Premier Zhao. If those meetings went well, he would meet with Deng. During each meeting, Howe had to get the right answers to the same questions. Howe was a lawyer by training and thought of it as a complex piece of litigation, where, by the end of the case, it was just as important not to get wrong answers that would conflict with earlier witnesses as it was to get the right answers.

HOWE'S DELEGATION, including Ambassador Evans, was whisked directly to the airport after meeting Deng to catch a flight to Hong Kong. Youde had been insisting for weeks that the British government could not just drop an agreement in Hong Kong's lap and expect people to accept it. He encouraged Howe to make a speech during his stopover in the colony. Shortly before Howe's visit, Youde himself had informed Legislative Councilors that Britain would not continue administering Hong Kong after 1997. One member broke down and cried.

Howe, Youde, Evans, Cradock, and McLaren spent the next day and a half in the governor's study, going over what Howe would say at his press conference. There were long discussions about what should or should not be "unveiled." Every word was carefully chosen. Then, on Thursday, April 20, Howe sat beneath the lion-and-unicorn coat of arms of the British government in the Legislative Council chambers and said that "it would not be realistic to think of an agreement that provides for continued British administration in Hong Kong after 1997." Though the news had been expected, it came as a jolt, like hearing that a terminally ill relative just died.

Howe said that the British negotiators were seeking an agreement based on China's concept of one country, two systems that would secure a high degree of autonomy for Hong Kong for fifty years after 1997. They wanted "arrangements that will provide for the maintenance of Hong Kong as a flourishing and dynamic society, and an agreement in which these arrangements will be formally recorded." China, at that point, was committed to only her twelve points, so he could not be too specific about the terms of the agreement. He said nothing that had not already been revealed to delegations visiting Beijing. Coming from the British foreign secretary, they seemed to carry greater weight.

During the speech, Howe made an explicit pledge to develop a democratic government in Hong Kong "during the years immediately ahead." He ruled out holding a referendum to determine if Hong Kong people accepted the agreement and refused to say whether or not Britain would go back to the negotiating table if Hong Kong was not satisfied.

When the stock market opened following the long Easter weekend, the Hang Seng Index dropped just forty-six points. Most newspaper editorials stressed the need to face reality. Civil servants in the colony were not reassured. Using the names of three of the principal players on the British side, a group of them summed up the talks this way: "Howe Youde Luce Hong Kong."

Round thirteen was held at Diaoyutai on April 26 and 27, at the same time President Reagan was staying there on his first state visit to China. (The compound was taken over by one hundred advisers and security people.) Although Zhou had been suspicious of Britain's intentions when he was told at the very end of Howe's trip that the foreign secretary intended to make a public statement on the talks in Hong Kong, he was delighted that the British had committed themselves publicly to withdrawing from Hong Kong. He believed for the first time that they were negotiating in good faith.

"After the rain, the sky is clear, and the garden has been washed," he declared buoyantly at the start of the round.

Richard Evans continued to push for a clause that would make the Joint Declaration legally binding. Zhou continued to resist. Despite the obstacles that lay ahead, Youde felt for the first time that it might be possible to secure an agreement by the end of September. The talks, he believed, had entered a new phase.

Chapter 8

The First Step Towards Democracy

T HE BRITISH Parliament would have to decide, in the end, whether to accept any agreement on Hong Kong reached by the British and Chinese negotiators. During the first year and a half of talks, MPs had held just a single, brief adjournment debate on the issue (ironically, after London had agreed conditionally to sever all ties with Hong Kong). MPs were as much in the dark as the people of Hong Kong. When they requested information, the government refused to say anything more than the general statements issued at the end of each round (though they were later told that they could get a private briefing at the Foreign Office if they wanted one). George Robertson, Labour's foreign affairs spokesperson, told an interviewer at the time: "We are almost impotent because we don't know what is going on, so it is useless to raise the issue."

Another reason for Parliament's lack of interest was that Hong Kong was not an important issue for winning votes. The colony had not established an effective lobby to sway public opinion and pressure Parliament, as residents of the Falklands had done earlier. John Walden, a retired Hong Kong civil servant, wrote letters to all forty-six members of the Legislative Council suggesting that they set up a small office in London to lobby MPs. He estimated that it would cost no more than £100,000 a year. He received polite rejections from two Councilors; the rest did not respond. (Umelco finally set up a permanent office in London, separate from the Hong Kong government's office, after the Beijing massacre in 1989.)

In the wake of Howe's announcement in Hong Kong, Parliament could no long ignore the issue. Neil Kinnock, the leader of the Labour Party, initiated a half-day debate on Hong Kong to be held May 16, 1984. Chung realized that this was the Executive Council's opportunity to go public with its demand for a detailed, legally binding agreement that would be acceptable to the people of Hong Kong. He chaired several special meetings of Umelco to work out a position paper that a delegation would carry to London. The paper made no demands on Britain, but raised some difficult questions that local residents were concerned about. Would the essential elements of the Basic Law, the "mini-constitution" under which Hong Kong would exist after 1997, be enshrined in the Sino-British agreement? If not, how could Britain ensure that China would stick to the accord? Would the British run Hong Kong up to 1997 without interference from Beijing? Could it maintain a residual presence in Hong Kong after 1997 to ensure that China would abide by the agreement? What would happen to British subjects born in Hong Kong? Would they be handed over to China along with the land and buildings? The paper also questioned how the British government planned to test the acceptability of the agreement to the people of Hong Kong, and what it intended to do if the agreement was found to be unacceptable.

Three days before leaving for London, Chung gave the governor a copy of the position paper, knowing it would be passed on to London. On May 9, Youde summoned Chung to Government House and showed him a letter from Howe, asking Umelco to withdraw the paper. The British government knew it would have trouble selling any agreement to Parliament. It was asking MPs to hand over six million subjects to a communist totalitarian regime. The Umelco paper raised difficult points and would only make it tougher to get an agreement ratified. Chung knew exactly what Howe was doing, and he was not going to be intimidated.

"I cannot withdraw it without consulting my colleagues," he said. "I can ask them, but it would be better if you did it yourself. We are leaving tonight, and there isn't much time."

"No, it is your business, and I will accept Umelco's decision."

Chung released a copy of the Umelco paper to the press before the delegation left for London that evening. The paper was an embarrassment to the Chinese government as well. It wanted to wrap up an agreement quietly with Britain and responded by trying to discredit Umelco.

"The statement is considered here as an attempt to obstruct the conclusion of an agreement by the Chinese and British governments on the Hong Kong issue at an early date," said a Xinhua dispatch. "It is therefore detrimental to Hong Kong's stability and prosperity and runs counter to the views and wishes of Hong Kong compatriots."

The left-wing press in Hong Kong argued that Umelco's request for a residual British presence after 1997 would violate China's sovereignty. Moreover, the Basic Law and China's policies for Hong Kong after 1997 were strictly an internal affair. The British government and Parliament should have no say in them.

WHEN Chung and his colleagues arrived in London, they found that Howe had personally briefed the British press and MPs that Umelco would demand residency in the U.K. for all British passport holders in Hong Kong. The result was a hostile reception.

The delegation met members of the All Party Hong Kong Parliamentary Group and other MPs interested in Hong Kong in the ornate Grand Conference Room of the Parliament building on May 11. Chung pushed hard for Britain to safeguard the interests and freedoms of Hong Kong people. His blunt style did not go over well. The message, as the MPs understood it, was: The British government has sold us out—now what are you going to do about it?

Former Governor MacLehose, who had been given a seat in the House of Lords upon his retirement, felt the delegation was making a bad impression. He reprimanded the Councilors for exaggerating the seriousness of the situation, sounding like a teacher lecturing naughty students. He said that their trip was "badly timed and ill-conceived."* Chung and his colleagues felt betrayed. MPs who did not know Hong Kong well would take Lord Mac-Lehose's view. After the meeting, they bitterly denounced the former governor in interviews with journalists.

As MacLehose was leaving Parliament, a young reporter from Hong Kong spotted him in the octagonal central lobby, under the gaze of the patron saints of the United Kingdom and Ireland. "What do you think of Umelco's comments?" she asked.

MacLehose looked down at her haughtily and said: "I never comment on what my friends say about me."

Umelco's position was weak. None of its members were democratically elected and they could not claim to speak for the public. Still, they were the only representatives that Hong Kong had. Chung appealed directly to the people of Hong Kong for support. Standing in the streets of London, he told a Hong Kong television reporter: "If people think we do represent their will, they should speak out. If they don't speak out now, they will probably never have the chance."

During the next few days, over a hundred telegrams and telexes were received at the Portman Intercontinental Hotel in London's West End, where the delegation was staying. Hundreds more poured into the Umelco office in Hong Kong. "You have precisely defined the doubts of Hong Kong people and the safeguards which we seek in any agreement now being negotiated," said one. "Kindly ask Lord MacLehose to jump into a lake," said another.

The delegation met Prime Minister Thatcher at 10 Downing Street the day before the debate and briefed her on the main concerns of the Hong

* MacLehose denies making these remarks. Three Umelco members present confirm them.

Kong people. She listened carefully and committed herself to nothing. Foreign Secretary Howe planned to host a banquet for the delegation at 7:45 that evening at Admiralty House, a government hospitality center near the Foreign Office. Chung and his colleagues gathered in their hotel beforehand to discuss tactics. They wanted to show Howe that if they did not represent the people of Hong Kong, at least they could speak for them. Each member chose ten of the best telegrams to bring to dinner.

Howe sat at the head of a long table. Cradock, Wilson, Clift, and Luce were also present. After the meal, Howe stood up and gave a brief speech about Britain's commitment to Hong Kong. When he finished, Chung responded.

"Sir Geoffrey, some of your colleagues in Parliament say that we do not speak for Hong Kong people. Of course, we are not elected. But we try to reflect as accurately as we can the thoughts and feelings of the people in Hong Kong. I have several telegrams here that we received this week. I would like to read a few aloud."

Chung pulled out the telegrams from his pocket and read. Some were harshly critical of the British government and the Foreign Office. Howe grew noticeably annoyed. When Chung had finished several, Howe stopped him.

"That's enough, S.Y.," he said. "I get your point."

Chung later told friends that that moment was the highlight of all his trips to London.

As many as a hundred MPs filled the green leather benches of the House of Commons during the debate. Geoffrey Howe stood at the dispatch box facing the opposition benches and delivered the opening address. He said he understood Umelco's concerns for British nationals in Hong Kong who would lose their connection to Britain after 1997, but held out little hope for them. "I have to say that I do not believe that either this Parliament, or a successor, would favor changes which stimulated emigration from Hong Kong to the United Kingdom, or elsewhere. That is a further reason why we are looking for an arrangement which would allow Hong Kong people to enter and leave the territory freely and at the same time to provide a secure future for them there. That must remain our prime objective."

Several Labour MPs attacked Thatcher's handling of the Hong Kong issue. Denis Healey, Labour's shadow foreign secretary, said that her visit to Beijing in September 1982 gave new meaning to the phrase "a bull in a China shop."

Former Conservative Prime Minister Heath did not want Britain to continue fighting with China over Hong Kong, so he tried to undermine the credibility of members of the Umelco delegation by portraying them as lapdogs. "These unofficial members, appointed by the governor, do not represent the people of Hong Kong," he said. "They never have done and they never will."

Chung and his colleagues were sitting in the Visitors' Gallery in the balcony above the intimate chamber. When Heath got up to leave shortly after finishing his speech, Chung jumped from his seat, ran down the staircase lined with etchings of historic Parliamentary sessions, and caught Heath in the book-lined corridor.

"Mr. Heath, do you remember me?" he asked.

"Of course, I remember you, S.Y."

"No, I mean do you *remember* me?"

"Whatever are you talking about?"

"In 1972, you appointed me to the Executive Council. If I do not reflect the views of the Hong Kong people, you should not have appointed me."

Most of the twenty-three MPs who spoke saw little advantage in going against the government on the issue. Britain's bargaining position was weak. It would be difficult for the Foreign Office to get an agreement that fully would satisfy the people of Hong Kong. It would be even more difficult for them to explain to their working class constituents why it was necessary to allow three or even six million Hong Kong Chinese to live in the U.K. This one was best swept under the green carpet of the Commons.

Hong Kong was looking to the elected Parliament to safeguard its interests and was bitterly disappointed. The *Far Eastern Economic Review* called the debate "a gala display of hypocrisy" and said "most MPs followed the Foreign Office line so closely they were in danger of causing a traffic jam."

WHILE BRITISH MPs were going through the motions of debating Hong Kong's future, Chinese legislators were meeting at the second session of the sixth National People's Congress in Beijing. During the conclave, Geng Biao, a vice-chairman of the Standing Committee of the National People's Congress and former defense minister, told journalists from Hong Kong that China would not send troops there after 1997 and that residents would not be required to pay any defense costs. The British negotiators had been trying to get the Chinese side to see that it would help confidence in Hong Kong if they did not station troops there. Some reports claimed that Beijing had agreed to this, others that they did not. Geng appeared to be clearing up the confusion. People in Hong Kong welcomed the news.

Four days later, Hong Kong reporters were invited to attend the opening of a meeting at the Great Hall between Deng and NPC delegates from Hong Kong and Macao. As the group took their seats in a semicircle around Deng, he announced that he had something to say to the journalists.

"I want to squelch a rumor," he said, his face flushed with anger. "Huang Hua and Geng Biao have been talking bullshit. What has been said about the question of stationing troops in Hong Kong is not the view of the [party's] Central Committee. You go and publish this bit of news: Troops *will* be stationed in Hong Kong. It is part of Chinese territory—why shouldn't we station troops there?"

Deng's statements were broadcast almost immediately by radio stations in Hong Kong. The Hang Seng Index, which was up in early morning trading, shed thirty points by the mid-day recess. What prompted the tirade is unclear, particularly since Huang had not spoken on the stationing of troops in Hong Kong.* Some political observers in Hong Kong believed that the issue was still being discussed with Britain and that Deng wanted to strengthen China's bargaining position before round fifteen. Others said he was under pressure from the generals because of their declining influence and cuts in the defense budget. Whatever the reason, Chinese officials dealing directly with Hong Kong tried to effect damage control. Xinhua released an edited version of Deng's remarks, leaving out the harsh rebuke of Huang and Geng and stating simply that China had "the right to station troops in Hong Kong."

The British had raised this issue repeatedly, but by this point they realized that the Chinese were not going to make any concessions. They were hoping now for a commitment that China would maintain only a token force, as Britain had.† The talks, however, were fast reaching an impasse over another important issue. Deng did not trust the British. He feared that they would milk Hong Kong dry during the transition period, or entrench pro-British people in positions of power to continue their control over the colony. He was pushing personally for the two sides to set up a joint monitoring committee to oversee Hong Kong affairs during the years approaching 1997.

---

* There were rumors that Deng was angry at Huang because as Foreign Minister he had backed the recall of Deng's daughter from an assignment to the Chinese embassy in Washington because her English was not good enough. Deng reportedly made a self-criticism in front of the party elders for wrongly accusing Huang.

† The British made no headway, and in the end, the Joint Declaration said that China had the right to station troops in Hong Kong. The British tried to get a commitment that the troops would be based in outlying areas. When they failed, the Hong Kong government announced that the British naval base in Central District would be moved to an offshore island, and the old site would be redeveloped. The Chinese objected vehemently to the move. The issue had still not been resolved in late 1993.

Chung was adamantly opposed to the creation of such a body. He believed that China would use it to interfere in Hong Kong's affairs before the exchange of sovereignty, that it would become "a shadow government." He was strongly supported by the other unofficial Executive Councilors. Even the governor shared his concerns. Youde did not want to have to govern with China constantly looking over his shoulder. He objected privately to the term "transition period." He saw it as a hand-over of sovereignty in 1997, not a gradual devolution of power.

Cradock and Ambassador Evans believed that there was some value in having a body that would serve as a source of contact during the transition, a vehicle for exchanging information and resolving disputes. They agreed that it should not become "a Trojan horse." Evans pushed for explicit and detailed terms of reference for the committee, which would guarantee that it would not interfere in Hong Kong affairs before 1997. Zhou refused to accept Britain's conditions.

THE BRITISH team was divided over who should head the working group that would draft the Joint Declaration. Ambassador Evans could not do it because he already had a heavy workload. Howe wanted a lawyer, someone who could master the legal issues involved, but Cradock argued against it. "A lawyer might be very good with the law," he said, "but he's got everything to learn about the Chinese." He wanted someone who spoke Mandarin and understood the Chinese. He recommended David Wilson, one of the Foreign Office's most capable China experts. Howe eventually agreed. Wilson would be based in Beijing and be directly answerable to Cradock. He would be, in effect, the number two man on the British team.

The working group would have people with more direct knowledge of Hong Kong. In addition to Wilson, who served as political adviser under MacLehose, it would include Robin McLaren, the current political adviser; Gerry Nazareth, the Hong Kong government's chief law draftsman; Fred Burrows, the Foreign Office legal expert; and William Ehrman, a first secretary at the British embassy (who later became political adviser).

The Chinese team would be led by Ke Zaishuo, a mousey man with white hair, a broad smile, and an unusually gregarious personality for a Chinese diplomat. He was a member of China's formal negotiating team and was known primarily as an expert in maritime law. Apparently he was the best negotiator available.

The working group first met on June 18, at the International Club, a popular spot in Beijing for low-ranking diplomats and foreign students. It was only a few blocks from the British embassy, making it more convenient than Diaoyutai, which was an hour's drive away. The mood in the working group was completely different from the plenary rounds. The first thing the British did at the start of each day was remove their suit jackets to encourage a less formal atmosphere (and because it was hot in Beijing and there was no air-conditioning in the room). The club was not, however, the ideal place to hold formal negotiations. It was noisy, and the upstairs conference rooms were not secure. During an early meeting, journalists from Hong Kong camped outside the door and could hear everything the negotiators said. The talks were moved to a room further down the hall and a guard posted outside the door to keep reporters away.

The working group began putting the agreement together based on the exposition the British had done since round five. The two sides negotiated the English and Chinese texts simultaneously, the first time this had ever been done in a major treaty with China. The British team felt both texts were equally important, and it wanted to avoid negotiating an agreement and then negotiating the translation, a standard Chinese tactic.

The Chinese team would not budge on its twelve points. These had been handed down from "the leadership" and had to be included in the main body of the accord. China's policies towards Hong Kong after 1997, the heart of the agreement, would be spelled out in an annex. The body of the Joint Declaration was drafted quickly. There were only two major sticking points. Britain wanted a clause stating that the accord would be legally binding on both sides and another that said the annex was equal to the main text. Ke refused to accept these two points. The first would mean China was signing, in effect, a treaty. The second would mean that she was including her policies towards her own territory in an agreement with a foreign country.

IN EARLY JUNE, Umelco announced that three senior members of the Executive Council—S.Y. Chung, banker Q.W. Lee and business executive Lydia Dunn—would visit China later that month. Unknown to the people of Hong Kong, the three had been holding secret talks with Xinhua's Xu Jiatun since January. The informal discussions were held over dinner, usually every fortnight.

China did not officially recognize the Hong Kong government, or its two main Councils. Britain did not formally recognize Xinhua as a consulate. The Executive Councilors and Xinhua representatives were privy to the secret negotiations. The informal meetings, held at Xu's invitation, helped to improve communication and foster understanding. The Executive Councilors knew Xu was reporting to Beijing, and he, no doubt, knew they were reporting to the governor.

After Howe announced that any agreement with China would not provide for continued British administration, Xu surprised the three Executive Councilors by informing them, over dinner in the Xinhua dining hall, that the "Chinese leadership" wanted to invite them to Beijing. After consulting the governor, the three accepted, in principle, on three conditions: They wanted to know who issued the invitation, in what capacity they would go, and whom they would see. Xu relayed the demands to Beijing. Meanwhile, Umelco was preparing to send a delegation to London for the debate in the House of Commons. Three days before the group was to leave, Xu told Chung that China had accepted his conditions and that the three would be expected in Beijing in a few days. The Chinese government obviously knew that the Parliamentary debate was scheduled for May 16. It is not clear if Xu knew that the Umelco delegation was preparing to leave on May 9. Xinhua had extensive intelligence gathering capabilities. He may have wanted to distract Umelco, or to test its priorities.

Chung discussed the invitation with his colleagues and then told Xu that they had to go to London. There would be no second chance to lobby Parliament, whereas they could travel to Beijing at any time. After they returned from London, Xu did not renew the invitation for two weeks. When he did, Chung stepped up his demands. They wanted to go in their official capacity, and they wanted to see Deng Xiaoping. Xu resisted. They held several secret meetings, some lasting deep into the night. In early June, they reached a compromise. The three Executive Councilors could use their official titles, but they would not be going on official business. Xu said they could announce in their press release that they would meet Deng Xiaoping in Beijing.

IT WAS A historic occasion. Never before had members of the Executive Council had a formal meeting with the leader of China. Every newspaper in town dispatched a reporter to Beijing to cover the event. A battery of television cameras was set up at the back of the Sichuan Room in the Great Hall and wires snaked across the carpet. When the Executive Councilors arrived, Deng was already there, accompanied by Ji Pengfei and several of his deputies. Chung was wearing a tie with the Chinese characters for Hong Kong on it, in case there was any doubt about whose interests he was representing. He bowed deeply as he shook the Chinese leader's hand.

"Is this the first time you've been to Beijing?" Deng asked in Mandarin.

"This is my first time," Chung answered in Cantonese.

"We welcome your coming in a private capacity. I hear you have quite a lot of views. We are willing to listen to them."

Chung was taken aback. It was agreed that they would be coming as Executive Councilors. He stood his ground.

"We three unofficial members of the Executive and Legislative Councils feel greatly honored to have this opportunity to call on Chairman Deng and other national leaders," he said.

Deng told his guests that he was aware of their recent trip to London. He welcomed them to speak their minds. But first he had a few things to say. China's policies were "firm and unchangeable." Whether they were understood by few or many "we believe they coincide with the interests of Hong Kong's five million [sic] people. We've heard many different opinions, but we don't recognize that they represent the interests of the people of Hong Kong." Britain and China will settle Hong Kong's future, without interference. "There have been references to a 'three-legged stool.' There are no three legs, only two."

When he finished making his point firmly and publicly, the journalists were ushered out of the room.

Chung thanked Deng for "telling us frankly about the Chinese government's policy towards Hong Kong" and read from a prepared position paper, which explained that residents were worried that low level cadres responsible for Hong Kong might interfere with the local administration. While they had faith in Chairman Deng and the present leadership, they feared that future leaders might revert to extreme leftist policies and renege on the promise of one country, two systems.

"When you say Hong Kong people don't have confidence, that is really your opinion," Deng admonished. "You do not have faith in the People's Republic of China. You say you trust only me—that is empty talk! The country's policy has been approved by the National People's Congress. If you have no faith even in that, then what is there to talk about?"

Deng said the people who ruled Hong Kong would have to be "patriots," people who respected the Chinese race and sincerely supported China's recovery of Hong Kong. "It doesn't matter what ideology they espouse—capitalism, feudalism, even slavism. They don't need to believe in socialism. You speak of 'Beijing people ruling Hong Kong.' You may say they are Beijing people. But I call them Hong Kong people, for their task is to make Hong Kong thrive. I've said many times that Beijing will not be sending people to Hong Kong. If you say that patriots are Beijing people, so be it."

Deng continued to press his point. Chung could do little more than clarify Umelco's position and express the hope that Deng would understand the concerns of the Hong Kong people. He gave the Chinese leader a copy of the position paper, which included some proposals for boosting confidence in Hong Kong. Deng told the three to take up these specific points with Ji. The meeting ended at 11:25 A.M.

The next day, the front-page headline in the *South China Morning Post* said: HUMILIATION! DENG TURNS ON UMELCO THREE. Another paper said they had received a "Deng-lashing." It was a humbling experience for Chung, following closely on the heels of the debacle in London. Umelco's stature, however, was enhanced by his willingness to stand toe to toe with China's strongman.

THE FORMAL rounds of talks in Beijing became "exceedingly dull," according to one member of the British team. The real negotiations were going on in the working group. Ambassador Evans presented new, more concise papers, which would be used by the working group to draft the annex. The two sides continued to differ over the joint monitoring body, though the Chinese team softened its position by permitting the committee to act as liaison between the two governments.

In the working group, Wilson and Ke had virtually finished the main body of the agreement. Ke still refused to insert a clause that would make the accord binding, so the two sides moved on to the annex and began elucidating China's policies towards Hong Kong after 1997. After agreeing that the legal system, including British common law, would remain unchanged, Wilson and Ke discussed Hong Kong's constitutional arrangements. The subject was a minefield of complexities. According to the Royal Instructions and Letters Patent, the governor ruled Hong Kong by decree and made virtually all decisions. In practice, sophisticated conventions had been adopted to make the government less autocratic. "It was difficult to explain the system to the Chinese," says one British negotiator, "because they probably preferred the theory to the practice."

The Chinese team had proposed during the early rounds that the future legislature would be "constituted by elections or consultations to be held locally," that the governor* would be appointed by Beijing "on the basis of the results of elections or consultations to be held locally," and that the governor would then nominate principal officials, who would also be appointed by Beijing. The British team wanted to include provisions for a Western-style democratic government, with an elected governor and legislature. Given the Communist's propensity to dictate everything and given China's poor human rights record, this would be crucial for securing the support of Parliament and the people of Hong Kong. The talks could founder on this one issue alone. Wilson pushed hard but got nowhere. The issue was put aside "for further consideration."

The question of accountability was equally important. Wilson and Cradock knew that Deng would oppose having an executive that was account-

---

* The official text uses the term "chief executive," presumably because the Chinese felt "governor" was associated with the British.

able to an elected legislature. Beijing wanted to exercise control over the special administrative region and protect China's sovereign rights; a Western-style democratic government would be too much like having an independent Hong Kong. They apparently decided to slip the term accountability into the agreement by telling the Chinese side that Hong Kong's civil service was already accountable to the Legislative Council. It had to seek approval for all public expenditure and proposed laws, and it had to answer questions about policy in the Council. The Chinese team was instructed to maintain existing systems, so it agreed to insert the term, though the definition was not spelled out.*

As the hot and dry Beijing summer approached, there was tremendous pressure on Wilson and his team to finish the agreement by September. The working group met all morning every day, including Saturday and Sunday. In the afternoon, the British team drafted an account of the meeting and resulting recommendations, which was telexed to Hong Kong and London. The General Duties Branch in Hong Kong consulted senior civil servants and, when necessary, Executive Councilors, then fired off replies to London. Cradock's team, seven hours behind, pored over these cables and then filed instructions to the negotiators. On several occasions, there was strong disagreement between London and Hong Kong over how to proceed. After consultations, new instructions had to be given over an unsecured telephone line. Eventually a leapfrogging system was developed where two issues were worked on alternately, giving London more time to respond. The working group made progress in drafting the complex economic provisions to be included in the annex and continued working right through the formal rounds.

In London, Percy Cradock was also feeling the pressure. It was early July. There were only two more months before the deadline expired, and the two sides were deadlocked over several crucial issues. Governor Youde and Ambassador Evans flew to London to discuss strategy with Thatcher, Howe,

---

* I was not able to clear up completely the confusion surrounding the question of accountability to my own satisfaction. Rumors in pro-China circles had it that the British negotiators told their Chinese counterparts that "accountability" meant to make an account to. A Hong Kong academic with a good relationship with the Chinese leadership said that after the negotiations, he was asked by a Chinese official to provide definitions of "accountability," which were brought back to Beijing. The academic said the Chinese had no idea what the term meant in the Western political context. The editor of one of the pro-Beijing newspapers in Hong Kong said he asked Lu Ping, one of the Chinese negotiators, if the Chinese had accepted this definition from Britain. Lu denied that they had, but as the journalist pointed out, he could have been covering up for a mistake. The most common story, and most plausible, is that the British negotiators told their Chinese counterparts that under the current system, the governor is accountable to the Legislative Council. The timing of when the Chinese agreed to put the term into the accord is also unclear.

and Cradock. Cradock believed that Howe would have to make another trip to Beijing if the two sides were to reach an agreement by September. Youde argued against it. He felt that Howe would be under pressure to make concessions. He and his advisers in Hong Kong still believed that Britain should not be held to any deadline unilaterally imposed by China. Again, Cradock got his way. The Chinese government welcomed the idea, and a trip was scheduled for the end of the month.

IF HONG KONG were handed over to China with the existing colonial system intact, Beijing would appoint the governor, all Executive and Legislative Councilors, and all senior civil servants. It would control every aspect of the administration and might not be as benign as British rulers had been. This always worried the British. When MacLehose returned from Beijing in 1979 with a vague indication that Deng wanted to take back Hong Kong in 1997, London introduced elected local bodies called District Boards. They had no power and could only advise the government on mundane matters such as garbage collection and park maintenance. It was a half-measure aimed at preparing Hong Kong for the possibility of self-rule, while not diluting MacLehose's decision-making power.

In October 1983, immediately after Britain made the decision to sever all ties with Hong Kong after 1997, Chief Secretary Haddon-Cave got Youde's permission to begin exploring ways of making the Hong Kong government more representative. The goal was to create a self-perpetuating system of selecting Legislative and Executive Councilors. There was also talk of erecting "roadblocks," which could keep Beijing from interfering too often and too directly in Hong Kong's internal affairs.

Haddon-Cave was more familiar with economics than with politics. During his term as Hong Kong's financial secretary, local Chinese called him *Choy Sun* (God of Fortune). With his puffy, white cheeks, thin blond hair combed neatly across the top of his head and Coke-bottle glasses, he looked like a prim school boy who was always confident he was the smartest kid in his class. He often gave long, didactic speeches in the Legislative Council (described by one wag as "crushingly boring") and earned a reputation for being impatient with those who could not grasp his arguments. Describing his policy as "positive non-interventionism," he was a strong proponent of minimum government interference in the economy. During the great boom of the late 1970s and early 1980s, he nurtured a climate of almost total freedom, refusing to rein in speculators, control the money supply, or peg the Hong Kong dollar. One writer said he had a way of "cloaking the verging chaos of economic laissez-faire in a mantle of reason."

He was born in 1925 in the Australian state of Tasmania. His father was

a British advertising executive, his mother a native Australian. He was educated at Cambridge and, after a brief stint in academia, joined the British
Colonial Service in 1952. His big break came in 1961 when both the governor
and the financial secretary of Seychelles, a group of tiny, British-controlled
islands in the Indian Ocean, were picked up by a "killer wave" and drowned.
He was brought in from East Africa and made financial secretary at the age of
thirty-six. A year later, he was transferred to Hong Kong, where he held a
variety of posts related to the economy and industry before becoming financial secretary. He saw himself as serving the interests of Hong Kong, not
Britain. He believed firmly that the government's job was to manage without
making mistakes. The less it interfered in private enterprise, the less chance
it had of disrupting things. He applied the same cautious approach to political reform. Rather than propose sweeping changes, he would proceed step
by step.

Britain had taken many colonies down the path to independence. This
was usually done through the "membership system." The governor would
choose appointed Legislative Councilors to run government branches. They
would become civil servants on a "sixty-second contract"—that is, they could
be dismissed or resign with sixty seconds' notice. They would gradually
learn to take over the government machinery. When they were elected, they
would become ministers in a traditional parliamentary government. Governor Youde and the Old China Hands in the Foreign Office supported the
move towards a more representative system. Fears about the Communist-
Nationalist rivalry no longer mattered. That would be Beijing's problem.
The Foreign Office had to ensure that the people of Hong Kong could
administer their own affairs after the hand-over. That would be the key to
getting Parliament's support for an agreement with China. Youde felt the
method used in other colonies would not work in this case. Hong Kong was
not ready, and China might object to such a radical change in the system.

Haddon-Cave decided to deal with only the method of constituting the
Executive and Legislative Councils. Their relationship with each other and
with the civil service would be looked at later. How do we man the Councils?
That was the question he sought to answer. The solution he came up with
was to preserve the balance of forces in the Legislative Council by introducing elections on the basis of occupational group. Instead of the governor
picking doctors, lawyers, engineers, bankers, and businesspeople to sit on the
Council, these groups would elect their own representatives. The proportion
of the public represented in the Council would be small at first. It could be
expanded with the introduction of democratic elections at a future date.

Chung and his fellow Executive Councilors saw the need to replace the
appointment system to insulate the government from interference by Beijing,
but they were divided over whether Britain should push China for very

detailed arrangements, or write some flexibility into the accord being negotiated. Chung himself did not have much faith in Britain's ability to introduce a democratic government before withdrawing. Most previous attempts in Africa had failed. He felt the Hong Kong system should evolve gradually to avoid disrupting the local economy.

At the negotiating table, China was resisting Britain's demands to include provisions for a democratic government in the agreement. But the British were not entirely hostage to Beijing's whims. London still ran the colony. Though Youde had hoped China would agree to an elected government before the Hong Kong government made a move, he forced the issue in July when he unveiled in the Legislative Council a Green Paper entitled *The Further Development of Representative Government*. China did not see a copy of the document until a day before it was published. Britain was handing her a fait accompli.

The goal of the reforms, according to the Green Paper, was "to develop progressively a system of government the authority for which is firmly rooted in Hong Kong, which is able to represent authoritatively the views of the people of Hong Kong and which is more directly accountable to the people of Hong Kong." This, Youde and Haddon-Cave hoped, would insulate the Hong Kong government and make any agreement reached with China more acceptable to the people of Hong Kong and to Parliament.

The document proposed that six Legislative Councilors would be elected by functional constituencies in 1985 and twelve in 1988. An electoral college comprising all members of the District Boards, Urban Council, and a proposed Regional Council, would elect six of its own members to sit on the Legislative Council in 1985 and twelve in 1988. The new elected members would replace appointed members. The Green Paper also proposed that in 1988 Legislative Councilors would elect from among themselves four candidates to sit on the Executive Council, providing the first constitutional link between the two bodies. Three years later, a majority of eight unofficial members of the Executive Council would be elected from among Legislative Councilors.

The document suggested that a review of the political structure be held in 1989 to consider further changes to the composition of the Legislative Council and to examine the functions of the two Councils. It held out the possibility that democratic elections* would be introduced some time in the future. Although the Green Paper did not spell out the goal of the

* The Green Paper tried to make the functional constituencies appear more democratic than they were by describing them as "indirect elections." Elections by universal suffrage became synonymous in Hong Kong with "direct elections." Throughout the rest of the book, I have substituted the word "democratic" for "direct" to avoid confusion.

reforms, the proposals were clearly a step towards a Western-style democracy.

"Our proposals recognize the complex balance of interests which lies at the foundation of Hong Kong's success," Youde told the Council. "They seek to maintain the best features of the systems which have served Hong Kong well in the past. At the same time, the proposals recognize the political realities of Hong Kong . . . and the need to maintain our good relationship with our mainland neighbor."

The following day, a spokesperson for the Chinese Foreign Ministry said of the Green Paper: "The plan was drafted by the British side. The Chinese side undertakes no obligation to it." It was a very mild statement compared to the blasts that had followed the Lobo motion and Jardine's Bermuda bombshell. Although Zhou Nan was suspicious of everything Britain did, he apparently did not make the connection between the Green Paper and the negotiations. China made no formal objection and did not raise the issue at the negotiating table.

The Hong Kong government gave people only two months to submit their views on the proposals. It had to move swiftly to get legislation in place, amend the Letters Patent and Royal Instructions, and publish an electoral role in time for the first elections to be held by September 1985. Reactions to the document were mixed. Groups campaigning for greater democracy dismissed it as a cosmetic exercise aimed at giving Hong Kong the appearance of democracy while maintaining power in the hands of the civil service. Members of the Executive and Legislative Councils, however, were overwhelmingly in support of the slow pace of reform. T.S. Lo summed up their feelings when he told a reporter: "It is not the right time for boldness—it's time to be sensible and cash in on the best we've got now."

ASSESSING OPINION in Hong Kong on the forthcoming Joint Declaration would be a tricky exercise. Britain could not be perceived as forcing an unacceptable agreement on the people of Hong Kong. But Hong Kong could not be given veto power over the accord. Britain could not return to the negotiating table demanding more concessions because China would not tolerate it. But Britain also could not hand over the colony without an acceptable agreement because world opinion would turn against her.

On the day that Youde presented the Green Paper in Hong Kong, Geoffrey Howe appeared in the House of Commons to reveal the method Britain would use to assess the acceptability of the Sino-British agreement to the people of Hong Kong. When the draft agreement was completed, it would be published immediately in Britain and Hong Kong as part of a

White Paper, which would explain the background to the negotiations, the constraints imposed on the negotiating teams, and the implications of the terms of the agreement. A special office, supervised by independent monitors, would be set up in Hong Kong directly under the governor to "collate and assess" public opinion. The objective was to provide the British government and Parliament with an accurate assessment of public opinion in Hong Kong towards the agreement before authorizing the foreign secretary to sign it. In a written answer to a question submitted by one MP, Howe ruled out holding a referendum, saying that such an arrangement would have "very real drawbacks."

Chapter 9

The Sprint for the Finish Line

A S GEOFFREY Howe rushed off to Beijing for the second time in four months, there was speculation in the press that the talks were foundering. There were only two months to go before Deng's deadline. Howe's trip, said the London *Times*, "has all the signs of a desperate mission."

Howe arrived in a nervous Hong Kong on July 26 for a twenty-four-hour stopover before proceeding to Beijing. It was already close to ninety degrees when he arrived at the government secretariat at nine o'clock the next morning for a meeting with the Executive Council. Howe wanted to consult Chung and his colleagues before going to Beijing. He explained that it might not be possible to get a legally binding agreement since Chinese opposition was strong. He hoped that the Council would be realistic and endorse the Joint Declaration, even if it was less than what they wished for.

Chung was highly suspicious of Beijing's intentions and promises (one British diplomat thought him almost paranoid) and he feared that the Old China Hands would wrap up the deal before the end of September, regardless of Hong Kong's interests. Before the meeting, and throughout the negotiations, he reminded his colleagues: "Our interests are not the same as those of the Foreign Office." He knew the Chinese did not trust Britain, and he was particularly concerned that Beijing would use the joint monitoring committee to begin taking over the colony prior to 1997.

Britain needed the Executive Council's support for the Joint Declaration. It had been privy to the secret negotiations, and if it rejected the accord, surely the people of Hong Kong would not accept it. Chung used this as leverage against the Foreign Office. He insisted that the accord must be legally binding. He was prepared to accept the joint monitoring committee as long as it came with a written guarantee that it would not become an organ of power before 1997.

Chung had earlier proposed that the joint monitoring committee continue for thirteen years beyond 1997, like "a mirror image." If the Chinese could have a monitoring committee before 1997, why couldn't Britain have one after? Cradock had advised Howe that this was unrealistic, since China opposed even a residual British presence. Such a demand would only sour the atmosphere of the talks. Now Chung pressed Howe directly.

"If you don't ask for it, you will not be able to face history and say you fought for the best deal possible," he said. "I'm not saying you will get it. But you must have the courage to try."

THE CHINESE TEAM, as Cradock had predicted, was feeling the pressure of the deadline. There was a lot of work still to be done in the remaining two months. Deng wanted his agreement by September and gave the word that his team should do what was reasonable and necessary to produce an accord on time. Shortly after Howe arrived, Zhou invited Cradock to lunch. It was an unusual move, since the two foreign ministers were holding face-to-face talks. The British team discussed the invitation and decided Cradock should attend alone.

The lunch was held in an elegant dining hall furnished with rare antiques in one of the larger villas at Diaoyutai. Over a traditional Chinese meal, Zhou began, for the first time, to talk seriously. "We've got a limited amount of time," he said. "Unless we get the major issues settled while Foreign Secretary Howe is in Beijing, we are going to miss the deadline."

He laid out the concessions China was prepared to make. The joint monitoring body would not be an organ of power. The agreement would be detailed and binding. The annexes would have equal force to the main body of the agreement. The exact wording and details of these arrangements would be worked out during Howe's visit. Cradock said that he thought Howe would accept Zhou's proposals, but that they would also have to be approved by the prime minister. (Cradock thought of Howe as Spenlow in Charles Dickens's David Copperfield. Whenever he was asked for something, Spenlow would say that he would like to agree, but his partner, Jorkins, was a hard man and wouldn't go along. Thatcher was a very effective Jorkins.)

The lunch paved the way for real progress to be made. The following day, Howe and Wu set up two groups to discuss the specific issues Zhou had raised. The first, led by Evans and Zhou, was to draft a separate annex that would spell out the terms of the joint monitoring body. The other, led by Wilson and Ke, was to draft clauses that would make the agreement legally binding and at the same time uphold China's principle that she was not negotiating with a foreign power over policies to be applied to her own territory. The two groups met separately at the Diaoyutai State Guest House in the afternoon. "It was like a train station," said one member of the British team. "People were running from room to room, trying to make sure they were where they were supposed to be when they were needed."

Howe sent a long cable to Prime Minister Thatcher laying out the Chinese proposals and his views on them. It took her forty-eight hours to respond. During that period, there was intense pressure on the Chinese team. They had made major concessions and would be in trouble if significant progress was not made while Howe was in Beijing. Cradock and his team were able to use the situation to their advantage. They exerted maximum pressure to get most of the details they wanted. By the time Thatcher responded, the main body of the agreement and the annex on the joint monitoring body were all but complete.

In Hong Kong, the Executive Councilors were eagerly awaiting news from Beijing. No cables were received for thirty-six hours. It was a period of bitter frustration and anxiety for members of the General Duties Branch and the Executive Council. One civil servant felt that the British negotiators were deliberately keeping Hong Kong in the dark because they feared that Haddon-Cave, who was opposed to the joint monitoring committee, would cable Thatcher in London and advise her to reject any compromise. In fact, events in Beijing were moving too swiftly. Youde suggested that Howe brief the Executive Council in person when he returned to Hong Kong.

On the third day of Howe's visit, Evans was replaced as leader of the first ad hoc group by Anthony Galsworthy, head of the Hong Kong department and a close adviser to Cradock. Significant progress was made. The British team agreed that the body, now called the Joint Liaison Group, would be based in Hong Kong after July 1, 1988. Howe pushed for its continuation for a period after 1997, against Cradock's advice. As a quid pro quo for allowing the body to be based in Hong Kong, the Chinese side agreed that it would not be disbanded until January 1, 2000.

Wilson's group was also able to put the finishing touches on the main body of the agreement. The Chinese government agreed that during the transition period, the British government would administer Hong Kong "with the object of maintaining and preserving its economic prosperity and social stability." The key clauses stated that the two governments "agree to implement the preceding declarations and the Annexes to this Joint Declaration" and that the agreement and its annexes "shall be equally binding."

That morning, Howe met Prime Minister Zhao Ziyang in Zhongnanhai's Hall of Supreme Brilliance, a traditional Chinese building with a steep roof of green tiles, columns hugged by menacing dragons, and eaves decorated with elaborate wood carvings. It was once used by Ming and Qing emperors to discuss with their generals the outcome of major battles and was now a place for meeting special state guests. The Chinese were obviously grateful to Howe for helping to settle the Hong Kong question and were according him the status of friend (Deng remarked after one meeting with Howe: "I can trust that man").

During the ninety-minute talk, Zhao reassured Howe that the Joint Liaison Group would not have any role in administering Hong Kong whatsoever. It would merely facilitate liaison, consultation, and exchange of information on issues relating to the transfer of sovereignty. Howe raised the issue of posting troops in Hong Kong. Zhao made it clear that Beijing would exercise its right to station troops in the enclave. Howe did not push the point, but commented that there was no threat to the security of the colony. Britain had only kept a token presence there, the main duty of which was to help patrol the border and prevent illegal immigration. This job could easily be handed over to an expanded police force. Howe left believing that if the Hong Kong government boosted the local police force, China might also maintain only a token military presence in the colony.

There were no further meetings of the ad hoc groups. Howe took the afternoon off to go sightseeing at the Summer Palace with Cradock and Zhou. They took a boat tour around scenic Kunming Lake. Beijing was enduring its worst heat wave since the 1950s, and Howe's shirt was soaked with perspiration as he snapped pictures like any other tourist.

Howe, Cradock, and Youde were delighted at the outcome of the trip. They had gotten virtually everything they wanted. It was clear that an agreement could be reached by September unless something unforeseen arose. Publicly, however, they played down the significance of the visit. There was still a lot of work to be done, and they did not want the Chinese to think the agreement was in the bag.

When the delegation returned to Hong Kong, it convened immediately with members of the Executive Council. Howe briefed the Council while Cradock and Youde listened in silence. When he finished, Chung stood and said: "Sir Geoffrey, in light of what you have achieved in Beijing, I think we can commend the agreement to the people of Hong Kong in good conscience." It was exactly the endorsement Howe was looking for.

BEFORE LEAVING, Howe held another press conference in the Legislative Council chamber. Sitting in the same seat where just four months earlier he had broken the bad news that Hong Kong would not be administered by Britain after 1997, he now spelled out the good news. Britain and China had agreed on a framework and key clauses of an agreement that would preserve Hong Kong's unique way of life. The agreement and its annexes would be legally binding. The arrangements, which would apply in Hong Kong for fifty years after 1997, would be "prescribed with sufficient clarity and precision to command the confidence of the people who live, work, trade, and invest here." However, he said, there were still matters of substance to be negotiated, notably issues relating to land leases, nationality, and civil aviation.

Towards the end of his speech, Howe came to the sensitive issue of the Joint Liaison Group. He said it was necessary to maintain consultations throughout the transition period, and so Britain had agreed to the creation of the group. It would have three functions: liaison, consultation on the implementation of the agreement, and exchange of information. It would not be an organ of power. The Chinese leaders had given him "firm and specific assurances on these points."

The speech was received with mixed emotions. The *South China Morning Post* said it contained "a lot to approve and welcome." Setting up the Joint Liaison Group so long before the exchange of sovereignty, however, was "like inviting the undertaker in before the patient has succumbed."

When the Xinhua News Agency reported Howe's speech, it quoted him directly, but replaced the word "agreement" with the term "Joint Declaration." This created confusion in Hong Kong because neither Howe nor the British negotiators had referred to a joint declaration at any point. Although they had agreed to the term, the British refused to use it because they clung to the hope that the Chinese side might give in and call the accord something else. Ambassador Evans later confirmed that the agreement would be a joint declaration. "But that will not affect its status as an international agreement between Britain and China," he told reporters. It would be "the highest form of contract between two countries."

THE TEMPERATURE in Beijing was a brutal ninety-eight degrees when the British team arrived at the Diaoyutai compound for the start of round twenty. The negotiators were in a relaxed mood after the breakthrough achieved during Howe's visit. Evans complimented Zhou on China's admirable performance so far at the Los Angeles Olympics. Zhou said China had a lot to learn from Britain in track and field and then asked how Hong Kong was doing. The colony had never won a medal. "We are trying very hard and expect to do very well in future Olympics," Youde said sheepishly.

The round marked the start of the sprint for the finish line. Evans began presenting papers on the three major outstanding issues: civil aviation, land leases, and nationality. There were other sticking points, particularly the issue of elections which Wilson had gone back to again and again without success, and the human rights provisions.

Wilson and his team were given a ten-day vacation after Howe's visit. When they returned to Beijing in mid-August, Wilson was concerned that they might not make the September deadline. The two sides agreed to set up another group to handle the three outstanding issues mentioned by Howe. Dubbed the "ad hoc" group to distinguish it from the working group, it was led by McLaren for the British and Lu Ping of the Hong Kong and Macao Affairs Office for the Chinese. The ad hoc group was split from the original group which continued drafting Annex I on China's policies.

The only International Club conference room available for the ad hoc group was inferior to the one being used by the working group, even though Lu Ping was Ke Zaishuo's superior. Despite China's "classless society," the Communists were very conscious of seniority and rank. When the two groups later moved to the Diaoyutai Guest House, Lu's group was given a room that was superior to that of Ke's.

The question of land leases proved a major headache. No detailed record of transactions existed. Some Crown leases had been granted for ninety-nine years, some for 999. Some residents of the New Territories had special rights; some did not. Lewis Davies and his staff at the General Duties Branch spent months sorting out the complexities. Lu agreed that leases in the New Territories could be issued beyond 1997 after the Joint Declaration came into effect. The major question was what to do with revenue from land sales before 1997. China feared that the British would sell off all the undeveloped land and abscond with the money, depriving the future government of an important source of revenue. After some debate, the two sides decided to split the revenues equally. The Hong Kong government would also be restricted from selling more than fifty hectares (about 125 acres) each year. The two sides agreed to set up a Sino-British land commission to oversee all matters relating to land leases during the transition period. The terms of reference for the commission were put in Annex III.

The ad hoc group turned next to the crucial and controversial issue of nationality. The Chinese government considered all Hong Kong Chinese to be citizens of the People's Republic, and it did not permit dual citizenship. The Executive Council was demanding that Hong Kong residents maintain some form of British nationality. The Chinese team recognized that a concession in this area would help to maintain confidence in Hong Kong. During a dinner at Diaoyutai one evening, Zhou told Evans that the Chinese government would "keep one eye closed"—Hong Kong residents could continue to travel on Hong Kong "travel documents" after 1997. They would be entitled to British consular protection when abroad. Inside China and Hong Kong, they would be treated as Chinese citizens. The British government could not continue issuing British Dependent Territory Citizen passports to Hong Kong residents after 1997 because Hong Kong would no longer be a dependent territory. It had to create, by an act of Parliament, a new type of Hong

Kong passport. It would be transferable for one generation. This was a relatively meaningless gesture, but gave the people of Hong Kong a psychological link with Britain.

McLaren and Lu also had to work out a method for linking the British passport with the right to live in a Chinese colony. The document would not be accepted by third countries if it was not clear where the holder should be deported to. The Chinese team could not accept Britain issuing passports that would entitle people to live in a Chinese territory. McLaren suggested instead that the future Hong Kong government issue identity cards, entitling people to live in Hong Kong. Britain could stamp in the "travel documents" that the holder had an ID card, which allowed him to live in Hong Kong.

Lu refused to put the nationality arrangements in Annex I of the Joint Declaration because if China were to state her formal policies towards Hong Kong, she would have to state the nationality law and nothing else. The two sides agreed to exchange memoranda, in which each side would state its own position. "We were papering over cracks," says a British negotiator.

THE PRESS WAS focused on the three issues being handled by the ad hoc group, since other issues had not been publicly released. However, important work was also being done by the original working group. One of the first topics it tackled after the break was human rights. The Chinese team was willing to spell out that the people of Hong Kong could enjoy specific rights and freedoms. But it was resolutely opposed to including a clause stating that the International Covenants on Civic and Political Rights and on Economic, Social, and Cultural Rights would be applied to Hong Kong. Burrows, the Foreign Office's legal expert, was keen to see the U.N. covenants included in the document. As the deadline grew closer, the British team made a big push for them. The Chinese side agreed to a compromise: They would remain in force "as currently applied." Because the covenants included the right to representative government and self-determination, Britain had applied them to Hong Kong with reservations.

Burrows also pushed for clauses that would enable Hong Kong to independently negotiate agreements in fields outside foreign relations and that would allow all treaties signed by the British government to continue to apply to Hong Kong. He tried to place such clauses in at least six different places in the text. The Chinese team was opposed on the grounds that this would infringe upon China's sovereignty. He was finally able to slip the two clauses into the section of Annex I on Hong Kong's international rights and obligations. Beijing committed itself to upholding 140 years of agreements signed by Britain on behalf of her colony. The Chinese team hated the entire section, but these two clauses were the most difficult to accept.

ZHOU NAN was getting anxious; six weeks remained and still some major hurdles needed to be cleared. He had little to do except direct the Chinese negotiators because most of the work was being done by the two working groups. He suggested at the start of the next round that the two working groups work alongside the plenary session at Diaoyutai. Zhou moved into one of the villas for the remainder of the negotiations so that he could give instructions to the Chinese team. During breaks in the discussions, Lu and Ke would go upstairs to talk with him. "No doubt," says one British diplomat, "the [conference] room was bugged, and he [Zhou] had his ear to the receiver the whole time."

Evans and Zhou went through the parts of the agreement drafted by the two subgroups. The legal experts changed a word or two. No issues were reopened for negotiations.

The pressure on the working groups, by contrast, was intense. The British negotiators worried that something might go wrong and the whole agreement would unravel.

By early September, the only outstanding issue for the ad hoc group was civil aviation. Britain had always considered Hong Kong to be a domestic airport for purposes of negotiating international air services agreements. Evans and Zhou had agreed during the formal sessions that Hong Kong should remain an international aviation hub separate from China. But the Civil Aviation Administration of China (CAAC), China's national flag carrier (at the time) and its ministry of aviation, took a tough line and demanded that it be allowed to negotiate landing rights for Hong Kong. The British wanted Hong Kong to negotiate its own air services agreements after 1997. Time was running short, and the Chinese side did not have time to debate the issue internally. Deng told CAAC officials that they could not get everything they wanted. The section was worded to recognize Chinese sovereignty over Hong Kong and at the same time give the colony enough autonomy to enable it to remain a regional hub.

WHEN ROUND TWENTY-TWO ended on September 6, there were only a handful of outstanding items to be resolved. The joint communiqué said that another round would be held, but gave no date. Journalists were told that it would depend on the progress made by the two subgroups.

One outstanding question was how to constitute the legislature. Wilson had made "a big push" for the Chinese team to drop "consultations" as a method of returning the governor and legislators, but Ke would not budge. "They were testing our bottom line," says one British negotiator. The British team was in a difficult position. Without an elected government, Parliament and the people of Hong Kong might feel that the agreement was worthless, that there would be no way to exercise a high degree of autonomy or safeguard human rights. If the British diplomats pushed too hard, the Chinese might withdraw previous concessions. They took the issue to a higher level.

In mid-September, Howe wrote to his Chinese counterpart, Wu Xueqian. The letter, delivered to Zhou by Evans, spelled out Britain's position on four or five outstanding issues. In it, Howe insisted that the governor and legislature be democratically elected. Two days later, Wu invited Evans to dinner at Diaoyutai. It was a cool evening, and a full moon lit the gardens of the compound. During the meal, Wu made concessions on all the issues Howe raised. He agreed that the legislature would be "constituted by elections," but refused to define the term in any way, or to drop consultations as a method of selecting the governor.

Evans cabled Hong Kong and London late that evening. The staff in the communications center at Government House woke the governor at 2 A.M. Youde met his assistant Davies and the clerk of the Executive Council, Robert Upton, in his study.

"What do you think?" Youde asked Upton, referring to the offer on elections.

"I think it's pretty good," Upton said.

Davies agreed.

"I think it's the best we're going to get," Youde concluded.

AS THE FINAL DETAILS were being hammered out in Beijing, the Executive Council was meeting every day in Hong Kong. The Councilors studied each section of the draft agreement. The pressure was tremendous. They had to make sure that its provisions would be acceptable to Hong Kong. Their comments were passed on to bleary-eyed staff at the Foreign Office in London and on to the negotiators in Beijing. The British side was able to work fast because it had "a secret weapon:" a Chinese-language telex machine. (The Chinese negotiators were using typewriters and carbon paper.)

Youde flew to London on September 15 and was joined, two days later, by the unofficial Executive Councilors, who were to brief Thatcher on their views before she presented the accord to her Cabinet. They woke early on September 19 and spent the morning in a stuffy room in the Foreign Office examining the last-minute changes agreed on by Howe and Wu. That evening, they went to 10 Downing Street for their "historic" meeting with the prime minister. After the usual photo call, they proceeded to the Cabinet Room.

Chung explained that he and his colleagues had some reservations about the accord, particularly the nationality provisions. They were also concerned that political reforms not proceed too quickly. He made it clear that they would give their full support to the accord, but said they hoped the British government would not wash its hands of Hong Kong now that the agreement was completed. Thatcher assured them that her government would continue to give Hong Kong high priority.

The next day, the Cabinet endorsed the accord.

THE BRITISH government geared up to sell the document to the people of Hong Kong, Britain, and the world. The political adviser's office in Hong Kong drafted background information for the White Paper. The government printer in Hong Kong would publish one million copies in Chinese and another 250,000 in English. British embassies around the world briefed London's allies on the content of the agreement. Support from overseas would be crucial to its success.

On September 22, 1984, the British and Chinese governments released the following statement:

> The second phase of the Sino-British talks on the question of Hong Kong, which began in July 1983, has now been concluded. The text of a joint declaration on the question of Hong Kong will be initialled by the chairmen of the two delegations (Sir Richard Evans and Mr. Zhou Nan) at 10 A.M. on 26 September 1984 in Beijing.

The following day, members of the British team went to the Foreign Ministry to proofread the English and Chinese texts of the Joint Declaration. When both sides were satisfied with every last word and character, the copies were bound with a red ribbon and sealed with wax. The negotiators shook hands and took a group photo. Y.P. Cheng, the interpreter for the British side, felt sad that the historic negotiations were over and wondered what he would do the next day.

Chapter 10

"A Masterpiece of Drafting"

T HE TEXTS were initialled by Richard Evans and Zhou Nan in a solemn, twenty-five-minute ceremony in the Great Hall of the People. It brought to an end two years of tough negotiations and a roller coaster ride for the people of Hong Kong. Governor Youde had traveled over 175,000 air miles, the equivalent of circling the globe more than seven times. Evans had driven more than 2,500 miles between the British embassy and Diaoyutai, roughly the distance from Beijing to Hong Kong and back. Executive Councilors had made five trips to London and held more than seventy meetings just on the negotiations. The Hong Kong Department in London received some 4,000 telegrams from Hong Kong and Beijing and sent about 1,700 to each. After the two teams had exchanged a champagne toast, Ji Pengfei hosted a lunch of pigeon eggs and stewed abalone in the Hebei Room of the Great Hall. Then Youde was whisked back to Hong Kong in a private jet.

The afternoon sky over the colony was draped with dark clouds. Radio stations recounted the major events of the last two years: Thatcher's momentous visit to Beijing, the typhoon, the currency crisis, Howe's trips to China and his press conferences in Hong Kong. Perceptions of the mood in the colony varied. The pro-Beijing *Ta Kung Pao* said people were "optimistic," the pro-establishment *South China Morning Post* characterized Hong Kong as "resigned." Whatever the mood, people wanted to know their fate. Hundreds lined up in the rain that evening to get a copy of the agreement.

At precisely 7 P.M., the governor convened a special session of the Legislative Council. It was the most anticipated day in Hong Kong's history, and the chamber was packed with senior officials, their wives, MPs sympathetic to Hong Kong, and of course, dozens of journalists. Youde said that the Joint Declaration would enable local residents "to continue to plan their lives, work, and raise their families in Hong Kong in peace and security with their rights and freedoms protected under the law." He commended the agreement to the Council because "it provides for the continuation of those elements which the community of Hong Kong have made clear they regard as essential."

The document was released simultaneously, and within ninety minutes, more than 175,000 copies had been snapped up. Many distribution centers ran out of copies long before they were due to close. Another 850,000 copies were printed by the Hong Kong government. Xinhua also printed English and Chinese copies of the draft accord (on yellow paper, so it would not be confused with the British White Paper). Its version contained no introduction or explanatory notes. Where the British White Paper referred to the accord as a "draft agreement" between Britain and China, the Chinese version called it the Joint Declaration. Staff stood at the entrance of Xinhua until 11 P.M., distributing copies to passersby.

The average Hong Kong resident was more relieved than elated. It was as if the entire city had been on trial for two years. Geoffrey Howe had announced the guilty verdict in April. Now they learned they had received a suspended sentence. Businesspeople and professionals found the Joint Declaration to be remarkably detailed, particularly the economic provisions. They felt it offered at least a chance that life under a communist regime would not be intolerable. Many put their emigration plans on hold. Older Chinese did not know much about international law and they had been uncomfortable with the constant antagonism between Britain and China during the past two years. They wanted harmony, and that was what the agreement seemed to bring.

The 8,000-word accord was greeted with almost universal praise in the media. The pro-China newspapers led the chorus of approval. *Wen Wei Po* said the agreement had created "a bright future for Hong Kong people." *Ta Kung Pao* claimed that leaders from Britain and China had "rectified gloriously a historic error." The independent *Ming Pao* daily declared that Hong Kong people got one hundred percent of what they wanted. Even Derek Davies of the *Far Eastern Economic Review,* one of the harshest critics of the British Foreign Office, was full of praise. He said the Joint Declaration was "a masterpiece of drafting" and provided "the most solid possible foundation on which the community of Hong Kong and those who trade with and invest in Hong Kong can go on building prosperity." The British press was equally effusive. The influential *Financial Times* said the Foreign Office's only advantage was that Beijing wanted Hong Kong to remain stable and prosperous, "and it has played that card for all it is worth and with great skill."

International reaction to the agreement was positive. Japan's acting foreign minister said it was "the first constructive step forward for the future of Hong Kong." Washington strongly backed the accord. Secretary of State George Shultz said the United States government would support Hong Kong's participation in international bodies after 1997 and accept travel documents issued by the future administration. The lone dissenting voice, as expected, came from Taiwan. Nationalist Premier Yu Kuo-hwa said the Joint Declaration was "a disgrace in human history."

As the days passed and commentators examined the fine print, there was some concern about the constitutional provisions which were conspicuously vague. After all, there were huge differences between what "elections" meant in Britain and what it meant in China, where there was one candidate approved by the party for every seat. Unnamed sources were quoted in the press as saying that the issue was raised right at the end of the talks and that there was no time to define the term, which was not true. The British negotiators did not explain that China had refused to stipulate that elections meant democratic elections. They did not explain that China had committed itself to a legislature with very limited powers to call the executive branch to account. Britain and China had agreed, at the Foreign Office's request, that the two sides not reveal anything about the content of the negotiations after they were concluded. It is hardly surprising, then, that the question of what type of political system Hong Kong would have after 1997 would be the most contentious issue of the transition period.

On october 15, 1984, three days after Irish Republican Army terrorists tried to assassinate Prime Minister Thatcher by bombing a Brighton hotel where the Conservative Party conference was being held, the Legislative Council in Hong Kong began a two-day debate on the Joint Declaration in accordance with the infamous Lobo motion. Although the Chinese government had opposed giving the Councilors a say, the debate would be to China's benefit. The Councilors were not ratifying the accord, or even recommending that Parliament do so. Instead, they were selling the agreement to the people of Hong Kong. Senior Councilor Roger Lobo, one of the last members of the great Portuguese trading families in Hong Kong, introduced a motion commending it to the people of Hong Kong.

"We have a good agreement, and it is now up to the people of Hong Kong and the international community to make it work," he said. He added that if Hong Kong did not remain stable and prosperous, there would be no reason for China to keep the promises made in the Joint Declaration. This would become a common refrain in the years ahead. The businesspeople who dominated the Council felt the Hong Kong people should work hard not to provoke China instead of worrying about the future or fighting for a better deal.

Most of the speakers supported the accord, albeit with reservations. John Swaine, who spoke so eloquently about the nationality issue during the Lobo motion debate, shocked his colleagues and visitors in the packed gallery by declaring that the Joint Declaration was "the best of a bad deal." He said that

Britain "went to the negotiating table with one arm tied behind her back. She disabled herself a long time ago when she closed the door to Hong Kong . . . by a series of immigration and nationality acts which turned the Hong Kong passport holder into a second-class citizen. If you don't want them, how hard will you negotiate on their behalf? Just as important, what is the Chinese [government's] perception of your negotiating stance?"

Swaine admitted that there were many admirable features included in the Joint Declaration. But he questioned whether Beijing could be trusted to implement them. In view of his reservations, he said he could not recommend the agreement to Hong Kong and abstained from voting. Only one other member, trade unionist Chan Kam-chuen, abstained.

Responding for the Hong Kong government, Chief Secretary Haddon-Cave said that the Joint Declaration was not just the best possible agreement the British negotiators could get—it was a good agreement, period. Picking up on the theme Lobo opened the debate with, Haddon-Cave concluded that Hong Kong's future prosperity depended on people taking a positive approach to the agreement and making it work.

The Council formally commended the agreement to the people of Hong Kong.

MEMBERS OF THE Executive Council convened one Tuesday in late October to discuss the political reforms to be spelled out in a White Paper. The situation had changed since the Green Paper was released. The Chinese government had agreed that the legislature would be constituted by elections, but refused to define the term. Chief Secretary Haddon-Cave felt the Hong Kong government had to move quickly to introduce a more representative system of government before Beijing had a chance to consider the election issue carefully. He wanted to step up the pace of reform and introduce a small number of democratically elected seats in 1985 in addition to the functional constituencies and electoral college proposed in the Green Paper. Although there was a growing demand for such elections, this sparked a serious rift within the Executive Council.

The unofficial members accepted that elections could insulate Hong Kong from communist interference after 1997. Some agreed with Haddon-Cave that it was essential to spell out a series of changes to be introduced steadily during the transition period, leading to a much more representative system. S.Y. Chung, banker Q.W. Lee, and businessman S.L. Chen argued vehemently against proceeding too quickly. They wanted a step-by-step approach, with a review after each stage to see if the government was on the right track.

Chung wanted Hong Kong to develop a unique system of government. He did not accept that a beggar should have the same rights as the most wealthy tycoon and believed that elections should be held as in a company, with the largest shareholder getting the biggest say. He also felt that there should be no changes to the method of constituting the Executive Council. It was an advisory body, and the governor should be allowed to pick his own advisers. Moreover, letting Legislative Councilors elect from among themselves members to sit on the Executive Council might give pro-China forces a way into the decision making. They were the best organized political group in the colony. They could win a majority of seats on the Legislative Council and then vote their own members onto the Executive Council. That would give Beijing a direct hand in running Hong Kong.

Chung was particularly worried about the Hong Kong government's ability to govern effectively during the transition period. He felt the government should maintain a majority of appointed members to ensure that it could get legislation approved. He argued that in clause four of the Joint Declaration, Britain had agreed to administer Hong Kong during the transition period "with the object of maintaining and preserving its economic prosperity and social stability."

"How can you make that promise if you give up more than fifty percent of the seats in the legislature?" he asked. "You cannot afford to make a mistake because the Chinese will say that you broke your promise, and they will interfere."

Haddon-Cave, sitting to the right of Youde, said that the government would have to work with the elected element to preserve stability. He felt that the danger of not getting a representative system in place was greater than the danger of moving too quickly and getting it wrong. If the colonial system were not replaced, the system of "benign patronage," as he called it, would be replaced by something very much less benign. China would find it easy to sweep away conventions that had protected the Hong Kong people from abuses under British rule, but she would have much greater difficulty scrapping a functioning democratic system that had the support of the people of Hong Kong.

Lydia Dunn, a Haddon-Cave protégé, and a few other unofficials felt Chung, Lee, and Chen were being too cautious. Youde let all members have their say. He took a more passive approach to the Executive Council than MacLehose had. During this period, he complained to one former senior civil servant about the Executive Council's opposition to the proposed changes. When the civil servant said he should go in there and tell them what's what, Youde replied: "Things don't work like that any more."

After one of the fiercest debates the Executive Council had ever seen, a compromise was struck. Haddon-Cave and his supporters agreed that democratic elections would be put off until 1988. In return, Chung, Lee, and Chen accepted that the number of representatives returned by functional constituencies and the electoral college in 1985 would be doubled. The government would maintain its majority by increasing the size of the Legislative Council from forty-eight to fifty-six. A political review would be held in 1987, instead of 1989, so that the changes introduced could be assessed before proceeding. All proposed changes to the Executive Council would be shelved until after the review. By then, however, China would realize that Britain was handing her a fait accompli, and the window of opportunity would be lost.

Although he had gotten the Executive Council's approval to introduce democratic elections to the Legislative Council in 1988, Haddon-Cave did not state this explicitly in the White Paper. He feared that the Foreign Office would object on the grounds that it might cause a confrontation with China. Instead, he only hinted at the government's intention. The White Paper read: "With few exceptions the bulk of public response from all sources suggested a cautious approach with a gradual start by introducing a very small number of directly elected members in 1988 and building up to a significant number of [democratically] elected members by 1997." Regarding changes to the Executive Council, the White Paper stated that although there was substantial support for the introduction of a ministerial system, the issue raised important constitutional questions. The subject would be "addressed further at a later stage."

Chen was head of the Legislative Council's constitutional affairs panel which conveniently recommended all the changes that had already been agreed on by the Executive Council. When the White Paper was published on November 21, journalists reported that the government had bowed to all of the panel's demands. It was an official secret that the Executive Council had approved the introduction of elections in 1988.

The public's reaction to the White Paper was mixed. A joint conference of more than eighty organizations found it "most disappointing" because it lacked a long-term schedule for introducing a truly representative system. The *South China Morning Post* called it a "first, cautious step forward—not very enterprising, but at least safe." In London, some MPs criticized it for not going far enough. Robert Adley, head of the Anglo-Chinese Parliamentary Group, said it did little or nothing to "satisfy the aspirations for democracy in Hong Kong."

IN mid-November, a few days before the White Paper was published in Hong Kong, Ambassador Evans called on the Chinese Foreign Ministry to give Zhou Nan a copy as a matter of courtesy. His instructions were not to debate its content. If Zhou objected to the proposals, Evans was to remind him that the Joint Declaration stated clearly that the British government was responsible for governing Hong Kong up to June 30, 1997.

The Chinese government, by this time, had examined the implications of the reforms and was disturbed by them. After 140 years of autocratic colonial rule, Britain was changing the nature of the game. It was okay for London to rule without input from local residents, but not for China. Zhou saw it as a sign of Britain's insincerity and was particularly annoyed by the phrase "a government more firmly rooted in Hong Kong," which he took to mean that Britain was intending to hand sovereignty to the people of Hong Kong, not to China. China's position was that sovereignty and administration had to be handed to her, and she would delegate the latter to Hong Kong people.

Zhou told Evans that the White Paper preempted the Basic Law, which would spell out the future political system. He impugned Britain's motives. Leaders in Beijing could not come out publicly against the White Paper because people would accuse them of being insincere in their promise that Hong Kong people would rule Hong Kong. In addition, any attempt to force Britain to reverse the proposals would undermine the Hong Kong government's ability to govern during the transition. Beijing could not afford to do that because investors would quickly lose confidence in the Joint Declaration.

Zhou felt tricked. He believed London was trying to extend its influence over Hong Kong beyond 1997. Local Chinese residents elected before 1997 would make a name for themselves and probably continue in office after the hand-over. Most of them would be British-trained and have close connections with the U.K. The Chinese government would not be caught napping a second time.

THE HONG KONG government's Assessment Office, which would collect opinion on the Joint Declaration, had been formally organized on September 1, 1984. Youde chose Ian MacPherson to head it, a tall, quiet Scot who had spent most of his career in the Hong Kong civil service. The two independent monitors appointed to oversee its work were Simon Li, an urbane high court judge and the most senior Chinese legal figure in the colony, and Sir Patrick Nairne, a distinguished former British civil servant. Residents were given six weeks to send their opinions to the office, two weeks less than they had to comment on the Green Paper on representative government. The Office solicited direct submissions from organizations and individuals and monitored media reports, opinion polls, and speeches made by appointed and elected officials of local bodies.

The assessment was meant to give the Joint Declaration some credibility. One Labour MP visiting Hong Kong called it "a farce" and "a sick joke." The people of Hong Kong were given a cruel choice: Be handed over to a communist totalitarian regime with this agreement, or be handed over with no agreement. Residency in the U.K. was not an option. If people did not like parts of the accord, that was too bad. Britain's White Paper on the Joint Declaration said that the Chinese government had made it clear that negotiations could not be reopened. In fact, a Chinese official told journalists, during a background briefing at Xinhua two days before the agreement was initialled, that the negotiations could be reopened if both sides agreed to it. It was the British team that did not want to return to the negotiating table because "we felt there would be things that they would want to renegotiate and the whole thing would unravel," according to one of the most senior negotiators.

Even if the people of Hong Kong rejected the agreement, the White Paper made it clear that all of Hong Kong would revert to China on July 1, 1997. The Chinese government had said that it would publish its own plan for Hong Kong. The White Paper explained that there was no guarantee that it would include all the elements included in the draft agreement, nor would it be a legally binding agreement between two countries. Britain claimed that the choice Hong Kong people faced was not one she sought to impose on them, but one "imposed by the facts of Hong Kong's history." The White Paper said in bold type: "Her Majesty's Government believe that the agreement is a good one. They strongly commend it to the people of Hong Kong and to Parliament."

Officials in Hong Kong said the public could express its concerns about any aspect of the accord. These would be passed on to the British government and perhaps discussed in the Joint Liaison Group. Though it was highly unlikely that Britain would get further concessions from the Chinese, many residents took the opportunity to express their frank views on the Joint Declaration, which were included in the Assessment Office's thirty-two-page report published on November 29. The Office had received only 2,494 direct submissions. Almost 680 came from organizations ranging from the American Chamber of Commerce to the Hair Dressing and Makeup Trade Workers Union. The rest were from individuals. Over thirty organizations and 360 individuals rejected the draft, an astonishingly high percentage given the alternative.

The report said that Hong Kong people were concerned about the possibility of "undue interference by China," about the feasibility of the one country, two systems policy, about the status of children born to British Dependent Territory Citizens after 1997, about conscription into the Chinese military, and about the stationing of the People's Liberation Army in Hong Kong. Some respondents felt that the provisions for selecting the future governor were not sufficiently clear and detailed. They said the governor should be returned by election, not consultation, and that he or she should be appointed by the legislature, not Beijing. The provision for the Hong Kong legislature to be constituted by elections was "hailed by many as far-sighted and progressive." The report recommended that the administration push forward with its plan to introduce a more representative system of government.

Many people were bitter about the choice they were given. One individual wrote that he was from the middle class and did not have the means or the desire to emigrate. He said he accepted the agreement, but with reluctance and with reservations about the feasibility of its implementation. He added:

> My heart is not truly at ease, and I have no full confidence in our future. The whole thing has not been a very fair play to us because we have not had any say and there is no other alternative other than not to have an agreement at all.

The nationality provisions of the agreement came in for particularly harsh criticism. "Britain cannot simply rescind a historic and moral responsibility of looking after its subjects," said one individual. "These people are legally British and cannot be made stateless." Another said: "With one stroke of the pen, you have stripped us of our identity and slotted us into racial categories—an unforgivable act."

The Assessment Office concluded "that most of the Hong Kong people find the draft agreement acceptable." In fact, it had no way to make such a claim since it did not conduct an opinion survey and did not know what the vast majority of people thought. However, the conclusion was "unreservedly" endorsed by the two independent monitors.

THE STANDING COMMITTEE of China's National People's Congress approved the Joint Declaration on November 14, 1984. The House of Commons was scheduled to debate the draft accord three weeks later. Chung and his Umelco colleagues decided to send another delegation to London. They would give "a soft thumbs-up" to the draft and point out the concerns being expressed in Hong Kong. Their position paper stressed that the ultimate success of the Joint Declaration depended on people's confidence that it would be implemented faithfully and that outstanding matters of concern be resolved satisfactorily. They urged the British and Chinese governments "to take steps to reassure the people of Hong Kong in these respects."

In early December, as the Umelco delegation left for London, there was a great sense of anticipation in Hong Kong. The Parliamentary debate on the accord and Thatcher's trip to Beijing to sign it would be history in the making. Chung was not content to bask in the glory. He had fought to secure a viable future for Hong Kong, and now he wanted to safeguard the colony's interests over and against the British and Hong Kong governments' determination to push through political reforms during the transition period.

When the delegation met Prime Minister Thatcher at 10 Downing Street just hours before the debate on December 5, Chung briefed her on Hong Kong's concerns and made a special plea for prudence in introducing political reforms. He said there might be pressure from some MPs to introduce a parliamentary system "in total and in haste." This might jeopardize Hong Kong's stability and prosperity. He pointed out that although there would be a high degree of autonomy, this was not independence and any move towards a full parliamentary system could be counterproductive. Hong Kong was not suited to adversarial politics because of its unique status and the political constraints on it. He pleaded for the colony to be given a chance to develop its own style of representative government, though he did not say what this should be. "Hong Kong," he said, "cannot afford the risk of making mistakes."

DOZENS OF Hong Kong residents studying in the U.K. lined up on a chilly Wednesday afternoon outside the St. Stephen's entrance to the Palace of Westminster to watch the historic debate on the Joint Declaration. It was delayed by more than two hours because Thatcher's administration was facing a revolt over the contentious issue of student grants. Members of the Umelco delegation passed the time anxiously in their hotel. At 4:30, they left for the Parliament building and proceeded straight to the Visitor's Gallery.

Though their decision would affect the lives of six million people in Hong Kong and perhaps change the balance of power in Southeast Asia, no more than fifty of the 650 members of the House of Commons remained in the neo-Gothic chamber when the debate on the Joint Declaration finally came up in the order papers. Geoffrey Howe opened the proceedings by reassuring MPs that the Joint Liaison Group would "in no sense be a shadow government," that there would be "a form of British nationality" for Hong Kong people who would otherwise become stateless after 1997, and that the more than three million Chinese in Hong Kong eligible for British nationality would retain a link with the U.K. even though they would not be allowed to reside there. He could not allay fears about conscription into the military, or about whether the People's Liberation Army would be stationed in Hong

Kong, because these were matters for Beijing to decide. But he said the Chinese government was aware of the concerns in Hong Kong and would "act prudently."

Some MPs brought up the issues raised by Umelco. Most spent the evening congratulating Howe, the Foreign Office, and the British government. There was so much congratulating that the *Far Eastern Economic Review* said the debate was more like "a quiet celebration in one of London's gentlemen's clubs."

The Joint Declaration was endorsed by the Commons.

THATCHER ARRIVED in Beijing at 8:20 P.M. on Tuesday, December 18, 1984, wrapped in a heavy coat and fur hat to protect her from the biting cold. No doubt recalling the furor over the remarks she made to reporters last time she was in the Chinese capital, she strode past some 200 journalists waiting at the airport without acknowledging them and proceeded directly to the Diaoyutai State Guest House.

The next day, the British prime minister was treated to the most lavish reception ever staged for a visiting head of state by the People's Republic. Hong Kong had never been a domestic political issue in China. Following the successful conclusion of the negotiations, the reformist faction led by Deng Xiaoping, Hu Yaobang, and Zhao Ziyang received a tremendous boost. It had successfully negotiated the return of sovereign Chinese territory from a major Western power and at the same time, ensured that the capitalist enclave would continue to serve the interests of the motherland. Deng was going to play up the agreement for all it was worth.

There was little political capital to be made in Britain, however. Thatcher, the Iron Lady, the Great Anti-Communist, could not have relished going down in history as the prime minister who had handed six million people over to a communist totalitarian government. There were rumors that she did not want to go to Beijing to sign the Joint Declaration and had to be convinced by her advisers that she would give the accord added respectability in the eyes of Hong Kong and the world.

After the elaborate welcoming ceremony and talks with Zhao, Thatcher met Deng in the Fujian Room of the Great Hall of the People, the same room in which the two leaders discussed Hong Kong back in September 1982. Deng told her that the Hong Kong question had cast a shadow over Sino-British relations for 150 years. "Now that this shadow has been cleared," he said, "cooperation between the two countries and friendship between their peoples shine with brightness."

Shortly after 5 P.M., some one hundred guests from Hong Kong, wearing red ribbons, strolled into the Western Main Hall of the Great Hall of the

People. They stood in rows on each side of the room. Then, officials of the British and Chinese governments, including the members of the two negotiating teams, came in and took their places in four rows behind a large table covered with a green velvet cloth. Deng Xiaoping, wearing a tailored, gray Mao suit, stood in the center of the front row, flanked by Geoffrey Howe and Chinese President Li Xiannian.

Thatcher wore a black velvet suit with a white, floral-print blouse, a diamond broach, and a string of pearls; Zhao a conservative Western-style suit. At exactly 5:30, they sat at the table. Attendants presented them with the large volumes. They each signed, and after the official seals were applied, exchanged copies. Flashes lit up the room as the press and some guests captured the historic moment on film. The two leaders gave brief addresses, which were not translated. Champagne was poured. Thatcher clinked glasses first with Deng, the architect of the one country, two systems policy. Then, dignitaries from both sides exchanged toasts. The entire ceremony lasted just fifteen minutes.

As the guests filed out of the hall, Thatcher walked back to the table, picked up the pen she had used to sign the accord, and put it in her handbag.

PART TWO

Chapter 11

The Beginning of the End

A S HE WATCHED Margaret Thatcher and Zhao Ziyang carefully affix their signatures to the large, leather-bound copies of the Joint Declaration under the bright glare of the television lights, the thin, middle-aged lawyer from Hong Kong was ambivalent. Like all Chinese, he was proud that China was recovering territory lost under humiliating circumstances and erasing a black mark on her history. He was hopeful that Hong Kong could play an important role in helping the motherland to modernize, to provide a higher standard of living for her people. But he was worried. There were so many unanswered questions: How would Hong Kong people run their own affairs? How would the theory of one country, two systems work in practice? Would China stick to the agreement? What could Britain, or anyone else, do if she did not? What kind of leader would take over after Deng Xiaoping died?

The lawyer knew, too, that there would be demands on people like himself and those standing next to him. The signing of the Joint Declaration marked not just the beginning of the end of British rule, but the start of a long transition period. During the next thirteen years, many of the questions that filled his head would be answered. And the answers would depend as much on Hong Kong people as on Beijing. Educated professionals could no longer afford to sit back and let mandarins sent from a faraway capital run things. They would have to get involved, make their views known, even run for political office.

Though Martin Lee did not realize it, he was already involved, as much by virtue of his birth as by his position within Hong Kong society. He was a prominent lawyer, three-term chair of the Bar Association, and an influential man within the legal community. Beijing needed support from people like him for the one country, two systems experiment to work. Xinhua had targeted him for United Front work during the Sino-British negotiations, and his presence at the signing ceremony indicated that he was among those the Chinese government would depend on during the transition period. He was also important to Beijing for historical reasons. His father, Li Yinwo, had been a general in the Nationalist army.

Li Yinwo was born into a prosperous family in Guangdong Province. In the early 1900s, he went to France to study, becoming the first Chinese to receive a doctorate of pharmacy from Lyons University. He was active in the Chinese student community, as was another urbane young man named Zhou Enlai, who later became China's premier under Mao Zedong. Li was as opposed to Communism as Zhou was in favor of it. The two once spent twenty-four hours straight trying to convert each other. Having failed, they shook hands and parted friends. Years later, they found themselves on opposite sides in the Chinese civil war.

Martin was born in Hong Kong in 1938 while his mother was vacationing in the colony. Intensely patriotic, General Li did not want his son to be British and prohibited his wife from registering the birth. The deteriorating situation on the mainland after Japan's invasion of northern China in 1937 forced the family to stay in Hong Kong. When the Japanese seized the colony in December 1941, Martin, his brother, and five sisters were sneaked out in baskets carried by coolies. The family settled in Guangzhou, where they stayed after Japan's defeat in 1945.

During the civil war, General Li was a member of the Anti-Corruption Yuan and saw firsthand the extent of graft within the Nationalist government and the ruling Guomindang. By the time the Communists crossed the Yangtze River, he was so disgusted that he refused to flee to Taiwan. He moved his family instead to Hong Kong. He and his wife agreed that if the Red Army invaded the colony, they would take the first ferry across the harbor and jump. They hoped that by killing themselves, they would save their children.

The Communists did not invade, but they were keen to woo disaffected Nationalists. Once a year, Zhou Enlai sent an emissary to Hong Kong to try to persuade General Li to return home to help to build the New China. Li disliked the Communists because they rejected the family as the basic unit of Chinese society. He refused to return and moved his home each year in a vain attempt to shake Zhou's messenger.

General Li lost everything when he fled to Hong Kong. Because of the U.S. trade embargo with China, the colony's economy was severely depressed, and he could not find a job. He gave private lessons in Chinese to earn money and later took a job teaching higher Chinese studies in the evenings at a high school. One of his pupils was a young Eurasian nurse named Han Siuyin, who was working on a novel called *A Many-Splendored Thing*. (Han gave General Li the typewriter she used to write the book. It was lost during one of the family's annual moves.)

General Li was a man of great principle—he had been an incorruptible official in a government riddled with corruption. Martin remembers as an eleven-year-old boy when a man came to the door with a bag full of money for the family to use to escape to Taiwan. His mother angrily sent the man away. Perhaps because of the extent of corruption within the Guomindang, General Li considered money something dirty. Once, when one of his students came to him because she could not afford to pay the high interest on a loan, General Li told Martin's brother to lend the girl the money, without interest, so she could pay back the bank. Martin protested that if his brother lent money to every student who needed a loan, he would soon be bankrupt. His father insisted.

General Li gave his children a clear sense of right and wrong and inspired them with the belief that the strong should stand up for the weak. Martin's brother supported Martin during his last year of law school. After Martin established his practice in Hong Kong, he helped to put his brother through medical school. Like his father, Martin Lee was a man of integrity. He possessed a fearlessness that was rare among Chinese, who are taught to avoid confrontation because it might cause a loss of face.

Having failed to win over his father, the Communists pursued Martin. When he received an invitation to dinner at Xinhua during the Sino-British negotiations, he barely gave his reply much thought. What was the harm? They were Communists, not lepers. Lee also believed that the relationship was a two-way street. They could try to convince him that China's policies were best for Hong Kong, and he could try to convince them that if the Chinese government were to recover the colony, it had to maintain the rule of law after 1997. Lee brought one official to his office during the talks to show him his law books and the system of precedents, which depended on British common law. Later, he took the same man to the law courts to show him how the system worked in practice. At one banquet, he encouraged Xinhua's representative on the Chinese negotiating team to set up the Court of Final Appeal in Hong Kong after 1997, a proposal that found its way into the accord.

Lee had very clear ideas about Hong Kong's future. The Joint Declaration should be fully implemented by the British and Chinese governments. He saw Hong Kong acting as virtually an independent state. Beijing would control only the two areas reserved for it under the accord: foreign affairs and defense. Everything else would be for the people of Hong Kong to decide. He feared, however, that Beijing would want a say in some, perhaps many, internal decisions. Even if Chinese leaders were faithful to their promises, low-level cadres might exert undue influence on the Hong Kong government, or abuse human rights. They could kill Hong Kong without Beijing ever knowing why. Thus, he believed that it was critical for the colony to develop a truly democratic government well before 1997. This was the only way to guarantee that Hong Kong could exercise the high degree of autonomy promised by Beijing. Cadres could manipulate individuals, but not the will of six million people.

This view was shared by many pressure groups, which sprang up in 1984 to express their views on the future. The groups were dominated by young people from the working class who had managed to get into one of the colony's two universities, secured a good job, and were in the vanguard of the growing middle class. By Western standards, they were middle of the road. They understood that it was vital to maintain Hong Kong's vibrant economy. Businesses had to keep expanding to provide jobs for an expanding work force. The colony was too small and had too few natural resources to support an extensive welfare system. They believed, however, that Hong Kong was now a rich society (the standard of living was twenty times higher than that on the mainland) and more could be done to improve the standard of living and to help those who had not shared in its success.

Almost half the population lived in public housing apartments that were a mere 300 to 400 square feet. Children slept in the same bedroom as their parents, separated by only a curtain or dresser. Often bunk beds were stacked five or six high. In the older buildings, the kitchen was a gas stove on the balcony. Some of these projects were built dangerously close to oil depots or chemical factories.

The colony had no social security system. Many old people had to work well into their eighties or depend on their children. Single men were allotted twenty-four square feet in public housing projects. They built cages around their bunks to lock in their few worldly possessions. Journalists from around the world photographed them living like dogs in a kennel, and compared them with the rich living in opulent palaces on the Peak, driving around town in Rolls Royces. (It is commonly said Hong Kong has more Rolls-Royces per capita than any other city in the world.)

Many of the young pro-democracy activists successfully ran for seats on the District Boards. They pushed the government to improve conditions for the poor and were moderately successful. They felt that political development had not kept pace with economic development. They wanted a more representative government—not just to keep Beijing at bay, but to bring a wider spectrum of society into government and rub off some of the rough edges of Hong Kong's ruthless capitalist system.

The pressure groups were small, weak, and divided. Martin Lee would give them a voice, an articulate, rational voice. Given his stature within the community and his willingness to stand up to London and Beijing, he would become the unofficial leader of the pro-democracy movement and the champion of the people. Within five years, he would be more recognizable than the governor and more popular than many pop stars.

WITH HONG KONG's future sealed, businesspeople resumed their frenetic money making. In the months that followed the signing, Hong Kong came to life like one of the millions of battery-powered toys it exports annually. With the future settled, companies began reinvesting again. Exports soared. Banking reforms introduced in 1977 helped to turn the colony into the world's third largest financial center, after New York and London. The quintessential Oriental city that Westerners saw in Hollywood movies was physically transformed into a modern metropolis, as sophisticated as New York or Tokyo. Traditional tile-roofed buildings and two-story prewar apartments, with their character-covered pillars, were torn down to make room for newer, higher, and more sophisticated skyscrapers. Corner shops selling rice from a barrel, pigeon eggs, and assorted dried foods were replaced by slick boutiques finished in chrome, marble, and neon.

Beijing led the investment drive, pumping an estimated $5 billion into the colony. There was talk of an economic takeover. It was not so much China taking over as Hong Kong surrendering. Major companies offered Chinese state investment firms shares at friendship prices, believing that this would protect them after 1997. Beijing would not force a company out of business if it owned a percentage of that company. Journalists called it Red Capitalism, and it made many businesspeople sleep a little more soundly at night.

The Joint Declaration gave new impetus to the economic integration of Hong Kong and South China. Local businesses, confident about the future, shifted light industrial manufacturing across the border. They designed the products, imported the raw materials, and shipped them to Guangdong. There, an army of Chinese laborers churned out goods, which were shipped back to Hong Kong for packaging and marketing. China benefitted from increased employment and the transfer of technology. Lower production costs kept Hong Kong exports competitive, and enabled factory workers to move into white collar jobs, where they could earn more.

Hong Kong profited from its position on the doorstep of China in other ways. Foreign companies looking to trade with the mainland set up offices in the colony, where they would have access to international transportation and telecommunications links. They hired and trained local Chinese, who were better at making contacts across the border.

Many businesspeople—expatriate and Chinese alike—were drunk with optimism. The Joint Declaration protected private property, the free flow of capital, Hong Kong's position as a free port, and more. China would stick to the accord, they would tell doubting reporters, because it was in her interest to do so. China's leaders were practical; they needed Hong Kong to further their modernization program. This belief was reinforced by the situation in China. The reform movement initiated by Deng was at its peak. Thousands of joint ventures with foreign companies, many from Hong Kong, were now earning needed foreign exchange. Under Deng, China had become self-sufficient in grain and was exporting raw cotton. For the first time in almost 200 years, she had a stable, responsible government. If the reformers could continue to make progress, Hong Kong would not just survive under Chinese rule, it would flourish.

Some businesspeople talked of a "reverse takeover." China would not absorb Hong Kong and make it socialist; Hong Kong's capitalist spirit would infect the mainland and turn it away from Communism. Businesspeople dreamed about one billion Chinese with the same work ethic (and hunger for consumer products) as their brethren in Hong Kong. The image had a hypnotic effect.

THE BRITISH government began the legal process of withdrawing from Hong Kong on January 10, 1985, when it published the Hong Kong Bill, which declared that Britain would give up all claims to sovereignty and jurisdiction over Hong Kong from July 1, 1997. Under the new law, Parliament would create a passport for the people of Hong Kong, one which would maintain the facade of British nationality, but at the same time end Britain's responsibility for them. British Dependent Territory Citizens in Hong Kong would be issued a new passport after 1997, which would identify them as British Nationals (Overseas). It would neither enable them to live in Britain, nor state that they had the right to live in Hong Kong. It could not be passed on to children born after 1997. Thus, Britain's link with Hong Kong would die with the last holder of such a passport.

The nationality issue was a powder keg under Hong Kong, and virtually any spark could set it off. Britain was, after all, handing over her subjects to a communist totalitarian regime every bit as brutal as the one in Moscow. The U.S. and major European powers had quietly acquiesced to this because the Cold War had reached new heights under the presidency of Ronald Reagan (Mikhail Gorbachev would not become leader of the Soviet Union for another two months), and China was the key to NATO's foreign policy. If she could be pulled into the world community, the Soviets would be further isolated. The future of six million Asians was not as important as a strategic alliance with Beijing. Britain knew, however, that she was in a precarious position. Although she had cleverly double-locked her door before starting negotiations with China, a collapse of confidence in the colony, the reemergence of radical leaders in China, or a determined campaign for British nationality by Hong Kong residents could turn world opinion against her.

T.S. Lo threatened to light the nationality fuse when he resigned from the Executive and Legislative Councils over "Britain's failure to accept its obligation to British subjects in Hong Kong." The news, speculated about for weeks, was revealed in a brief, matter-of-fact government statement, released on February 12, 1985, which said that Governor Youde had accepted Lo's resignation. The colony was stunned. Lo was the first person in Hong Kong's history to resign in protest, and his departure marked the end of an era: He was the last member of the Cantonese aristocracy to serve on either of the two Councils.

As a Eurasian, Lo was particularly sensitive to the nationality issue. His father had been educated at Oxford, but could not join the Hong Kong Club or play tennis at the Cricket Club before the war. Throughout the secret negotiations, he had stressed the importance of Britain's obligation to her subjects in Hong Kong. He suggested that Britain grant Hong Kong people the right to live in the U.K. and give them staggered dates by which they would have to take up that right, thus avoiding a huge influx all at once. He suggested that Britain convince the United States and other countries to take in Hong Kong people, or that China and Hong Kong set up a joint committee to examine the problem after the signing of the Joint Declaration. All of these ideas were rejected by the Foreign Office. During his last appearance in the Legislative Council on July 25, 1984, Lo called an adjournment debate on freedom of movement and talked of the need for "a fire exit, a safety net," for the people of Hong Kong, who were being "thrust into the unknown."

Though silently applauded in all sectors of the Chinese community, Lo's resignation did not spark a wave of protest over Britain's handling of the nationality question because there was still a great deal of optimism about Hong Kong's future and because Lo's decision was a personal one. He would not lead a campaign for Britain to give Hong Kong people residency, though he did set up a privately funded company to help people who wanted to emigrate.

As strongly as he felt about the nationality issue, Lo's decision to turn his back on the establishment was as much a political move as a symbolic protest. He was growing increasingly frustrated with Umelco, particularly Chung's dominance of it. An incident during the Sino-British negotiations was the last straw. Members agreed to keep secret Xu Jiatun's invitation for Chung, Lee, and Dunn to visit Beijing. When it was leaked, some Councilors questioned the journalist involved. He claimed that he got the information from

Lo. Chung alerted the government that there had been a breach of confidentiality, but no evidence surfaced to suggest the leak had come from Lo.

"It's obvious that the leak came from one of us," Chung told his colleagues. "Now we cannot trust each other, so we will not discuss sensitive business within Umelco any more."

Shortly thereafter, Lo resigned. In his confidential letter to the governor, dated October 24, 1984, he said he did not believe that Britain had lived up to her obligations to her people and that he did not have any faith in democracy in Hong Kong. He added that he did not like his Umelco colleagues speaking for him. He did not respect them because they were appointed by the governor and were his "creations."

Youde summoned Lo to Government House and told him very firmly that his resignation would have to be considered formally and accepted or rejected. These were sensitive times, Youde said, and it would be better to deal with the situation later; he would consider the matter in five or six weeks after his vacation. He did not formally accept Lo's resignation until February 1985.

Lo could have remained in Umelco despite being distrusted by his colleagues, but he was angry at London's handling of the nationality issue, and he foresaw other problems. Britain and those aligned with her would become less influential during the transition, while those aligned with Beijing would become more so.

Even before his resignation was announced, he made a private trip to Beijing to meet Chinese officials to "see if they were people I could work with." In late 1984, he approached a Xinhua official, explained that he had resigned from the Executive and Legislative Councils and that he wanted to go to Beijing in a personal capacity to meet Chinese officials responsible for Hong Kong affairs. He said he wanted to stay at the Diaoyutai State Guest House. Lo made the proposal as a test: If Beijing officials would not give him that respect, then it probably would not be worth establishing a relationship. (Lo apparently had few qualms about switching allegiances, which is not all that surprising since the aristocracy had always had a love-hate relationship with the British. Aristocrats depended on the British for their position and influence within the society, but also resented them for it.)

Although the Chinese government distrusted Lo because of his close relations with the British, it understood the use of having a man of his intellect, experience, and family background on its side. The trip was arranged for late January. Lo was treated, much to his delight, like a state guest. At a banquet hosted in his honor, he felt he should make a toast to the forty-odd people gathered in the hall. He did not speak Mandarin well, but stood and wished everyone "a long and prosperous life." The group of Communists went dumb. Even in the age of reform, prosperity was considered a capitalist sin. There was an "awful silence." But Lo refused to sit down.

"Prosperity is no bad thing," one aging cadre said finally. "Let us drink to prosperity for all."

During the trip, Chinese officials gave Lo "the clearest impression that China's interests coincided with Hong Kong's prosperity." It was the message he wanted to hear. Hong Kong had a future under Chinese rule.

Lo did not share Martin Lee's views on how Hong Kong should be run after 1997. He distrusted elections because he believed the common man had neither the intelligence nor the education to choose the best leaders. The elite should run Hong Kong. Businesspeople and professionals knew what was best for the colony. They would act as compradors for the Communists the way the aristocracy once had for the British imperialists.

At the press conference on the day his resignation was announced, Lo told reporters that moves towards representative government were neither necessary nor viable. "Hong Kong people should spend less energy and time in politics," he said, "and concentrate more on business, which is more helpful to China. If Hong Kong can suit the needs of China, then it will have a better future. If not, its future will not be as bright."

He said that the system of having an all-powerful governor appointed by London had worked well. Since Hong Kong was to be governed by China after 1997, the simplest approach would be to replace the British-appointed governor with a local person acceptable to China. "Why change the system? I think the change will do more harm than good."

There was a strong element of self-interest to this view: The rich and powerful would maintain their influence in government (Lo himself was an obvious candidate to become the first post-1997 governor), and Hong Kong would continue to be run for the benefit of private industry. There was, perhaps, also a Confucian element to it: The rich and educated would rule in the interests of everyone. The average citizen would obey the laws, work hard, and enjoy the benefits of a capitalist society.

Lo's vision of the future, which was shared by many powerful businesspeople, did not take into account that Hong Kong was changing rapidly. The rich were no longer the only ones who could afford an overseas education. Many middle-class residents now had the opportunity to attend university in the U.K., U.S., and Australia. They did not accept the elite's right to rule. Like Lee, they feared that the future sovereigns might not be as benign as the British had been, and they put more faith in the Western ideals of democracy and the rule of law than in Confucianism. The Hong Kong establishment would be slow to perceive that the promise of elections and the fear of abuses after 1997 had galvanized young professionals and intellectuals and altered the political equation.

DURING THE negotiations, the British government never raised the possibility of shortening the transition period. Margaret Thatcher and Geoffrey Howe assumed that it was London's obligation to administer Hong Kong up to 1997, and that the Hong Kong people wanted them to do so. Beijing did not request an earlier hand-over apparently because it feared this would spark panic and perhaps because it could use the time to learn more about how to run Hong Kong. While the length of the transition period would give each side time to prepare Hong Kong for the change of sovereignty, it also provided plenty of time for things to go wrong.

London wanted, above all, to maintain cordial relations with China. This was necessary for strategic reasons (Thatcher had aligned her foreign policy more closely with that of the United States than any British prime minister since World War II). It also hoped to win business contracts in China. Most important, it wanted to avoid a diplomatic row that would undermine confidence in the Joint Declaration, perhaps precipitate an economic crisis, and lead to calls for Britain to grant the people of Hong Kong residency in the United Kingdom. (On a personal level, Percy Cradock and other senior Foreign Office diplomats had been involved in, or witnessed, difficult decolonizations in Africa, some resulting in bloodshed. They wanted to get out without having a disaster. A Hong Kong official based in London says there was definitely a "finish-line mentality.")

Not everyone, however, believed that cordial relations was the paramount concern. Chief Secretary Haddon-Cave and other senior civil servants continued to put the interests of local residents above those of the British government. They were eager to foster changes that would maximize Hong Kong's chances of surviving the transfer of power. It was Haddon-Cave (with Youde's consent) who began revamping the colonial political system as soon as Britain agreed conditionally to withdraw from Hong Kong. After the agreement was signed, he started to look at other areas.

An apolitical, relatively honest, and efficient civil service was one of the cornerstones of the colony's success. At the end of 1984, only two percent of all civil servants were expatriates, but they held eighty percent of the top posts. They would all have to be replaced by Chinese because foreign nationals were prohibited from holding senior positions under the Joint Declaration. Haddon-Cave knew that Chinese bureaucrats would be more susceptible to pressure from Beijing. He began to turn government departments into autonomous bodies (a practice developed during previous decolonizations). The Hong Kong government would create authorities to run public hospitals, housing estates, and other large departments. Trustworthy locals and in some cases retired expatriate civil servants would be appointed to run them. This would minimize the possibility of the new regime ruining everything.

Haddon-Cave also wanted to liberalize the draconian measures introduced during the 1967 disturbances. He feared that leaving these on the
books would give China the means to repress the local population. Prior to
the signing of the Joint Declaration, few people in Hong Kong knew how
much power the governor possessed, or cared. Although the government
regularly detained people without trial, deported undesirables without giving
them recourse to the courts (usually those gathering intelligence for Taiwan),
and censored films on political grounds without the legal authority to do so,
people were protected from widespread abuses by the democratically elected
Parliament in Britain, from which the governor derived his authority. As
Richard Margolis, then assistant political adviser, puts it: "Hong Kong enjoyed the fruits of democracy without cultivating the tree." After 1997, the
colony would no longer enjoy this protection. It was imperative to limit
Beijing's ability to infringe upon human rights.

China was opposed to any fundamental changes in Hong Kong's system.
During the negotiations, the Chinese team insisted that when Beijing agreed
to maintain "existing systems" in Hong Kong, that meant existing in 1984.
China did not want to give Britain a blank check to reform the government
before 1997. The British team insisted that Hong Kong was a dynamic place,
and there would have to be evolution during the transition period. The issue
was never resolved.

Percy Cradock and the Old China Hands knew that Beijing would object
to dramatic changes in Hong Kong and that it wanted to maintain some type of
appointment system. Yet Hong Kong and Parliament had been led to believe
that the colony would have a democratic government. The Foreign Office
would allow the Hong Kong government to take a few small steps down the
road to democracy, as long as it could secure Beijing's consent. They knew that
any changes that made the colony a better place to live under Chinese rule
served Britain's aim of keeping Hong Kong residents out of the U.K. (One
Executive Councilor claims they were also concerned about their place in
history.) They were prepared to go along with moderate changes as long as
China did not object. The problem was that many people in Hong Kong shared
Lee's desire to see a fully democratic system introduced before 1997. When China
inevitably opposed such moves, London would be caught in the middle.

Youde was the Foreign Office's point man. Though he had initially
supported changes to the political system, he began to backpedal as Beijing
raised objections. According to one insider, Haddon-Cave was not asked to
stay on after he reached retirement age in mid-1985 because he and Youde
clashed about how far reforms should go. Youde chose as his new chief
secretary David Akers-Jones, whom one Executive Councilor describes as "a
dove" when dealing with China.

The differences of opinion on reforms emerged in public in May 1985, when the Hong Kong government published the Powers and Privileges Bill to prepare for the introduction of elected members to the Legislative Council. In addition to giving legislators more power to demand information from the government, the bill granted them immunity from civil or criminal charges relating to any written or oral statements made in the Council, a customary privilege in the Commonwealth countries. It also made it a criminal act to show "intentional disrespect" to Legislative Councilors or to publish reports of meetings held in private.

Pro-China newspapers complained that the purpose of the bill was to turn the Legislative Council into a full-fledged parliament, similar to Britain's (a gross exaggeration). Several editorials demanded that Britain halt all reforms because China alone would determine Hong Kong's post-1997 political system.

Some pressure groups misunderstood the bill's intent and claimed it infringed on civil liberties. A few charged that Britain was toughening legislation because she had promised to hand over a docile Hong Kong. The government was forced to amend the bill heavily before it was enacted. The incident showed how nervous Hong Kong was about the transfer of sovereignty. Local residents wanted laws liberalized to the greatest extent possible. This made confrontation with Beijing inevitable.

Despite the growing tension below the surface, Britain and China were keen to present an image of harmony. On May 27, 1985, the two sides exchanged instruments of ratification of the Joint Declaration in a simple ceremony in villa 12 of the Diaoyutai State Guest House. The accord came into force three days later and was registered with the United Nations on June 12.

Zhao Ziyang visited Britain in early June. There was talk of "new vistas" in Sino-British relations. He discussed mainly trade and economic issues. Britain was eager to sell more goods to China, particularly weapons. The implementation of the Joint Declaration did come up, but there was not much said because, according to Zhao, "we share identical views on this question."

Chapter 12

"The First Symphony of National Reunification"

C HINA'S MAIN task during the transition was to draft the Basic Law, the mini-constitution under which the future Hong Kong Special Administrative Region would exist. Martin Lee knew that the charter would be crucial. It would spell out how the Joint Declaration would be implemented, the type of political system Hong Kong would have, and the extent of Beijing's control over Hong Kong's affairs. He believed that, in some ways, how the Basic Law was drafted would be as important as what it said. The Joint Declaration had been negotiated with a foreign country, and China was forced to make concessions to keep the colony from collapsing. The Basic Law would be drafted by China, without British interference. If it was done in an open and democratic way and if Beijing generously interpreted the provisions of the Joint Declaration, the people of Hong Kong and foreign investors would have great confidence in the colony's future under Communist rule.

Lee encouraged the Chinese government, through his contacts at Xinhua, to draft the Basic Law as soon as possible. He believed that if the current government in Beijing was sincere about the promises it had made in the Joint Declaration, then it was best to get those incorporated into the charter before the political situation in Beijing changed. If the Basic Law was only a public relations exercise, the Chinese government would still be under pressure to carry through with their promises to maintain confidence. (He subsequently learned that the British government had encouraged Beijing to delay the drafting, apparently to enable Britain to change the system in Hong Kong before China set it in stone.)

Beijing decided to proceed immediately. It also bowed to pressure from Hong Kong activists to include a number of local residents on the drafting committee. This was done to give the document credibility and perhaps because Chinese officials recognized that they did not yet fully understand how the colony worked. It was an important concession because it gave the people of Hong Kong, for the first time, a direct say in their future.

The Hong Kong members of the Basic Law Drafting Committee would be selected by Xu Jiatun and appointed by the Standing Committee of the National People's Congress. Beijing considered the drafting to be an internal affair; Britain would have no say in it. But Xu accepted suggestions from a wide variety of sources, including the Hong Kong government.

Beijing saw the drafting committee largely as an extension of the United Front, an opportunity to win friends and influence people in Hong Kong. The drafting itself would be simply a technical exercise of translating the provisions of the Joint Declaration into a legal framework, which would be handled by a selection of constitutional experts from the mainland.

The primary targets of the United Front were the Hong Kong tycoons, whom Beijing hoped to persuade not to leave the colony (as they had left Shanghai). For this reason, it appointed four of the wealthiest men in Hong Kong to sit on the Drafting Committee. Three of them were given the added tribute of being named vice-chairpersons of the committee, along with a left-wing publisher, and four eminent mainland drafters.

Martin Lee and three other lawyers were also chosen. One had given up her practice for a political career; one was a solicitor who was overtly pro-China; and one was a High Court judge who, although competent, was not considered by some members of the legal fraternity to be outstanding.

The other Hong Kong members were selected from virtually all sectors of the society, ostensibly as unelected representatives. Many of them had been courted during the Sino-British negotiations. Some, like Martin Lee, had family links to the Guomindang, but most were simply outstanding figures in their fields. They included the publisher of a leading independent newspaper, the heads of the Christian and Buddhist religions, the vice-chancellors of the two local universities, the president of the Medical Association, a prominent accountant (whose grandfather had been China's premier under the Nationalists), and the leaders of the largest teachers' union and the main rural association in the New Territories. Only five members of the Hong Kong contingent were considered overtly pro-China.

The official list of members was announced on June 18. It received almost no international press because the world media were focused on the continuing hostage drama involving a TWA airliner that was hijacked to Beirut and Algiers. The Basic Law Drafting Committee would be chaired by Ji Pengfei, the aging director of the Hong Kong and Macao Affairs Office, and consist of fifty-nine people, including twenty-three from Hong Kong.* The ratio of Hong Kong to mainland drafters was carefully chosen. The Chinese government wanted to have enough Hong Kong members to make their participation appear to be meaningful but not so many as to concede control over the committee's decisions.

The mainland side comprised eleven legal experts, fifteen government officials, and ten members described as "well-known people." The officials came from the Foreign Ministry, the Hong Kong and Macao Affairs Office, and Xinhua. Some had participated in the Sino-British negotiations, either directly or behind the scenes. They would not play an active role in drafting the Basic Law, but were simply there to look after China's interests in their area of expertise. Representatives from the Bank of China and the Ministry of Foreign Economic Relations and Trade were appointed to deal with economic matters.

The Hong Kong and Macao Affairs Office would oversee the drafting. Ji was a loyal member of the old guard and could be trusted to protect China's national interests. Because he was in poor health, much of the responsibility would fall to his two deputies on the committee, Li Hou and Lu Ping. The two were a natural good-cop/bad-cop team. Li was dour, serious, blunt, and prone to polemics. Lu was more outgoing and gregarious, willing to joke with reporters. He was known as Lulu to his friends. Early on, the drafters held ice cream parties in the evenings to encourage the mainland and Hong Kong members to get to know each other. The Hong Kong drafters would sometimes buy a bottle of brandy or cognac. Li never touched the stuff. Lu would indulge himself occasionally, and after a few sips, his pale face would turn as red as the Chinese flag.

Lu was instantly recognized by his great shock of white hair, which, it was said, lost its color prematurely when he was disgraced during the Cultural Revolution. British diplomats who sat across from him during the Sino-British negotiations say he was someone you could reason with. He could, however, be a typical bloody-minded Communist. After one meeting, a Hong Kong drafter explained his position to Lu and said: "I know you probably agree with me in your heart, but you can't say so because you have to stick to the party line." Lu replied: "No, I always believe in my heart that the party line is correct."

---

* Beijing never explained the odd number. Clearly, it intended to have sixty members, of which twenty-four, or forty percent, would be from the colony. A Xinhua official told the U.S. consulate in Hong Kong that the last place was reserved for someone who would represent Taiwan's interests, but Beijing had been unable to find anyone willing to accept it.

The party line was set at a higher level, sometimes as high as Deng himself. Li and Lu were there, in the end, to implement it. They could, however, influence policy. Along with Xinhua, they were the eyes and ears of Chinese leaders. How they explained the issues and what they recommended would influence the decisions made at a higher level. Lu, especially, understood that the Basic Law had to have the confidence of the people of Hong Kong and international investors if the colony were to remain prosperous. Throughout the drafting, he tried to balance the Chinese leadership's concerns about Hong Kong's becoming too independent with the need to look after the interests of all sectors of Hong Kong society to guarantee that the charter had popular support.

For the wording of the articles, Li and Lu would depend on the mainland legal experts, who were culled from various Chinese ministries and universities. In the beginning, these experts would disagree with one another, though they always made it clear that they were expressing their personal opinion. Gradually, as the Chinese government worked out its position on a key issue, the party line would emerge. Sometimes it was expressed by Li or Lu, sometimes by one of the experts. The other mainland drafters would sense it, seemingly instinctively (though they may have been informed without the Hong Kong drafters' knowledge), and fall into line.

The reaction in Hong Kong to the list of drafters was muted. Most people seemed surprised and pleased that Beijing had not chosen twenty-three pro-China figures from the colony. Some pressure groups complained that grass-roots organizations were not given enough representation. Many commentators felt that the inclusion of so many prominent businesspeople was acceptable given that their support was necessary to maintain Hong Kong's stability and prosperity. The *South China Morning Post* said that "Hong Kong people should have much to be content with" because the twenty-three Hong Kong members "represent a cross-section of the community and most of them are expected to speak up for the interests of the local people."

As HE SAT in the VIP room at Kai Tak airport waiting for the flight to Beijing on June 30, 1985, Martin Lee was not sure what to expect. Earlier that month, he received a letter stamped with the official seal of the Chinese government in red ink, confirming his appointment to the Drafting Committee. He was subsequently informed that the first meeting would be held in Beijing on July 1, exactly twelve years before China was to resume sovereignty over Hong Kong. He was not told whether he would be paid for his services, or if he would have to pay for his flight to Beijing and for his hotel room. (The drafters were not paid. The Chinese government gave them economy class tickets on CAAC and standard rooms in the Beijing Hotel. The vice-chairpersons flew first class and were given suites. If members wanted to bring along their wives, they had to pay for their tickets and meals.) A sense of uncertainty surrounded the whole affair.

A friend from the Xinhua News Agency approached him in the lounge. "Mr. Lee," he said, "we are going to be counting heavily on you for the legal aspects of the Basic Law."

Lee nodded, taking the comment as an apology for not appointing to the Drafting Committee any of the people Lee had recommended. Years later, he would recall the comment and reflect that there may have been something more behind it. His friend at Xinhua probably knew that he would have little support during the drafting from his Hong Kong colleagues.

When they arrived in Beijing, Lee and his fellow drafters were driven to the hotel in small four-seater vans. The drafters called them *mein bao che* ("loaf buses") because of their bread loaf shape. The four Hong Kong vice-chairpersons and Xu Jiatun were taken in shiny new Toyota Crowns. One Hong Kong drafter complained about the special treatment, so from the second plenum onward, all drafters were driven in private cars. The motorcade was given a police escort to the hotel. To Lee's embarrassment, it did not stop for red lights and drove on the wrong side of the road when there was a traffic jam along the two-lane road from the airport. So much for the classless society, he thought.

The Beijing Hotel was an imposing, gray, Soviet-style building with Chinese and European motifs. It was popular with businesspeople and foreign journalists because of its convenient location just east of Tiananmen Square. The rooms were awful, particularly when compared with the five-star hotels in Hong Kong, which were consistently rated among the best in the world.

On the morning of July 1, Lee awoke—still uneasy about what he was getting himself into. Would the Chinese government use the Hong Kong drafters for its own propaganda purposes? Or would it rely on them to make sure that the views of Hong Kong people were genuinely consulted and reflected in the Basic Law? He ate breakfast in the hotel with the Hong Kong drafters and one or two mainlanders who had flown in from the provinces for the meeting. At 9:30, they piled into the loaf buses for the two-minute ride to the Great Hall of the People on the western side of Tiananmen Square. Although he had been in the building to witness the signing of the Joint Declaration, Lee was no less impressed as he strode up the steps and between the massive columns. A woman from Xinhua who accompanied the drafters explained that she had been one of the thousands of people who helped to construct the building in the astonishing span of ten months between 1958 and 1959.

The Hong Kong drafters were led to a conference room with a high ceiling, tall windows with long red drapes, and a large emblem of the Chinese government on the back wall. The room was gray and somber, and to the Hong Kong drafters, who were used to the quaint customs of British colonialism, a little eerie. For so long, China had been cut off from the outside world, and one could only imagine the inner workings of the Communist Party. Now, here they were inside the citadel, in the building where China's future had been plotted for four decades, where Mao had launched the Great Leap Forward and where Deng had opened China's doors to the West. Who were these people? What would it be like working with them?

The vice-chairpersons' table occupied the center of the room with the chairman's table perpendicular to it. The rest were organized in a U-shape. At each seat was an ashtray, tea in a white porcelain cup, and a microphone. Staff of the committee's secretariat sat behind a wall at the back of the room and tape recorded all of the proceedings. (All meetings, including those of the Consultative Committee, would be recorded. No transcripts were ever provided, but detailed and accurate minutes were distributed the day after each session.) The men from Hong Kong wore business suits, the women skirts or dresses. The mainland—or "inland" members as they referred to themselves—dressed in short-sleeved shirts with open collars. Ji wore a heavy, long-sleeved gray shirt despite the summer heat. The mood was friendly, expectant. Photographers moved among the tables, snapping pictures as the drafters made acquaintances. Lee was extremely pleased. Several mainland drafters told him that the Basic Law would not be a success unless it was as acceptable to Hong Kong as the Joint Declaration had been. He believed that he was right to encourage China to draft the charter right away.

When the reporters were ushered out, Ji sat at his table, below the Chinese government emblem, and gave his opening address. He looked weak and his hands shook as he read from a prepared text. One Hong Kong member thought Ji would not live long enough to see the publication of the Basic Law, but during the drafting, he took up qi gong, a mystical Chinese art based on breathing exercises, and grew stronger. Ji laid out the timetable for completing the charter. A "discussion draft" would be released in early 1988 for Hong Kong people to comment on. It would be revised and then submitted to the National People's Congress (NPC) as a draft law. Hong Kong residents would get a second chance to comment on the charter in 1989. Final revisions would be made before the law was submitted to the NPC for approval in the first half of 1990.

The full Drafting Committee would not meet again until March 1986, when subgroups would be set up to tackle specific portions of the Basic Law. In the meantime, the Hong Kong members, including Xu Jiatun, would set up a consultative body in Hong Kong to collect opinions on the Basic Law. Ji said he hoped this could be done "at the earliest possible time." He promised that there would be full consultation on the drafts of the Basic Law. "Good, conscientious investigation has to be done, and full play will be given to democracy and solving problems through democratic consultation."

Ji made no mention of China's policy of Hong Kong people ruling Hong Kong, or that Hong Kong would be a highly autonomous Special Administrative Region. Lee was concerned, but not unduly, about the omission.

The purpose of the first plenum was for members to adopt procedures that would govern the drafting and discuss the general content of the Basic Law. The event was poorly organized, there was no agenda, and meetings were scheduled haphazardly. The Hong Kong drafters, accustomed to the efficient world of international business, were frustrated by the relaxed attitude of their mainland counterparts.

On the second day of the five-day session, members were divided into three discussion groups with about twenty members each. They met separately in smaller conference rooms, where Chinese officials met state guests. Members sat in large red sofa chairs organized in a circle. Lee was pleased by the attitude of the mainland drafters, who said they were *kong mong*— literally, Hong Kong blind. They would rely on the Hong Kong members to educate them about the colony and what was best for it. It was exactly what Lee wanted to hear.

The Hong Kong members, however, were a diverse group of people, most of whom did not know each other. They came from widely different backgrounds and had widely different views and opinions. "We were like a handful of sand," says one of them. "Let go and we would scatter and you would never get us back together again. The Chinese members were like mud. They stuck together."

The Hong Kong drafters were not afraid to give their views, and they got into heated debates over a number of issues, including the formation of the Basic Law Consultative Committee. Industrialist T.K. Ann was adamantly opposed to the idea. One of the Shanghainese who had fled to Hong Kong in 1949, he had served on the Executive and Legislative Councils. After being dropped by the British, he was courted by the Chinese government. Like T.S. Lo, he distrusted the masses. He said the members of the Drafting Committee knew what was best for Hong Kong, and there was no need to consult the population at large.

The Drafting Committee's secretariat arranged for Ann and two other Hong Kong drafters to meet the press during a break in the discussions. Ann told reporters that the only people who should be invited to sit on the Consultative Committee were those who agreed with his conviction that the lifeblood of Hong Kong was manufacturing, exports, and tourism. "We can't eat politics," he said. "We can't eat laws."

Many of the businesspeople and some of the professionals from Hong Kong agreed with Ann's view. Lee did not. He believed that all sectors of the society should be involved in drafting the Basic Law. He was not eager for a confrontation and said little.

During the five-day session, the drafters were given an opportunity to address their colleagues. Ann used the opportunity to oppose the consultative organ. He argued that it would be impossible for China to set up such a body in Hong Kong because, by law, all organizations had to be registered with the Hong Kong government. It would be a loss of face for the Chinese government to register an official body with the colonial administration.

One Hong Kong drafter suggested that the Hong Kong government would probably waive the registration requirement. Ann said that he wanted a commitment from the governor before the drafters agreed to set up the Consultative Committee. At 7 P.M. on July 4, four Hong Kong drafters went to his hotel room to call Youde, who was scheduled to fly to London at nine o'clock that evening. Maria Tam, the only one who sat on the Executive and Legislative Councils, made the call. Tam explained the situation and asked if Youde would waive the registration requirement. He said he would.

The next day, the Basic Law drafters formally voted to set up the Basic Law Consultative Committee. It would not be an official government body, and its members would not be appointed by the National People's Congress. Some Hong Kong drafters would be appointed to the consultative body. Despite these stipulations, which made the body little more than a post box for comments on the charter, the drafters decreed that it would be equal in standing to the Drafting Committee.

Deng was eager to take credit for the successful recovery of Hong Kong, and on the last day of the session, he appeared at the Great Hall with Communist Party chief Hu Yaobang, President Li Xiannian, and Peng Zhen, chairman of the Standing Committee of the National People's Congress. The four leaders shook hands with some of the drafters. Hu told them that they were composing "the first symphony of national reunification."

GRASS-ROOTS ACTIVISTS in Hong Kong objected vociferously to Ann's criteria for appointment to the Consultative Committee. They had been excluded from the Drafting Committee, and now they feared they would be excluded from the Consultative Committee. The result would be that the businesspeople would be free to transform Hong Kong from a British colony run by the rich for the rich to a Chinese colony run by the rich for the rich. The formation of the body became an important test, in their eyes, of whether Beijing was sincere in consulting all of the people of Hong Kong, or just the wealthy businesspeople.

When the drafters returned to Hong Kong, Ann took no action towards setting up the Consultative Committee, though he had been appointed chairman of the preparatory body. After a week, he received a formal letter from Youde waiving the registration requirement. Ann called a meeting on July 17. All twenty-three Hong Kong drafters sat around a large elliptical conference table in a spacious, ultramodern conference room on the top floor of the mainland-owned China Resources Building. (State firms operating in Hong Kong were quick to adopt local business practices, and there was no skimping on office accommodation.)

The first order of business was to arrange funding for the body. Members agreed that they would collect donations. (No details of the funding were ever released to the public. According to a confidential report prepared for the second plenum of the Drafting Committee, the Hong Kong drafters raised almost two million dollars. Most of it probably came from Xu's friends—businesspeople eager to cooperate with China.) The next step was to draft a constitution for the Consultative Committee. One person suggested that since it was a legal matter, the four lawyers should handle it. Xu agreed and suggested that his deputy, Mao Junnian, should "assist" them. (Mao was a local resident who had risen to a senior rank in the Hong Kong branch of the Xinhua News Agency.) Xu also recommended that Judge Simon Li be chairman of the subcommittee. No one objected.

Szeto Wah, the head of the Professional Teachers' Union, was one of the few grass-roots people appointed to the Drafting Committee. He wanted to see that a cross-section of society was represented on the Consultative Committee and asked to be a member of the subcommittee.

"If he's in, I'm out," said Simon Li.

Li was the epitome of the establishment in Hong Kong: a handsome, sophisticated man, who dressed impeccably and spoke with a perfect English accent. He apparently objected to Szeto because Szeto was an outsider, a troublemaker who had opposed the Hong Kong government on numerous issues. After an awkward moment of silence, Xu convinced Li to accept Szeto as a member of the subcommittee.

AT JUDGE LI's suggestion, the subcommittee met a week later in a conference room in the new Supreme Court building, a monotonously tall and gray building near the business district. In addition to the six Hong Kong drafters, an official from Xinhua's propaganda department attended to assist Mao Junnian. Dorothy Liu, the pro-China solicitor, said Xinhua was exerting undue control over the drafters. No one else objected, and the official was allowed to remain.

During the meeting, members agreed that the Consultative Committee would conduct "consultations." The Xinhua official suggested the term "democratic consultations." Dorothy Liu immediately protested. "This is a communist term," she said. "It does not belong in the constitution of a Hong Kong body."

"What is the harm?" asked Judge Li. "Just because red is the color of the Communist Party does not mean it is a bad color."

Martin Lee agreed with Li. They had agreed on consultations— democratic consultations seemed even better.

"You don't understand the historical background of this term," Liu replied. In China, democratic consultation is when the Communist Party informs minority parties of its policy.

The term was left in the draft constitution until it could be put before all the Hong Kong members.

The other members of the subcommittee were surprised by Liu's willingness to stand up to Xinhua and her criticism of communist terminology. They assumed, wrongly, that all leftists in Hong Kong were puppets of the Chinese government. Liu was, in fact, keen to raise her profile and fighting for the interests of Hong Kong was one way to do it.

Born in Hong Kong in 1934 to a wealthy family, she studied English literature at Oxford and obtained her law degree from Harvard. Because her father was considered pro-communist, she was shut out of the establishment. She dropped her English given name and became a rabid anti-colonialist. The only other source of power and prestige she could turn to was China. She did work for mainland companies in Hong Kong (she claims to have waived her fee when she negotiated Xinhua's purchase of its headquarters in Happy Valley). When China opened its doors to foreign investment, she helped to draft the laws governing joint ventures.

More courageous than clever, Liu liked to make bold statements that would attract attention and show that she was her own woman. She attacked Communists and colonialists alike. One Xinhua official dubbed her "the unguided missile." As the drafting proceeded, Liu shifted her position from attacking the Chinese government to supporting it on most issues. Conscious of the press interest, she flaunted her patriotism towards China the way a rebel in a winning cause flaunts his allegiance to an outlawed group. She kept a handsome portrait of Zhou Enlai displayed prominently behind the desk in her law office.

When all of the Hong Kong drafters met again on August 20, many felt the draft constitution read like a document handed down from Beijing. It said that the responsibility of the Consultative Committee was "to collect public views on the Basic Law and reflect them to the Drafting Committee" with the aim of drafting a charter that was "in line with the aspirations of the people of China, including Hong Kong compatriots."

Dorothy Liu again raised her objection to the term "democratic consultation," which was used nine times in the 1,200-word draft. Xu, his face red with anger, strongly rebuked her. He said the phrase was coined by the Nationalists, not the Communists. He rejected criticism of the draft, saying that Hong Kong people did not realize that Britain was transferring sovereignty and administration of Hong Kong to China, not to the people of Hong Kong. The right to self-government would be delegated by Beijing.

Lee did not speak Mandarin very well and could not catch everything Xu said, but he was shocked by the Xinhua director's vehemence.

The draft constitution was published in local newspapers later that week. Some pressure groups objected to a provision that said the Consultative Committee's executive board would be selected by "democratic consultation" with the drafters. They felt the businesspeople who dominated the Drafting Committee were leading the consultation process, rather than allowing the new organ to function independently. Political groups wanted the Basic Law drafters to give the public three weeks to voice their opinions on it. They argued that the drafting of the Basic Law was the first test of Beijing's policy of "Hong Kong people ruling Hong Kong" and should include full consultation. One vice-chairman said that the public was free to comment on the draft, but there would be no formal consultation.

Lee was growing increasingly uncomfortable with the way Xinhua and the business tycoons seemed to be controlling everything. When all twenty-three Hong Kong drafters met to approve the constitution on September 7, he proposed that the public be given more time to comment on the draft constitution. This was rejected. To make the consultation on the Basic Law more democratic, he proposed that some members of the Consultative Committee be elected and that the Drafting Committee give up the power to veto nominations from designated groups. These suggestions were rejected. To prevent a few powerful businesspeople from dominating the Consultative Committee, Lee also suggested that the term of office for the executive board be limited to two years. This was also rejected. The draft was approved with only superficial changes.

Chapter 13

"Somebody Has Deviated from the Joint Declaration"

A S A BOY, Martin Lee wanted to be a diplomat. His father patiently explained that Hong Kong was not a country and had no foreign service and that the British Foreign Office was unlikely to accept a Chinese. During his years at the Jesuit high school where his father taught at night, Martin chaired the debating team. His keen mind and excellent verbal skills won him many contests, and he began to think about becoming a lawyer. After graduating from Hong Kong University with a Bachelor of Arts degree in 1960, he taught high school for three years and saved enough money to study law in the U.K. He was called to the bar in England in 1965 and in Hong Kong a year later. He became one of the most successful lawyers in the colony. Within twenty years, he no longer needed to work to support his family.

Lee's ability did not escape notice. He was made a queen's counsel in 1979 and the Hong Kong government appointed him to several advisory committees dealing with legal issues. He was not, however, intensely political. During his years at Hong Kong University in the late 1950s, he was persuaded to run for the presidency of a union for liberal arts students; but he steered well clear of the main student union, which was dominated by what he called "professional students," who supported the Communists.

Under the reforms introduced in the Hong Kong government's White Paper of November 1984, the legal community would be given a seat in the Legislative Council. When a friend suggested that he run for it, Lee was hesitant. He had never wanted a career in politics. On the other hand, he felt that it was not enough to give Hong Kong a democratic system of government in the Basic Law. If elections were held only after 1997, the people of Hong Kong would not be prepared for self-government and Beijing would be able to manipulate the elections so that its people won. Elections had to be introduced well before 1997, and the Hong Kong government would probably have to be pressured into holding them. After discussing his feelings with some of his colleagues, he decided to run.

The election, held on September 26, 1985, was a low-key affair. Only 70,000 of the colony's six million people were eligible to vote. (Only 25,000 people, or less than one percent of the population, actually cast their ballots.) Often the constituencies were so small that the election was akin to running for the presidency of a social club. Six candidates were returned unopposed. Most sent personal letters to each constituent and met privately with key individuals whose support could swing the election.

Lee's main rival was an Oxford-educated Eurasian lawyer named Henry Litton, who had served seven terms as chair of the Bar Association. There was little to separate them on legal issues, so Lee campaigned on a democracy platform. He wanted a quarter of all legislators to be returned by universal suffrage in 1988, with a steady increase towards a fully elected legislature in 1997. He also wanted to see the post-1997 governor elected, rather than selected through consultations.

On election night, the votes were counted in an indoor stadium across from the Xinhua News Agency. The legal constituency was close. Around midnight, Lee was declared the winner. A reporter from a local newspaper cornered him at the back of the hall and asked what was the first thing he was going to do as a legislator. Lee said he would push for the introduction of democratic elections in 1988 so that he could be elected by the people next time around.

Though the election was the first to the Legislative Council in Hong Kong's history, it did not really change much. The functional constituencies were designed to ensure that those elected were conservative, well-educated, and pro-business (and thus pro-government). The government maintained a majority of appointed members on the Legislative Council, and the power to make policy was still firmly in the hands of civil servants. Moreover, the functional constituencies were, in some ways, a step backwards. A doctor appointed by the governor could act in the interests of the community at large. A doctor elected by his colleagues, however, would have to put the interests of his profession above those of the public. The functional constituencies also inhibited the formation of political parties, which could one day take over the administration of government. The interests of narrow constituencies would naturally conflict with those of a broad-based political party. The colonial practice of divide and rule had been institutionalized.

The election was significant, however, because it gave Lee another forum. He could now represent the people of Hong Kong with both the Hong Kong and Chinese governments. He gained confidence from his election and immediately became more outspoken. In his maiden speech to the Council, he outlined his ideas on political reform. They would become not just his agenda, but his life's work.

Lee was joined on the Legislative Council by several fellow Basic Law drafters, including Szeto Wah, who was elected by the teaching constituency. Szeto shared Lee's commitment to democracy and his fearlessness. With few others to depend on in the Council and on the Drafting Committee, the two would become as close as brothers.

At first, Lee and Szeto seemed an unlikely team. Lee was rich. He wore finely-tailored, conservative business suits, a solid gold watch on his wrist, and lived in a large apartment halfway up the Peak. He was thin and gave the impression of being weak. In fact, he possessed a limitless supply of energy and after his election he kept up a schedule that would have ruined most men half his age. His ability to debate ferociously in public was matched in private by the inner calm of a man doing what he believes is right. British author Dick Wilson said he had "a Nehru-like charisma."

Szeto, by contrast, was a man of the people. He was often seen clad in jeans and sneakers at the headquarters of the Professional Teachers' Union. Though well-educated, he wore old-fashioned glasses, had crooked, nicotine-stained teeth, and did not seem out of place walking the streets in the working-class district where the union was located.

Szeto was born in Hong Kong in 1931 and studied exclusively in the colony. He attended the evening school where Martin Lee's father taught and rose to be a grade school principal. He had met Lee only twice before the first plenum of the Basic Law Drafting Committee. During a teachers' strike in 1973, Szeto had formed an organization with leaders from other schools, which was declared illegal by the Hong Kong government. He needed help and recalled that his former teacher's son was a famous lawyer. General Li arranged a meeting. Martin did not seem interested in the teachers' cause, and Szeto came away from their first meeting with a bad impression.

Out of that strike was born the Professional Teachers' Union, the largest independent (neither pro-China nor pro-Taiwan) trade union in the colony. As its head, Szeto Wah was a powerful man in labor circles. He was active in social causes. Many of the young leaders of the grass-roots groups, the former student activists who now dominated the pro-democracy movement, learned from him and looked up to him almost as a father figure. He went up against the government from time to time, and like other troublemakers, he was labeled "pro-communist," a charge that was taken seriously by some because his brother was an employee of the Xinhua News Agency in Hong Kong.

Szeto and Lee met again at the signing of the Joint Declaration. Martin thought Szeto might not know most of the businesspeople and professionals present and offered to make some introductions.

At the time of the election, they still hardly knew each other. As they found themselves alone against conservatives on the Legislative Council and Drafting Committee, they were drawn to one another. They complemented each other well: Lee was analytical, Szeto emotional; Lee was articulate in English, Szeto hardly spoke it; Lee had no experience in mobilizing support, Szeto was a veteran of many campaigns. If Lee was the leader of the pro-democracy movement, Szeto was his general. Together they would transform the face of Hong Kong politics.

UP TO NOW, Beijing had been completely outmaneuvered on the reforms. The Hong Kong government had introduced fundamental changes to the political system, and Beijing had been powerless to stop it. Chinese officials were determined not to let it happen again.

In the months following the signing of the Joint Declaration, Xu reorganized the Xinhua News Agency along the lines of a government. Offices were set up around the colony, shadowing the government's district offices. Ten departments were created to handle such tasks as administration, propaganda, the economy, and foreign affairs. Their purpose was to monitor the Hong Kong government and provide information to Chinese officials when they needed to negotiate with Britain or speak publicly about the colony's affairs.

Xu himself adopted a higher profile so that he could voice Beijing's views on the issues affecting the colony. He was, in fact, staking China's claim to Hong Kong, letting the public know that there was another point of view to consider. (Journalists called him "the shadow governor.") During the next few months, he underwent a dramatic transformation, swapping his ill-fitting clothes and tinted glasses for well-tailored Western suits and designer eyewear. He dropped the communist dogma and became a smooth-talking, seasoned diplomat. He was highly sought after by companies eager to show their willingness to cooperate with China, by pressure groups looking to boost their credibility and influence, by politicians anxious about their post-1997 careers, and by journalists keen to know Beijing's views on the latest event. He seemed at times to be everywhere. He became a regular fixture in newspapers and on the nightly news. There were pictures of him cuddling babies in a working-class home, toasting tycoons at a cocktail party, shaking hands with movie stars at film openings, and shoveling a spadeful of dirt at the topping-out ceremony for the colony's latest skyscraper—his face always scrunched into a broad smile.

To outsiders, the change in China's top representative was miraculous and welcome. To insiders, it was superficial. Xu remained a die-hard Communist who executed his orders ruthlessly and worked for the best interests of China, the party, and his masters in Beijing. One former Xinhua employee describes him as "a nasty man" who was "a master of public relations." (When he took up his post in Hong Kong, the first thing he did was assure the staff that they were good comrades who had done good work. Then, he fired them one by one, condemning their work as "leftist and narrow." He drove Li Chuwen, a very capable deputy director, to the point of a breakdown because Li had criticized him. According to one former Xinhua employee, Xu set up companies in Hong Kong and used his position as China's chief representative there to get lucrative deals for himself.)

When he was asked about the historic election, Xu responded tersely: "We do not support it. We do not oppose it." He was, in fact, increasingly concerned about the calls for democratic elections and the Hong Kong government's determination to push ahead with the planned political review in 1987. He was determined to halt all reforms. Beijing demanded through all its diplomatic channels that reforms be discussed in the Joint Liaison Group. British diplomats pointed out that under the Joint Declaration, the Joint Liaison Group would discuss, during the first half of the transition period, only measures to enable Hong Kong to maintain its economic relations as a separate customs territory and "to ensure the continued application of international rights and obligations affecting Hong Kong."

Chinese officials claimed that the reforms infringed on China's sovereignty. How could China allow Britain to determine the political system of a territory of China? They feared that Britain would use the guise of democracy to entrench her own people in government before 1997. They seemed to assume that whoever held an election also manipulated it. At the same time, powerful businesspeople were advising Xu that democratic reforms would damage Hong Kong's stability and prosperity. Xu accepted T.S. Lo's vision of Hong Kong, with Beijing and the tycoons running it for their own benefit. The interests of the Communists and the capitalists were the same, and they forged an "unholy alliance" to oppose democratization in Hong Kong.

Who would determine the shape and nature of Hong Kong's political system after 1997? China felt that she had the sole right to do so. Martin Lee and other pro-democracy activists (who were unaware of the conflict behind the scenes) believed that Britain had promised to introduce "a truly representative government" in Hong Kong before 1997 and that this was the reason that the people of Hong Kong, and Parliament, had accepted the Joint Declaration. Thus, Britain had a responsibility and a duty to push the colony as far down the road to democracy as possible, regardless of China's objections. For Lee, it was more than just a question of whether the Hong Kong people would be able to run their own affairs for the benefit of all. It was a question of life or death. Without an elected government to protect them, the people of Hong Kong would be subject to the same random justice as the people on the mainland.

British diplomats had painted themselves into a corner. They knew that China opposed democratic elections, yet the government had encouraged the people of Hong Kong and Parliament to believe that the colony would have a democratic system of government after 1997 to get them to accept the accord. They duped the Chinese with the first Green Paper, but now the Chinese were on to them. The Hong Kong government had committed itself to holding a second political review in 1987. If it bowed to China's demand and put off the review, it would be perceived as a lame duck and find it increasingly difficult to govern during the transition. If it did not, there would be a major diplomatic row, which would undermine stability in Hong Kong.

In the weeks following the elections, several Hong Kong officials made public statements aimed at reassuring the Chinese government that changes would not be introduced too quickly and that its concerns would be taken into consideration. Youde decided that the next Green Paper, to be released in May 1987, would not lay out specific proposals or indicate the best direction for reforms to take. It would simply list options. This would enable the Hong Kong government to claim that it was not leading public opinion or preempting the Basic Law. If the Chinese and Hong Kong governments both consulted the public objectively, the Basic Law and political reforms should merge.

Beijing was not reassured and continued to insist that the subject of political reform be discussed at the next Joint Liaison Group meeting. The Hong Kong government, presumably with Youde's approval, switched tactics. Officials leaked information about the behind-the-scenes pressure to mobilize public opinion and force Beijing to back off.

In mid-November, Xu went to Beijing for consultations with his superiors. When he returned, he called a press conference, his first since arriving in the colony more than two years earlier. Hong Kong officials sensed that he would make a statement on political reform and decided to preempt him. On November 19, the day Ronald Reagan and Mikhail Gorbachev held their first summit in Geneva, the new political adviser, John Boyd, invited a journalist from the *South China Morning Post* to lunch. Boyd told the reporter that China was pushing for a say on political reform and that this was a dangerous precedent, which could possibly lead to Beijing assuming a role in administering Hong Kong before 1997.

The next day, the headline on page two read: PATH TO AN EARLY TAKEOVER. In the article, the writer, quoting an unnamed source, claimed that Beijing wanted to halt the reforms until the Basic Law was complete. After the charter was promulgated, Chinese officials would demand that it be discussed in the Joint Liaison Group. They would say that in the interests of a smooth transition, it should be implemented before 1997. "If this scenario is borne out," the article concluded, "China will have in effect recovered Hong Kong well before the lease [of the New Territories] runs out."

Boyd's maneuver backfired. When Xu met the press on November 21, he banged his glasses on the table repeatedly and declared: "The only way to ensure Hong Kong's prosperity and stability hinges on whether both parties will stick to the terms of the Joint Declaration. But it is not difficult for us to detect that somebody has deviated from the accord. We can't ignore this fact." He held up a copy of the Joint Declaration and said that it would be "most unfortunate" if "drastic changes" were made to the colony's political system before the completion of the Basic Law.

The remarks stunned the colony. The stock market index plummeted fifty points the next day.

Lee did not believe that Britain had deviated from the Joint Declaration, but that Xu's remarks constituted a breach of the agreement. The Chinese government clearly was trying to intimidate Hong Kong. What worried him most was the British and Hong Kong governments' failure to challenge Xu's claims. When asked if political reforms were a breach of the agreement, a Foreign Office spokesperson said: "We have no idea what is in Mr. Xu's mind. Both governments are fully committed to the Joint Declaration."

IF THE BRITISH and Hong Kong governments were unaware of what Xu was talking about, he was willing to spell it out for them. A day after his press conference, he held one of his regular secret meetings with S.Y. Chung, Lydia Dunn, and Q.W. Lee at Xinhua. Xu was unusually serious during the dinner. He said that the Hong Kong government's reforms were preempting the Basic Law. China could not allow Britain to develop a system that would extend beyond 1997. She would not accept another fait accompli. He added that if reforms proceeded too quickly, they might damage the colony's stability and prosperity. In particular, he demanded that democratic elections to the Legislative Council not be introduced in 1988.

"You don't have to convince me," Chung replied. "You are preaching to the converted."

Late that night, the three Executive Councilors went to Government House to inform Youde of what they had been told (as they did after every meeting with Xu). None of it came as a surprise to the governor. That day he had discussed Xu's statements with senior government officials and David

Wilson and Tony Galsworthy, two members of the Joint Liaison Group. The group agreed that political reforms had to be discussed in the Joint Liaison Group to avoid a diplomatic incident. If the Chinese government insisted that reforms be delayed until after the promulgation of the Basic Law, Britain could insist that the political review go ahead, but agree to put off all major constitutional changes. It was the easiest, but worst possible solution. It guaranteed that the coming political review would be meaningless. Instead of being seen as a lame duck, the Hong Kong government would be perceived as a deceitful lame duck.

The issue was put before the Executive Council. The unofficial members were split. Chung believed that Britain did not have the right to press ahead with reforms without China's consent. It was acceptable in 1984 when the two sides were negotiating and had to use whatever tactics they could to get the best deal, but now Britain and China were partners and had to cooperate.

Other members of the Council disagreed. They felt that Britain should maintain administrative control over the colony. Giving in to China on this issue would only lead to further demands. At the same time, they were not eager to see a rapid move towards a representative government—not because they would lose their privileged positions, but because they did not want to see anything disrupt Hong Kong's economy. Their opposition was half-hearted, and in the end, the Executive Council agreed that Britain should put off all major constitutional changes until after the promulgation of the Basic Law at China's insistence. None of them questioned the implications of this decision.

When the Joint Liaison Group met at Villa Two of the Diaoyutai State Guest House on November 26, the Chinese side, as expected, insisted that all reforms be delayed until after the publication of the Basic Law in 1990. After much acrimonious discussion, David Wilson said that the British government would put off "all major constitutional changes." The Chinese were satisfied. The agreement was kept a closely guarded secret. The British government did not want to admit to Parliament, or the people of Hong Kong, that it was no longer responsible for determining political reforms in the approach to 1997.

As LONDON AND Beijing tussled over political reforms, plans were continuing for the creation of the Basic Law Consultative Committee. Under pressure from grass-roots activists, the Hong Kong drafters agreed to expand the membership from 150 to 180. To avoid the problem Szeto had caused when forming the constitution subcommittee, Xu quietly appointed six Hong

Kong drafters to select the 120 people who would be invited to join the Consultative Committee and to designate sixty organizations which could choose their own representatives.

When the list of members was released on November 25, 1985, it was again dominated by businesspeople and professionals. Less than a quarter of the seats were given to labor and grass-roots organizations. Seven Basic Law drafters were appointed, leading some critics to charge that the Drafting Committee would be consulting itself.

The Basic Law Consultative Committee's job was to collect public opinion on the drafts of the charter. It would confer some legitimacy upon the Basic Law by enabling the Chinese government to say that it had consulted the people of Hong Kong—much the way the Hong Kong government's Assessment Office tried to confer legitimacy on the Joint Declaration. It would have no power over what went into the document. Its constitution prohibited it from informing the Drafting Committee of the number of submissions in favor of one option or another, reflecting the businesspeople's belief that the majority did not necessarily know what was best for Hong Kong.

The committee was also part of the United Front. Important people who could not be given a seat on the Drafting Committee were rewarded with one on the Consultative Committee (such as T.S. Lo, who had been too close to the British). During private discussions with U.S. consulate officials in January 1986, Lu Ping proposed that two Americans be invited to sit on the Consultative Committee as advisers. When this was reported to Washington, an official scrawled in the margin of the confidential cable: "This is taking United Front to the max."

The press, intellectuals, political commentators, and democracy activists were skeptical of Beijing's willingness to consult the people of Hong Kong and draft a Basic Law that accurately reflected their views. Journalists, in particular, suspected a sinister motive behind everything Beijing did. Xu's determination to direct the consultation only fueled this suspicion.

On December 6, all 180 members of the Consultative Committee met at its plush office on the eighth floor of the Lane Crawford House to elect the executive board. Before the ballot, shipping tycoon and Drafting Committee Vice-Chairman Y.K. Pao came in. Though he was not a member of the Consultative Committee, he was apparently invited by Xu because he was a vice-chairman. (He also owned the building.) Pao told members that the executive board should be made up of people loyal to China and Hong Kong, and should include some women and industrialists. Xinhua officials quietly spread the names of those it favored.

After the election, the winners were asked to stay behind "for coffee and tea." When most members had left, three vice-chairmen of the Drafting Committee—Y.K. Pao, T.K. Ann, and Xu Jiatun—entered the room. Pao took a piece of paper from his pocket. He proposed that Ann be named chairman of the Consultative Committee and that Xinhua's Mao Junnian be secretary-general. He recommended five prominent people to serve as vice-chairpersons. The names were seconded. There was a round of applause, and Pao quickly left the room.

When news of the "election" was leaked to the press, there was an uproar. Martin Lee feared that this was the kind of election Beijing wanted to see in Hong Kong after 1997. He told the press that it was invalid because only the executive board members themselves could nominate office-bearers. Moreover, the constitution called for at least a week's notice for an official meeting. Xu defended the method of selecting the office-bearers, claiming that "consultation is one form of election."

The selection of the officers was not much different from the way traditional Chinese companies chose directors. But there was little doubt that the names on Pao's list came from Xinhua. It indicated to people that Beijing was intent on controlling every facet of the Basic Law drafting. The most disturbing part of the incident, to some, was that the tycoons were willing to do Beijing's bidding.

In response to the outcry, the executive board called a formal meeting on December 11 and held fresh elections. Lo was nominated as a candidate for the chairmanship. He knew Xinhua had already made its choice in Ann and refused to stand. All other candidates declined nominations for the remaining posts, and the seven original officers were returned. The new polls failed to relieve anxieties in Hong Kong because they only proved that few individuals were prepared to defy Big Brother.

IN JANUARY 1986, Timothy Renton, the new British minister of state at the Foreign Office, went to Beijing for talks with Chinese officials. The issue of political reform had not been entirely resolved. The Hong Kong government had agreed to put off major constitutional changes, but the 1984 White Paper said another political review would be held in 1987 and that the question of democratic elections would be considered. If Britain failed to hold the review or to offer the option of democratic polls, it would damage the government's reputation at home and abroad.

Renton was an intelligent and capable Conservative who was first elected to Parliament in 1974. His star was rising under Prime Minister Thatcher, but there were plenty of shoals around Hong Kong where a career could crash. One misstatement could cause panic in the jittery colony and reverse his political fortunes. Renton studied his brief well and stuck to the Foreign Office line. He suggested that the two sides seek convergence between the political system that was evolving in Hong Kong and the system to be laid down in the Basic Law. The Chinese, believing there would be no major constitutional changes before 1997, including elections, agreed.

Before leaving Beijing, Renton told reporters that both governments "saw the need to keep closely in touch to avoid misunderstandings" and that "the principle of convergence will be the one that will guide us both."

Lee was stunned by Britain's decision to consult China about reforms in Hong Kong. A year earlier, Renton's predecessor, Richard Luce, had told the House of Commons that "it is firmly agreed [with China] that the British government will be responsible for the administration of Hong Kong until 1 July 1997. That includes responsibility for constitutional development."

Renton also told reporters that the political reforms introduced in the 1984 White Paper needed time to "settle down." This seemed to indicate that London had already agreed not to introduce democratic elections in 1988. (It had not, but was eager to reassure Beijing.)

Political commentators in Hong Kong believed that China had proposed the policy of "convergence" to limit the Hong Kong government's ability to alter the political system before 1997. In fact, the policy had been worked out by Wilson and Galsworthy. China was demanding that no reforms be introduced before the promulgation of the Basic Law. Convergence was an improvement because it implied that the political system being incorporated into the Basic Law would move towards the system being developed in Hong Kong and vice versa. Chinese officials either did not understand this or did not care what the British implied in public. What mattered was that London had agreed to put off all major constitutional changes until after 1990.

Thatcher was sympathetic towards those in Hong Kong who wanted democratic reforms. Britain's weak bargaining position had left her no choice but to hand back the colony, but introducing elections could help assuage the guilt she felt over it. She was advised against taking a tough stand on the issue by Cradock, who had moved into an office on the second floor of No. 10 Downing Street as her foreign affairs adviser.

Cradock was a diplomat and he saw things in diplomatic terms. It was not a question of whether the people of Hong Kong had the right to self-administration; it was a question of what was realistic. He argued that it was fruitless to introduce reforms against China's will because Beijing could "lay waste to Hong Kong" simply by publicly opposing routine decisions made in the colony. If Britain moved ahead and introduced political reforms, the Chinese government could create a major diplomatic storm, or could simply overturn the entire system and introduce something of its own design in

1997. Both of these scenarios were unacceptable because they would damage confidence in Hong Kong. For the Joint Declaration to work, he argued, the two sides had to cooperate.

Had Lee been aware of the British government's thinking, he would have countered that China would not dare to overturn a well-functioning democratic system because the move would shatter confidence in Hong Kong and kill the goose that laid the golden eggs. Even if the Communists were bloody-minded about the political system, Lee was prepared to take risks because he believed that without a democratic government Hong Kong did not stand much of a chance after 1997 anyway.

RENTON FLEW to Hong Kong by helicopter from Shenzhen on January 23. After private discussions with the governor and the Executive Council, he met with Umelco at 7 P.M. They gathered in the largest conference room in the new Legislative Council, a stately colonial building with a domed-roof and large doric columns, which used to house the Supreme Court. The building had been completely renovated, and the conference room boasted the most modern translation equipment. Pale yellow walls, ceiling fans, and window shutters with slats maintained the old-world feel of the building.

Renton tried to sell the Councilors on the policy of convergence. He stressed that Britain would not give in to China on points of principle in the Joint Declaration (she already had by giving China a say in the administration of Hong Kong before 1997) and that the coming political review would be "a serious one." "It is in everyone's interest," he said, "to ensure that both governments arrive at the crossing point at more or less the same speed and same time without a jolt."

Lee and Szeto asked how convergence could be achieved without bowing to whatever China wrote into the Basic Law. Renton was evasive. He offered no assurance that there would be democratic elections to the Legislative Council in 1988.

At a press conference before his departure, Renton tried to calm the storm his remarks in Beijing had whipped up. "By convergence, I mean two or more [parties] moving in the same direction in order to arrive at approximately the same place at approximately the same time." This did not mean that one party was inferior or superior to the other. "We are creating a set of railway lines that lead up to 1997. The Chinese will be creating a set of railway lines that lead on from 1997. The need is to see that those two railway lines meet together at a crossing point."

He stressed that the people of Hong Kong had to "come forward with their feelings and suggestions" on political reform. These would be used to shape a system that was "appropriate to the unique needs" of the colony. He refused to say what Britain would do if the people of Hong Kong wanted democratic elections to the Legislative Council in 1988 and China opposed them.

Lee could not see how there could be convergence when the Chinese government was insisting that the future political system must be the one spelled out in the Basic Law. As he saw it, Beijing was reinterpreting the Joint Declaration and reneging on the promise of "Hong Kong people ruling Hong Kong." Britain was abdicating her duty to introduce a representative government in Hong Kong and her responsibility to see that the agreement was faithfully implemented. He and Szeto launched a five-year crusade to ensure that the people of Hong Kong would enjoy the fruits of democracy after 1997.

Chapter 14

The Battle Lines Are Drawn

M ARTIN LEE left for Beijing with the other drafters on April 17, 1986, two days after U.S. jet fighters attacked Libya because of her support of terrorism. At the start of the second plenum, Vice-Chairperson Ann briefed the drafters on the establishment of the Consultative Committee. Then, the secretariat handed out an outline of the Basic Law. It broke the charter into a preamble and ten chapters dealing with everything from Hong Kong's political system and economy to its relationship with Beijing and the rights and obligations of local residents. It listed the issues to be tackled and spelled out some of the fundamental objectives of the charter.

That afternoon, drafters split into their discussion groups. Within the groups, members were divided over how the outline should be amended. Lee, Szeto, and a few other Hong Kong drafters wanted to get the highest level of autonomy for the future Special Administrative Region. The mainland drafters were there to see that the central government would be able to exercise sovereignty over Hong Kong. This basic conflict continued through all of the Drafting Committee's work.

Szeto proposed that an article be added to the outline to give Hong Kong all authority not specifically retained by the central government. He explained that this would give local residents confidence that Beijing intended to exercise sovereignty only in the areas of foreign affairs and defense. One of the mainland legal experts immediately opposed the idea: The concept of residual powers applied only to a federal system and China was *not* a federal republic.

As a lawyer, Lee was particularly concerned about upholding the independence of the judiciary and the rule of law in Hong Kong. He proposed adding an article to specify which parts of the Chinese Constitution would apply to Hong Kong. Without such a provision, he said, Hong Kong people would not know which laws they had to abide by. Several mainland members objected vehemently: The Basic Law would be subordinate to the Chinese Constitution; it would be inappropriate to include parts of the Constitution in the Basic Law. Lu Ping of the Hong Kong and Macao Affairs Office said that only the National People's Congress could say which provisions of the Chinese Constitution were applicable to Hong Kong.

On the third day of the plenum, the secretariat submitted a revised outline with over fifty amendments. There were no new articles on residual powers or on the relationship between the Chinese Constitution and the Basic Law. Lee and Szeto were angry that their suggestions had not been included.

That evening, eleven Hong Kong and five mainland drafters met the press in a sparsely furnished conference room in the Beijing Hotel. It turned into an open argument between some of the mainland and Hong Kong drafters. Lee declared angrily that he and several of his colleagues would vote against the outline if it did not include his proposal and Szeto's.

Senior Chinese leaders, no doubt, believed that the Hong Kong drafters would cooperate fully with their Chinese counterparts and that any disagreements would be worked out quietly behind closed doors, much the way Legislative Councilors worked with the British administration in Hong Kong. For the most part, they were correct. Some of the wealthy tycoons seemed to be willing to do whatever China's leaders asked. More than one of their Hong Kong colleagues felt the Basic Law did not really matter to them because they thought the Chinese government would rule Hong Kong with their help and cooperation. What really mattered was staying on the good side of those who held power in Beijing.

Though most of the Hong Kong professionals on the Drafting Committee felt the Basic Law was important, they would not confront the Chinese drafters. Instead, they would quietly try to persuade China to incorporate needed provisions into the Basic Law. Lee and Szeto were the only two drafters who were willing to stand up to Chinese officials. Some commentators believed that Lee's confrontational approach was a result of his Western education. Szeto, however, was even more confrontational but had not been educated overseas. At first, the two were eager to work with their Chinese counterparts through friendly persuasion. When it became clear that the Chinese drafters had some very definite ideas about the Basic Law and that many of the Hong Kong drafters were willing to cooperate regardless of Hong Kong's interests, the two found that open confrontation was their only choice. Their aggressiveness was born out of a desire to get the best deal for Hong Kong—the most autonomy, the greatest level of democracy, the best protection of human rights, and ironclad guarantees against interference by the Chinese government.

On the final day of the plenum, another draft of the outline, with thirty additional amendments, was distributed to members. An article would be added regarding the legal status of the charter and its relationship to the Chinese Constitution. The issue of residual powers was not included in the outline itself, but was covered in a memorandum. The compromise was enough to get Lee and Szeto to support the draft. (Residual powers was completely anathema to the Communists, who wanted to control everything from the center. Despite the promise to discuss it, the idea was never given serious consideration.)

A rumor spread within the committee that Ji Pengfei and his deputies had discussed the controversy over the two proposals the night before with Deng himself and that the Chinese leader agreed to concede to Lee and Szeto's demands. Basic Law drafter Dr. Raymond Wu believed that Lee's success after taking the issue public encouraged him to adopt such aggressive tactics throughout the drafting.

Whether the rumor was true or not, Chinese officials clearly wanted to maintain the appearance of harmony. A split between the Hong Kong and mainland drafters would damage the committee's credibility. To avoid this, members would not vote on a version of a clause until a consensus could be reached (which is why the charter ultimately took five years to complete). In this case, the mainlanders were successful. The final version of the outline was approved unanimously.

DURING THE plenum, the Drafting Committee's secretariat announced that five special issue subgroups would be set up to write clauses on: the relationship between the central and Hong Kong governments; the rights and obligations of Hong Kong citizens; the future political structure; the economy; and education, culture, and scientific and religious affairs. To make it appear that the Hong Kong drafters had an equal say, each subgroup would have a Hong Kong and a mainland convener, who would take turns chairing meetings. There were no nominations, no elections, not even consultations over who the conveners should be. The secretariat simply read out a list of names. Some of the Hong Kong members were not even notified in advance or asked if they would accept the appointment. (All five did.)

The eight vice-chairpersons formed, along with Ji, the Chairman's Committee, which would meet the day before each plenum to prepare the agenda. The rest of the drafters were asked to join one or two subgroups. Three of the subgroups had the comparatively simple task of codifying the terms of the Joint Declaration into the Basic Law to ensure that existing systems would remain in effect after 1997. In many cases, they copied passages from the accord verbatim. The relationship and the political subgroups were the most crucial. They had no existing systems to perpetuate and often the Joint

Declaration either did not cover these areas, or was vague because Britain and China could not agree on a detailed formula.

Lee was well aware of the importance of these two groups and signed up for both. Szeto joined him on the political subgroup, but because he was ostensibly the teachers' representative, he felt he had to join the education and culture subgroup. (Lee found the work of the relationship subgroup particularly frustrating and demoralizing. Without Szeto, he was often left standing alone against the other sixteen members.)

The Chinese government was also aware of the importance of these two subgroups and stacked them with officials who could be instructed how to vote. Li Hou and Lu Ping sat on both and played an important role in protecting China's interests.

In all but one case, the secretariat paired a strong mainland convener with a weak, malleable Hong Kong one. Only publisher Louis Cha, one of the most powerful men in Hong Kong publishing circles, had the intelligence and strength of character to stand up to the mainland drafters. Ironically, his appointment as coconvener of the political subgroup raised the most concern in Hong Kong.

Cha was short and stocky, with a square face and thin lips. He was born the son of a banker and landlord in Hangzhou, China, in 1924. As a young man he was liberal- and independent-minded. He defied his father and struggled across the country to study in the wartime capital of Chungking. After the war, he returned to Shanghai to study international law. He wanted to join the foreign service so he could go abroad. While in Shanghai, he saw firsthand the corruption and brutality of the Nationalist regime. Like many young intellectuals, he leaned towards Communism.

Cha never did join the foreign service. In 1947, he went to work as a translator for the *Ta Kung Pao* newspaper, which was then controlled by a businessman linked to the Guomindang. When the paper launched a Hong Kong edition in March 1948, he was posted to the colony. After liberation, *Ta Kung Pao* became a mouthpiece for the Communist Party. Cha stayed on, even after his father was executed by the new regime for capitalist crimes. (After Deng came to power, the case was reopened and his father was exonerated.) Cha was not trusted by the Communists because of his bourgeois upbringing and because he enjoyed going to the movies and listening to Western music. He watched in anger and frustration as many of his friends back home were either purged or sent to the countryside.

In 1955, *Ta Kung Pao*'s editor asked Cha to write a novel that would be published in the paper in installments. Cha chose the pseudonym Kam Yung ("Golden Mean"). Within twenty years, he would be considered one of the greatest living Chinese writers, with scholars on both sides of the Taiwan

Strait poring over his works. On the surface, his novels were about kung fu and sword fighting. However, he blended historical fact, religion, mysticism, and romance into a rich tapestry that depicted the complex and constantly shifting relationships between a large number of characters. His works could be read as pulp fiction, philosophical treatise, or political allegory.

Cha used the money he earned from his books to launch *Ming Pao* in 1959, principally as a vehicle for his fiction. Initially, his paper leaned towards the left. Then, in 1962, there was turmoil in Guangdong. China opened the border, and Hong Kong was suddenly inundated with thousands of refugees. The left-wing press played down the crisis and the pro-Taiwan journals blew it out of proportion for propaganda purposes. Cha's paper was one of the few that tried to get to the truth. Its independence and objectivity attracted intellectuals. Circulation jumped in a few months from a few thousand to 20,000. The paper made a profit for the first time that year and has done so every year since.

During the Cultural Revolution, *Ming Pao* harshly criticized the radical policies of the Chinese government. Cha launched a monthly magazine devoted to classical Chinese literature, philosophy, and history, in defiance of the Red Guards' call for the destruction of traditional Chinese culture. He became a marked man. After a prominent radio personality was burned alive, one of the smaller pro-Beijing papers ran a picture of Cha with the caption: "This man is next."

When Deng came to power, *Ming Pao* toned down its criticism of Beijing. Cha still opposed the communist system, but he commended the reforms being introduced. He was wooed by the Chinese government and was one of the first non-leftists in Hong Kong to be given a private audience with Deng, during which he told the Chinese leader frankly how he felt about Communism. After Xu arrived in Hong Kong in 1983, he personally courted Cha, passing him internal reports on the situation in China for background and inviting him and his family to dinner. The two became close friends. They were from neighboring provinces, spoke the same dialect, and shared a love of Chinese literature and *go*, a board game popular in China and Japan. They often spent long evenings at each other's homes, talking about everything except Communism, on which they differed strongly.

Cha's novels showed the brilliance of his mind and the complexity of his thinking. He was a student of politics, history, philosophy, and especially human nature. As a young man, he was a keen poker player and understood the game's psychological aspects. As brilliant as he was at grasping the complexities of human relationships, he was less successful at engaging in them. He was married three times, and was not particularly loved by his staff. There was always something cold and calculating about him. No matter how transparent his motives, people always suspected something else going on beneath the surface. As he became rich and influential, his progressive thinking stagnated and he became a staunch defender of the status quo. He feared that elected politicians would inevitably raise taxes. During the Sino-British negotiations, he argued that the important thing was to maintain freedoms and the rule of law in Hong Kong. He did not explain how this could be done without democracy.

Cha had doubts about joining the Drafting Committee. He knew how the Communists operated and that Hong Kong would have little leverage in bargaining with Beijing. He accepted the appointment because he felt he should give something back to the colony before he retired. Perhaps he also felt that helping to draft the colony's constitution would be the fitting end to an illustrious career. Whatever his personal motives were, journalists in Hong Kong believed that he was made convener of the important political subgroup because he was opposed to democratic elections.

A week before the plenum, Cha told a luncheon audience that local politicians could not prevent interference from Beijing because even if they organized strikes and riots, the Chinese government could send a flood of workers from the mainland to fill jobs and use the People's Liberation Army to crush any uprising. Since Beijing did not want to see professionals leave the colony, he argued that it would respect the views of representatives chosen by functional constituencies. This view differed slightly from that of most conservative industrialists, who felt those who created the wealth should determine how it would be used.

It is unlikely that Cha was chosen because of his conservative views, as there were others in the subgroup who were more conservative. He may have been appointed convener of the political subgroup because he was an important ally who could not be made a vice-chairperson. Or perhaps Xu pushed for him out of personal loyalty. It did not make any difference. Cha was not the type to steamroller his views through; his role in developing Hong Kong's political system was more subtle. He gave all sides a chance to air their views during subgroup meetings. As he did with the characters in his novels, he tried to manipulate the key players to bring about a resolution to the conflict between warring factions.

WHEN MARTIN LEE and the seven other Hong Kong drafters in the relationship subgroup arrived at the Shenzhen railway station, just across the border from Hong Kong, they were greeted by hawkers selling watches and other goods, taxi drivers offering rides, and by large, hand-painted billboards advertising Chinese-made home appliances. Capitalism was, indeed, spreading out from Hong Kong. (Just fifteen years earlier, during the Cultural Revolution, Hong Kong residents crossing into China at this station wore several layers of shirts and pants because that was the only way to sneak them in for poorer relatives in Guangdong.)

The drafters were met at the crowded station by officials of the Hong Kong and Macao Affairs Office and driven for twenty minutes to the Shenzhen Guest House, a Chinese government complex similar to Diaoyutai, but on a smaller scale. The rooms in the villas were simple and clean, an improvement over the Beijing Hotel. During all of the subgroup meetings, the drafters ate breakfast together, worked from 9:30 to 11:30, then stopped for lunch. Some of the older mainland drafters took naps, so the afternoon session usually started at three o'clock and ended at five.

At the first meeting, on May 31, 1986, members of the subgroup gathered in a modestly furnished conference room within the complex. Each of the other subgroups had to draft just one chapter, but they had to write three: chapter two on the relationship between the central and Hong Kong governments; chapter seven on external affairs; and chapter nine on the interpretation and amendment of the Basic Law. The conveners assigned members to write reports on the topics to be covered and then began discussing substantive issues.

One of the first questions to arise was who would have the authority to interpret the Basic Law. The Joint Declaration said that the Hong Kong Special Administrative Region would have the "right of final adjudication." Most legal experts and political commentators in the colony took this to mean that judges would interpret the Basic Law when trying cases. Several Chinese officials, including Ji, had stated publicly that the Standing Committee of the National People's Congress would interpret the Basic Law. Lee believed the issue was as crucial as getting the political system right. If China's legislature could interpret the Basic Law, the charter would offer no protection and no guarantees to Hong Kong. Whenever Beijing did not like a court ruling, it could simply reinterpret the charter.

During the meeting, a mainland drafter said that since the NPC would promulgate the Basic Law, it should have the right to interpret the charter. Lee pointed out that, under the Joint Declaration, Hong Kong would continue to use British common law after 1997. In common law countries, only the courts had the power to interpret the laws. He argued that after 1997, Hong Kong courts should have the power to interpret the Basic Law while hearing cases. When there was no case before the courts, the NPC could interpret the Basic Law at the request of the central or Hong Kong government. That way a litigant could not gain the upper hand in a case by asking for an interpretation.

"There shouldn't be a problem," said mainland legal expert Wu Jianfan. "The British government did not even raise the issue during the Sino-British negotiations."

Some of the other Hong Kong drafters proposed other formulas, which restricted the Hong Kong courts' power to interpret some portions of the Basic Law. By the end of the two-day session, most agreed that the Standing Committee of the NPC would have the right to interpret the Basic Law and that the Hong Kong courts should be able to interpret some provisions when adjudicating cases. Lee continued to oppose the formula because it was alien to Hong Kong, contrary to the one country, two systems concept, and would erode the independence of the judiciary.

THE POLITICAL SUBGROUP met at the Shenzhen Guest House at the end of June. Members began by looking at the basic elements of a political system. There was no discussion about how to give the future government legitimacy, or the functions of an elected legislature in a capitalist society. The businesspeople simply wanted to have the future government maintain pro-business policies. They wanted to retain a strong governor (chosen, of course, by the business community) because this was more efficient than a system of checks and balances. If there were a parliamentary-style government, legislation would get bogged down in political battles, and policies would change every time the ruling party lost an election.

Lee and Szeto were concerned mainly with protecting the people of Hong Kong from abuses. They opposed a strong governor because he could conspire with cadres in Beijing to deprive people of their rights and introduce policies aimed at keeping the population poor and the tycoons rich.

The mainland drafters did not express any opinions, and it was not clear what type of government they favored until the third day of the meeting, when Li Hou gave the Chinese government's definition of accountability. He said the executive branch would be required to submit periodic reports to the legislature, answer questions about policy, and seek approval for legislation and public expenditure. The legislature would also be able to impeach the governor and senior officials in the case of a serious breach of duty.

Lee and Szeto were stunned. This was not accountability in the Western political sense of the word. If this definition was accepted, the Legislative Council would have little more power than at present to make laws relating to policy. The future governor would be able to run Hong Kong as he saw fit. It seemed to them that Beijing wanted a powerful governor because if it controlled him, then it controlled the entire government.

Maria Tam was the only Hong Kong drafter who knew what definition Britain and China had agreed upon during the negotiations. Bound by law not to reveal the contents of the negotiations, she called on Britain and China to give their definition. Both sides stuck to their agreement not to reveal the contents of the talks. But Chinese officials felt tricked. Britain had given them a definition that was not accepted by most Hong Kong people.

DR. RAYMOND WU sensed that the political situation in Hong Kong was changing. The calls for democratic elections were growing louder, and it would not be enough for the tycoons simply to demand that the colonial system be maintained after 1997. Britain and China would be under pressure to respect the will of the majority. He believed that businesspeople and professionals had to organize themselves and propose an alternative to Western-style democracy and then sell it to Beijing and the people of Hong Kong. (He joined the political subgroup from its sixth meeting.)

In early 1986, Wu expressed his concerns to five colleagues on the Basic Law Consultative Committee. They agreed, and over the next few weeks, the six of them met regularly at a restaurant in a social club to draw up a political blueprint that would maintain the best features of the current system. Other conservative members of the Consultative Committee heard about the group and asked to join. As the membership grew, it needed to elect a chairperson. Although the businesspeople were fond of saying that they should run Hong Kong because they had made it successful, they did not want to give up their valuable time to get involved in politics. No one wanted to lead the group. Finally, one member suggested Vincent Lo, the head of a construction company. Lo was extremely reluctant. He was a businessman, not a politician, but he recognized that Hong Kong people needed to make sacrifices and eventually agreed.

As the head of the new lobby, Lo would be the main spokesperson for the business community, and Lee's chief political rival. At first, Dr. Wu did not believe Lo was right for the job. He was shy, hid behind a pair of large glasses, and hated to talk to the press. He did not seem to have the mettle to engage in the cut and thrust of politics. But he had two essential qualities that made him suitable for the job: the conviction that the businesspeople's view was right and the determination to get their message across to the public. Young, boyishly handsome, and eminently successful, he was also more palatable to the press than the crusty old men declaring that since they made Hong Kong successful they should run it. Though Lo agreed with the aging tycoons' view that a headlong rush into democracy simply for democracy's sake was dangerous, he did not share their arrogance and contempt for the man in the street. He was not politically ambitious. He had previously turned down a seat on the Legislative Council.

Lo was not a member of the aristocracy. His family came originally from Chiu Chow on the coast of Guangdong. His great-grandfather moved to Thailand during the Qing dynasty in search of a better life and established a small but successful trading company. Vincent's father, Lo Ying-shek, came to Hong Kong in 1938 seeking business opportunities. He found the colony an excellent base from which to trade, and eventually made it his home. In 1956, he expanded into property development almost by accident and made a fortune. His firm, Great Eagle, was incorporated in 1963 and floated on the stock exchange in 1972. It grew to become a major player in the local market.

Lo Ying-shek had nine children, six boys and three girls. The boys all shared two traits: They were independent-minded, and they were good businesspeople. Second son Lo Yuk-sui was the first to establish himself in the family business. He took over Great Eagle and ran it for several years. When the property market collapsed in the early 1980s, he and his father had different ideas about how to handle the crisis. To the astonishment of the business community, Lo Yuk-sui broke from the family firm and took two of its listed companies with him. He bought a controlling stake in Century City, an ailing property concern and was so successful in turning it around that he became known as "the Wizard of Century City."

In 1984, another son, Dr. Lo Ka-shui, returned from a successful medical practice in New York to take over the day-to-day running of Great Eagle (seventy-seven-year-old Lo Ying-shek remained chairperson). Though he knew little about the business, with his father's help, he made some bold moves and got the company back on its feet.

Vincent was born in Hong Kong in 1948. He studied economics at the University of New South Wales in Australia. After graduating in 1969, he returned to Hong Kong. His father wanted him to handle the family's textile business, but Vincent felt real estate was where the action was. When his father would not let him work for Great Eagle, he decided to find a job outside the family business. His mother felt it was not proper for him to work for someone else and convinced her husband to lend Vincent about $17,000 to start his own company.

In 1971, at the age of twenty-three, Vincent went into the construction business, which complemented the family's major activity, property development. A year later, he founded Shui On Construction Company Ltd. and adopted a seagull as his corporate logo after one of his favorite books, *Jonathan Livingston Seagull*. (He later named his first son Jonathan.) In 1974, Shui On was awarded its first open-tender contract for the construction of an upmarket commercial block in Wanchai. Vincent Lo was on his way.

He was a leading member of the new generation of Chinese entrepreneurs who were well-educated and familiar with Western management techniques. He understood the value of diversification, and throughout the 1970s, he expanded into construction-related businesses. In the 1980s, he bought restaurants, a photo developing chain, and dozens of companies in unrelated activities. Shui On was listed on the Hong Kong Stock Exchange in September 1984, and three years later, it sealed its image as a major player when it moved into Shui On Center, a blue glass facade skyscraper on the waterfront.

Vincent and his brothers controlled, at one point, nine companies listed on the stock exchange. One would expect to have seen them driving around town in Italian sports cars, flaunting their success at cocktail parties, and dominating the gossip columns, like the sons of other tycoons. But they avoided all forms of publicity. Though not entirely self-made men, they acted like it. They were smart, mature, and practical. Like other traditional Chinese children, they spent Sunday having a traditional Chinese meal at their father's house, talking business—never politics.

As a businessman with millions of dollars invested in Hong Kong, Lo was instinctively conservative. Hong Kong had no natural resources, other than its people and its harbor. If it were to continue to prosper, he felt, it would have to vigorously maintain the policies that had made it successful: low taxation, minimum government interference in industry, weak labor unions, an efficient bureaucracy, and the best physical infrastructure in Southeast Asia. Like many big businesspeople, he was almost paranoid about elections. He believed they would lead to political opportunists promising to raise the taxes of the rich and introducing social welfare benefits for the poor. The local economy would stagnate.

This view showed a shallow understanding of Hong Kong. Unlike in the West, most local residents worked for small companies, often family-owned, not mammoth corporations with faceless managers. They saw their boss arrive for work each morning in a chauffeur-driven Mercedes, and they envied him. They did not want to tax him out of existence because they saw themselves in his position one day, which is why they worked so hard. They were economic conservatives by nature. They admired Ronald Reagan and Margaret Thatcher and despised governments, such as those of Canada and Australia, that paid people who did not work.

Lo and his colleagues believed that Hong Kong's lack of natural resources and its precarious position on China's doorstep made it unsuitable for Western-style democracy. This ignored the fact that most people understood the situation and that Hong Kong was, in many ways, an ideal place for democracy to thrive. The society was homogeneous. About ninety-eight percent of the population was Chinese. They shared a common culture and beliefs. When Vincent Lo was a boy, people used to set up tables on the sidewalk and read or write letters for money. By 1985, the literacy rate was ninety-five percent, and they were out of business. (In Africa, by contrast, political parties had to use symbols on the ballots.) Dissemination of information was easy because the colony was so small and had hundreds of newspapers. Almost every family had a television, including those who lived on fishing boats, or in hillside shacks.

Nevertheless, Lo did not see himself as protecting only the interests of the rich and powerful. He believed that maintaining a favorable business environment was to everyone's benefit. As companies grew and became prosperous, salaries and the standard of living would rise. Jobs would be created for the expanding work force. Like S.Y. Chung, he thought of politics in business terms. A board of directors (the legislature) would monitor the performance of the chairperson (the governor), who would run the company (Hong Kong) to maximize profits for the benefit of the shareholders (the workers).

This was essentially how Hong Kong had been run by the British, and Lo believed now was not the time to experiment with change. China had agreed to uphold freedoms and maintain the colony's way of life because it wanted to continue reaping the benefits of the capitalist enclave. If elected politicians ran Hong Kong's economy into the ground, it would lose its usefulness to China, and Beijing would have no reason to treat it differently from the rest of the country. Economic success was a matter of survival, and since the current system worked, the less change the better.

THE NEW CONSERVATIVE lobby dubbed itself the Business and Professional Group of the Basic Law Consultative Committee. When it was launched in April 1986, it boasted fifty-seven members, including some of the colony's wealthiest tycoons, well-educated professionals, and a handful of expatriates. It grew steadily to include eighty-nine members and became known as the Group of 89.* (Though he was a member of the Consultative Committee, Louis Cha never joined because he did not want to compromise his position as head of the political subgroup and perhaps because it was his nature to work alone.)

Lo and several core members of the group held a press conference on August 21 to unveil their blueprint for the future political structure, which, they said, retained "the good aspects of the present system"—a powerful governor, an absence of political parties, and an independent judicial system. It called for the governor to be chosen by a grand electoral college made up of

* Hereafter, the organization will be referred to as the Group of 89, although it did not achieve its maximum membership until early 1989.

600 people. (Lo later announced that almost half of its members would be from the commercial, industrial, and financial sectors because "an environment conducive to business operating efficiently is a vital element in the overall well-being of all Hong Kong people.") The legislature would be composed of eighty members, half chosen by occupational groups, a quarter by the electoral college, and the remaining quarter by democratic election.

"While [the proposal] reflects the thinking of the business community," Lo said, "it is designed to be a government system that works for the welfare of all Hong Kong people."

Some journalists pointed out that the proposal was similar to one that had been floated the previous December by a pro-Beijing magazine. Lo denied that China had a hand in developing the political model. Some of his colleagues, however, boasted privately that it had Beijing's backing. A senior Xinhua official was said to have solicited support for the proposal among Consultative Committee members.

The next day, nineteen professionals, social workers, and community representatives on the Consultative Committee published a hastily developed political model. It proposed that the future governor be nominated by the legislature and elected by universal franchise. Half the seats in the legislature would be returned by democratic elections, a quarter by functional constituencies, and a quarter by an electoral college composed of District Board members.

The battle lines were drawn.

Chapter 15

Death of the Governor

WITH THE business community united behind a political blueprint, pressure was mounting on the grass-roots groups to cooperate. Each had its own views on the future political system. Some wanted an executive-led system, others a legislative-led one. Some wanted the legislature to be fully elected by 1997. Others preferred as little as one third direct representation. The nineteen Basic Law Consultative Committee members who had proposed that half the Legislative Council and the governor be returned by universal suffrage in 1997 worked feverishly to build a coalition that would support their political model. They insisted that they had to compromise to show the public that they were not rushing headlong towards democracy for the sake of democracy, that they were concerned about maintaining Hong Kong's stability and prosperity, and that they were prepared to compromise for the sake of unity.

After months of haggling, 190 leading pro-democracy activists formed the Joint Committee for the Promotion of Democratic Government on October 19. The group's short-term goal was to put pressure on the Hong Kong government to introduce democratic elections in 1988. In the long term, it would promote the political model proposed by the "Group of 19." The Joint Committee did not have the money or influence of the businesspeople, but many members had extensive contacts with the working-class people of their districts. They would rely on sheer numbers.

Szeto Wah joined the Joint Committee, but Martin Lee did not because he felt its political model was not progressive enough and because he wanted to maintain his independence as a Basic Law drafter. He was united with the young activists in the belief that democratic elections had to be introduced in 1988, so that Hong Kong would have a fully functioning democratic government in place before 1997. He attended many of the Joint Committee's functions and continued to be recognized as the unofficial leader of the pro-democracy camp. In fact, he was fast becoming the champion of the people and a statesman without a state. He never appeared to be a demagogue or an opportunist. He was an amateur politician speaking out for what was right, and that is the image he projected.

On November 3, the Joint Committee held a rally in a small open-air theater in Kowloon. Over 1,300 people attended, including representatives of over ninety community organizations. After a lengthy gestation period, the pro-democracy movement was finally born.

AS THE CONSERVATIVES and liberals were heading for a showdown over the future political system, Britain and China were on a collision course over the question of democratic elections in 1988. Xu Jiatun continued to meet local tycoons as part of the United Front. They advised him that reforms in Hong Kong should not proceed too quickly because elections in 1988 would lead to demands for more elections before 1997. Behind the scenes, the Xinhua director pressed the Hong Kong government for an assurance that it would not introduce democratic elections to the Legislative Council in 1988. Governor Youde refused to give it. Britain had already acquiesced when it agreed to put off all major constitutional changes until after the promulgation of the Basic Law. The 1984 White Paper, however, said that the issue of elections in 1988 would be addressed during the next political review. Failure to include it as an option in the coming Green Paper would lead to charges of a sellout by Britain, and the Hong Kong government would be seen as a lame duck.

The question of elections in 1988 had not been discussed at the second meeting of the Joint Liaison Group. The Chinese officials assumed that elections were a major constitutional change and would be put off. They felt Britain was reneging on a promise. As usual, when they got nowhere in private, they took the issue public. When the five Basic Law subgroups met at the Shenzhen Guest House in early November, Lu Ping used the opportunity to put across Beijing's views on the upcoming political review.

"It is better to wait to decide what changes should be made [to Hong Kong's political system] until after the draft Basic Law is decided," Lu told a gaggle of journalists thrusting microphones into his face. "By so doing, political reforms before 1997 can converge with the Basic Law."

The confrontation that Percy Cradock had wanted to avoid was now looming on the horizon. Britain was caught between the pro-democracy activists' demands for elections and China's opposition to them.

DURING SUBGROUP meetings held in August in Xiamen, a coastal city in Fujian Province, across from Taiwan, two fastidious Hong Kong drafters noticed that someone had gone through their suitcases and notes while they were out and others noticed that they were followed while walking around the city in the evenings. Lee suspected that the drafters' hotel rooms might be bugged, so he bought a detector at an electronics shop in Hong Kong. When he checked into the Beijing Hotel on November 28 for the third plenum of the Basic Law Drafting Committee, he located a listening device in a flower pot. (Later, when the subgroups met at newly built hotels in Guangzhou, he found bugs in the walls between the rooms.) He informed Szeto and a handful of other Hong Kong drafters whom he trusted. Whenever they discussed strategy before a meeting, they would go into the bathroom, turn on the faucets, and whisper. Sometimes, they would write notes to each other, then burn them, and flush them down the toilet. (Conspiracy was in the air. The Hong Kong newspapers were filled with stories about the Iran-Contra affair, which had just come to light.)

The agenda for the plenum said that the reports prepared by the five subgroups would be discussed. When the Hong Kong drafters assembled in the gray conference room in the Great Hall, they were told that only the reports of the relationship subgroup and the rights and obligations subgroup would be considered, even though drafters were supposed to be given one month's notice of a change in the agenda. Lee believed that the decision to postpone the discussion on the political structure was to avoid sending the wrong signal to the Hong Kong government. If the plenary session agreed that a measure of democratic elections should be included in the Basic Law, it might be seen as a green light for the Hong Kong government to introduce polls in 1988. Instead of pursuing a policy of convergence, as agreed with the British, Beijing was stalling. Political reforms could not converge with a system that did not exist.

On the morning of December 1, the drafters were given an opportunity to address the plenum on the relationship between the central and Hong Kong governments. Lee used the opportunity to push for the Hong Kong courts to be allowed to interpret all provisions of the Basic Law.

"The Joint Declaration has already laid down that the common law shall continue to apply to the Special Administrative Region after 1997," he said, his voice even and unemotional. "If we wish to uphold the integrity of the common law, then we must let the courts interpret all the laws of [Hong Kong], including the Basic Law." If the courts of the Special Administrative Region had the right to interpret only those provisions of the Basic Law that were within Hong Kong's autonomy, he argued, there would be endless debates over what was within its autonomy and what was not. Defendants in civil cases would delay their trials by calling for the NPC to rule on one clause or another. This would paralyze the legal system.

Though his reasoning was flawless, he received little sympathy. The mainland drafters saw this not as a legal issue, but as a question of sovereignty, and on sovereignty, they would never budge.

AFTER EIGHTEEN months of meetings, arguments, accusations, and counter-accusations, many people in Hong Kong were losing interest in the Basic Law. Even some journalists referred to it as the "Basic Bore." Press reports were sketchy and confusing because the drafters rarely resolved any important issues. More often than not, statements made by Chinese officials to the press overshadowed anything achieved during the meetings.

Many people in Hong Kong, including senior government officials, were disappointed with the performance of local drafters. About a third seemed to be fighting doggedly for the best interests of the colony. Another third, mainly the business tycoons, seemed willing to do and say whatever they thought would please China's leaders. The remainder did very little at all. Some of the Hong Kong members were grossly ignorant of issues outside their area of expertise. A few made proposals that were in violation of the Joint Declaration. They were amateurs with no experience in drafting a constitution. Some set up think tanks to help them. (Lee was supported by several prominent lawyers.)

The Hong Kong government could not get directly involved because China insisted that the Basic Law was an internal affair. Instead, senior officials offered local drafters covert support. Legal experts (including Fred Burrows, who had worked on the Joint Declaration and was now part of the Hong Kong government's legal department) regularly answered queries and commented on draft articles. Government departments provided information, statistics, briefings, and other services. Sometimes, the Hong Kong drafters would hide their briefing papers from one another, not realizing that they were holding the same material provided by the Hong Kong government.

The Chinese government was well aware of what was going on. Although it strenuously maintained that the British and Hong Kong governments had no role to play in drafting the Basic Law, Beijing realized that they knew more about running the colony than anyone. Seven Hong Kong drafters also sat on the Legislative Council and acted as a liaison between the two governments.

IN EARLY December 1986, as Basic Law drafters were meeting in Beijing, Governor Youde flew to the Chinese capital to attend an exhibition of Hong Kong products sponsored by the Trade Development Council and to hold talks with Chinese officials. Youde was relaxed and in good spirits as he toured the exhibition, even though he was anticipating a tough session with his mainland counterparts.

On the cool, crisp morning of December 4, Youde shook hands with the other members of the trade delegation, who were returning to Hong Kong. Then, he and Ambassador Evans drove to the Chinese Foreign Ministry for a meeting with Zhou Nan. Atop the agenda was the upcoming political review. Zhou reiterated that elections were a major constitutional change and had to be postponed. Youde insisted that the option of introducing elections in 1988 had to be included in the Green Paper. The only way elections could be put off was if that was what the people of Hong Kong wanted. The message was clear: If China wanted elections postponed until after 1990, she would have to mobilize her forces in the colony to sway the outcome of the political review.

It was a difficult meeting. "Zhou was at his bullying worst," said a Hong Kong civil servant who was briefed by the governor. "He gave Youde a real pasting."

Youde was nevertheless relaxed and cheerful that evening as he went over the day's events with aides. He enjoyed a nightcap with them before retiring to bed in the ambassador's residence. At 6:20 the next morning, a servant woke Evans and asked him to go to Youde's room. Evans knocked on the door several times. There was no answer. When he entered the room, Youde was not breathing. A doctor was summoned, and the governor was pronounced dead at the scene.

Evans telephoned Lady Youde, who had accompanied her husband to China and gone on to the northwest city of Xian. Then, he called Chief Secretary David Akers-Jones in Hong Kong and informed him of the news. Akers-Jones called a special meeting of the Executive Council, and at 9:25 that morning, the following bulletin was sent to all media organizations in the colony:

THE ACTING GOVERNOR, SIR DAVID AKERS-JONES, IS DEEPLY GRIEVED TO ANNOUNCE THAT HE WAS INFORMED EARLY THIS MORN-ING BY H.M. AMBASSADOR IN BEIJING OF THE DEATH OF THE GOV-ERNOR, SIR EDWARD YOUDE, IN HIS SLEEP LAST NIGHT.

The government-owned radio station interrupted its regular programming to announce the news. Flags at all government buildings were lowered to half-mast. The stock market plunged briefly, then recovered.

Youde was the first governor to die in office in Hong Kong. There was some confusion about funeral arrangements. The British government sent instructions that he be given a full state funeral modeled on the ceremony for former Prime Minister Winston Churchill.

AT 9 A.M. ON December 9, a guard of honor gathered outside Government House for the funeral. There were about 1,500 soldiers from the Gurkha Rifles, Coldstream Guards, Hong Kong Volunteers and representatives of the Royal Navy and Air Force. By ten o'clock, senior officials and the pall bearers arrived, all in black except for Chief Justice Denys Roberts, who was clad in the same red robe he wore for Youde's swearing in four and a half years earlier. Legislative Councilors, judges, and representatives of the consular corps took their places in the cortege outside Government House. At 10:25, a Gurkha sounded the bugle call, Royal Air Force helicopters flew past, and at exactly 10:30 Youde's coffin was loaded onto a carriage. The first shots of a seventeen-gun salute rang out as the procession began.

People lined the route to the cathedral, some in tears. Office workers watched from their windows as the coffin made its way slowly down Garden Road. Thousands more saw it on television.

When the procession arrived at St. John's Cathedral, the Coldstream Guards removed the coffin from the carriage, carried it down the narrow aisle, and set it on a black dais in front of the altar. An aide placed the governor's royal decorations on the coffin. Lady Youde added a wreath of lilies, freesias, and chrysanthemums.

Some 750 dignitaries and well-wishers crowded into the church. Akers-Jones said that Youde "developed a deep professional and emotional attachment to China and to the people of China. [His] interest in the Chinese language and literature filled many of his quiet moments."

Some Executive Councilors had spoken privately to Jack Cater about the Bramall affair. Some believed now that Youde may have lied to them. They were left to wonder how much else he might have hidden from them during the negotiations. Their doubts would remain personal. Sir Edward Youde was buried a hero.

Chapter 16

New Governor, Old Attitudes

G OVERNOR Youde's term was not due to expire for at least another six months. Suddenly, a replacement had to be found. S.Y. Chung knew that the choice would be crucial. China would inevitably demand a greater say in Hong Kong's affairs during the transition. Percy Cradock and the Foreign Office mandarins would want to give in to maintain good relations with China. Chung felt the next governor should be someone who could stand up to Beijing and London, and at the same time, keep the emerging political factions within the colony placated. He did not have a specific person in mind, but was thinking of someone like Lord Soames, the British MP who had handled Rhodesia's stormy passage to independence.

Chung called a special meeting of the unofficial Executive Councilors. They agreed with his thinking and decided to make their views known to Her Majesty's Government. On the morning of December 9, they met Foreign Office Minister Timothy Renton, who had flown out for Youde's funeral.

"We think that the time for a diplomat-governor is over," Chung said. "The next governor should be a politician of considerable standing, someone who can provide leadership during the transition period."

Renton did not say whether he agreed or disagreed, only that he would pass the message on to Prime Minister Thatcher.

In London, Thatcher was having trouble finding someone willing to take the post. Percy Cradock, an obvious choice, rejected the idea even before being asked. She approached former Foreign Secretary Lord Carrington, who was now secretary-general of NATO. He declined the offer.

Richard Evans and Alan Donald were tipped in the press as potential candidates. Neither would enjoy the support of the Executive Council. Evans was considered too weak, and Donald was distrusted now more than ever because of the Bramall affair.

Although Thatcher recognized that the Executive Council's request for a politician of standing was sensible, Cradock advised her to choose a diplomat, someone who understood the Chinese and would know how to deal with them. He recommended David Wilson, the Foreign Office's most gifted China expert. Thatcher accepted his advice, but over time she developed misgivings about Wilson. Years later, after she had been ousted as prime minister, she was heard to snort: "I never thought much of that David Wilson. He was just a bureaucrat."

On January 16, 1987, the British government announced that David Clive Wilson would be Hong Kong's next governor. At fifty-two, he was the youngest man ever appointed to the post. Tall and lanky with a large nose that became the delight of every cartoonist in the colony, Wilson was not ideally suited to the job. He preferred to work behind the scenes to achieve his objectives and was uncomfortable with the constant attention the governor was subjected to. Though warm and friendly in private, he appeared stiff and cold on television. He was barely able to conceal his contempt for the journalists who besieged him after every public function. He was portrayed in the press as arrogant, aloof, and as working more for the interests of Britain than those of Hong Kong.

Wilson was very much a diplomat-governor in the same mold as Edward Youde and Murray MacLehose. Like MacLehose, he was a member of the Scottish clique within the Foreign Office and had a passion for hill walking (he was a member of the team that climbed Mount Kongur in northwest China in 1981 and his goal after retiring was to climb all of the peaks over 3,000 feet in Scotland). He was born the son of a Scottish minister in Alloa, near Aberdeen, on Valentine's Day, 1935. After graduating from Oxford in 1958 with a master's degree in modern history, he joined the Foreign Service. He spent two years in Hong Kong studying Mandarin and was posted to Beijing, where he shocked good Communists by driving around in a red sports car. (During the Sino-British negotiations, he traveled, like locals, by bicycle.) When he returned to the U.K., he was introduced to a young teacher named Natasha Alexander in a Chinese restaurant and courted her by passing her books on Hong Kong and China. They were married in 1967.

Wilson resigned from the Foreign Service in 1968 to become executive editor of the *China Quarterly*, a prestigious academic magazine. People who worked with him considered him brilliant, though he sometimes ruffled feathers in his exuberance to get things done. He spent some time in New York as a visiting scholar at Columbia University and returned to the Foreign Office in 1974. He served as MacLehose's political adviser from 1977 to 1981. He was head of the Southern European Department when Cradock brought him into the Sino-British negotiations in 1984. At the time he was appointed governor, he was under secretary of state for Asia and the Pacific, much more junior than Youde had been when he took over. He would have to sell his policies to his superiors in the Foreign Office, which was not too difficult; he saw things much the way Cradock and the other Old China Hands did.

Wilson was chosen because no one knew more about Hong Kong's transition to Chinese rule. He had been at the MacLehose-Deng meeting in 1979 when Britain first broached the subject of commercial leases in the New Territories. He had personally drafted most of the Joint Declaration and had been the leader of Britain's Joint Liaison Group team, and his knowledge of China and Mandarin were unsurpassed in the Foreign Office. Despite these credentials, one colleague felt Wilson lacked the essential qualities of a good governor: compassion for local residents and an understanding of their needs and aspirations. He was a functionary, not a leader.

While he was serving as political adviser in Hong Kong, Wilson confided in colleagues that he would like to be governor of Hong Kong one day. When the news came, he was taken aback. He did not expect it so soon. Moreover, the nature of the job had changed since the late 1970s. With Hong Kong's future sealed, Wilson knew his job would be difficult. The Chinese culture taught that the letter of a contract is important, not the spirit. The Chinese reinterpreted the words and made steadily increasing demands to outmaneuver opponents. Wilson knew that Beijing would probably do this, and that its demands would be very difficult to resist. At a dinner he gave for a few friends and dignitaries shortly after taking up his appointment, Wilson asked if there were any single issue "on which I can safely oppose China." His guests could not think of one.

Wilson was an aristocrat, and like many of his kind, he joined the diplomatic corp to serve his country, to deal with matters of national interest and security. He did not see himself as a mere administrator, managing a city. He was not interested in sewage systems and traffic control (though he proved himself capable of mastering such issues when necessary). Those matters would be left to professional civil servants. His job would be to smooth the transition to Chinese rule, and the first task at hand was to defuse a possible confrontation between Britain and China over the questions of elections in 1988.

As HONG KONG was awaiting the arrival of a new leader, China was dispatching one of its own. In December 1986, thousands of students had taken to the streets of Shanghai and other cities to denounce corruption in the Communist Party and demand democratic reforms. The protests, though quickly quelled, gave conservatives within the party an opportunity to attack Deng Xiaoping.

The hard-liners felt reforms were getting out of hand. Farmland was being paved to make room for rural factories, reversing a trend towards increased crop production. The open-door policy was creating "spiritual pollution" and a proliferation of Western thinking. Venereal disease had returned. Corruption was rampant. If the reforms were not brought under control, they believed, the result would be chaos.

In January 1987, party leader Hu Yaobang, Deng's handpicked successor, was forced to resign. The Chinese government launched a campaign against "Western bourgeois liberalization." This marked the start of an open power struggle between the conservative and reformist factions within the Communist Party, which would reach a crisis point during the student demonstrations in the spring of 1989.

Hong Kong was shaken by the realization that the men who had engineered the one country, two systems concept were not in complete control of China. Hu's downfall coincided with a spate of newspaper reports in Hong Kong that senior Chinese leaders were opposed to democratic elections in the colony not just in 1988, but after 1997 as well. Most political analysts believed Beijing was taking a tougher line in foreign as well as domestic policy. They were not aware that the conservatives, who clearly had gained the upper hand in Beijing, had decided to follow the advice Governor Youde gave during his meeting with Zhou Nan in December 1985 and mobilize all their forces in Hong Kong. Pro-China journalists say the leaks were the start of a concerted effort to sway public opinion against elections in 1988.

Lu Ping stepped up the assault in February, when the five subgroups of the Basic Law Drafting Committee held meetings in Kunming, a dusty and increasingly industrial city in southwestern China. He told journalists that unless political reforms introduced by the Hong Kong government complied with the system laid down in the Basic Law, the Chinese government would overturn them after 1997. The most appropriate time to hold democratic elections, he said, was in 1991, a year after the promulgation of the Basic Law. Martin Lee was angry that the Chinese government was dictating to Britain when elections could be held. Other pro-democracy activists were pleased that China was at least prepared to allow elections before 1997.

During the political subgroup meeting from February 12 to 14, members discussed a report on the judiciary prepared by Judge Simon Li. The question of interpreting the Basic Law came up because the political subgroup had to draft the articles on the judiciary as well as the executive and legislative branches of government. Members argued over the difference between final adjudication (given to the Hong Kong courts in the Joint Declaration) and interpretation (a right claimed by mainland members for the NPC). As in the relationship subgroup, mainland members feared that the courts might "get it wrong" and make a decision that would harm China's national interests or damage relations with another country. One said the jurisdiction of the Hong Kong courts should be clearly circumscribed. Another proposed that the Basic Law spell out China's national interests and that the Hong Kong courts be prohibited from trying cases that related to them. Martin Lee, Maria Tam, and Dorothy Liu, the three Hong Kong lawyers in the subgroup, were appointed to look into the issue further.

AFTER THE education and culture subgroup meeting in Kunming, Szeto Wah was given some insight into the important role the Communist Party was playing behind the scenes. Ma Lin, the Hong Kong convener, wanted a copy of the minutes because the group was not scheduled to meet again until June. He feared that what had been discussed and agreed to would be forgotten by then. But he was a timid man and did not want to ask his mainland counterpart, Qian Weichang, for the minutes. He persuaded Szeto to go with him.

Although the minutes had already been printed by the secretariat, Qian refused to release them. The Drafting Committee planned to hold a world-wide contest to choose the best flag and emblem for the Hong Kong Special Administrative Region. Within the minutes was a list of the people who would judge the entries. Though it had been finalized during the meeting, it had not yet been approved by a member of the Communist Party. (The only two party members in the subgroup were absent.)

"There is no harm in giving us a copy," Szeto said. "The minutes will not be made public. No one will see the list except the drafters."

"I can't," Qian replied.

Szeto persisted, and Qian finally took the minutes to Lu Ping, a party member, who said they could be distributed.

DAVID AKERS-JONES took over as acting governor until David Wilson's arrival. He was succeeded as chief secretary by David Ford, a psychological warfare expert who had been brought into Hong Kong during the riots in 1967. (Ford has denied in interviews that he ever received psy-war training, but a senior official under whom he served in 1967 says he did.) Ford brought with him a reputation for toughness, which was widely welcomed. Unfortunately, it was not matched by an understanding of, or a commitment to, the people of Hong Kong.

Ford was born in north Wales in 1935. As a boy, he dreamed of being a lawyer, using his intelligence and wit to win great courtroom battles. After leaving school, he was called up for military service and posted to Malta. When his term of national service was about to expire in 1955, he decided that he enjoyed the army and applied for a regular commission. He was trained as a commando and posted to seventeen countries in five years, either for exercises or to fight in small brushfire wars. He saw action in the jungles of Borneo in 1964 when Indonesian troops infiltrated Malaysia as part of Sukarno's *konfrontasi*.

After being sent to staff college in Pakistan, he was bound for a desk job in Singapore when he received orders in September 1967 to go to Hong Kong. He was met at the airport by Bob Locking, Jack Cater's assistant, who took Ford to the colonial-style Repulse Bay Hotel and briefed him until 2 A.M. Major Ford reported for work at the Special Duties Unit at seven that morning. As resolute as he was shrewd, he played an important role in getting Hong Kong through that difficult period.

Ford remained in Hong Kong for five years, on loan from the military. He finally severed his links with the army in 1972 and made Hong Kong his home. He soon caught the eye of the governor. While most civil servants were intimidated by MacLehose, Ford spoke his mind. He was made director of Information Services, a post he was ideally suited for. Though relatively junior in rank, Ford was invited to sit in on Executive Council meetings and internal governmental meetings at the highest level, which was viewed with suspicion—and not a little jealousy—by many of his colleagues.

In 1977, Ford was temporarily assigned to Northern Ireland. When he returned to Hong Kong two years later, he was promoted to secretary for information. He was considered an outsider by the old colonialists, who resented his close relationship with MacLehose. He served briefly as Hong Kong's commissioner in London, filling in until Jack Cater could take the post. During that period, he made connections with the right people in the British government, which would serve him well as chief secretary.

In the early 1980s, he was sent to the Royal College of Defense Studies, a prestigious school for top military people and civil servants. Ford returned to Hong Kong in 1983, ready to continue his ascent to the top. Chief Secretary Haddon-Cave had other ideas. He felt Ford did not have enough administrative experience for a senior post and should "dirty his hands in a big department." He made him director of housing, which was, in effect, a demotion. There, Ford opened up policy to public debate, worked tirelessly, and earned the respect of many of his colleagues. In 1985, he was made secretary for the civil service, responsible for managing the 170,000-strong bureaucracy.

Ford was smart, hard-working, and ambitious. Some of those who worked with him say he was a brilliant public servant, but lacked ideals and vision. As one would expect from a former military officer, he was autocratic, and because he entered the civil service at a senior rank, he never served as a District Officer, where he could get to know the local people. He started in Information Services, the government's propaganda arm, where his job was to sell the administration's policies to the press and public. He took a similar approach as chief secretary. Instead of making the civil service more responsive to the public, he defended it aggressively from criticism. His loyalty seemed to be to the public service, not the people it was supposed to serve.

Ford probably did not see his lack of knowledge of the Hong Kong people as a handicap. As the former head of Information Services, he knew how the government could influence public opinion. He knew too that the local Chinese were relatively conservative and passive and would go along with almost any policy that would not disrupt their businesses or private lives. Ford seemed to focus on community leaders and influential individuals, those who shaped how society thought. He established contacts with key people in all sectors. He remained chummy with Martin Lee even after Lee became the Hong Kong government's most outspoken critic. He courted Vincent Lo, and he opened back channels to pro-China figures. By selling the government's policies to these people, he could accomplish the administration's objectives.

In March 1987, Ford got his first test as chief secretary. As part of Haddon-Cave's plan to liberalize local laws, the government decided to scrap an ordinance passed in 1951 because of fears that the newly victorious Chinese Communists would try to subvert the colonial government. The law made it an offence to publish anything "subversive" and gave the Hong Kong government the power to suspend publication of any newspaper, search its offices and seize its printing presses. It was used only three times, each time during the 1967 riots. The administration wanted to retain one controversial clause which made it a crime for anyone to "maliciously publish in any newspaper false news which is likely to alarm public opinion or disturb public order." This was included in a new Public Order (Amendment) Bill.

When the government published the draft bill in December 1986, local publishers, journalists, and legal experts welcomed the decision to relax restrictions on the press, but objected vociferously to a clause that said malice would be presumed and the burden of proof would be on the accused to show that he took "reasonable measures to verify the truth of the news." As with the Powers and Privileges Bill, the public wanted the Hong Kong government to go further in liberalizing the law. Opposition to the bill escalated as it passed through legislative stages. Journalists dubbed it the "Press Gag Law." Some political observers charged that Britain was retaining the "false news" clause at China's request, a charge both governments vehemently denied.

Though Ford had dealt with the press extensively as director of Information Services, he failed to comprehend the depth of emotion journalists felt on the question of censorship with 1997 looming. The adverse reaction caught him by surprise. Nevertheless, the bill had been approved by the Executive Council, and he would see it implemented. He refused to delay passage.

When the bill was debated in the Legislative Council on March 11, eleven members, led by Martin Lee, spoke out against it, particularly the false news clause. Ford staunchly defended it, saying "the community is entitled to protection from irresponsible reports which have serious consequences for the stability of this territory."

Towards the end of his speech, he came to what he called "the nub of the matter"—the fear that China would abuse the law after 1997. "Sadly," he said, "if . . . a future government is determined to restrict press freedom, the absence or presence of a law would not inhibit it."

When the votes were counted, the bill passed forty-four to twelve. Only one appointed member voted against it. The others wound up in the embarrassing position of having to reverse their vote when the government decided to repeal the law in December 1988.

DAVID WILSON arrived in Hong Kong on April 9, 1987, to take up his post as Hong Kong's twenty-seventh governor. Some observers thought he might dispense with the usual colonial regalia to avoid offending China. But tradition was tradition. Like Youde, he arrived in a plumed cocked hat, tropical white uniform with gold epaulets, and a sword at his side. (Aside from anachronistic, he looked somewhat comical; his uniform was as wrinkled as an old sailor's face.)

Censorship was still uppermost in the minds of local journalists. Many of the 200 or so gathered at Queen's Pier to cover the governor's arrival wore badges that said: DON'T GAG THE PRESS. The major issue on Wilson's mind was political reform. "If there is to be change, it should be prudent and gradual," he told the dignitaries gathered in City Hall for his swearing in. "It must not disrupt the steady progress we have been making, nor the stability which we prize."

Wilson shared Percy Cradock's view that it would be senseless to push ahead with political reforms against China's will. Perhaps he also wanted the opportunity to establish his own administration. He clearly came with misgivings about the wisdom of introducing democratic elections in 1988.

He was not the kind of man who would consider whether the people of Hong Kong had an inalienable right to self-government. He was a realist, a pragmatist. He considered only what could be achieved, and it was patently obvious to him that the Hong Kong government could not introduce elections in 1988 without provoking a major confrontation with China.

THE STORM WAS gathering. Pro-China newspapers kept up a constant barrage of antielection editorials. During the fourth plenum of the Basic Law Drafting Committee in April 1987, the drafters were told that Deng Xiaoping would address them during the session. Xu Jiatun had apparently convinced China's strongman that the issue of political reform in Hong Kong was crucial and warranted his attention.

On the fourth day of the meeting, the drafters were discussing Hong Kong's future flag and emblem when work was suspended. They waited for several minutes before Deng entered the conference room. With a cigarette in his left hand, he shook hands with each and every member of the committee, stopping to chat with some of the tycoons he knew personally.

Deng took a seat next to Ji Pengfei and began to speak without any prepared notes. "I have three vices," he said. "I drink, I spit, and I smoke," at which point an attendant placed a spittoon beside his chair. He told the drafters that the Basic Law would determine whether the one country, two systems concept would work well. It would be an example for both Macao and Taiwan. He said the status quo would be maintained in Hong Kong for fifty years after 1997, then added that there would be no need to have any changes for another fifty years after that.

Rambling, as he often did, Deng said that if Taiwan were not recovered, the Americans and Japanese would conceive "wicked ideas" to control it. He said China would remain socialist and would not turn to capitalism or "wholesale Westernization." Then, he got to what was really on his mind: political reform in Hong Kong. He warned that democracy might not be good for the colony. "The people who will rule Hong Kong [after 1997] must love the motherland and love Hong Kong. Can universal suffrage definitely produce such persons?" he asked sternly.

Deng said he did not think that Hong Kong should copy the system of separation of powers from Western democracies. "Each country must find a system that best suits its needs. Also, do not expect Hong Kong to be controlled by Hong Kong people alone. The central government will not interfere with its daily management. But when the interests of the State are being endangered, the central government will not stand aside. We can stand people scolding the Chinese Communist Party or China, but we cannot accept people who want to use democracy to turn Hong Kong into an anticommunist base."

The political subgroup had already agreed that there should be separation of powers, though it had not come up with a formula. When coconveners

Louis Cha and Xiao Weiyun met the press after Deng's address, they back-tracked. "We may not have studied [the principle] comprehensively," Cha told reporters. Xiao said that Deng was correct in saying that Hong Kong was not a country, so separation of powers was inappropriate.

Martin Lee felt Deng was trying to intimidate people in Hong Kong. Who was going to come out in favor of democratic elections in 1988 when the highest authority in China opposed them? He decided to respond to Deng's speech the next day. That evening, after dining with several Hong Kong journalists (instead of his fellow drafters), Lee and his personal assistant returned to their musty hotel room on the tenth floor of the Beijing Hotel to prepare a speech on the draft articles discussed during the plenum, while they waited for an official transcript of Deng's speech. (Although his Mandarin had improved a little, Lee was unable to catch everything Deng had said.) Around midnight, a Hong Kong journalist passed him a copy of Deng's speech. It did not include his remarks about Taiwan, elections in Hong Kong, or separation of powers.

At about 2 A.M., Lee and his assistant finished the speech on the articles. Lee woke a member of the secretariat and asked him to make copies and distribute them in the morning.

Then Lee returned to his room to prepare a second speech. Whispering and passing notes because of his concern about listening devices, Lee briefed his assistant on what he wanted to say and then went to bed. When the assistant finished the draft, he woke Lee. Lee suggested several changes and went back to sleep. When the second draft was finished, Lee got up and his assistant went to bed. He spent the early hours of the morning struggling through the speech in Mandarin, so that he could deliver it without translation, which took too long.

The committee had introduced a ten-minute limit on speeches to give everyone a chance to speak. When Lee saw T.K. Ann at breakfast the next morning, he said that he would go over the limit by about five minutes. Thinking that Lee would be delivering the long speech on the draft articles, which by now had been circulated, Ann said it would be all right.

When it was his turn to speak, Lee went up to the chairman's table and sat in front of the microphone. "Members," he said, "I have prepared some opinions on the drafts of chapters two, seven, and nine. But after meeting the Chinese leader yesterday, I feel there is something very important for me to say to you. I've decided to deliver my original speech in written form. I hope everyone can spend time to read it, and I hope that members of the subgroup will give serious consideration to my views."

Lee said he believed that Deng had three concerns: that if Hong Kong were given too much autonomy, it would jeopardize the one country, two systems policy and national reunification; that even if it did not jeopardize unification, it would damage the interests of the central government and the Communist Party; and that an autonomous and democratically elected government could ruin Hong Kong's economy and thereby hurt the nation. Like a defense attorney undermining the prosecution's case, Lee addressed each of these worries.

The political subgroup has agreed on a balance of power after discussing the issue at length, he said. "Should we waste all these efforts just because the Chinese leader expressed his opinions?" He claimed Deng was out of touch and said he hoped that "we can help him to understand the practical issues of the Basic Law throughout the drafting process."

Lee said he agreed with Deng that Hong Kong should reform its political system gradually and not simply adopt a Western system. That is why he wanted only a quarter of the Legislative Council returned by universal suffrage in 1988 and supported a legislature returned by a variety of means in 1997. (This was not his original position, but there was now no hope of achieving a fully elected legislature by 1997, and it was useful for him to adopt a more moderate stance.)

As for Deng's statement that the future leaders of Hong Kong had to be "patriotic," Lee questioned how the word should be defined. "Some people like to charm those in power with their sweet talk, . . . We could say they love their country, but they love their wealth and assets even more. To sweet talk is not difficult. But does this benefit the nation? How many times does our leader listen to this every day?"

"Mr. Lee," Ann interrupted, "your time is up, and you have not addressed us on the Basic Law."

"I am winding up my speech now," Lee said and then continued speaking for several more minutes.

It was common courtesy for all members to applaud at the end of every speech. When Lee finished, only three Hong Kong drafters clapped. As he returned to his seat, he could see that the faces of the mainland members had gone white. No one ever confronted Lee or refuted his arguments. He was simply cold-shouldered by the mainland drafters and the members from Hong Kong who had aligned themselves with Beijing.

WILSON AND FORD were in a difficult position. The previous administration had agreed to put off all major constitutional reform until after the publication of the Basic Law. They had to carry out a political review, but could not cover the most important aspects of Hong Kong's political system: the function, powers, and composition of the Executive and Legislative Councils, and the governor's role as head of the legislature. Ford's deputy, John Chan, filled the Green Paper with minor proposals regarding the composition and role of the District Board and municipal councils and even such nonsense as whether elections to these bodies should precede or follow Legislative Council elections. The only important issue dealt with was whether or not democratic elections to the Legislative Council should be introduced in 1988. Youde and Haddon-Cave had already secured the Executive Council's consent to do so, but both were gone, and the political situation had changed.

When the draft Green Paper was presented to the Executive Council, the unofficial members went through it line by line, writing and rewriting much of it. The aggressiveness of Lee and his followers in recent months had made Chung and some of his colleagues even more conservative. Chung believed that the role of the appointed Legislative Councilors had changed. Once they were the only check on the executive branch of government. Now that role was being played by the elected members. The appointees had to be, in effect, the government's party, and they had to maintain a majority if the administration was to continue to work efficiently. In listing the options for changes to the composition of the Legislative Council in 1988, he made certain that the Council maintained a majority of official and appointed members no matter what the public decided. (With so many hands in it, the Green Paper was a mess. When Governor Wilson arrived on the scene, he gave it to Bob Pierce, the assistant political adviser, to clean up.)

The Green Paper, entitled *The 1987 Review of Developments in Representative Government*, was published on May 27, 1987. The businesspeople and pro-China forces praised it. The pro-democracy camp condemned it. Lee claimed that by omitting any changes to the functions and powers of the Executive and Legislative Councils, the Hong Kong government was reneging on its promise to introduce a truly representative system. He could have organized a boycott of the review in protest, but that would only play into China's hands. Lee and his followers concentrated virtually all their efforts on trying to force the Hong Kong government to introduce a small number of democratically elected legislators in 1988 and hoped that pressure for further changes would build.

THE POLITICAL review had to be seen to be genuine. If people believed that the Hong Kong government had manipulated the results to avoid a confrontation with China, its credibility would be destroyed. Akers-Jones had already decided to set up a survey office, similar to the Assessment Office, which would be separate from the government machinery and be monitored by a former Legislative Councilor and a retired civil servant. Ford knew that most

Chinese were conservative politically and they would be cowed by Beijing's continuing propaganda barrage. He instructed the Survey Office to make the review as wide and as aggressive as possible (in marked contrast to the collection of opinion on the Joint Declaration, which was passive). The Survey Office was instructed to "receive and record all views expressed in writing by September 30, 1987, including those submitted directly to [the Survey Office] or through established consultative channels." It was to submit an "impartial and accurate" report to the governor before October 31.

The Survey Office would monitor debates, minutes, and submissions from the District Boards, the municipal councils, and the Legislative Council; invite organizations and individuals to submit their views; monitor media reports; collect signature campaigns and comment on their methods. It could conduct its own public opinion surveys and make note of other surveys.

The government printed almost two million copies of the forty-eight-page Green Paper, including half a million in English. They were distributed to the public through 300 outlets around the colony. Braille copies and audio cassette tapes were prepared in both Chinese and English. Advertisements were aired on radio, television, and in movie theaters, and were run in most major newspapers. The post office even created a special frank, urging people to submit their views. This would be the biggest consultation exercise in Hong Kong's history, dwarfing that done on the Joint Declaration.

Chapter 17

The Deal Is Done

THE SUMMER of 1987 was the season of politics. In the United States, Democratic presidential candidates were already gearing up for the following year's election. Margaret Thatcher was romping to a postwar record third term as Britain's prime minister. Mikhail Gorbachev was overhauling the Soviet system and allowing multicandidate elections. Student demonstrators were taking over the streets of Seoul to demand the resignation of Chun Doo Hwan and constitutional reforms in South Korea. And in Hong Kong, Martin Lee and his supporters launched a campaign to try to force the government to introduce democratic elections in 1988. They took to the streets in a desperate attempt to enlist the support of the silent majority. On a sweltering Sunday morning, Lee could be seen handing out leaflets in front of a Japanese department store. Dressed in his usual dark business suit, sweat dripping from his brow, he greeted each person with a smile and a handshake. Not a politician seeking votes. An idealist seeking *the vote*. He was there to convince the public that his way was not the right way, but the only way to protect Hong Kong after 1997. Many people he met on the streets, in the housing estates, at shopping malls said thanks. Thanks for fighting for Hong Kong. Thanks for saying what few other politicians had the courage to say. This gave him the strength to carry on.

China countered with a propaganda blitz of her own. The procommunist newspapers kept up a constant barrage of antielection editorials. Left-wing trade unions encouraged their members to speak out. Hecklers were sent to pro-democracy rallies. The local branch of the Bank of China instructed its employees to sign a form letter denouncing democratic reforms. Xu Jiatun reportedly boasted that he could raise "50,000 soldiers" to counter the pro-democracy lobby.

Hong Kong's powerful tycoons allied themselves with Beijing. The privately run stock exchange encouraged its members to oppose polls on the grounds that they would be against the interests of investors. Ronald Li, its chairperson and a founding member of the Group of 89, dismissed democracy as "nothing more than a head count." Although the businesspeople claimed they opposed confrontational politics, there was no shortage of confrontation. They portrayed Lee as a political opportunist, a man championing democracy to gain popularity and secure a position in an elected, post-1997 government. One businessperson dubbed him "Martyr Lee."

The liberals countered by claiming that the tycoons were Beijing's puppets, that they were willing to sell out Hong Kong for the sake of protecting their assets and maintaining their personal relationships with Chinese leaders. Vincent Lo was accused of doing Beijing's bidding so that he could become the first Chinese governor after 1997.

The Hong Kong government was caught in the middle. With Chinese officials and even Executive Councilors, such as S.Y. Chung, denouncing elections in 1988, it struggled to convince the public that the consultation on the Green Paper was genuine. In mid-June 1987, Chief Secretary David Ford told *Asiaweek*, a regional news magazine, that the introduction of democratic elections was "not a major constitutional change" to which China should object. He added that if a majority of people in Hong Kong favored such elections in 1988, the administration would recommend to London that they be introduced.

Chinese officials responded harshly to Ford's remarks. Li Hou told *Outlook*, a mainland news magazine, that if the Hong Kong government "rashly introduces elections next year," it would "naturally fail to observe convergence with the Basic Law." He warned that such a move would be a breach of the Sino-British Joint Declaration.

On June 20, Chinese Foreign Minister Wu Xueqian made an unscheduled stopover in Hong Kong to meet Governor Wilson at his private residence in the New Territories. Although the meeting was billed as a courtesy call, some reports said Wu pressed the Hong Kong government not to introduce elections the following year. Pro-democracy activists were outraged by what they saw as blatant interference in Hong Kong's affairs. Investors reacted nervously to the worst signs of discord between Britain and China since the signing of the Joint Declaration. The Hang Seng Index fell fifty-five points in the first two trading days after Wu's visit.

The massive outcry against Li's remarks and the fall of the stock market forced Beijing to backtrack. Li claimed that he had been misquoted in *Outlook*. He denied having said that the introduction of universal suffrage in 1988 would contravene the Joint Declaration, but insisted that it would "fail to observe convergence with the Basic Law." (Critics dared the Hong Kong government to prosecute *Outlook* for publishing false news.)

Tension was high when five homemade bombs went off around the colony in as many weeks. The worst attack occurred on July 8 in a crowded chrome and glass shopping center in a middle-class residential district of Tai Koo Shing. No one was killed, but the public was stunned by newspaper photographs of a boy, not more than five or six years old, standing in his underwear crying. His clothes had been blown off and his skin singed by the heat of the blast. Hong Kong had not seen such acts of terrorism since the 1967 riots.

As THE TRAIN rumbled through the lush rice paddies of Guangdong and past small clusters of traditional Chinese homes with tiled roofs, Martin Lee was reminded of just how different China was from Hong Kong. Different economic systems, different political systems, different legal systems, different worlds. Lee was leaving the maelstrom in the colony for the tenth meeting of the political subgroup in Guangzhou. He had been optimistic about the chances of getting a good Basic Law for Hong Kong. But Deng's speech at the last plenum and the recent remarks by Li had left him wondering if he was wasting his time.

The next day, July 31, the subgroup members began preparing a report for the fifth plenum. They adopted Li's definition of "accountability," which would seriously restrict the legislature's power to oversee the policies and activities of the governor and civil service. Lee was furious. He believed that Beijing was maintaining Hong Kong's colonial system so that it could rule unchecked through an appointed governor, the way Britain had for almost 150 years.

Members of the subgroup had proposed six different formulas for constituting the first post-1997 legislature, including proposals from the Group of 89 and the Joint Committee. Since they could not agree on any one proposal, Lee requested that all the models be included in the subgroup's report. When this was rejected, he suggested putting them in an annex to the report. This was also turned down. After the meeting ended on August 2, Lee told a Hong Kong television reporter that the subgroup's definition of "accountability" was in breach of the Joint Declaration and attacked members for not coming to an agreement on the selection of the governor and the legislature. He implied that these issues were ducked because China feared that if the subgroup agreed to include any element of democratic elections in the draft Basic Law, it would enable the Hong Kong government to introduce polls in 1988.

That evening, the eight lawyers in the relationship and political subgroups held a meeting in their hotel to try to define the jurisdiction of the Hong Kong courts by adding an article to the section on the judiciary in chapter four of the Basic Law. Mainland legal expert Wu Jianfan proposed that the courts be prohibited from interpreting the Basic Law in cases concerning defense, foreign affairs, and "the executive acts of the central government." Lee strongly objected to the term "executive acts," which could be construed to refer to almost anything, including the arrest of someone who had criticized the Communist Party. Such a formula would leave the courts virtually powerless to protect the public from abuses by Beijing.

The following day, all the members of the two subgroups met to consider the new article as well as the original one (in chapter nine) on the power of the National People's Congress to interpret the Basic Law. Wu Jianfan patiently explained that if Hong Kong had not been given the power of final adjudication in the Joint Declaration, the mainland drafters would not insist on restricting the courts' power to interpret the Basic Law. In sensitive cases, the central government had to have some way to correct wrong decisions. Wu suggested that in cases involving foreign affairs and defense, plus a few other cases that might have "serious repercussions," the Standing Committee of the National People's Congress should have the power to issue an interpretation that would overturn decisions previously rendered. This would occur only very rarely, not more than once or twice a year. All he wanted, he said, was "to drill a small hole" in the power of final adjudication to enable the NPC to remedy "a wrong interpretation."

Mainland members gave examples of when the Standing Committee might need to exercise the power of interpretation. One referred to the case of *Spycatcher*, the book by a former British secret agent which London tried to prevent from being published on the grounds that it contained national secrets and could damage Britain's intelligence network. The drafter pointed out that in such a case, if a Hong Kong court approved the publication of a book containing Chinese state secrets, under Lee's proposal, Beijing would be powerless to halt publication. The situation was particularly dangerous because under the Joint Declaration foreign judges could be invited to sit on the Court of Final Appeal. They might not have China's best interests at heart.

Lee argued that such a formula would seriously erode the power of final adjudication and would be a breach of the Joint Declaration. "If one case can be overturned by the Standing Committee of the NPC," he said, "then no case would be immune."

The issue was left for further consideration.

THE BASIC LAW was taking shape. During the fifth plenum, held at the Great Hall from August 22 to 26, the secretariat handed out drafts of the preamble, general provisions, and first nine chapters for members to discuss.

A coordinating committee headed by Vice-Chairpersons Y.K. Pao and Hu Sheng was set up to compile the articles into a draft charter.

It was becoming abundantly clear to Lee that the Chinese drafters had a bottom line on the question of interpreting the Basic Law and that he had already reached it, but it was a crucial issue, and he resolved to continue the fight. When the drafters were allowed to address the plenum on the afternoon of August 25, Lee took his seat next to Ji Pengfei and challenged Wu Jianfan's position on the issue. He argued forcefully that the question of interpreting the Basic Law had nothing to do with the power of final adjudication, but was related to the independence of the judiciary.

"In any country where the judiciary is independent of the government," he said, "there is the possibility that some judgements handed down by the courts would not please the government and would thus be considered to be 'wrong.' But that government would not destroy the independence of its judiciary by interfering with the decisions of the courts, though it might, if necessary, change the laws in question so as to ensure that there would not be a similar decision in the future."

Lee said that the NPC's Standing Committee should trust the courts of Hong Kong and accept their interpretation of those provisions in the Basic Law that were within the limits of Hong Kong's autonomy. When a case dealt with an area outside Hong Kong's area of autonomy, such as foreign affairs or defense, the Standing Committee could make an interpretation after the case was completed to avoid similar decisions from being made. It could even amend the relevant provisions of the Basic Law where necessary, without affecting judgements previously rendered.

If the interpretation of the Standing Committee were given retroactive effect, he said, every time someone lost a case, he would appeal to Beijing. This would erode the authority of the courts and spell the end of Hong Kong's power of final adjudication. He proposed a practical solution: Whenever a case came up which called for an interpretation of the Basic Law, Hong Kong's attorney-general could appear on behalf of the government to avoid a wrong interpretation.

Lee said drafters should have confidence in the Hong Kong courts. Otherwise, they could not assure the independence of the judiciary and fulfill the promise of "a high degree of autonomy." In that event, the people of Hong Kong would not have confidence in the Basic Law, or the policy of one country, two systems.

Dorothy Liu leapt to Wu Jianfan's defense. She said that no one in her two subgroups—the relationship and political subgroups—tried to reduce the power of final adjudication of the Hong Kong courts. No one indicated that they did not trust Hong Kong judges. No one said they did not respect the independence of Hong Kong's judiciary. Obviously referring to Martin Lee, she said that it would be unfortunate if "any drafter" misled the public by insinuating otherwise. "Some people" have suggested that the Standing Committee's power of interpretation should not be given retroactive effect, she said. They should "admit to the public that their proposal is inconsiderate."

IN HONG KONG, Xu Jiatun was doing everything possible to convince the government not to introduce elections in 1988. He informed Governor Wilson, through back channels, that Beijing would "make sure things work out for [Britain] after 1997" if she did not introduce polls the following year. Xu's messenger made it clear that China would not oppose a small number of democratically elected seats being introduced in 1991. It was an attractive deal. Britain would avoid a confrontation with China, and the Hong Kong government would maintain some credibility.

Wilson scheduled his first visit to Beijing since becoming governor for September 23. If he could strike a deal with the Chinese, the issue of political reform could be put to rest. When the Executive Council discussed his visit at a regular Tuesday meeting that month, Wilson brought up the issue.

"Based on the submissions received by the Survey Office so far, it appears that a majority are not in favor of introducing elections to the Legislative Council in 1988," he said. "I would like to use this as the basis for my negotiating position in Beijing." He added that he knew what he was doing was "dangerous" because the consultation period was not yet over.

Wilson also knew that the Executive Councilors were all conservatives who were uneasy about democratic elections and as eager as he was to avoid a confrontation with China. They took the bait.

S.Y. Chung, always the most conservative on the issue of political reform, argued that introducing elections the following year was too risky. The governor had only been in office for six months. He had to maintain control of the legislature to administer the colony effectively. Chung said "the short pain is better than the long pain," meaning that if elections were put off, there would be an uproar, but it would die down quickly. If elections were introduced in 1988, the Hong Kong government might have trouble governing through the rest of the transition period. He did not question Wilson's assertion or demand to see the Survey Office's material. For Chung, it was not necessary to heed public opinion. It was necessary to govern effectively and to maintain an environment conducive to economic prosperity. Idealism and democratic rights had no place in a city whose success was as precarious as Hong Kong's was.

Lydia Dunn and several other members felt Chung was being too cautious. Having democratic elections did not mean that radicals would take over the Legislative Council and cause instability. They argued that China should not be allowed to dictate the pace of democratic development in Hong Kong. At the same time, they were not keen to see elections introduced in 1988, or to have a confrontation with China. No one questioned whether it was ethical to make a decision before seeing the Survey Office's report on public opinion. After a brief discussion, the Council agreed that the governor could negotiate on the basis that democratic elections would be put off at least until 1991.

DURING HIS two-day stay in Beijing, Wilson informed Vice-Foreign Minister Zhou Nan that the initial results of the political review indicated that most people in Hong Kong were in favor of democratic elections, though not in 1988. Zhou said that the Chinese government would not object to a small number of democratically elected seats being introduced in 1991—if the Basic Law included some measure of elections. He had taken a small but important step forward. While maintaining China's original position that the Basic Law alone should determine the future political system, he had opened the door just enough to give Britain a way out. Chinese officials on the Drafting Committee would make it clear that the Basic Law would include some measure of democratic elections. London would then be free to introduce elections in 1991.

The deal was done.

AMIDST ALL THE tension over the future political system, Hong Kong's economy continued to roll on like a runaway train. Growth in gross domestic product consistently reached double figures. The Hang Seng Index soared to almost 4,000 (compared with 1,173 on the day the Joint Declaration was signed), as companies and banks announced record profits. The tremendous prosperity created a genuine middle class. Expatriates joked about the "Chuppies" (Chinese Yuppies). By 1987, they could be seen on every street corner in Central District, wearing Giorgio Armani suits, carrying a mobile phone in one hand and a Louis Vuitton briefcase in the other. They worked for Hong Kong trading companies, British business consultants, American computer firms, and Japanese banks, and they were fluent in the techno-jargon of international business.

The cockiness of the early 1980s returned. But it received a jolt on Monday, October 19, when the New York Stock Exchange plunged 508 points, a fall unprecedented in the short careers of the colony's young financial professionals. The world's financial markets were thrown into panic. Hong Kong, twelve hours ahead of New York, knew that share prices would plummet when the market opened the next morning. Late that evening, the exchange's executive board voted to close the market for four days, ostensibly to clear a backlog of paperwork, but in reality to avoid a massive sell-off. The colony's financial secretary approved the move, which was harshly criticized by investors around the world. When the market opened the following Monday, the Hang Seng Index plunged 1,120 points.

Some speculators had purchased index futures on margin, putting up only a fraction of the price. It appeared that many would not be able to pay brokers, and some houses would go under. The entire futures market was in danger of collapsing. The Hong Kong government hastily organized a $250 million rescue package. It was supported by Beijing, through the Bank of China.

A week later, the Legislative Council held an adjournment debate on the controversial closure of the exchange and the Hong Kong government's decision to use taxpayers' money to bail out speculators. Martin Lee was in Guangzhou for a meeting of the relationship subgroup, where, as usual, he was making little headway on the courts' power to interpret the Basic Law. He decided to skip the afternoon session on the last day and jumped in a taxi for the railway station in Shenzhen. He got the next train to Kowloon but was too late to speak on the issue. When he did get a chance to address the Council later that afternoon, he attacked the Hong Kong government's handling of the affair. David Ford, sitting in for the governor, reprimanded him for digressing from the subject at hand. After the legislature was adjourned, Lee fired off to the press.

THREE DAYS LATER, Lee was back in Guangzhou for an important meeting of the political subgroup. He made another attempt to limit restrictions on the jurisdiction of the Hong Kong courts. He proposed that the courts be allowed to try all cases except those "formerly excluded under Hong Kong's previous legal system." He received little support. The group formally adopted Wu Jianfan's earlier proposal to restrict the courts from dealing with cases concerning defense, foreign affairs, and "the executive acts of the central government."

On the second day of the meeting, Lu Ping suggested holding a vote on the method of choosing the governor and constituting the legislature. It was the first time a mainland official had proposed a vote on the political structure. Unaware of the nature of the discussions between Governor Wilson and Zhou Nan, the Hong Kong drafters were surprised and confused by the change of policy.

Five drafters supported the Group of 89's proposal for the governor to be selected by a grand electoral college. Martin Lee, Szeto Wah, and publisher Louis Cha voted to have him elected by universal suffrage. (Cha claimed to have converted to the democratic cause, but Lee and Szeto remained highly suspicious of his motives.)

Two mainland and five Hong Kong drafters voted for the Group of 89's proposal for half the legislature to be returned by functional constituencies, a quarter by universal suffrage, and the remainder by an electoral college. Only Lee and Szeto backed the model favored by the Joint Committee for the Promotion of Democratic Government, which called for half the legislature to be returned by universal suffrage.

After the meeting, the conveners said they wanted to get an idea which models were the most popular within the subgroup. In reality, the vote was taken to pave the way for the Hong Kong government to introduce democratic elections in 1991. Although the most conservative model got the most votes, it still included a measure of such polls.

ON NOVEMBER 4, the Hong Kong government's independent Survey Office released its report—a massive, three-volume tome weighing almost ten pounds. The Survey Office had received, by the September 30 deadline, over 130,000 submissions, compared with 364 for the 1984 Green Paper on representative government and 2,494 on the Joint Declaration. In addition to two public opinion surveys commissioned by the Survey Office, 166 private surveys were conducted on various aspects of the Green Paper. Pressure groups organized twenty-one signature campaigns.

Over ninety-five percent of all submissions dealt with the issue of democratic elections to the Legislative Council, far more than any other subject. The results stunned Lee. A table in the report showed that 39,000 people favored elections to the legislature in 1988 and 94,000 opposed them. China's mobilization of her forces was successful. Over ninety percent of some 70,000 preprinted letters were against polls in 1988. Almost 23,000 came from the pro-Beijing Federation of Trade Unions alone. One prominent leftist boasts privately: "We built the step that the British used to climb down."

Lee was outraged. He demanded to know why the preprinted letters were included in the tabulations, but the results of the signature campaigns, which showed that 225,000 people favored elections in 1988, were included at the end of the chapter, almost as an afterthought.

The Survey Office's terms of reference said they should be handled separately. But the report clearly gave more weight to statistics that showed people were against elections in 1988. One group that had conducted its own public opinion survey lodged a formal complaint, claiming that the Survey Office and senior government officials had grossly misrepresented its findings. The group asked which year was most suitable for the introduction of democratic elections to the Legislative Council. It listed each year from 1987 to 1997. The results showed that most people preferred 1988. The Survey Office grouped all those favoring other years as being against elections in 1988.

What outraged Lee the most, what convinced him that the whole consultation was designed to get the result the government wanted, were the two surveys conducted by AGB McNair, a professional market research company.

The Survey Office's terms of reference said that it was to collect opinions on the "issues discussed in the Green Paper." It instructed AGB McNair, which won an open tender, to conduct opinion surveys on "the options" in the Green Paper. The company was to find out not what people thought about representative government and the need for checks and balances, but their opinions on the specific, highly-technical options raised in the Green Paper.

At the start of the summer, AGB McNair conducted interviews with ten focus groups. It quickly became clear that it would be impossible to conduct a comprehensive survey on the entire Green Paper because it was too long and complex. The government had already distilled the options into a summary chapter, and the company suggested basing its questionnaire on that. The commissioner of the Survey Office agreed. AGB McNair stuck rigidly to the wording of the Green Paper, even though it knew that the result would be a badly worded questionnaire. When one expatriate suggested ways to improve the English version, the senior executive in charge told him the company had to adhere to the wording of the summary chapter because any changes it made might be attacked as an attempt to lead or misrepresent public opinion. Although the company and the government claim this was AGB McNair's decision, an executive in the firm says that the government was ultimately responsible for the decision to stick to the badly worded summary chapter.

The two surveys were conducted between July and September 1987. Only two percent of respondents said they were against democratic elections to the Legislative Council. About twenty percent concluded that elections were desirable, but not in 1988. Only twelve to fifteen percent said they wanted polls to be introduced in the coming year. These results conflicted with eight other surveys conducted by professional market research firms on behalf of newspapers and other organizations, which found that those in favor of elections in 1988 outnumbered those against by almost two to one.

Lee claimed that there was blatant bias because the questionnaire had made it as difficult as possible for respondents to choose democratic elections in 1988. They were given three opportunities to oppose such elections. If they chose option four, they were given six more options, which included introducing democratically elected members in 1988. He charged that this "screening" was done to ensure that a majority would not choose elections in 1988. He was supported by the Hong Kong Statistical Society, a group that included government statisticians.

"Some options in the Green Paper consist of questions with multiple concepts and are spelt out in relatively complicated language," the Society said in a press release. "They are therefore not very suitable to be directly used as options in the questionnaire." It added that some questions were "loaded because listed options have rather different degrees of complexity" and that some choices were not mutually exclusive, but because of the design of the questionnaire, appeared to be so.

A senior executive at AGB McNair and a senior civil servant at the Survey Office both say privately that any survey conducted on the Green Paper would be biased because the document itself was biased. By drafting the Green Paper in a way that discouraged people from favoring the introduction of democratic elections in 1988 and forcing the research company to conduct a survey on the options in the document, the Hong Kong government ensured that the results would justify putting off elections until 1991.*

Chief Secretary Ford defended the Survey Office a week later in the Legislative Council. In a blatant attempt to intimidate liberal legislators before the scheduled debate on the Survey Office report, he sharply rebuked Martin Lee and a labor representative for accusing the Hong Kong government of relinquishing its authority and of deceiving local residents. Ford said the two had done a grave disservice to the community by trying to undermine the government's credibility. He warned that "those who continue to make [accusations against the government] in the misguided belief that they are dealing with a lame duck will learn that they have a tiger by the tail—and not a paper tiger either."

A month later, Ford was knighted for his loyal service to the British government.

WHEN THE Legislative Council debated the Survey Office report on November 18, Martin Lee delivered a long, searing speech pointing out again and

* At least six people resigned from AGB McNair in the wake of the controversy. The company was absorbed into a conglomerate, and three senior executives who worked on the Green Paper survey were posted to Taiwan. The Survey Office commissioner was given a promotion and transferred to a department where he would be out of the limelight.

again the flaws in the AGB McNair surveys, using testimony from experts he had consulted to back up his charges. "Can our people be blamed for suspecting that these two surveys had been conducted for and on behalf of the government with the sole object of ensuring that the results would not justify the introduction of [democratic] elections in 1988?" he asked. "Can our people be blamed for . . . concluding that this political review is nothing but a fraud?"

At the end of his speech, he said that if all of the information in the report—*all* of the surveys, individual submissions, and signature campaigns—was taken as a whole, it showed that the public was in favor of elections in 1988. "Sir," he concluded, "let this administration show us its undaunted mettle and restore its credibility with us to the full by coming to the only correct decision in the circumstances: Give our people the vote in 1988."

The appointed members staunchly defended the Survey Office report, but could not dispel the belief that the government had conspired to thwart the public's democratic aspirations.

Ford told the Council that the AGB McNair surveys were only a small part of the Survey Office report and that the Executive Council would consider all of the information before making recommendations to the governor. Neither Lee, nor anyone else outside the highest level of the government, knew that the Executive Council had already made its decision, without seeing the biased questionnaire or the misleading statistics.

GOVERNOR WILSON flew to Beijing in early December to discuss political reforms. The furor over the Survey Office report actually strengthened his hand because it was clear that if the Hong Kong government did not commit itself to introducing democratic elections before 1997, there could be instability in the colony.

During a two-hour meeting on the afternoon of December 3, Wilson briefed Vice-Foreign Minister Zhou Nan on the report and on the Hong Kong government's plans for constitutional reform, which would be laid out in a White Paper to be released in early 1988. He said that it would not introduce elections in 1988, but the results showed that people were overwhelmingly in favor of having elections before 1997. Zhou stuck to the position spelled out during the governor's last visit.

After the meeting, Wilson told reporters from Hong Kong that Zhou had informed him that China was "not opposed to some element of [democratic] elections in Hong Kong before 1997 if this is provided for in the Basic Law." He was being economical with the truth. By omitting that Zhou had stipulated 1991, it appeared that the Hong Kong government was free to introduce polls in 1988.

When Wilson returned to Hong Kong, he said he would be following closely the outcome of the Basic Law Drafting Committee's next plenum, which would be held in Guangzhou later that month. He was making it appear, for China's sake, that reforms were converging with the Basic Law. In fact, even if the drafters approved democratic elections in principle, there was no guarantee that they would be included in the final draft. There were still two consultation exercises to be held.

LEE'S PLANE touched down at Kai Tak airport early in the morning on December 11. He was returning from London, where he had been lobbying Parliament on the issue of elections. He had a few hours to shower, change his clothes, and organize the notes he had prepared on the plane before catching the No. 94 train for Guangzhou at 2:21.

Lee and the other Hong Kong drafters were met at the Guangzhou station and driven through sooty streets to the towering 843-room White Swan Hotel on Shamian Island, where European traders had their warehouses in the eighteenth and nineteenth centuries. The hotel was owned by one of the Hong Kong drafters and boasted a Chinese garden, complete with a waterfall, in the lobby. The mainland drafters preferred this hotel to some of the other new five-star hotels because of the park across the street where ancient banyan trees grew. The Hong Kong members enjoyed the luxurious rooms. When Lee checked into room 2135, he hardly noticed its commanding view of the Pearl River.

On the afternoon of December 13, the drafters broke into their discussion groups to consider the formation of the first post-1997 government. The issue was important. Martin Lee felt that if China's proxies controlled the first government they could revise the electoral laws, even the Basic Law, to entrench themselves in power. That seemed to him to be exactly what China wanted to do. During a political subgroup meeting in October, Li Hou had proposed that China's National People's Congress set up an organizing committee consisting of people from Hong Kong and the mainland to oversee all aspects of the formation of the first government. It would be like the Basic Law Drafting Committee and would set up "a widely representative body" similar to the Consultative Committee to choose the first governor and legislature.

Vincent Lo wanted to avoid any bumps in 1997, which might upset investors or cause instability. His Group of 89 had proposed that the last colonial legislature become the first post-1997 legislature. Picking up on British Minister Renton's railway tracks analogy, the press dubbed this the "through train" proposal. Virtually all of the Hong Kong drafters, including

Lee and Szeto, supported the idea. Ke Zaishuo of the Foreign Ministry told his discussion group that the Chinese and British governments had to cooperate to achieve a smooth transition. Ji Pengfei was not a member of any group, but had been listening in. He chastised Ke. "We have our ideas," he said. "[The British] have theirs. They cannot be trusted."

The "through train" was temporarily derailed.

The next day, when the drafters turned to the composition of the first legislature, there was still a vast gap between the viewpoints of the liberals and conservatives from Hong Kong. No vote was taken. The drafters merely agreed to include the various political models raised in the political subgroup, all of which included a measure of democratic elections in 1997, in a preliminary draft of the Basic Law. (The Chinese drafters were prepared to do this now because Wilson had assured Beijing that elections would not be held in 1988. In doing so, they undermined their own argument that elections should not be introduced that year because they might fail to converge with the Basic Law.) The committee had approved democratic elections to the Legislative Council in principle. This was the green light that enabled Governor Wilson to write into the White Paper that elections would be introduced in 1991.

Chapter 18

Basic Flaws

I T WAS A desperate mission, but Martin Lee never wasted a moment calculating the chances of success. This was not a chess game, nor even a civil case with millions of dollars at stake. It was a battle for survival, Hong Kong's survival, and every effort had to be made, every last possibility exhausted, no matter how high the odds had been stacked against him. The House of Commons had agreed to hold a debate on Hong Kong on January 20, 1988. It was only an adjournment debate; no motion would be filed, no vote would be taken. Lee decided to return to London anyway to lobby for the introduction of democratic elections in 1988. If enough MPs came out strongly in favor, if enough newspapers supported his cause, if he could appeal to the democratic instincts of Parliament and the nation, perhaps Margaret Thatcher could be moved to force the Hong Kong government to introduce polls later that year.

While in London, Lee requested an audience with Geoffrey Howe to press for democratic elections. The foreign secretary had rejected a similar request in December, but this time he accepted. During the forty-minute meeting, Lee attacked the British government for breaking its promise to introduce a more representative government in Hong Kong. Howe cross-examined him, demanding: "What's your best point?"

Lee had only circumstantial evidence. He did not know that back in 1984 the Executive Council had approved the introduction of democratic elections in 1988. He did not know that Britain had agreed to put off all major constitutional changes at the second Joint Liaison Group meeting. He did not know that the Executive Council had been hoodwinked into postponing the introduction of democratic elections in 1988 without even seeing the report that was supposed to be the basis for its decision. He was barred legally from obtaining the evidence that would have proved his case.

In Hong Kong, Lee had told reporters that one reason more people were leaving the colony was because, without the protection of a democratic government, they feared for their future. Howe said that Lee should not say publicly that Britain had betrayed the colony, or that people were emigrating because of concerns over 1997. "Otherwise you will be doing a great disservice to Hong Kong."

Lee left dejected. Then Howe added injury to the insult. His office released a statement saying that he had seen Lee and refuted claims that Britain had reneged on her promise to introduce a democratically elected government well before 1997. Lee felt that he had been used, that Howe had seen him only to show Parliament that the government had heard Lee's arguments and rejected them.

As HE WATCHED the debate from the visitor's balcony, Lee was not just disappointed, he was angry. To these men, Hong Kong was a political issue, and not a very important one at that. They were debating the future of Hong Kong people the way they would debate the poll tax, or public spending on sanitation. They would not put their political careers on the line for six million Chinese in a faraway colony.

Like the people of Hong Kong, MPs were asked to accept the Joint Declaration on the grounds that the British government intended to make the Hong Kong government more representative during the transition period. MPs were allowed, and perhaps encouraged, to believe that when the agreement said the legislature would be "constituted by elections," that meant democratic elections. (Labour MP George Foulkes recalls that when Parliamentarians were briefed by the Foreign Office on the Joint Declaration, they were told the legislature would eventually be elected entirely by universal suffrage.) MPs had ratified the accord. They felt they had some responsibility to the people of Hong Kong, but the debate was a perfunctory exercise.

Some MPs who spoke did come out in favor of introducing democratic elections in 1988. Former Prime Minister Edward Heath, always happy to oppose Thatcher on any issue, said that "unless action is taken quickly now," Britain would not be able to hand over Hong Kong with an experienced representative government. Equally content to oppose the government, the Labour and Liberal Parties came out in favor of elections, in large part due to Lee's lobbying. Labour's new shadow foreign secretary, Gerald Kaufman, said that polls should be introduced as soon as possible and that the entire Legislative Council should eventually be returned by universal suffrage.

Conservative MP Robert Adley, who always appeared to put Britain's relationship with China before the interests of Hong Kong, said the colony's "prosperity and stability are based firmly and simply on autocracy, not democracy." This was true, but ignored Parliament's own role in ensuring that it was a benevolent autocracy.

Thatcher supporters turned the tables on the pro-democracy activists. Peter Blaker, chairman of the Hong Kong Parliamentary group, said the loss of confidence in Hong Kong could be a result of "the activities of the delegation of democracy, who are stirring up fear."

Howe defended the British government's policy, saying that the idea that Britain had forsaken Hong Kong for the sake of her relations with China was "a grotesque distortion." London's primary aim, he said, was to secure the firmest foundation for the future of Hong Kong. "It certainly cannot be founded on confrontation between Britain and China." He rejected charges that London had broken its promise to introduce democratic elections and hinted that such polls could be introduced in 1991, but only "a modest proportion—certainly not going all the way."

WHEN DAVID FORD submitted the White Paper on political reform to the Executive Council, there was no heated debate, as there had been in 1984. The decision to put off elections until 1991 had already been made. How the elections were to be conducted and how many seats should be introduced were the only questions remaining. S.Y. Chung was convinced that the administration should maintain a majority of appointed members. Ford did not push for the greatest level of representation, as Haddon-Cave had. The Council decided that ten members returned by universal suffrage in 1991 should replace the ten currently being chosen by the electoral college. Although there was no evidence in the Survey Office report to suggest that the public preferred this arrangement, the Executive Councilors preferred it because it retained the existing ratio of elected to appointed members in the Legislative Council.

Ford's job was to sell the White Paper to the public. It was a job he was well trained for. First, to get the public used to the idea that elections would not be introduced in 1988, senior government officials leaked word that they would be put off until 1991. Then, to minimize the expected adverse reaction to the White Paper, it was released on February 10, 1988, the eve of the Lunar New Year, the biggest holiday in the local calendar, when almost a million people leave to visit relatives in China or vacation abroad. The paper, entitled *The Development of Representative Government: The Way Forward*, stressed that the move towards representative government should be "prudent and gradual" and that the system developed "should permit a smooth transition in 1997 and a high degree of continuity thereafter." In at least six different places, it emphasized that changes must take into account the drafting of the Basic Law. It announced that ten democratically elected seats would be introduced to the Legislative Council in 1991 but said nothing about how the other forty-six members would be chosen. Senior officials were leaving their options open because, according to one, they did not want "any more hostages to ransom."

The only modifications to the composition of the Legislative Council in 1988 would be to replace two appointed members with two members elected by expanded medical and financial constituencies. The governor would remain its president. Various insignificant changes were made to the composition of the District Boards and municipal councils. The most comprehensive consultation exercise in Hong Kong's history, which cost millions of taxpayers' dollars and politicized the community, produced no fundamental changes to the colonial political system. Trying to salvage the government's reputation, Governor Wilson described the changes as "far-reaching and important" and promised that they were only "the first step."

Lee was extremely disheartened by the White Paper. It was even worse than he had expected. He thought the democratically elected members would replace appointed members, not indirectly elected ones. The government had made sure that it would maintain its appointed majority until at least 1994 and thus would be able to push through unpopular legislation. For the first time, Lee expressed disappointment that he had not received more support from the people of Hong Kong. He told one reporter, "[They] ought to wake up." But he did not sit around licking his wounds. Two days later, he joined 500 demonstrators and publicly burned copies of the White Paper.

Vincent Lo, on the other hand, was immensely pleased with the White Paper. Like S.Y. Chung, he wanted the government to maintain a majority in the Legislative Council so that policies would remain unchanged and legislation could be processed efficiently. Xu Jiatun was also pleased. He had helped to satisfy the concerns of his powerful friends in Hong Kong and his superiors in Beijing. But the White Paper settled only the question of elections in 1988, not the underlying issue: How much autonomy would Hong Kong have after 1997?

WHEN THE MEMBERS of the Basic Law Drafting Committee gathered in Beijing in April 1988 for the seventh plenum, everyone felt that history was being made. After almost three years, they were about to release the first draft of the charter Hong Kong would live under until 2047. Members proposed amendments during the day and spent the evenings lobbying each other at dinner time, over coffee, or in the drab rooms of the Beijing Hotel. Minor changes in the wording of the articles were made right up until the last morning of the plenum. The secretariat worked furiously to include all the amendments and produce a final draft ready to be endorsed.

On the afternoon of April 28, the drafters gathered in the Great Hall to cast their ballots. As he waited for the votes to be tallied, Martin Lee felt frustrated. Few of his suggestions had been accepted. Shortly before 6 P.M., the results were announced: Every article had passed. That evening, the first draft of the Basic Law was released simultaneously in Hong Kong and Beijing. The mainland press played up the event. The *People's Daily* said the principles in the Basic Law "will have a positive influence on the great task of completing national reunification."

STUCK IN A cramped economy-class seat, Lee went through the draft on the plane back home. What disturbed him as he made his notes was the emerging pattern. The Chinese drafters, in every case, had defined as narrowly as possible the powers given to Hong Kong in the Joint Declaration and restricted its ability to exercise the high degree of autonomy promised. Beijing would have the power to apply national laws directly to Hong Kong, to veto local laws passed by the Hong Kong legislature (without giving any reasons), and to force the Special Administrative Region to pass legislation to prohibit "any acts that would undermine or subvert the Central People's Government." The local legislature would also have to enact laws to give effect to mainland statutes relating to defense, foreign affairs, and the "expression [of] national unity and territorial integrity."

Beijing would have the power to amend the Basic Law, except those portions dealing with the principles laid down in the Joint Declaration. Before the Hong Kong legislature could propose an amendment, it would have to obtain the approval of the governor and two-thirds of the local delegates to the National People's Congress.

Lee's pleas for Beijing to respect the authority and independence of the local courts had been ignored. The courts would be prevented from hearing cases that dealt with "defense, foreign affairs, [and] the executive acts of the Central People's Government." To him, this meant the courts would be powerless to try mainland officials who may have violated the laws of Hong Kong, even the Basic Law. The courts would also be restricted from interpreting portions of the Basic Law dealing with defense, foreign affairs, and "other affairs" that were Beijing's responsibility. Nowhere in the draft were these "other affairs" defined.

The draft also referred to a "Basic Law Committee," which would be set up to advise the NPC on important matters relating to the relationship between Hong Kong and Beijing. The draft did not spell out the nature and composition of the committee, or its terms of reference. Though Lee had succeeded in getting the issue in the draft structure of the Basic Law, the question of the Basic Law's relationship to the Chinese constitution was never adequately addressed.

Chapter four on the political system was written to give the Hong Kong legislature little more power than at present. It would have no authority to propose bills relating to government policy or public expenditure. The governor could dissolve the legislature if it insisted on enacting legislation that he refused to sign, or if it failed to approve the budget or pass "important bills" proposed by the government. The legislature would have no power to investigate the actions of executive authorities or call them to testify before its committees. It could impeach the governor with a two-thirds majority, but the decision would have to be approved by the NPC.

Lee believed that it was essential not just to provide for a high degree of autonomy in the articles of the Basic Law, but to have an elected government with the will to exercise it. The draft included five options for selecting the first post-1997 governor, among them the Group of 89's grand electoral college and the Joint Committee's proposal for one man, one vote. There was no explanation of how the electoral college would be formed, and Lee feared that it would be manipulated by Beijing. The percentage of democratically elected seats in the four options for the legislature ranged from twenty-five to fifty. Without strong support from the public, he would not be able to force the Drafting Committee to adopt the most democratic proposals.

He was extremely concerned about the formation of the first government, which was dealt with in an annex to the draft. Beijing would appoint—albeit indirectly—the first governor and the first legislature. This, he believed, was a breach of the Joint Declaration and seriously undermined the chances of Hong Kong ever having a government that would have the will to exercise a high degree of autonomy.

The businesspeople on the Drafting Committee were so paranoid about elected officials destroying Hong Kong's economy that they had even tried to constitutionalize the colony's economic policies. The Basic Law stated that the future Hong Kong government be required to maintain its policy of low taxation and to limit spending to about fifteen percent of the gross domestic product. Lee thought this absurd.

Lee was also worried about the human rights provisions in the draft. Article Thirty-nine said: "The rights and freedoms enjoyed by Hong Kong residents shall not be restricted unless prescribed by law." Since at most only half of the legislature would be democratically elected under the current draft, the people would not be able to oust politicians who restricted their freedoms. He felt that the two United Nations covenants on human rights should be given the force of law in Hong Kong, a proposal the mainland drafters consistently rejected as an infringement upon China's sovereignty.

The next day, major newspapers in Hong Kong gave the Basic Law unprecedented coverage. There were full reproductions of the entire draft— ten chapters, comprising 172 articles and three annexes, a total of more than 35,000 words. Academics, legal experts, and political commentators dissected it. Most agreed with Lee's view that it did not give Hong Kong enough autonomy and democracy.

Vincent Lo and the Group of 89 were relatively satisfied with the draft. They were unconcerned with Beijing's power to interfere in Hong Kong's affairs. Although the degree of democracy still had to be determined, they were pleased that the articles on the political system guaranteed that the future administration would remain efficient and not get bogged down in party politics.

Editorial comments on the draft depended on where a paper stood on the political spectrum. The pro-Beijing *Wen Wei Po* said the Basic Law would play an important role in boosting confidence in Hong Kong's future. The pro-Taiwan *Sing Tao Jih Pao* pointed out that Tibet had been given similar promises of autonomy. Yet, during the past few months, Tibetans had been protesting Chinese oppression.

Opinion in London was split along party lines. John Marek, Labour's spokesperson on Hong Kong, claimed the draft failed to live up to the principles of the Joint Declaration. Conservative MP Robert Adley described the draft as "a remarkable document—far, far better for Hong Kong than anyone could have imagined."

THE FIVE-MONTH consultation on the draft Basic Law began immediately. The Consultative Committee spent $385,000 to encourage the people of Hong Kong to submit their views. It prepared a video explaining the background to the Basic Law and sent it to high schools throughout the colony. An international advertising company was hired to create a low-key campaign featuring soft-focus shots of adorable children and doting parents with a voice-over urging people to "get to know the Basic Law." The two local television stations, after some prompting by the government, agreed to air the commercials 3,000 times, free of charge. One of the colony's biggest pop stars was recruited to sing a jingle. A total of 450,000 copies of the draft charter were printed in Chinese and English. They were distributed through 900 outlets around Hong Kong, including subway stations and most major banks.

As with the consultation on the Green Paper, Lee knew that he would have to rely on numbers to overcome the influence of the business community. Only an overwhelming demand for a democratic government would sway Beijing. Lee believed that most people were in favor of such a system; the problem was how to get them to say so. Beijing had already ruled out a plebiscite on the draft Basic Law. Lee believed, despite the controversy over the AGB McNair surveys, the next best thing was a professional opinion poll. This, too, was ruled out.

Conservatives on the Consultative Committee's executive board were concerned that the issue of elections would dominate the consultation exercise the way it had the Green Paper survey. To prevent this, one month would be devoted to each of the five broad areas covered by the Drafting Committee's subgroups. Members of the public were invited to write to the Consultative Committee's office or voice their opinions directly to committee members during meet-the-public sessions. Although all 450,000 copies of the draft Basic Law were quickly snapped up, people were largely apathetic about the draft. The Consultative Committee received only one hundred submissions from individuals during the first month. Seminars attracted as few as ten people.

A private opinion poll conducted by a professional research firm found that seventy-five percent of respondents were aware that the Basic Law had been published. But seventy percent had not read any of it, and almost sixty percent said they would not submit their views because they felt their opinions would not be seriously considered. Political commentators lamented that people seemed more interested in the latest tips on emigrating than on the future mini-constitution.

Lee blamed the Consultative Committee for the lack of interest. He said that its failure to conduct an opinion survey, combined with the way the Group of 89 was pushing its views, gave people the impression that what they had to say was unimportant. Vincent Lo argued that the public's apathy was further proof that Hong Kong was not ready for self-government.

With most of Hong Kong sitting on the sidelines, the consultation would once again be a political battle between pro-democracy activists and the "unholy alliance" of conservative businesspeople and pro-China forces. The Group of 89 was by now well organized and enjoyed support that stretched beyond the Consultative Committee and into the boardrooms of many of the colony's largest businesses. Lo believed the governor's post would be the most important in the future government. How he or she was selected would affect the nature of the future administration. To keep the message simple, the Group of 89 focused on its proposal for selecting the future governor by a grand electoral college. It sent letters to 600 influential social and professional organizations asking their views on the grand electoral college. The letters said the group believed that the organizations "should have some form of representation in the electoral college" and that they would be free to determine how their representatives should be chosen should they be given a seat on the college. That failed to pique their interest. Out of the 600 professional and community organizations targeted, only a few dozen groups took up the offer to discuss the grand electoral college.

The pro-democracy camp also concentrated their efforts on the political structure, but appealed to the working class. The Joint Committee for the Promotion of Democratic Government held a "Run for Democracy" on June 13, 1988. It was followed by exhibitions, slide and video shows, seminars, drama performances, and public opinion surveys at the district level. The purpose was to expand awareness of the draft Basic Law, promote universal suffrage, and prepare for a letter-writing campaign towards the end of the consultation period. Lee and Szeto published a seventy-page booklet, which proposed alternatives to forty articles and the three annexes of the draft. In early June, Lee led a delegation to London to lobby Members of Parliament to get more involved in ensuring that the Basic Law conformed to the terms of the Joint Declaration. Both Houses agreed to debate the draft Basic Law.

IN LATE JUNE, as Hong Kong held meetings, marches, debates, speeches, forums, rallies, and signature campaigns on the Basic Law, Lord Glenarthur, the new British minister of state at the Foreign Office, flew to Beijing for talks with Chinese officials. Tall and handsome, with a sonorous baritone voice, Glenarthur looked like a stereotypical aristocrat in a 1940s Hollywood movie. He was seen in Hong Kong as a political lightweight, someone ignorant of the facts, lacking experience in dealing with the Chinese government, and totally dependent on the Foreign Office. While in the Chinese capital, he met Chinese Vice-Foreign Minister Zhou Nan to discuss a range of bilateral issues, including the Basic Law. Glenarthur said that his government had an obligation to make sure the charter conformed to the terms of the Joint Declaration. Zhou stuck to his government's formal position. "It is our responsibility."

As a matter of principle, Beijing did not want to give Britain any say in the Basic Law. It had agreed that the charter would reflect the terms of the Joint Declaration. But it needed to make sure that the charter would maintain the confidence of local and foreign investors, and Britain knew more about how to do that than either Chinese officials in the Hong Kong and Macao Affairs Office or the Basic Law drafters. Zhou agreed that Chinese and British legal experts could discuss the draft, but insisted that there would be no negotiations and that the Chinese government would not be bound by Britain's recommendations. Glenarthur accepted this because the Foreign Office diplomats believed it to be the most China would offer. They accepted

220 • *The Fall of Hong Kong*

that Britain would not be able to guarantee that the Basic Law conformed to the Joint Declaration.

Legal expert Fred Burrows had personally pushed to have the two United Nations covenants on human rights put into the Joint Declaration. When he met his Chinese counterparts, one of the crucial provisions he wanted amended was Article Thirty-nine, which "whittled away the U.N. covenants to nothing." One Chinese legal expert admitted that the article was poorly drafted. He told Burrows that the mainland drafters had been pressured into accepting it by their Hong Kong counterparts. "We only put it in," he said, "to get some peace." (When the rights and obligations subgroup met after the consultation period, the mainland members agreed to scrap Article Thirty-nine. Journalists, unaware that the British legal experts had met with their Chinese counterparts, assumed that committee members had bowed to pressure from the public.)

THE CONSULTATIVE COMMITTEE received 73,000 submissions on the Basic Law during the five-month consultation period. Over 66,000 responses were organized by pro-democracy groups. The rest included commentaries in the media, less than a thousand individual submissions, and ten private opinion surveys. Many residents were daunted by the length and complexity of the draft Basic Law. Many more did not submit their views because they felt that Beijing would not heed them.

One of the few comprehensive professional opinion surveys on the draft was commissioned by the *South China Morning Post*. The results indicated what Martin Lee had always believed: The public wanted a more democratic system. About sixty percent of respondents said the governor should be chosen by universal suffrage. Only sixteen percent approved of the grand electoral college. Almost eighty percent believed the Basic Law should include economic guidelines stipulating that the future government would maintain a policy of low taxation, balanced budgets, and no trade tariffs, indicating that the Group of 89's fear of the free-lunch crowd was misplaced. Over all, less than half of those polled were confident that the draft Basic Law would implement effectively the one country, two systems policy.

THE CONTROVERSY over democratic elections increased anxiety in Hong Kong and fueled a growing exodus of businesspeople and professionals to the United States, Canada, and Australia. Hong Kong had long been a stepping stone to the West. During the 1970s, an average of 10,000 to 15,000 people per year left the colony to join family or establish new lives overseas (some people joked that Hong Kong was the world's only self-sustaining refugee camp). In the early 1980s, as concern about the colony's future increased, so did the number of people leaving. According to government figures, about 100,000 emigrated between 1980 and 1984.

After the signing of the Joint Declaration, the number of people leaving declined briefly. There was hope that Hong Kong could prosper and enjoy freedoms under Chinese rule. When Xu Jiatun banged his spectacles on the table at his press conference in November 1985, he shattered that illusion. Though not imbued with a strong fundamental belief in democracy (it was not in Britain's interest to encourage democratic aspirations), local residents saw Beijing's determination to force the Hong Kong government to put off elections as a sign that it would not live up to the spirit of the Joint Declaration.

In 1987, the number of people emigrating jumped to at least 30,000. Because many of those leaving were skilled managers and professionals, the phenomenon became known as the "brain drain." Finanical, accounting, and information technology companies were hit hard because professionals in these areas were in demand in many developed countries and their skills were easily transplanted. The Hong Kong Bank lost eight percent of its 670 local executives to emigration, triple the number in 1986. (It had no such problems before that year.) By 1989, Singapore would overtake Hong Kong as the number two foreign exchange center in Asia (after Tokyo) because so many dealers had emigrated. To hold on to experienced Hong Kong traders, many international banks posted them to Singapore, Australia, or Canada, where they could eventually apply for residency. The Hong Kong government itself was finding it impossible to implement its localization policy because experienced staff were leaving the colony or moving to the private sector where salaries were going through the roof. It resorted to recruiting Hong Kong Chinese in Canada.

The exodus was the most powerful indictment of Britain's policies towards its last important colony, and as such, the Hong Kong government refused to recognize it as a problem. Officials, including Governor Wilson, stated publicly that this was a historical phenomenon and that press reports were blowing the situation out of proportion. As more articles were being written, David Ford decided that the administrative officers, the elite grade of civil servants, should be told "the truth" about the brain drain. He instructed Donald Tsang, a high-flyer in the General Duties Branch, to give briefings in small groups. His message: The brain drain had nothing to do with 1997; it was simply that destination countries had raised their immigration quotas, and people were leaving to join family overseas, as they had always done. One expatriate civil servant says the talk was "complete bullshit."

In May, the government finally acknowledged the problem and set up a "task force" to determine the number of people leaving and their background, and, if possible, to propose countermeasures. Since the government kept no statistics on the number of people emigrating, or asked people why they were going, its task force had very little information to go on. Its only sources were the Immigration Department's aggregate statistics for arrivals and departures, applications for Certificates of No Criminal Conviction (required by most destination countries), and information from foreign consulates in the colony. Based on this sketchy data, it determined that about 30,000 people had emigrated in 1987 and estimated that 45,000 people would leave in 1988. It refused to release any information about how it had arrived at these figures. Most journalists accepted them as being accurate. However, senior government officials admitted privately to foreign diplomats that the actual number of people leaving each year was "probably about 10,000 higher."

When Wilson gave his second annual address to the Legislative Council in October, he said the government had to do something about the brain drain. He emphasized that it would not prevent people from leaving. Freedom of movement was a fundamental human right guaranteed in the Joint Declaration. The government would learn more about which groups of people were leaving and boost local education and training programs to "fill the gaps." It would increase the number of university graduates each year and improve contacts with those who had already emigrated to inform them of opportunities in Hong Kong. It all sounded very good, and the business community was pleased. But it ignored the fundamental reason that people were leaving—fear of the Communists.

Chapter 19

Striving for Consensus

THE BASIC LAW Consultative Committee was given seven weeks to prepare reports for the drafters on the opinions gathered in Hong Kong. The Drafting Committee's five subgroups would meet in mid-November to amend the charter before presenting it to the eighth plenum in January 1989. Pressure was mounting on the political factions to compromise over the future political system. The public was tired of the bickering, and Chinese officials hinted that if Hong Kong could not reach a consensus, the Basic Law Drafting Committee would impose its own ideas on the colony. In a last ditch effort to break the deadlock, the main groups held a frenetic series of meetings.

After listening to the governor's address to the Legislative Council, Martin Lee drove to the office of Szeto Wah's Professional Teachers' Union, which had become the headquarters for the Joint Committee for the Promotion of Democratic Government. Lee's refusal to join the umbrella organization and his tendency to monopolize attention from the press created some friction with other leading liberals.

Pressure from the Group of 89 was also splitting the Joint Committee. It had revised the membership of its electoral college to include more grassroots bodies and to allow them to elect their own representatives. Vincent Lo, showing himself to be a wily politician, claimed that the liberals had not made a single concession on the political structure, while his group had made many. In September, he turned the heat up on the Joint Committee another notch when he announced that the Group of 89 favored ultimately choosing the governor through universal suffrage—as long as there was a fifty percent turnout of eligible voters in the Legislative Council elections to show that people had matured enough politically to choose their own leader.

Lee argued that it would be impossible to achieve a fifty percent turnout unless the elections were meaningful and rejected Lo's charges that the liberals had not made concessions. The Joint Committee, he said, had already compromised by agreeing to just half the legislature being returned by universal suffrage in 1997. Anything less and the public would not have adequate representation.

Lo was winning the public relations war by portraying the liberals as uncompromising. Some members of the Joint Committee felt it was time to make concessions, but Lee believed it was still too early. There was another consultation to be held, and if they made concessions now, they would be forced to make more later. He believed that the Joint Committee should stand firm and show the drafters both ends of the political spectrum.

The Joint Committee had to elect a team to negotiate with the other political groups. Lee was a Legislative Councilor, a Basic Law drafter, and perhaps the only man who could unite the fractious pro-democracy camp. He agreed to join so that he could lead the team. Szeto Wah and four others were also elected. After much internal squabbling, the Joint Committee came up with a negotiating position: It would not compromise on the composition of the legislature, but would accept having the governor elected for the second term in 1999.

One of the first rival organizations the Joint Committee team met was the "Group of 38 Educationalists." In early 1986, a high school principal got together with the heads of twenty-nine other schools and several teachers to work out a moderate political model for Hong Kong. The group held its first meeting in April 1986 and completed a proposal in the summer of 1987. It attracted little attention because the educationalists had neither the money of the Group of 89, nor the grass-roots support of the Joint Committee. In 1988, the educationalists began to play a larger role in the political debate for two reasons: As the consultation progressed, more political organizations were moving towards the middle ground their group occupied, and a key member returned from England, where he had been taking a teaching course.

Cheng Kai-nam was a sincere-looking man with bright eyes, an engaging smile, and prematurely gray hair. He was friendly, open, and frank about his pro-Communist views, which cost him personally. Before the signing of the Joint Declaration (and to some extent after it), "leftists" were ostracized by the establishment and criticized harshly by the proestablishment media. They could not join the civil service. They were not invited to sit on government committees or to become members of certain social clubs, and they would never be granted royal honors. More than just opponents of the colonial administration, they were outcasts. Cheng accepted that this was the price he had to pay for his allegiance to China.

He was born in Hong Kong in 1950. His pro-China affiliation began when he attended a leftist high school. Six were set up in the colony after the Communist Revolution in China by supporters of the new regime. They were attended by the children of Chinese officials, employees of mainland companies, and parents who could not afford to send their children else-where. Cheng studied at Pui Kiu Middle School during the riots in 1967. Like other students, he took part in demonstrations and made propaganda material. It was a violent, passionate time. He was sixteen and he knew little about politics except that the Communists were good and the colonialists were bad. As he grew older, he grew more moderate. He came to believe in a form of socialism that embraced democracy and the rule of law. He strongly supported the reforms initiated by Deng Xiaoping.

When Cheng graduated from Pui Kiu in 1968, he took a job teaching language at the school, though he had no formal training. He joined the Federation of Education Workers, a union (although it was not formally registered as such) for left-wing teachers. The Federation, though patriotic and sympathetic to China, was not directly linked to any mainland organization and did not take orders from Beijing. Cheng was blessed with boundless energy and was active in social causes throughout the 1970s. He was an intellectual who loved Hong Kong and cared about its people. He did not mind the pro-China label, or that he was denied credit for his social work because of it.

He was elected to the Federation's executive committee in 1977 and became its chairperson in 1985. He boosted its membership to 4,600 and expanded it to include teachers from non-leftist schools. China hoped that he could challenge Szeto as the leading unionist in the teaching field. Although this was a long way off, he was becoming an important figure in left-wing circles. He was intelligent, handsome, moderate, and committed to Hong Kong—in short, someone who was more palatable to the people of Hong Kong than the old hard-line Communist supporters. When the Federation was given a seat on the Basic Law Consultative Committee, Cheng was elected to fill the position. (He likes to make the point that he was *elected*, not invited, but Xinhua made sure that the Federation was nominated to send a representative, which guaranteed his participation.) In 1986, he joined the Group of 38 Educationalists. Some political commentators believed he had a direct line to Beijing because he was the head of an important pro-China group. In fact, the Federation of Education Workers and the Group of 38 Educationalists were largely ignored by Xu Jiatun and Lu Ping because they had no clout.

When Cheng returned from studying in England in the summer of 1988, he threw himself into the Basic Law consultation, giving some sixty talks on the first draft alone. He believed that the stalemate between the liberals and conservatives created an opportunity for the Educationalists. By charting a moderate course, they could break the deadlock over the future political system. At the same time, Cheng would establish himself as a legitimate political figure and create a platform for moderate, pro-China groups.

Martin Lee and the team from the Joint Committee met Cheng Kai-nam and the Educationalists on October 27, 1988, at the Consultative Committee's headquarters. The two sides rejected the Group of 89's proposal for the governor to be democratically elected only after a fifty percent voter turnout. They wanted a clear timetable for electing the governor spelled out in the Basic Law. They could not agree on anything else.

It was not surprising that the meeting achieved nothing. Lee believed it would be a tactical mistake to compromise with the Educationalists because he would be forced to make further concessions to bridge the gap with the businesspeople. Moreover, he did not trust Cheng. Lee believed that Cheng was operating under orders from Beijing, or at least that he had China's interests at heart more than Hong Kong's. This simplistic view was wrong and was indicative of the way Lee saw the political battle: People were either for him (and therefore for Hong Kong), or they were against him. As far as he was concerned, Cheng was against him.

VINCENT LO headed the Group of 89's six-member negotiating team. He met Lee and the Joint Committee's team on November 1 at the Consultative Committee's headquarters. Lo said that his group could not accept having the governor democratically elected before the third term (and some members favored the fifth). It was clear to Lee that the two sides were miles apart. The meeting broke up with the groups no closer to a compromise.

Lo felt that the liberals were being unreasonable. If he could isolate them, he might be able to pressure Beijing into accepting the views of the majority of local political groups. A day after meeting with the Joint Committee team, Lo invited representatives from all the other major political organizations to a meeting at the Consultative Committee's office in Lane Crawford House. He tried to sell them on the electoral college, which was the foundation of the Group of 89's proposal. Other issues were open for compromise. Cheng opposed the idea of holding a meeting without one of the major players; it would put China in a difficult position because the Joint Committee enjoyed a lot of grass-roots support. Other groups felt it was too early to compromise and little progress was made.

The Group of 89 and the Joint Committee met again on November 9. Lo put forward three general principles, which he hoped could be used as guidelines for achieving a compromise. Szeto Wah rejected them because they called for the governor to be selected by "an adequately representative body," and not universal suffrage. "Then there is no point in continuing," Lo said. The meeting broke up after just ten minutes. The first round of negotiations had produced no results.

GOVERNOR WILSON flew to Beijing on November 2, 1988, to discuss the formation of the first post-1997 government with Chinese officials. Li Hou and Lu Ping had visited Hong Kong in September as part of the Basic Law consultation. During a meeting at Government House, Wilson told them that there was a widespread feeling in Hong Kong that legislators and senior civil servants serving under the British should be allowed to carry on after 1997. Fresh elections would cause unnecessary disruption and uncertainty. He was aware of the Chinese government's concerns about sovereign rights and proposed that, instead of simply continuing on after 1997, the last legislature under the British government could be dissolved on June 30, 1997. The same members would then be endorsed by a preparatory committee set up by the Chinese government, take a new oath of allegiance on July 1, and the body reassembled. The press later called this the "Lo Wu" solution after the last train station on the Hong Kong side of the border. (Before 1979, passengers had to disembark there, walk across a bridge to the Chinese side of the border, and get on another train to continue their journey to Guangzhou.)

During a two-and-a-half-hour meeting at the Chinese Foreign Ministry the following day, Zhou Nan told Wilson that China agreed in principle to the Lo Wu proposal, provided details could be worked out to the satisfaction of both governments. Wilson was pleased. He said the Hong Kong government would introduce a four-year term for Legislative Councilors from 1991 (in accordance with a decision made by the Basic Law Drafting Committee). Thus, Councilors elected in 1995 would continue on until 1999, avoiding the need for an election in 1997.

The two sides had to work out only a method of electing legislators under British rule while giving due recognition to Chinese sovereignty. Wilson made several suggestions. Beijing could set up a preparatory committee in Hong Kong in early 1995 to oversee the elections, or there could be "dual elections" monitored by Britain and China. There were practical difficulties with each proposal. Wilson wanted only to show Zhou that there were ways to achieve a smooth transition and address China's concerns about sovereign rights. The two agreed that the Basic Law should not include details on the formation of the first government and that the two governments should hold further discussions on the issue. It was a breakthrough. Britain would be able to guarantee a smooth transfer of administration.

TWO WEEKS BEFORE the political subgroup was to meet in Guangzhou, Cheng and four other Educationalists went to the headquarters of *Ming Pao* in the industrial area of North Point. They wanted to sell Louis Cha on their moderate political model. Unknown to the group, Cha had been working on

his own political model. As coconvener of the subgroup, he had been instructed to prepare a report on amendments to the political structure proposed by members. He decided to go further. He believed he could bridge
the gap between the Group of 89 and the Joint Committee, not by adopting a
moderate proposal, but by creating a political blueprint that would include
the best aspects of all the proposals put forward so far. It would be a tapestry,
like one of his novels. The result, he hoped, would be a satisfactory climax to
the long political battle.

Using his editorial resources at *Ming Pao*, Cha compiled information on
all the political models and came up with a composite model. The pace of
democratization would be slow to satisfy the conservative businesspeople. A
series of referendums would ensure that Beijing would not go back on its
word. This, he believed, would satisfy Lee and his supporters. Cha wanted
to be sure his model had the support of the Chinese government, so he held a
private meeting with Xu Jiatun in Shenzhen to inform the Xinhua chief of his
plan for a proposal based on a series of referendums.* Xu supported the idea
as long as the pace of reform was slow.

When Cheng presented his group's model, Cha said very little about it.
He left the room and came back with copies of his own proposal.

"What do you think of this?"

The five sat around a large marble coffee table in the spacious, book-
lined office. Even before he finished reading, Cheng said it was unacceptable.

"What's wrong with it?" Cha asked.

"The pace of democratization is too slow. People will not wait twenty-five
years for a fully elected legislature."

After the meeting, Cheng realized something had to be done before Cha
presented his model in Guangzhou. He called the leaders of all the major
political groups and suggested holding a conference to give them each an
opportunity to air their views. Then, Cha would see his proposal was not in
line with the thinking of most groups. Lee and Szeto believed Cheng was
laying a trap on orders from Beijing: Cha would threaten to introduce his
ultra-conservative model, and they would be forced to make concessions to
prevent him from doing so.† Cheng pleaded with Szeto to attend, saying it
would be a disaster if Cha presented his model to the subgroup without
revision. Szeto and Lee refused. Instead, they invited Cha to hold separate
talks with the Joint Committee's negotiating team.

* Cha revealed in a television interview that he had met Xu to discuss his proposal. In
an interview with the author, he denied that the meeting took place, but said Xu was in
favor of holding a referendum to determine the pace of political reform.

† Cheng denies that he was acting on orders from Beijing, and there is no evidence to
indicate otherwise.

Cheng's meeting was held on the afternoon of Saturday, November 12, at the Consultative Committee's office. Ten political groups were present, including the Group of 89 and Cheng's Educationalists. (Although Lee and Szeto did not attend, two other pro-democracy activists represented the Joint Committee.) A total of sixty-nine people huddled around the large conference table. The Chinese-language press dubbed it the *Mo Lum Dai Wiu* (Kung Fu Congress), after gatherings described in some of Louis Cha's novels. Cha was asked to chair the meeting. He opened by explaining that there was an urgent need to compromise. The mainland drafters were very conservative and would not accept a radical proposal for the future political structure. If the groups present could not reach a consensus, Beijing would impose a system that was acceptable to no one. Each group was given a few minutes to explain the merits of its proposals. The exercise was largely a formality, since everyone present was already familiar with everyone else's model. Cha did not give his opinions or reveal the contents of his own proposal.

After almost three hours of discussion, the groups were no closer to a consensus. As he was leaving, a disgusted Vincent Lo told Cheng: "You shouldn't negotiate with the radical groups—it's useless."

That evening, Cha went to Lee's law office. Sitting at the small, round conference table with the Joint Committee's negotiating team, he praised the liberals for sticking to their democratic ideals and said that a few years ago most Hong Kong people were not in favor of having a legislature returned by universal suffrage. The men in this room had changed that. But it was time to reach a compromise that was acceptable to Hong Kong and to Beijing.

"Mr. Lee and Mr. Szeto should realize the situation now in the political subgroup," Cha said. "It is impossible that your proposal will be accepted, especially the part on holding a general election for the governor before July 1, 1997. The subgroup is going to hold a four-day meeting, and we are running out of time. Right now, I'm going to raise a compromise proposal. I hope things will work out if each party is willing to give in a bit. We should leave a leak in the Basic Law so that the chance of carrying out general elections within the fifty-year time frame still exists. As for the pace of progress, I'm afraid it has to be pretty slow. All of you will think my proposal is extremely conservative."

Lee responded that they understood the situation, but would stick to their principles to the end. Cha was disappointed. Before the subgroup meeting, he made slight amendments to the model he had shown Cheng. He did not make major changes because he felt that for any proposal to be accepted, it "must get the best for the majority of people in Hong Kong without making China lose face." He deliberately made the proposal conservative so that it would not be rejected by the political subgroup right away. If it were accepted as the basis of discussion, Lee and Szeto could push for concessions. The result would be a satisfactory compromise.

Cha faxed a copy of his proposal to Xiao Weiyun in Beijing before the mainland convener left for Greece on official business. Xiao faxed back to say that Cha should use his own name to raise the proposal for discussion in the subgroup meeting. Cha agreed because he felt it would avoid the image that the mainland drafters were dominating the proceedings. Two days before the meeting in Guangzhou, he distributed copies of his proposal and other working reports, a total of 108 pages, to the other Hong Kong drafters in the subgroup. He requested that they not reveal the contents to the press until after it had been discussed by the subgroup.

MARTIN LEE boarded a train to Guangzhou on the afternoon of November 15, and turned his thoughts from the political system to Hong Kong's future relationship with China's central government. He carried a report from the Consultative Committee that showed most people wanted Hong Kong to have a greater level of autonomy. Many of the proposals he had made had received significant support. He wondered if the mainland drafters would make any substantial concessions.

The next day, Chinese officials in the relationship subgroup agreed to list, in an annex to the draft, seven national laws that would apply to Hong Kong.* The article giving the National People's Congress the power to veto laws passed in Hong Kong was revised to say that the NPC would return unacceptable legislation for amendment. The subgroup also dropped the clause empowering China's State Council to instruct the Hong Kong government to enact laws relating to defense, foreign affairs, and laws that "give expression to national unity and territorial integrity." Meeting in his hotel room with reporters that evening, Lee dismissed these changes as a "facelift." He claimed that as long as the issue of interpreting the Basic Law was not resolved, all other changes were insignificant.

The subgroup had spent much of that first day discussing the jurisdiction of the Hong Kong courts and their authority to interpret the Basic Law. Lee continued to push for the widest possible jurisdiction. On the second day of the meeting, the Chinese legal experts finally gave some ground. Instead of prohibiting the courts from trying cases involving "defense, foreign affairs, and executive acts," they would be allowed to hear all cases except those involving "acts of state" (a common law phrase referring to government poli-

* These dealt with China's flag, emblem, capital, national day, nationality law, and territorial waters, as well as diplomatic immunity and the election of Hong Kong deputies to the National People's Congress.

cies on national rights). Although the NPC would retain the right to interpret the Basic Law, the courts would be allowed to interpret the charter unless the outcome would affect the central government. In such cases, the courts would have to adjourn and seek an interpretation from the NPC. It was an improvement, though much less than Lee had hoped for.

The subgroup also clarified the definition of subversion, spelled out some guidelines for the formation of the Basic Law Committee, which would advise Beijing on the interpretation of the charter, and added a clause to clarify that the Hong Kong government would be responsible for maintaining public order in the Special Administrative Region. Mainland officials were quick to play up the significance of the changes. Li Hou told reporters: "The original provisions in the first draft were never intended to allow Beijing to interfere [in Hong Kong's affairs]. We hope that the amendments can help to clear up the anxieties."

ON FRIDAY, November 18, the day the relationship subgroup concluded its meeting, several newspapers in Hong Kong published details of the political model Louis Cha planned to present formally to the political subgroup the following day. The proposal was even more conservative than Lee had feared. Cha divided political development into three fifteen-year stages. During the first stage, the governor would be chosen by a grand electoral college similar to the one proposed by the Group of 89. Only a quarter of the legislature would be returned by democratic elections, the rest by functional constituencies and the electoral college. A referendum would be held in 2012 to see if a more democratic electoral college should be introduced to elect the governor and if the percentage of democratically elected legislators should be raised to half. A second referendum would be held at the end of the second stage in 2027 to see if the Hong Kong people supported returning the governor and the entire legislature by universal suffrage. If it was not passed, one man, one vote would be introduced automatically in 2041, just six years before the end of the fifty-year period of the one country, two systems policy.

Cha flew to Guangzhou that afternoon and arrived at the hotel at dusk. He was besieged in the lobby by a group of Hong Kong journalists, who grilled him about the proposal. Cha was furious that one of the drafters had leaked it, but defended it bravely, saying it was "very democratic" and would satisfy the pro-democracy camp because it contained referendums. That evening, he did not have dinner with the other drafters. Instead, he held a meeting with his coconvener Xiao Weiyun, Li Hou, Lu Ping, and Xinhua's Mao Junnian. Li and Lu feared that the proposal would alienate a large segment of Hong Kong society. They said the pace of democratization should be stepped up. After the five-month consultation period, the political sub-group should make some concessions to the pro-democracy camp. Cha was surprised. A real compromise could finally be reached.

The five agreed that political development would be cut from three stages to two and the introduction of universal suffrage would be moved forward. Cha went back to his hotel room and began cutting and pasting. It was after one o'clock in the morning when he finished revising his proposal.

At the start of the meeting the next morning, the drafters did not discuss the views of the Hong Kong people on the political models in the first draft. (Szeto believes few of them actually read it. Certainly none of them paid heed to the overwhelming demand for greater democratization.) Li suggested that they examine Cha's revised proposal because it was a composite of the nine models in the first draft. Dorothy Liu objected initially, but she later threw her support behind Cha's proposal. Lee and Szeto refused to take part in the discussion because they felt the subgroup was ignoring the views of the public. They sat through the meeting in defiant silence.

There was no time for members to hash out a compromise. For the first time, they voted whenever opposing views could not be reconciled. By the end of the first day, they agreed that in 1997 Beijing would appoint a sixty-member preparatory committee, made up of people from Hong Kong and the mainland. This committee would then establish an "election committee" comprised of 400 Hong Kong residents, which would choose the first gover-nor from among several candidates. The membership of the election commit-tee would be doubled to 800 members after the first term. Sixteen members voted in favor; Lee and Szeto abstained.

On the second day of the meeting, the subgroup agreed that a quarter of the legislature would be returned by democratic elections in 1997. A referen-dum would be held to see if the entire legislature should be returned by universal suffrage in 2012. The results would have to be approved by the National People's Congress. One mainland drafter who was a member of the Congress objected. "A referendum carries such force that no one can disallow it," he said. "How could the NPC do so without causing a major controver-sy?"

Members spent most of the rest of the meeting discussing the technical problems of holding a referendum. The mainland members were finally satisfied that all of the problems could be solved. But the subgroup had spent so much time dealing with the annex on the formation of the first government that there was little time left to discuss the articles in chapter four relating to the powers and functions of the governor and legislature. Lee requested that the meeting be extended. This was denied. Instead, on the last morning, each article on the political structure was read out by the staff of the secretariat, and members were given an opportunity to propose amendments. Since there was no time for explanations, few changes were approved.

The new political model, which was essentially a more liberal version of Cha's original proposal, was passed with only Lee and Szeto opposed. A referendum would be held in 2011 to determine if the governor and the entire legislature should be returned by universal suffrage the following year— fifteen years after 1997 and a full twenty-seven years after Geoffrey Howe said Hong Kong would develop a representative government "during the years immediately ahead." (If the referendum was not passed, another would be held ten years later.) The Chinese officials on the subgroup, eager to end the political factionalism in Hong Kong, called it the "mainstream proposal."

After the meeting, Li told a group of reporters that "unless there is very strong opposition" from the people of Hong Kong, the drafters were unlikely to revise the model substantially after it was submitted to the National People's Congress. Margaret Ng, publisher of Cha's *Ming Pao*, concluded in her weekly column for an English-language paper: "Things are looking grim for democracy in Hong Kong."

LEE AND SZETO reacted to the conservative political blueprint the only way they could: by organizing street demonstrations. At 4 P.M. on Saturday, December 3, over fifty pro-democracy activists gathered outside the Xinhua headquarters in Happy Valley to stage a twenty-four-hour fast—one hour for each year democracy would be delayed by the mainstream proposal. Among them was fifty-seven-year-old Szeto Wah, wearing blue jeans and a denim jacket. "We have to unite," he said. "We have no money and no power. The only thing we can depend on is unity, and I hope all of us will struggle hard on the long and difficult road to democracy."

As evening came and it grew chilly, the organizers handed out blankets. Protestors, including Szeto, snuggled up in sleeping bags as a dozen police officers watched over the bed-in.

The next day, Martin Lee, joined by his wife Amelia, led a protest march from Victoria Park to join the fasters at Xinhua. During the ninety-minute procession, some 600 demonstrators sang songs and held up banners saying: We want democracy in 1997; Democracy delayed is democracy denied; and A whole generation is being deprived of its political rights. When they reached Xinhua, the marchers and fasters tore up copies of the Basic Law and threw them into a large rubbish bin. Szeto set them alight.

"We have become the pioneers of the democratic movement in China," Lee told the crowd. "We hope the torches of democracy will light up every corner of China. Today's action is not only aimed to fight for democracy in

234 • *The Fall of Hong Kong*

Hong Kong, but on the mainland. We hope Hong Kong, after 1997, can become a special *democratic* region of China."

This is exactly what the Chinese government feared.

THE MAINSTREAM proposal caught the Group of 89 by surprise. Vincent Lo called a meeting at his plush Wanchai office in early December to discuss it. In the beige-colored conference room on the eleventh floor, members said they were prepared to move forward the referendum to determine if the governor should be elected by universal suffrage. However, they wanted a separate referendum to be held in 2010 to determine if the entire legislature should be returned by one man, one vote. They insisted that the referendums should not be valid unless there was a fifty-percent turnout of eligible voters.

The future political system was by no means set in concrete, and Lo continued to work to forge a consensus with other groups. That month, the Group of 89's negotiating team met with the Educationalists four straight nights at Lo's office, from seven to ten, to hammer out a compromise on the electoral college. Cheng Kai-nam insisted that the college should be formed by democratic elections, something the businesspeople were not prepared to accept. During one meeting, he found himself alone in the men's room with one of the Group of 89's negotiators.

"If you go along with our electoral college," the businessman said as they stood at the urinals, "I can persuade my colleagues to accept one-third of the legislature being returned by [democratic] elections."

Cheng rejected the offer. He believed there was a better way to break the deadlock than to isolate the liberals. As a leading leftist, he had insights into how the Communists worked that none of the other political players had. While outsiders saw the Chinese government as a monolith, he realized that there were differences between Xu Jiatun and Lu Ping and that this could be exploited to Hong Kong's benefit.

Xu was heavily influenced by the people around him, the powerful businesspeople in Hong Kong. He was deeply opposed to too much democracy before and after 1997. (Indeed, he had led Louis Cha to believe that his proposal had to be extremely conservative to be accepted by Beijing, when the Hong Kong and Macao Affairs Office was prepared to accept something more moderate.) Lu Ping was more practical. He realized that for Hong Kong to remain prosperous, the Basic Law had to have the confidence of the population as a whole. He emphasized over and over at Drafting Committee meetings that the interests of all groups had to be looked after.

Cheng believed that if he could drum up support for a moderate proposal, Lu might convince Chinese leaders that the way to break the deadlock over the political system without alienating the businesspeople or the liberals was to take the middle road. While the subgroups were meeting in Guangzhou, Cheng contacted a wide variety of political groups representing all sectors of society to ask them if they were interested in working out a moderate political model with his Educationalists. Nine said yes. Some represented professionals, some labor. None was committed to specific principles. What bound them was a desire to come up with a political blueprint that would work for Hong Kong and that would end the years of struggle between the two major political factions.

The ten groups met at the Consultative Committee's headquarters to work on their political model. Within a few weeks they came up with a moderate proposal: A third of the legislature would be elected by universal suffrage in 1997 and two-thirds by functional groups. By 2001, the entire legislature would be democratically elected. The governor would initially be selected by a democratically formed electoral college and eventually be returned by one man, one vote. It was not earthshaking, but it might be acceptable to Beijing and the people of Hong Kong.

THE CHAIRPERSON, vice-chairpersons, and subgroup conveners of the Basic Law Drafting Committee were scheduled to hold a meeting in Guangzhou from December 6 to 8, to study the amendments to the draft Basic Law proposed by the subgroups before the revised text was submitted to the eighth plenum. In protest of the mainstream proposal, a prominent priest and an academic staged a fifty-hour fast to coincide with the meeting. Instead of camping outside the Xinhua building, they sat at the Star Ferry concourse, where thousands of people, many of them tourists, passed each day to travel between Hong Kong Island and Kowloon.

The protests failed to move the drafters. They endorsed the mainstream proposal without amendment. Lu Ping told reporters that it could be changed only if there was a consensus in Hong Kong. Li Hou strongly rejected suggestions that Beijing wanted to manipulate the Hong Kong government after 1997. He said this was just "a conspiracy theory." When asked about the fasts in Hong Kong, the usually serious official quipped: "The government warns its citizens that hunger strikes are hazardous to health."

The Joint Committee decided to keep up the protest action at the Star Ferry when the meeting in Guangzhou concluded. Lee and Szeto realized that the chances of having a truly democratic government in Hong Kong were now almost nil. Their only chance was to mobilize the masses. Volunteers took turns fasting at the Star Ferry and collecting signatures of people opposed to the mainstream proposal. They would keep up the action until the eighth plenum of the Drafting Committee opened in Beijing in early January. On New Year's Eve and New Year's Day, hundreds of volunteers stood at the entrances of all the subway stations in the colony and collected 90,000 signatures of people in favor of holding a referendum on the future political system.

CHINESE LEADERS had more on their minds than the Basic Law. The economy was fast getting out of control. The introduction of free-market forces had exacerbated corruption and created spiraling inflation. Cadres were buying steel and other needed commodities at artificially low prices from the state and reselling them on the black market for huge profits. Crop production continued to decline, and supplies of meat and produce shrank. Farmers were selling their goods in street markets for exorbitant prices. The standard of living of workers in the cities was falling for the first time since Deng launched the reform movement. Intellectuals were being affected the most, and they were growing restless.

In September 1988, the State Council introduced measures to cool the overheated economy. Limits were placed on capital investment and imports as the central government fought to regain control of the economy. Deng and the reformers were under pressure from conservatives within the Communist Party. In an effort to curtail inflation, which was estimated by some Western economists to be as high as 40 percent, the central government introduced price controls in Beijing on December 3 and later in Guangdong. It was a major setback for Zhao Ziyang, who believed the answer was more reform, not less.

The only bright spot for Deng was a thaw in relations with the Soviet Union. The two communist giants had agreed to hold a summit in Beijing the following spring, the first in more than two decades.

Chapter 20

"Only One Thing Matters—a Valid Nationality"

T HE EIGHTH PLENUM of the Basic Law Drafting Committee was to open at the Garden Hotel in Guangzhou on January 9, 1989. Pro-democracy activists ended their thirty-three-day "relay fast" at 3 P.M. on January 7. The following day over one hundred demonstrators gathered in the tourist area of Tsim Sha Tsui East. Waving flags and banners, the group marched along the harbor-front promenade, where tourists and lovers gazed at the spectacular view of the Hong Kong skyline glistening in the distance. At the Kowloon railway station, they gave a rousing send-off to an eighteen-member pro-democracy delegation, which was going to Guangzhou to present to Ji Pengfei the 90,000 signatures of people in favor of holding a referendum on the political system before it was written into the Basic Law.

The delegation was not able to see Ji, but was given a ninety-minute audience with Lu Ping. Lu said that holding a referendum on the political structure was a good idea because it would reveal the views of the silent majority. There were, however, legal and technical problems with doing so under British administration. How could China enact laws establishing the eligibility of voters? "We can't have such laws now," he said. "The Basic Law will not take effect until [after] June 30, 1997. Should we follow the laws of the British administration?" He insisted that it was "a matter of sovereignty."

A week before the plenum, Martin Lee wrote to Li Hou in Beijing suggesting that the Drafting Committee should not make it appear that everything had been settled by the Drafting Committee. He specifically requested that the drafters not vote on each article. He feared that if votes were taken, it would appear that further changes were unlikely, and the people of Hong Kong would lose interest in the second consultation period. Lee's request was not only ignored, but the Chairman's Committee decided that all amendments had to be seconded by at least four members and passed by a two-thirds majority. Lee was furious. The decision meant that amendments that had a lot of support in Hong Kong but not among the drafters could not be included in the second draft. The Chairman's Committee was, in effect, limiting the discussion to proposals the drafters felt were acceptable.

On the second day of the plenum, the discussion groups met in separate, brightly lit banquet halls in the hotel to consider the second draft of the Basic Law. It did not include details on the formation of the first government. Instead, it said that the first administration would be set up in accordance with a resolution passed by the National People's Congress. This was in accordance with the agreement reached by David Wilson and Zhou Nan.

"Who suggested this?" demanded Dorothy Liu. "This has never been discussed. Where did this 'empty proposal' come from?"

"It was not proposed by any one person; it was proposed by a country," Li Hou said, admitting that the proposal came from Britain.

When members were given a chance to address the plenum, mainland legal expert Wu Jianfan said that a proposal to boost the Hong Kong courts' power to interpret the Basic Law would undermine the authority of the NPC. The courts' power of interpretation should not exceed the scope of Hong Kong's autonomy, he said. "If you restrict the power of the central authorities, how can it impose all laws, including the Basic Law, which is part of the constitution, in all provinces and cities?" He added that "powers that can be granted to [Hong Kong] have already been granted."

Martin Lee and Szeto Wah had drafted thirty-one amendments that they wanted to propose at the plenum. Lee spent his evenings knocking on doors on the special floor of the hotel reserved for the drafters. Some of the Hong Kong drafters with whom he was still on speaking terms gave him a hearing. (He went alone because Szeto Wah felt the effort was futile.)

Lee was able to get three more seconders for sixteen of the thirty-one proposals. One amendment he was unable to present would have replaced the mainstream political model with that of the pro-democracy camp. Only one other drafter, Hong Kong businessman Graham Cheng, supported the suggestion.

By 5:30 P.M. on the third day of the plenum, the secretariat had received fifty-three proposed amendments. One of the most crucial came from industrialist Cha Chi-ming. If passed, it would require two-thirds of Hong Kong's legislature, the governor, and the Standing Committee of the NPC to agree to a referendum before it could be held under the mainstream political blueprint. The proposal also required the referendum to be passed by at least one-third of all eligible voters for it to be valid. If written into the Basic Law, it would virtually guarantee that there would never be full democracy in Hong Kong.

On January 13, the fifty-two drafters present—three were absent and four had died—held two rounds of voting. In the morning, they passed just ten amendments. None of those proposed by Lee and Szeto received the required thirty-seven votes. The drafters rejected amendments to the political system proposed by members of the Group of 89 and by supporters of the moderate alliance.

While the votes were being counted, Lee went to the rest room. When he returned, he met a mainland drafter from the Hong Kong and Macao Affairs Office at the back of the hall.

"What do you think?" Lee asked.

"Big headache."

"Why?"

The mainland official said he knew there would be a lot of objections to the political system in Hong Kong. Beijing was prepared to make some concessions on the mainstream proposal after the second consultation. Cha Chi-ming's amendment would make matters worse.

"I hope it's voted down," he said. "I personally voted against it."

Cha's proposal for restricting the referendum was passed by exactly two-thirds of the committee.

In the afternoon, the drafters approved 156 of the 159 articles in the revised draft. They met the next day to hammer out compromises on the remaining three. Articles 106 and 107 dealt with economic policy guidelines. Apparently at the Hong Kong government's request, Maria Tam suggested putting them in an annex to the draft, rather than making them part of the constitution. A coconvener of the economic subgroup, Wong Po-yan, had proposed constitutionalizing the economic policies, and he opposed diluting them. As a compromise he suggested that they remain in the text and be reworded to make it clear that these policies were not legally binding. His motion was passed.

After lengthy and at times heated debate, the drafters could not agree on the article restricting the jurisdiction of the Hong Kong courts. The original article was put in the second draft intact with a note to indicate that it was the only article not passed by a two-thirds majority.

A month later, the draft Basic Law was passed by the Standing Committee of the National People's Congress. It received almost no international press, although hundreds of foreign journalists were in China covering U.S. President George Bush's state visit. The media were more interested in the diplomatic row caused when Bush invited Fang Lizhi to a banquet at the American embassy, and the dissident astrophysicist was forcibly prevented from attending by Chinese police.

When the second draft was published in Hong Kong on February 27, 1989, it was seen as a significant improvement. The main problem now was the political system. The press called the amended political structure the "Cha-Cha model" after its two main architects. Lee called it "a great leap backwards." Szeto said the Joint Committee would take the fight for democracy to the streets. Chinese officials tried to defuse the controversy. Li told reporters that the model would definitely be amended if the various political groups in Hong Kong reached a consensus.

THE BRAIN DRAIN received almost as much coverage as the Basic Law during the spring of 1989. There were articles in the local press about companies losing key employees, about the impact of having to recruit and train new people, about Hong Kong losing its competitiveness because of the high wages companies had to pay to maintain staff. The international press picked up on some of the more bizarre and unfortunate aspects of the phenomenon, such as people digging up the remains of deceased relatives and shipping them to Canada, or families leaving behind retarded children because that was the only way they could get immigrant visas. One of the most common stories was about the *tai hung yun*, or "astronauts." These were executives who moved their families overseas, then returned to Hong Kong where they could earn more and enjoy better prospects for promotion. They would "commute" once or twice a month to their new country of residence to see their wives and children. It exacted a heavy price on many marriages.

Surveys indicated that the continuing exodus could become catastrophic. They revealed that as many as a third of all people in Hong Kong and half of all professionals wanted to leave before 1997. The Hong Kong government and businesspeople pointed out that nowhere near that number could leave because destination countries had strict quotas. Still, emigration became big business. Consultants—some legitimate, some shady—flooded into the colony and set up shop wherever they could find office space. For a handsome fee they would do little more than fill out forms. Companies held exhibitions to promote property and investment opportunities abroad. A bilingual magazine called *The Emigrant* was launched to offer information on getting a visa, plus investment advice and tips on how to cope with life in a new country. It was an instant success.

The French government caused a stir when a Hong Kong newspaper revealed that France was giving citizenship to employees of major French companies doing business in Hong Kong. The passports, which came with no strings attached, were to help firms retain key staff. But many of those who got passports promptly resigned; since they were now less likely to emigrate, they could earn more money elsewhere.

Britain was coming under increasing pressure to ease fears in Hong Kong and stem the brain drain by issuing passports to all 3.3 million people born in the colony. In January, the Portuguese government had announced that Portuguese citizens in Macao, most of whom were ethnic Chinese, would be given European Community passports. Thus, they would be able to live anywhere in the European Community, including Britain. It was the bitterest of ironies that Chinese in Macao could escape to the U.K., but Hong Kong Chinese could not. Under an agreement similar to the Sino-British Joint Declaration, Portugal agreed to return Macao to China on December 20, 1999. Unlike the Sino-British deal, the accord said that Portuguese citizens in Macao would maintain their nationality and their right to live in Portugal. At the time, the British government pushed Executive Councilors to come out against this provision. S.Y. Chung convinced them not to "fall into the Foreign Office's trap."

Letters demanding the right to live in Britain began to appear almost daily in Hong Kong newspapers. One signed by eight students from the local university said: "Today, only one thing matters—a valid nationality and passports to enable people to flee Chinese Communism. . . . Political reforms, democracy, even universal franchise to elect a legislature and chief executive do not matter any more."

Some of Britain's most prestigious newspapers criticized the Thatcher administration for not giving the people of Hong Kong British citizenship. It had been so stingy that it refused to allow in some thirty widows of men killed defending Hong Kong during World War II. Lord Wyatt, a newspaper columnist and former Labour MP, called for a debate on the subject in the House of Lords. Members of the Executive and Legislative Councils wrote to him requesting the British government adopt a more liberal interpretation of the "special cases" clause within the Nationality Act. (Only eight Hong Kong civil servants had been granted British citizenship in the previous five years under the clause.) Other groups called for full nationality for all British subjects in Hong Kong.

Many MPs who spoke during the debate were in favor of giving more Hong Kong people the right to live in Britain. But they were expressing a personal view. The Lords had no power to alter government policy. Lord Wyatt explained that most Chinese residents wanted to stay in Hong Kong. They would only do so "if they have the key to what might become a communist prison." He accused the British government of making it deliberately difficult for Hong Kong Chinese to enter the U.K. and said this was a "monstrous injustice."

Lord Geddes pointed out that 3.3 million Hong Kong residents was nothing compared to the 250 million European Community passport holders who would be given the right to live in Britain after 1992, and Lord MacLehose warned that the nationality issue was "harming Britain's reputation . . . among [her] best friends in Hong Kong."

Lord Glenarthur, responding for the government, said that under no circumstances could it change its well-stated policy. "There would not be sufficient support in this country for large-scale immigration from Hong Kong," he declared. "Nobody could predict with any accuracy the effect of granting U.K. citizenship would have on the economy."

He ignored all arguments that the granting of citizenship would bolster confidence in Hong Kong and keep people from leaving. In a minor concession, he said that the Home Office would consider the plight of the war widows. A Hong Kong columnist described his speech as one "combining feeble reasoning with total heartlessness."

NEGATIVE COMMENTARIES in the British press calling the Hong Kong government a lame duck, and news reports about the thousands of well-heeled refugees fleeing the colony gave an impression in the U.K. that Hong Kong was unraveling, that the transition to Chinese rule was going all wrong. Members of Parliament could no longer ignore the problem. They, after all, had consigned the people of Hong Kong to this fate. The standing Foreign Affairs Select Committee, which monitors Britain's overseas relations, decided to investigate the government's implementation of the Joint Declaration. A day before the Lords debated the nationality issue, the Select Committee grilled Foreign Secretary Howe and Governor Wilson in the House of Commons.

Howe said it would not be possible to give Hong Kong people British citizenship, even though many of them would never take up the right to live in Britain. He was very careful when answering questions about political developments in Hong Kong and the move towards representative government. He said that the pace of evolution was in line "with what most Hong Kong people probably want" and that a system had to be developed that would last beyond 1997. He raised the possibility of enacting a bill of rights to protect the people of Hong Kong from abuses after 1997. "The Basic Law itself contains explicit provisions on human rights," he said. "The possibility of going beyond that is certainly still open."

Wilson flew to London, avoiding the embarrassment of having to give open testimony in Hong Kong. He looked relaxed as he entered the Commons' Grand Committee Room. He was well prepared and easily fended off questions from the MPs. He submitted separately a written background briefing on the brain drain, which stated that the number of people leaving in 1989 would fall to 42,000 from 45,800 the previous year. Given that senior officials told foreign diplomats that the number of emigrants was underestimated by 10,000, the Hong Kong government was apparently misleading Parliament.

Wilson's submission to the committee appeared to be the start of a concerted campaign by the Hong Kong administration to reverse the negative
press coverage of the brain drain. Three weeks later, in response to a question
in the Legislative Council, a senior civil servant said that the number of
people emigrating to Canada in 1989 would fall by more than 8,000 to about
16,400. The commissioner for Canada responded that the calculations of
Hong Kong officials "were presumably designed to support their own argument." Another Canadian official said that even the Canadian Commission
did not know how many visas would be issued for any given year because the
decisions were made in Ottawa.

Mike Rowse, head of the Hong Kong government's task force, responded
that his unit used a variety of criteria to arrive at its estimate, so it was in a
better position than the consulates to make a forecast. The task force was, in
fact, a joke. It consisted of two people, a policy secretary and a statistician.
Its sources of information, other than the consulates, were very imprecise,
and its attempts to gauge the extent of emigration were half-hearted at best
and deliberately misleading at worst.

When it was revealed in early 1990 that the Canadian Commission had
issued over 20,000 visas in 1989, Rowse insisted that not all of those would be
taken up immediately. He maintained that arrivals in Canada would be closer
to his figure. When the arrival figure was published, it was also over 20,000.
The Hong Kong government admitted that its estimates for Canada were
wrong, but said that the overall figure of 42,000 was correct because the
estimates for the United States and Australia were too high. In other words,
it got the figures for all three countries wrong but the total correct.

The task force claimed its figures were accurate to within one percent.
However, they did not include professionals who were transferred overseas
and then applied for citizenship, tourists who found jobs overseas and stayed,
or students who attended foreign universities and did not return. The task
force claimed that these figures were impossible to obtain. However, figures
released by the U.S. Immigration and Naturalization Service in May 1990 at
the author's request showed that the number of workers, students, and tourists from Hong Kong who obtained residency had risen steadily since the
signing of the Joint Declaration. In all, almost 10,000 people who were not
included in the Hong Kong government's emigration statistics left the colony
permanently for the United States between 1982 and 1989. Another 3,000
found back doors into Canada. It is likely that many more entered Australia
and other countries without being recorded as emigrants, or obtained foreign
passports that enabled them to flee in the event of a crisis.

One of the most worrying aspects of the brain drain was the fact that
many of the people who were leaving were not unskilled workers, but well-

trained executives and professionals who were taking lower paying jobs overseas in order to live in continued freedom. Nurses were taking jobs at McDonald's restaurants in Canada. Accountants were working in Chinese restaurants, and airline mechanics were collecting welfare.

The government claimed that only a quarter of the emigrés were in the "professional, technical, administrative, and managerial" category of the work force. Here again, it hid the true extent of the problem. Another twenty percent of those leaving were businesspeople and entrepreneurs. In many families, both spouses were professionals, but one was listed as a dependent. All told, well over half of those who emigrated in 1987 and 1988 had skills that Hong Kong desperately needed to maintain.

Chapter 21

Two Systems in Conflict

O N APRIL 15, 1989, a black-bordered picture of former Communist Party chief Hu Yaobang appeared on Chinese television, accompanied by somber music. The disgraced leader had died early that morning of a heart attack. In a statement, the party's Central Committee praised Hu as a "long-tested, loyal communist fighter, great proletarian revolutionary, statesman" and "outstanding leader." That evening students covered notice boards at Beijing University with posters hailing Hu as a champion of democracy. "A true man has died—false men are living," said one. "Mr. Hu, your death is a great blow against the struggle of the people of China for democracy and freedom," said another.

Two days later, 4,000 people gathered in Tiananmen Square to mourn Hu. About 600 students marched for four hours from Beijing University to the square, carrying a six-foot funeral wreath to lay at the Monument to the People's Heroes. "Long live Hu Yaobang!" they chanted with fists raised. "Long live democracy!"

Police took photographs of the demonstrators, but did not attempt to stop the unauthorized rally. The crowd dispersed peacefully in the evening. The students returned the following day, and over the next few weeks, Tiananmen Square became the center of dissent in China.

As the demonstrations in Beijing began, the eleven British MPs on the Foreign Affairs Select Committee flew into Hong Kong to gather views on Britain's implementation of the Joint Declaration. Public hearings were held in the old Legislative Council building adjacent to the government secretariat. The musty chamber, with horseshoe-shaped benches and a large rostrum where Geoffrey Howe sat to tell Hong Kong that Britain would withdraw in 1997, had not been used in four years. It was chosen because the government anticipated that a large number of journalists and citizens would want to sit in on the hearings. The journalists came; the public was indifferent.

The hearings represented a unique opportunity for Martin Lee and his supporters. They believed that British MPs had remained apathetic while the Old China Hands in the Foreign Office planned and executed Britain's Hong Kong policy. The Thatcher government had convinced the people of Hong Kong to accept the Joint Declaration by promising that they would run their own affairs through an elected government and enjoy a high degree of autonomy. Now it was clear that China had very different ideas about how Hong Kong would be run after 1997. If the pro-democracy camp could convince Parliament that a corresponding change of policy was needed, that democracy had to be introduced (or that Britain had to give them an escape route in case things went wrong), perhaps things could be turned around and a disaster avoided.

Unfortunately, there would be no change of policy. Hong Kong was too divided to present a convincing case. And the Select Committee itself was a perfunctory exercise—a shallow attempt by Parliament to exorcise its guilt at having quietly acquiesced while the Thatcher administration handed six million people over to a communist regime. Though its members came, ostensibly, to hear opinions in Hong Kong, they often seemed intent on lecturing to those giving evidence.

The one issue on which Hong Kong was united was nationality. Businesspeople believed giving all 3.3 million British subjects in Hong Kong an escape route would stem the brain drain. Committee members dismissed this as unrealistic. They rejected arguments that people were leaving only to get foreign passports that would provide insurance against a catastrophe after 1997 and that by giving people the right to live in the U.K., they would be inclined to stay in Hong Kong.

On the second day of public testimony senior Executive Councilor Lydia Dunn made an emotional plea for passports. "I sometimes wonder what the British people feel when they read about Hong Kong's British subjects scurrying around the world to find somewhere else to take them in," she said, her voice cracking. "It would do so much to help families . . . to commit themselves to a future here . . . if they could be guaranteed a home . . . of last resort in Britain. It would be a decisive gesture. . . . It would be the honorable course."

She broke down and cried. After about fifteen seconds, she composed herself, and resumed her presentation. Committee Chairman David Howell said he was impressed with her deep feelings. But apparently not enough to recommend nationality be given to the people of Hong Kong. Some members of the committee later told British diplomats in Beijing that they were repulsed by her outburst.

Martin Lee followed Dunn, and the MPs used the opportunity to refute, rather than listen to, Lee's accusations that the British government had failed to live up to its promises. After a rambling speech in which, as one journalist put it, Lee "drifted at times in a tide of mixed metaphors," the MPs grilled him.

"I must put it to you very strongly that you are wrong, that you produced no evidence [that the British government deceived the people of Hong Kong]," said Labour MP Peter Shore. "One has to be very careful when you attack the British government's good faith as distinct from its wisdom. If a government is thought to be dishonest or deliberately misleading people, it is a grave matter indeed."

In a statement that sounded as though the committee had reached its conclusions before the hearings even started, Shore said that after reading the 1984 Joint Declaration he saw "nothing whatever to back up your contention that there was any clear promise or commitment to . . . one-person-one-vote democracy. Therefore, I do not think that you have any right at all to accuse the British government of deliberately misleading the people."

Lee explained that he never accused British officials of misleading the Hong Kong people. "They promised us democracy in good faith. They really wanted to give it to us. I believe that. But when there was a strong objection from China, they decided that they did not want to confront China."

Shore said that was "a very much less serious charge than the grave one with which you began your statement."

The British government had, in fact, misled the people of Hong Kong and Parliament into believing that the colony would have a Western-style, democratic government after 1997. It never revealed that China had opposed defining the term "elections" in the Joint Declaration as "democratic elections." (Various Foreign Office diplomats claimed they never attempted to define the term, which was a lie.) The Hong Kong government had also reneged on its promise to introduce democratic elections in 1988. Had members of the Select Committee wanted hard evidence, they should have demanded access to the stacks of Foreign Office files and the minutes of Executive Council meetings. The MPs, in fact, did not want to know the truth: that the British government had led the people of Hong Kong to believe that they would enjoy full democracy in order to get them to accept the Joint Declaration, and that it then manipulated public opinion in the colony and used questionable surveys to justify not introducing elections in 1988 to avoid a confrontation with China. Although they may have sympathized with Hong Kong's plight, they did not want to see a massive influx of Hong Kong Chinese into the U.K., which would rile voters perhaps at the cost of some political careers. Incredibly, some of them said they were surprised by the "enormous bitterness" they encountered in Hong Kong towards the British government.

After the hearings concluded, the MPs continued on to Beijing. Chinese officials, eager to avoid anything that might disrupt the smooth transition prepared by Beijing and London, were on their best behavior. Li Hou told the MPs that Beijing would be willing to increase the pace of democratization in the Basic Law and "do whatever Hong Kong thinks is best." Zhou Nan said that China would not object to Britain's granting nationality to her subjects in Hong Kong. The MPs came away believing the situation was not as bad as people like Lee were saying.

As PART OF the second consultation on the Basic Law, delegations of mainland drafters were scheduled to visit Hong Kong in April, May, and June. The first, led by Lu Ping, arrived while the Select Committee was taking evidence in the colony.

Cheng Kai-nam had persisted in his efforts to create a moderate proposal that could bridge the gap between the business community and pro-democracy activists. After the eighth plenum in January, representatives from the ten moderate groups met every Tuesday for ten weeks to develop a comprehensive position paper that would explain their political model. On April 27, Cheng and several other moderates met Lu and Xinhua's Mao Junnian at the Consultative Committee headquarters and submitted their nineteen-page proposal on the political system. It called for the referendum to be scrapped because it would "only extend the political debate for another decade and bring about more uncertainty and instability." Instead, it proposed that an electoral college be formed through democratic elections to select the governor for the first two terms. In 2007, he would be elected by universal suffrage.

Lu told the moderates that their ideas would be considered. Cheng was not satisfied. He felt that Xu Jiatun was supporting the businesspeople and undermining the chance for a consensus. He wanted to see Lu privately, but Xinhua was handling all of the arrangements for the delegation. After the meeting, Cheng spoke to one of Lu's assistants, whom he knew well. The friend agreed, after much prodding, to set up a meeting at a restaurant on the fifth floor of Lane Crawford House.

Cheng waited in the restaurant for more than thirty minutes. Lu did not show; he felt it was not safe to meet in such a public place. A second meeting was arranged that night at the Chinese office of the Joint Liaison Group on the sixth floor of the China Resources Building in Wanchai. Cheng explained that his plan was to hold talks with the conservatives and liberals. He said he believed that a consensus could be reached. Lu seemed to like the idea. It was a way for China to extricate itself from the controversy over the political system without losing credibility. "Your proposal is acceptable in principle," he said. "Perhaps it can be modified. I can't make any promises." Cheng left encouraged.

WHILE CHENG was trying to create a role for the pro-China forces by bridging the gap between liberals and conservatives, Dunn was trying to do the same for Omelco.* She had taken over as the senior member of the Executive Council when S.Y. Chung retired in July 1988. As such, she was now the head of the body and the most influential woman in the colony. The British press called her "the Iron Lady of the East." Although Omelco had been left on the sidelines as the Basic Law Drafting Committee and the Consultative Committee determined Hong Kong's future constitution, she believed that it could seize a leading role in determining the political system by reaching its own consensus.

Dunn was born to a traditional upper-class Chinese family in 1940. Her grandfather was one of the biggest tea merchants in China. He left his native Guangdong to settle in the commercial center of Shanghai and anglicized his surname (Deng). Lydia's mother, Bessie, was the seventh daughter in a large family. One of the few Chinese girls to receive a formal education, she was said to be very beautiful and very tough. Lydia was heavily influenced by her and even adopted for a brief period her habit of wearing silky *cheongsams*.

The Dunns moved to Hong Kong when the Japanese invaded China proper. After the war, they returned to Shanghai, where Lydia got her early education. But the Communist Revolution drove them back to Hong Kong permanently. Lydia's father set up a printing company and liked to boast that he introduced offset printing to the colony. Bessie Dunn insisted that her three daughters receive the best possible education. Lydia went to a prestigious convent school in the colony before being sent to Berkeley, where she studied business administration. When she returned to Hong Kong in 1963, she joined a division of Swire, a traditional, white-male-dominated British firm, as a trainee. She worked hard, showed a flair for business, and rose rapidly to become a director in 1973 and managing director three years later. She was the first female ever to be asked to sit on the board of the colonial-minded Hong Kong Bank.

---

* In 1986, the unofficial members of the Executive and Legislative Councils changed the name of their organization from Umelco to "Omelco"—for Office of the Members of the Executive and Legislative Councils—because the term "unofficial" was misleading.

Dunn was an inveterate antique collector and became a director of Christie's auction house when it opened a branch in Hong Kong. She was driven around town in a white Cadillac, which stood out conspicuously in a city with few American cars (Hong Kong follows the British practice of driving on the left side of the street).

After being appointed to the Legislative Council in 1976, she developed a reputation among junior civil servants as being a snob. Although she often refused to take their calls, she was absolutely solicitous towards senior British officials. It was said her Oriental charm captivated them. She was not a beautiful woman. Her eyes were too far apart, her nose too flat, and she wore too much makeup. But she dressed fastidiously, spoke flawless English, and carried herself with tremendous confidence.

As well as being a savvy businessperson, she was a clever politician. Her willingness to join government committees and her loyalty to the colonial establishment won her a promotion to the Executive Council in 1982. She became the undisputed leader of a new generation of local politicians when T.S. Lo resigned from the two councils.

One person who worked closely with Dunn said that despite her Western veneer, she was a "most intensely Chinese person" who played the role of "a powerful boss who expects to exercise authority without question." In return for unquestioning obedience and loyalty, she rewarded her supporters with unfailing kindness and generosity, but she was absolutely ruthless with those who questioned her judgement.

Dunn was taking over as senior politician at a crucial time. Britain had abdicated her role of determining the future political system. The Executive Council's influence had been greatly reduced from the days of the Sino-British negotiations. Now Hong Kong people were negotiating with China on their own behalf. Omelco included members of the Group of 89 and the Joint Committee. If they could come to an agreement on the future political system, perhaps the two groups would accept it. And if the two groups accepted it, perhaps China would too.

Dunn called four special, in-house meetings in May 1989, in the colonial-style committee room of the Legislative Council building. They did not go as well as she had hoped. Most members watched passively as Lee and Szeto argued with conservatives from the Group of 89. Dunn acted as referee. At times, it was difficult just to get them to focus on the issues.

ON THE SAME day that Omelco was arguing over the political system, Soviet leader Mikhail Gorbachev arrived in China for a four-day summit. Hundreds of foreign journalists flew to Beijing to cover the visit. Two days later, they focused on a bigger story. Over a million people jammed into the center of Beijing as farmers and factory workers turned out in support of students for the biggest antigovernment demonstration since the 1949 Revolution. After Gorbachev left, events unfolded quickly. On May 19, Premier Li Peng declared martial law, and Communist Party chief Zhao Ziyang was forced to resign.

More than a million Beijing residents poured onto the streets to block the approach of 200,000 soldiers sent to quell the student protest. Factory workers, teachers, and housewives formed a human barricade in front of convoys of trucks and tanks. They pleaded for the soldiers not to open fire on the students and gave them food and cigarettes. People Power had come to China.

The next day, Typhoon Brenda slammed into the South China Coast one hundred miles southwest of Hong Kong. High winds and heavy rains battered the colony's steel-and-glass office towers, massive public housing blocks, and flimsy squatter huts. Shops and offices closed. The Saturday horse races at Happy Valley were canceled, and public transportation came to a halt. Stuck indoors, people turned on their televisions and watched as events unfolded 1,300 miles to the north in Beijing. They watched along with the rest of the world as two Chinese bureaucrats pulled the plug on Cable News Network's live satellite coverage and a curtain was drawn over the city. They feared communist hard-liners would use the military to crush the dissent.

Hong Kong's reaction was as surprising as it was swift. Pro-democracy activists rallied in support of the students. Some 50,000 people braved the typhoon that evening and gathered in Victoria Park on the north side of Hong Kong Island. Many wore yellow headbands that said "Support the Beijing Students," or t-shirts scrawled with "Long Live the Democratic Movement." At six o'clock, the demonstrators began marching through flooded streets towards the Xinhua News Agency.

The leaders of the march arrived outside the twenty-one-story building at 7:15. About 300 police officers kept the demonstrators on the far side of an iron railing that divided Queen's Road East. But as more and more people arrived, the police relented and the crowd filled both sides of the four lane street and the sidewalks for more than half a mile. They closed their umbrellas and sat on the pavement. Leaders of the march called on Chinese officials not to use violence against the students.

At about 8:30, the rain began to fall more heavily. The leaders of the march asked people to go home. About 200 protesters stayed behind. They demanded that Xu Jiatun come out to meet them. When he did not appear, the protestors stood facing the brown marble facade of the entrance to the news agency and sang the Chinese national anthem before leaving.

The following day, as the crisis in Beijing deepened, organizers in Hong Kong called another rally. One million people—almost a fifth of the colony's entire population—took part in a march through the city-center. They gathered at noon in Chater Garden, a small park squeezed between the skyscrapers of Central District. Independent minibus and taxi drivers ferried students from college campuses to the demonstration free of charge. Long derided as money-hungry and politically apathetic, the people of Hong Kong had been transformed by the spirit of the student movement in Beijing.

Even Hong Kong residents loyal to Beijing supported the student demonstrators. Members of pro-Beijing trade unions marched alongside everyone else. Xinhua employees published a letter calling for Li Peng to step down and asking each Hong Kong family to write ten letters and make ten phone calls to relatives in China to tell them the truth about the student movement. *Wen Wei Po*, a pro-communist newspaper funded by Beijing, published a stark, four-character editorial, which said: "Deep grief, bitter hatred!"

As the crowd wound its way eastward through the main thoroughfare across northern Hong Kong Island, its ranks swelled. Shoppers left department stores, store-owners closed early, and construction workers climbed down from their scaffolds to join the march. The police struggled to cope with the huge crowd as traffic came to a standstill. Most of the demonstrators were under forty. Some pushed children in strollers or carried them in harnesses on their backs. Many wore white headbands, a symbol of mourning in Chinese culture. Others carried banners that said: Li Peng step down; Long live democracy; and It is not a crime to love your country. Those too old to walk in the intense heat lined the streets and waved encouragement from overpasses. Some people draped banners from their windows or blared such patriotic songs as "Be a Brave Chinese" and "Descendants of the Dragon" from their stereos. Journalists and souvenir-seekers snapped photos from every vantage point.

On Monday, there was panic in Hong Kong's stock exchange. The market plunged almost eleven percent as local and foreign investors anticipated a bloody confrontation in Beijing. Over eight billion dollars was wiped off share prices. But the crackdown never came. Share prices bounced back nearly ten percent on Tuesday amid speculation in the local press that Li Peng would be forced to resign.

THE EVENTS IN Beijing and the massive protest in Hong Kong dramatically changed the political situation in Hong Kong. Louis Cha had sat in his living room and watched a news report on Li Peng and President Yang Shangkun's address to the nation. He decided almost immediately that he would resign from the Basic Law Drafting Committee. The next morning, he sat at his desk and drafted a brief letter explaining his decision. He sent it to Xinhua to be passed on to Ji Pengfei, chairman of the Drafting Committee, and Wan Li, chairman of the National People's Congress.

Early on Sunday, May 21, Cha issued a brief statement to the press announcing his resignation. Critics accused him of using the situation in Beijing to escape responsibility for his political model. Some of his conservative allies on the committee say he was disillusioned after having been accused unfairly of doing Beijing's bidding and was looking for a way out. Ji Pengfei wrote back to ask Cha to reconsider. The letter was delivered personally by Xu Jiatun. Cha, of course, refused. He dropped out of the public eye and was considering selling *Ming Pao* and emigrating to Canada.

Another Hong Kong drafter, Reverend Peter Kwong, had watched on Saturday morning as the Chinese leadership imposed a news blackout on Beijing. The Anglican bishop, a down-to-earth man who introduces himself simply as "Peter," was not opposed to martial law, but to the Chinese government's censorship of the news. He spent all day Sunday considering whether he should resign. Would the move do more harm than good? The Basic Law was almost finished. There was little more that he could contribute. On Monday, Kwong announced that he had resigned from the Drafting Committee, the Consultative Committee, and its nineteen-member executive board.

The same day, the Consultative Committee held a special meeting to discuss the crisis. It issued a brief statement, which said members felt "deep regret and concern" over events in China. "These events have profoundly affected our consultative efforts, and we are temporarily unable to carry out our work as planned."

Omelco met again at 9 A.M. that morning. The mood was markedly different. Most of the people sitting around the large conference table were affected deeply by the local outpouring of support for the students in Beijing. Some thought the demonstrations marked the beginning of the end of Communism in China.

Dunn opened the meeting by asking if the events in Beijing had changed the way members felt about the Basic Law and "the Joint Declaration itself." Martin Lee was greatly encouraged by the local demonstrations (which he and Szeto had led). Although people were not marching for democracy in Hong Kong, it showed they cared about political issues, about freedom and human rights. He said that in light of recent events, the pace of democratization should be increased. Half the legislature should be democratically elected in 1991 and the entire body in 1997. An appointed businessperson said that the discussion on the Basic Law should not be "influenced by emotions

254 • The Fall of Hong Kong

aroused by what was happening in China." He argued that the functional constituencies had served Hong Kong well and should not be scrapped.

Some of the other businesspeople had been moved by the demonstrations in Hong Kong and were prepared to accept a faster pace of democratization. (At one point, a member said to a Group of 89 stalwart: "My god, you sound like a liberal.") Dunn sensed that it might be possible, finally, to reach a compromise. She kept members at the negotiating table. Two days and many arguments later, most Omelco members were agreed that half of the legislature should be elected by universal suffrage and half by functional constituencies in 1997 and that the entire legislature should be elected by universal suffrage in 2003. Though held together only by Dunn's stubborn insistence, it was a consensus. Even Lee and Szeto accepted the new model.

There were still differences over the composition of the legislature in 1999. Dunn continually urged liberals and conservatives to compromise. "Only by achieving a consensus can Omelco effectively provide leadership for the community, obtain its support, and present a strong case to the Basic Law drafters," she said.

At another in-house meeting on Saturday, May 27, thirty-five members discussed the selection of the future governor. Most members had already agreed that the governor should be elected by universal suffrage in 2007. Dunn said this needed to be reconsidered because Omelco had already agreed that the entire legislature should be democratically elected in 2003. She suggested that members consult their constituents before committing themselves.

DURING THE WEEK, the real drama in Beijing was played out behind the heavy wooden gates of Zhongnanhai, the ancient compound where China's senior leaders lived and worked. The party leadership was divided over how to deal with the student movement. Hard-liners were prepared to use violence to suppress the dissent. Others favored a conciliatory approach. As the two sides argued, soldiers camped outside the city, and an eerie calm settled over Tiananmen Square.

Hong Kong watched anxiously as the stalemate continued in Beijing. On Saturday, May 27, over 150 entertainers, including most of the colony's biggest pop stars, held a twelve-hour concert to raise money for the students in Beijing. Large chrome bins were put at the entrances, and people dropped money into them as they arrived. Over $1.5 million was collected to buy food and medical supplies, bringing the total raised in Hong Kong to more than $3 million since the demonstrators first occupied Tiananmen Square in mid-April.

The next day, a second march around the city was organized and even more people turned out. As the protesters marched down the Eastern Corridor, an elevated highway along the harbor-front, the mood was buoyant, even festive. Friends held hands and snapped photos in front of the procession of colorful flags and banners. It seemed the students had won. Li Peng had been disgraced by the army's failure to carry out his orders. He would have to step down. Political reforms would have to be introduced in China. The future looked bright.

As the days slipped by without incident in Beijing, life in Hong Kong began to return to normal. Then on Sunday, June 4, people woke to learn that Chinese troops had moved into Tiananmen Square during the early hours of the morning and brutally crushed the student movement. Early reports were sketchy, but it was clear that dozens of students had been killed. Activists in Hong Kong hastily organized a gathering at the Happy Valley Race Course, the largest outdoor stadium in the urban area. By noon, the main road into the racetrack was choked with people, most dressed in white or black, the colors of mourning in the East and West. It was hot and humid. Bodies were pressed close together, forty or fifty across from the gates of the storefronts to a high cement wall of the Football Club. On the other side of the wall, British expatriates ate hamburgers and lounged by the pool.

A girl in a blue and white shirt and jeans wept openly as she read the *Tin Tin Daily News*, which reported that at least fifty-seven people had died in Beijing. A young man in a gray t-shirt shouted: "We don't recognize the Chinese government." A heavy-set man wanted "blood for blood."

As the crowd approached the entrance to the race course, a young, frail woman standing on the back of a truck shouted hoarsely into a megaphone: "Long live democracy!" and "Chinese butchers step down!" The crowd repeated her words in blind, monotonous anger. Another woman on the back of the truck implored people to give blood to the Red Cross as soon as they could.

The crowd filed orderly into the stadium, crossed the dirt track, and sat on the grass field in the center of the race course. A makeshift stage had been set up in front of the large outdoor television screen, which was normally used to broadcast replays of the horse races. Democracy activists gave speeches as an endless tide of people streamed in. When a group marched in waving the red, white, and blue Nationalist flag of Taiwan, many people cheered. Another man carried the Communist Chinese flag. But instead of the five stars on the normal red background, they were set starkly against a black backdrop.

"I will not leave Hong Kong in 1997, even if Li Peng is still premier," Szeto Wah yelled, his voice cracking with emotion. The crowded erupted into applause.

"Protect Hong Kong," he declared. "If Hong Kong collapses, no one will be left to fight for democracy."

Szeto called for a general strike on the following Wednesday for Hong Kong people to show their support for the murdered students in Beijing. As he stepped off the stage, he collapsed from heat exhaustion and was brought to a nearby Red Cross tent.

The organizers showed news footage from Beijing on the giant outdoor television. Many people could not see the tanks rumbling through the streets of Beijing, or the abandoned vehicles of the People's Liberation Army set ablaze. They could only hear the gunshots, screams, and sounds of mass confusion and panic. Many wept openly. At 3:45, the organizers broadcast over the public address system a live phone call from a local television reporter in Beijing. The reporter said 2,600 people had been killed during the night and 10,000 injured. The figures hit the crowd like a water cannon.*

A local student leader gave an emotional speech imploring people to send the news of the Beijing massacre back to China any way they could. Then Martin Lee took the stage.

"Put away your guns and your sticks," Lee said, addressing Chinese leaders. "If you kill one Chinese, one hundred will stand up for him. If you kill one hundred, one million will stand up for them."

He told the crowd that he and Szeto would not resume their work on the Basic Law until China had a regime that enjoyed the support of the people.

At 4:30, the organizers asked for a moment of silence for the dead. The only sounds were those of people crying and a helicopter buzzing overhead.

Over 200,000 people sat for five hours under an angry sun and listened to emotional speeches from other politicians, community leaders, and movie stars. At five o'clock, thousands more were still waiting to get into the stadium. The organizers had no program left, so they invited anyone to come on stage and address the crowd. Several people could barely speak because they were so overcome with emotion. Most vowed that they would not let the students in Beijing die in vain. The mood quickly turned anti-communist. One man said that since he was a boy his mother had told him not to believe anything the Communists said. She had told him about an eighteen-year-old girl in Guangzhou who was forced to stand naked on a platform in the street after the Communists seized the city in late 1949. She went home and committed suicide by drinking kerosine. His mother had seen the Communists kill a three-year-old boy because his father was a capitalist. Other people related similar stories.

After the rise of Deng, many people in Hong Kong, even those who had

---

* Later reports put the figure at no more than 200 to 300 dead.

fled the communist regime, believed that China had changed, that the brutal days of Mao Zedong were gone forever, that China's desire to prosper and modernize would force the leaders to behave in accordance with accepted international standards. The bullets that killed innocent students in Beijing shattered those illusions forever.

THE MASSACRE OF innocent protestors in Beijing threatened to undermine the smooth exchange of sovereignty over Hong Kong. It exposed the nature of the government that Hong Kong was being returned to and exposed the lie that Beijing would abide by the Joint Declaration and respect human rights because it was in its own economic interest to do so. The aging leaders had sent in the troops knowing that it would cost them billions of dollars in investment, trade, tourism, and human resources.

Lee called on Britain to renegotiate the Joint Declaration to make Hong Kong part of a Chinese confederation, independent in all but name. Other activists demanded a fully elected government by 1997. By far the loudest cries were for Britain to provide a place of refuge for her subjects.

British diplomats in the Foreign Office were horrified by events in Beijing. They knew there would be a brief period of panic in Hong Kong, and their immediate concern was to get the colony through the crisis. They were unified in their view that they could not tear up the Joint Declaration or renegotiate it. China would be in no mood to entertain new demands and would probably take back some of the promises already made. They drafted a statement for Prime Minister Thatcher, which was released on the evening of June 4: "I understand the deep anxiety presently felt by the people in Hong Kong and admire their steadfastness in the face of these latest tragic events. Britain will continue to stand by its commitment to a secure future for Hong Kong. And we are confident the Chinese government will continue to abide by their obligations under the 1984 agreement."

The statement did nothing to reassure Hong Kong. No one knew who represented the Chinese government. Beijing was in chaos. There were reports of fighting between troops loyal to different factions within the leadership and rumors that Deng was dead or dying, that Li Peng had been shot, and that the children of senior leaders had been flown to Switzerland.

On Monday, June 5, angry housewives, shop workers, and office clerks, lined up at some of the thirteen mainland-owned banks in Hong Kong to withdraw their money. Some hoped the collapse of the Chinese-owned banks would send a message to the octogenarians in Beijing. Others were afraid of losing their life savings. The Hong Kong government warned people not to withdraw their funds because it could damage the entire banking system.

Thatcher appeared in the House of Commons the following day to answer questions on her government's handling of the crisis. She expressed "utter revulsion and outrage" over the massacre in Beijing and said Britain would do everything possible to reassure the people of Hong Kong (everything except give them residency in the U.K.). The best she could offer was a promise to implement the Nationality Act with "more flexibility."

Foreign Secretary Howe announced that Britain was suspending arms sales to and high-level military contacts with China. The Foreign Office later said that discussions with China on the future of Hong Kong, including Joint Liaison Group meetings, would be suspended indefinitely. The Chinese government responded that Britain would be "held responsible for all possible consequences."

THE STUDENT MOVEMENT in Beijing unified Hong Kong's pro-democracy groups in a way that nothing else had been able to. They came together under the umbrella of the Hong Kong Alliance in Support of the Patriotic Democratic Movement of China. Most leaders of the Alliance were leaders of the Joint Committee for Democracy. People who had previously found the liberals too abrasive and aggressive suddenly joined the organization. These leaders were now viewed as the only ones capable of mobilizing the people of Hong Kong. They had been the ones to organize the massive protests under difficult conditions and with great speed.

The Alliance called for a general strike on Wednesday, June 7, to show Hong Kong's anger at the crackdown in Beijing. It planned to hold a number of rallies that day. Many schools were organizing marches and political seminars (though this was illegal), and other groups prepared to stage their own protests. Everywhere anger and rage seethed below the surface. The situation was volatile, and in the early hours of Wednesday, trouble finally erupted.

On Tuesday evening, minibus and truck drivers who were not associated with the Alliance held a slow drive down Nathan Road, the main thoroughfare through the heart of the congested Kowloon Peninsula. Cars and buses covered with pro-democracy stickers converged in the commercial and residential area of Mong Kok at seven o'clock. Protestors honked their horns and yelled anti-Beijing slogans. By midnight, traffic was paralyzed. Some people left their cars to continue the protest. They were joined by a group of youths, who threw bottles at police and yelled to passers-by that "the police are using force in Mong Kok." When the youths attacked shops, the police moved in with baton charges and teargas. The violence lasted more than four hours. Fifteen demonstrators were arrested. News footage of the clash, which was shown around the world, gave a grossly distorted image of the situation in the colony.

Alliance leaders had received anonymous phone calls and facsimile messages warning that rallies would be disrupted. They heard rumors that Beijing had sent 3,000 people to infiltrate and discredit the pro-democracy movement in Hong Kong, but thought mainland forces were trying to dissuade them from holding massive protests. After the riot in Nathan Road, they called off all activities planned for that day. The pro-democracy groups believed that maintaining law and order was paramount. During the massive demonstrations, they had had hundreds of volunteers on hand to make sure things did not get out of control. The so-called radicals had proved themselves to be incredibly level-headed.

Some businesspeople criticized the general strike, saying it had no purpose. Szeto told people to follow their consciences. Many used the occasion to show how deeply they had been affected by events in Beijing. Most shops closed. Some owners plastered slogans in support of the mainland students across their iron gates. Thousands of factory workers, clerks, and manual laborers stayed away from work. Movie theaters canceled their morning and afternoon shows. Gold dealers stopped trading for fifteen minutes, and a performance of the Spanish National Ballet was canceled because stagehands refused to work.

Thousands of people joined an impromptu march to the Xinhua News Agency. Local students had set up an altar in front of the building. At times, the line was more than a mile long as people waited patiently to pass in front of the altar, bow three times (a sign of respect for the dead), and sign a petition. Many people gave money or laid flowers and wreaths.

WITH HONG KONG facing the first real crisis of the transition, Governor Wilson left for London on the day of the strike to hold urgent discussions with Thatcher, Howe, and senior Foreign Office officials. Wilson was as horrified as anyone in Hong Kong by the bloody crackdown in Beijing, and he realized the effect it would have on Hong Kong. During the massive demonstrations in the colony, he took a private car and drove around to see them. He was aware of the great hopes people had for real change in China (though he thought them somewhat naive). Now, as he sat in the first class cabin on his way to London, he was aware that Hong Kong would be affected on two levels. There would a sense of despair, maybe even panic, but it would fade quickly. On a deeper level, people's view of China had changed, and therefore, their perception of their future under Chinese rule would be dramatically altered. The British government had to take steps to repair the damage.

Shortly after his plane touched down in London, Wilson held a rare breakfast meeting with Howe and Lord Glenarthur at the foreign secretary's official residence (Wilson hated breakfast meetings, but time was short). The governor briefed the ministers on the situation in Hong Kong. There were three obvious areas where Britain could help to restore confidence: speed up the pace of democratization, enact a bill of rights, and give Hong Kong residents a place to go in case of an emergency. He said that flexibility on the nationality question would be the best way to reassure Hong Kong. He raised several suggestions, including that all 3.3 million British subjects in Hong Kong be given the right to enter Britain, rather than British citizenship. This was rejected.

When the governor held a private meeting with Thatcher and Howe in the prime minister's study on June 9, it came down to a numbers game. How many people would have to be given the right to live in Britain to stem the brain drain and avert a crisis? At least a quarter of a million, Wilson said. Thatcher was aghast. She had run on an anti-immigration platform, and she was not about to break a political promise now. She said Britain could take 150,000, no more.

Wilson and Howe both appeared for a second time in front of the Foreign Affairs Select Committee and played "good cop/bad cop" to win back some credibility for the Hong Kong administration. Howe refused to budge on the nationality issue. When asked what the British government would do if the Chinese used the same force and brutality in Hong Kong after 1997, he said Britain would have a responsibility to take refugees from Hong Kong into Britain. This gave Hong Kong residents little assurance since, at that point, China would be controlling the exits. Wilson followed with an impassioned plea for Hong Kong people to be given the right to enter Britain and won kudos from every sector in the colony.

In BEIJING, people went about their daily routines in stunned silence as calm returned to the city. It quickly became clear that Deng Xiaoping was still in control of the country and had ordered the brutal crackdown. The Communist Party purged Zhao Ziyang's supporters and rounded up dissidents. Having had their hopes crushed, the people of Hong Kong did not just return to their money-making ways. They had supported the students, and they would continue the fight. A small group of well-organized activists set up an underground railway to spirit student leaders out of China. "Operation Yellow Bird," financed by secret donations from businesspeople in Hong Kong, was successful in getting some of the most-wanted dissidents to the West. Though no one knew about Hong Kong's role in getting the students to the West, it was the colony's finest hour. Even the triads (organized crime groups) helped by bringing the dissidents out on high-speed boats used for smuggling.

The official Chinese media launched a propaganda blitz to convince the rest of the country that there had been no massacre in Beijing and that the disturbances were caused by "counter-revolutionaries." Hong Kong people tried to counter the cover up. Those with facsimile machines sent reports of the massacre to people in China. Some risked arrest by carrying newspapers and videotapes across the border. When the Beijing authorities set up a hot line for people to report counter-revolutionaries, Hong Kong residents continuously rang the number to tie up the lines.

On June 9, Chinese state-run television said that Hong Kong and the United States had paid rioters to take part in the violence. A few days later, Chinese television showed a videotape, taken by hidden surveillance cameras, of student leader Wu'er Kaixi having an expensive dinner with Hong Kong journalists at a Beijing hotel. The authorities claimed the dinner took place while other students were on a hunger strike. China Central Television also indicated that a Hong Kong unionist, who was caught before he could pass $130,000 to students in Tiananmen Square, had engaged in subversion. (He was released after signing a confession.)

Deng's one country, two systems concept was in danger of failing before it was implemented. The two systems, which had existed side-by-side for four decades with a British buffer, were now in open conflict. In a speech congratulating soldiers on their performance during the turmoil, Deng said: "I was told a million people paraded in Hong Kong. Do not be scared. Compared to a billion people, a million is nothing."

PRESSURE ON Britain to give Hong Kong residents the right to live in the U.K. became intense. A group of businesspeople donated money to hire professionals to lobby foreign governments to take in as many Hong Kong people as they could. They planned to hire Saatchi and Saatchi, the advertising firm that had bolstered the British Conservative Party's image, to appeal to people in the U.K. to offer Hong Kong a lifeboat. T.S. Lo's new political group, the New Hong Kong Alliance, announced that it would investigate the possibility of taking legal action against the British government to restore Hong Kong people's right to live in the U.K. (China soon opposed London's plan to give some Hong Kong people British nationality and Lo quietly dropped the idea of suing London.)

Lydia Dunn and senior Legislative Councilor Allen Lee flew to London to lobby Thatcher and Howe. During their trip, they appeared on numerous radio and television programs to spread the message that Hong Kong people needed—and were entitled to—an escape route. They argued if people had a British passport, or even just the right to live in Britain, they would be enabled to remain in Hong Kong. Allen Lee pointed out that it would take three 747 jumbo jets eight years to transport all of Hong Kong's British subjects to Britain. The idea that Britain should give people the right to live in Britain so that they could stay in Hong Kong was confusing and bound to fail. When Dunn and Lee met Thatcher on June 23, all they received were tea and sympathy.

THE FOREIGN AFFAIRS Select Committee released its report on June 30, in advance of a trip to Hong Kong by Geoffrey Howe. The massacre in Beijing had made it clear in the most dramatic terms that a change of policy was needed, and the Select Committee was prepared to recommended giving the people of Hong Kong half of what they wanted. The report said that the pace of democratization should be speeded up. Half of the Legislative Council should be elected by universal suffrage in 1991 and the entire body by 1995. The first post-1997 governor should be chosen by a democratically constituted electoral college six months before the hand-over. Every governor thereafter should be chosen by universal suffrage.

The committee's proposals were not binding on the British government, and many people in Hong Kong felt that the proposal for a fully elected government had come too late. The only thing that mattered now was getting British nationality, but that was something the committee was not prepared to give. Instead, it recommended that Britain lead an international effort to provide sanctuary for Hong Kong residents in the event of a catastrophe after the transfer of sovereignty. It should grant nationality, with the right to live in Britain, to key people in the civil service, police, and other sectors of society as a way of keeping them in Hong Kong (it did not specify how many), as well as to widows of war veterans and minorities who would become stateless after 1997. An editorial in the *South China Morning Post* said the committee's report "completely evades the issue of Britain's moral responsibility."

THE PURPOSE OF Howe's visit in early July was apparently to show the people of Hong Kong that the British government was concerned about them. The people, in turn, geared up to exert maximum pressure on Howe to grant local residents the right to live in Britain. A group of businesspeople planned to air a forty-five-second commercial on the nationality question. It featured a handsome Chinese boy in a British-style school uniform with a voice-over saying: "There's no point in being almost British." The commercial was produced by a local advertising agency free of charge. And a local television station offered to run it without charge during Howe's trip. The Hong Kong government, however, banned the ad under the broadcasting code, which prohibited political or religious issues being advertised on television. To many, it seemed that the colonial administration was censoring the ad to avoid embarrassment to Howe and the British government. Reports that senior officials warned rank-and-file civil servants not to participate in rallies during the foreign secretary's trip solidified the impression.

The Alliance planned to hold a massive demonstration at the airport. Only a few hundred people showed up to jeer as Howe was driven by. Most people in Hong Kong felt they were entitled to the right to live in Britain, but saw little point in campaigning for something they were unlikely to get. It was more useful to spend the day standing in line at the American, Canadian, or Australian consulate to get an immigrant visa.

On the day Howe arrived, he was ambushed by the *South China Morning Post*, which featured a front-page story claiming that Britain would benefit from letting in Hong Kong residents. The paper commissioned a study by a team of British economists, who found that an influx from Hong Kong would fill the skills gap in the labor market, improve Britain's balance of payments by absorbing many of Hong Kong's export-oriented industries, and create "the largest housing boom the U.K. has ever seen." The economists concluded that "the economic costs are not dramatic" and that Britain could deal with even the worst-case scenario: all 3.3 million subjects arriving.

The following day, Howe gave a speech to a gathering of community leaders at the newly opened Convention and Exhibition Center, a glittering chrome and glass building designed as a showcase for Hong Kong's economic prowess. Howe admitted that only a small number of Hong Kong people would go to the U.K. "But the plain fact is that there is simply no way that a British government could grant to several million people the right to come and live in Britain." In words that rang hollow to most local Chinese, he said the nationality issue had nothing to do with race. It was simply a practical problem of an enormous scale. He did not explain why the British government had made no attempt to study the problem, or why it would not give the *Post*'s study serious consideration.

Towards the end of the speech, six liberal District Board members, led by teacher Lee Wing-tat, stood up and unfurled a large banner, which said: "Shame on the Thatcher Government—Irresponsible and Hypocritical Government." The television cameras swung around and journalists scurried for position as security men converged on the group. "Don't touch me," Lee barked. When Howe finished his speech, Lee yelled that it was "bullshit" and an "insult to the Chinese people." The group walked out yelling, "Shame! Shame!" Some guests clapped enthusiastically.

That afternoon, Howe went for a walk in the bustling Causeway Bay shopping district. The public appearance was organized to show that everything was normal in Hong Kong and that the people did not hate the British. Ringed by security men and chased by journalists, he strode confidently into the Great Wall Herbalist Store. The owner gave him almost eighty dollars worth of bird's nest for making soup. The irony of a large Chinese sign in the store's window slipped most of the British media. It said: Emigrating—Big Clearance Sale.

Before leaving for London the next day, Howe gave a brief press conference. Leaning forward and resting both elbows on the podium in the government's antiseptic press room, he read a prepared statement outlining seven measures Britain would take to help to restore confidence in Hong Kong. He was so dispassionate that he could easily have been reading the telephone directory. His proposals included alerting Britain's allies of the need for international support for Hong Kong; introducing a bill of rights; speeding up democratization; and ensuring that the Basic Law conformed to the Joint Declaration. He said that Britain would introduce a flexible nationality package that would allow certain categories of Hong Kong people to qualify for the right to live in Britain, but would not reveal any details about the scheme.

There was little that Howe could say to satisfy the journalists. Britain had committed itself to handing six million people over to a murderous regime. There was no going back. He admitted candidly that Britain could not force China to stick to the Joint Declaration.

During a debate in the House of Commons after Howe returned to London, MPs reaffirmed that they were not in favor of granting Hong Kong people the right to live in Britain. Their message: It was up to China to restore confidence in Hong Kong.

Chapter 22

"A Matter of Honor"

D URING THE lead-up to the massacre, the people of Hong Kong were focused almost entirely on events in Beijing. Now they returned to thoughts about their own future. Thousands lined up outside foreign consulates to apply for immigrant visas. The number of applications handed out by the Australian consulate rose from fifty a day before June 4 to 1,000 after. At Exchange Square, twin, sleek skyscrapers on the harbor-front, the landlord had to draft a freight elevator into service to cope with the crush of people trying to get into the Canadian Commission on the eleventh floor.

On July 10, the Singapore commissioner in Hong Kong announced that his country intended to broaden immigration to take in 25,000 Hong Kong people and their families over five to eight years. The scheme would allow in blue-collar workers, technicians, craftsmen, skilled laborers, and office clerks. A quasi-government company that handled immigration requests for the commission set up a booth in a major shopping center to hand out visa applications. People began lining up outside at 3 A.M. the day after the announcement was made. Within an hour of opening, the booth handed out over 12,000 applications. Suddenly, it started to rain. Those still lined up outside surged forward, and the booth was trampled. The police moved in to restore order, but hundreds of people ignored calls for them to leave. Many jammed into the upstairs office of the commission itself. The crowd dispersed when signs were posted informing people that they would have to write in to receive application forms. Within a week, the company received 30,000 letters.

The nature of the emigration problem had changed. Previously, people were interested in leaving Hong Kong only if they could go to the United States, Canada, or Australia. In the panic that followed the crackdown in Beijing, people looked for any exit. The tiny Central American nation of Belize (formerly British Honduras), which offered passports for $23,800 with no residency requirement, saw a surge in enquiries. It was later revealed that the Panamanian consulate, which was run by a relative of General Manuel

Noriega, had sold some 3,000 passports illegally to panicked residents. Countries such as Jamaica, Tonga, and Gambia were now being considered in the desperate scramble for foreign passports. The *South China Morning Post* published a chart detailing the requirements for obtaining residency in forty different countries.

Everyone was talking emigration, at work, over *yum cha*, and between games of squash. Executives who once traded investment tips now prided themselves on being up on the latest escape route—from the Marshall Islands (which was freely associated with the United States and could lead to residency there) to American Indian reservations.

Thousands of residents applied for British Dependent Territory Citizen passports in case London gave all its subjects in Hong Kong the right to live in the U.K. Each night, several hundred people camped outside the Immigration Department's golden office tower in the tourist area of Tsim Sha Tsui to make the daily quota of 530 applications. The department also handled one hundred applications a day by appointment. The quota was soon filled until the following March.

The frenzied push for passports was an overreaction in a city known for overreacting. The lines outside the consulates would soon grow shorter. But the world now knew Hong Kong people were looking for a way out. In the months following the crackdown in Beijing, representatives from South Africa, Paraguay, Guam, Curacao, and half a dozen other countries arrived in Hong Kong to offer residents the chance to exchange their money for a second passport.

Businesses redoubled their efforts to cash in on people's fears. An exhibition of Canadian property attracted 20,000 visitors. One seminar was so popular that Xinhua complained it was damaging to Hong Kong's stability and prosperity. Travel companies organized investment tours to Australia and Canada. Banks set up personal banking departments to cater to rich Hong Kong residents who wanted to invest overseas. Dozens of companies launched immigration-linked funds.

Head-hunters descended on Hong Kong like vultures. Each week, there were articles about another sector being stripped of its talent. SINGAPORE HAS FORMULA TO LURE LOCAL CHEMISTS, said a typical headline. Already suffering from low pay, atrocious working conditions, and poor prospects for promotion, nursing was one of the hardest hit professions. Hospitals from Singapore, the United Kingdom, and the United States recruited hundreds of nurses from Hong Kong between July and December. As an added incentive, most offered to help successful applicants to obtain residency.

Surveys conducted in the months following the Beijing massacre revealed that the emigration problem could spiral out of control: sixty percent of lawyers, seventy-five percent of pharmacists, eighty percent of accountants, eighty-five percent of property surveyors, and ninety-nine percent of government doctors intended to leave before the transfer of sovereignty. Many had applied to leave even before the upheaval and said they would not stay in Hong Kong even if China became more democratic. It looked as though Hong Kong might become a ghost town by 1997.

ON THE SAME day that the Singapore commissioner announced changes to his country's immigration policy, Xu Jiatun and members of the Basic Law Consultative Committee met Ji Pengfei in Beijing. There had been calls in Hong Kong and London for China to delay passage of the Basic Law so that it could be improved further. The Chinese government resolved that there would be no delay and that Hong Kong would not be given more democracy and greater protection of human rights because of the June 4 crackdown. Ji told the delegation that it could extend the consultation period to the end of October, but the Basic Law would be promulgated in 1990 as planned.

When the delegation returned to Hong Kong, Xu called a meeting of the Hong Kong Basic Law drafters. All were invited except Louis Cha and Reverend Peter Kwong, who had resigned, and Martin Lee and Szeto Wah, who had suspended their work. Twelve of the remaining eighteen Hong Kong drafters attended the meeting at the Xinhua headquarters on July 15. Xu explained that promulgation of the Basic Law could not be postponed. Several Hong Kong members wanted to delay the final plenum and hold more subgroup meetings, so that the draft could be revised in light of recent events. Former Legislative Councilor Rayson Huang was the strongest proponent of this view. He had been the head of the Hong Kong University and was outraged by the massacre of students in Beijing. He lost his fear of the mainland drafters and argued strongly that the final plenum should be delayed. "You cannot pretend that June 4 didn't happen," he said. "You cannot pretend that the atmosphere has not changed."

Some of Huang's colleagues felt that delaying the plenum might do more harm than good. China might take back some of the concessions it had made in the Basic Law. In the end, the drafters agreed to delay the last plenum and allow the subgroups to hold up to three more meetings. The public consultation resumed on July 20, after a forty-three-day suspension. The subgroups of the Drafting Committee would meet in December and January to revise the draft before the final plenum in February. The political factions had until then to reach a consensus.

ON JULY 24, the British government announced a major cabinet reshuffle. Thatcher removed Howe as foreign secretary because of differences over Britain's policy towards the European Community and gave him the largely symbolic post of deputy prime minister. She chose her treasury secretary, John Major, to replace him. Although few in Hong Kong were sad to see Howe go after his recent performance in the colony, there was some concern about Major's lack of experience; he was just forty-six years old and had never held such an important post. Lord Glenarthur also resigned as minister of state at the Foreign Office. Francis Maude, a thirty-six-year-old lawyer and up-and-coming Conservative MP, became the fifth minister handling Hong Kong affairs in seven years.

Three months later, Major would be replaced by Douglas Hurd, the fifty-nine-year-old home secretary who had held the Tory line on immigration from Hong Kong. Unlike Major, Hurd had real experience in international diplomacy. After graduating from Cambridge, he joined the Foreign Service and was posted to Beijing. He served in the United Nations and in Rome before leaving the Foreign Office in 1966 for a career in politics. He published a scholarly work on the second Opium War, which led to the cession of Kowloon, and several thriller novels, including one about the last days of colonial rule in Hong Kong. Hurd's skill would be tested almost immediately. A major battle was looming again over the pace of democratization in Hong Kong. The Executive Council was demanding that more democratically elected seats be introduced in 1991 to boost confidence. Chinese officials were insisting that the pace of reform should not be increased because of the Tiananmen incident.

Like everyone else in Hong Kong, Lydia Dunn was deeply affected by the massacre in Beijing. She had gone along with the British government's decision not to introduce elections in 1988 against China's will, and now she regretted it. Appeasement had achieved nothing. It was time to stand firm. Hong Kong was united in its demands for greater representation. The Omelco consensus paved the way for the Hong Kong government to introduce more seats in 1991. She was supported by David Ford. Even Governor Wilson realized that the situation had changed.

Omelco had considered the composition of the legislature only in 1997 and beyond. Dunn called an in-house meeting at 6 P.M. on Wednesday, July 26, to discuss the changes that should be introduced in 1991 and 1995. If members could reach an agreement, she could use this to pressure the Hong Kong and British governments into introducing more democratically elected members.

Thirty-two of the forty-nine unofficial members of the two councils attended the meeting in the Legislative Council building. One conservative member opened the discussion by proposing that the legislature be expanded to sixty members and twenty each be returned by universal suffrage, functional constituencies, and appointment in 1991. Martin Lee, always eager to push for the greatest level of representation (and to assume the strongest bargaining position), said he supported the proposal made by the Foreign Affairs Select Committee, which called for half of the legislature to be democratically elected in 1991 and the entire legislature in 1995. Another member who represented the colony's social workers said he agreed that a third of members should be returned by universal suffrage in 1991, but said that two-thirds should be democratically elected in 1995, instead of half, as stipulated in the original Omelco consensus.

The discussion quickly degenerated into a shouting match between Lee and Szeto and two members of the Group of 89. Dunn struggled to maintain order. One businessman claimed that people did not have much confidence in the effectiveness of a fully elected legislature. Another said the Group of 89 had already compromised by allowing half of the legislature to be elected by universal suffrage in 1997.

"People in Hong Kong have lost confidence after June 4," said Martin Lee. "They feel that full democracy should be introduced before 1997. The liberals will no longer accept Omelco's earlier consensus. But I am prepared to accept a third of all legislators returned by universal suffrage in 1991 and two-thirds in 1995."

Dunn said there was broad agreement that a third of the legislature should be elected by universal suffrage in 1991. Two views had emerged regarding 1995: A majority wanted half of the members returned by universal suffrage. Lee, Szeto, and other liberal members were demanding that two-thirds be democratically elected.

"I urge you to put aside your personal views and try to reach a consensus," Dunn pleaded.

Lee realized that it was time to compromise. Twenty democratically elected seats in 1991 was a significant improvement over the ten originally planned by the Hong Kong government. Half in 1995 was what the Joint Committee had always pushed for. If he could strike a deal now, perhaps the Hong Kong government would introduce more seats, and China would be forced to accept a faster pace of reform. He said that for the purpose of reaching a consensus, he would accept "no less than half" of seats being democratically elected in 1995. The Group of 89 members objected vehemently, saying they had already compromised when they agreed to "no more than half" in 1995. Others felt Lee's wording could accommodate the views of all members. At that point, Lee and one of the most conservative businesspeople left to attend dinner engagements.

Dunn proposed that members accept Lee's compromise: twenty members would be returned by universal suffrage in 1991 and "no less than half" in 1995. All of the remaining thirty members supported her motion. When the acrid meeting broke up at 8:30, Dunn remained seated at the large conference table. As the others filed out, she broke down and cried.

OMELCO HAD laid out reforms in Hong Kong up to and beyond 1997. It was a major breakthrough. But Beijing would have none of it. Li Hou and Lu Ping saw it as a British plot to pressure China into allowing a faster pace of reform. They insisted that the Basic Law Drafting Committee would not even consider the Omelco consensus. Omelco members, including Basic Law drafter Maria Tam, abandoned it like a sinking ship.

Moderate leader Cheng Kai-nam knew that the Chinese government would be in no mood to make concessions to Hong Kong. It had lost credibility and all the good will it had built up since Deng came to power. Cheng believed, however, that if he could recover the initiative lost because of the events in Beijing, perhaps he could still unite Hong Kong behind a political model, and perhaps, just perhaps, Beijing would feel compelled to accept it. It was a long shot, but he had to try.

As a leftist, Cheng was in a difficult position. During the demonstrations in Beijing, he openly supported the students, which meant that he opposed the Chinese government. He had searched his heart and decided that he loved China more than he loved the Communist Party. He believed that the students were patriotic and had the best interests of the motherland at heart. His Federation of Education Workers joined the Hong Kong Alliance, and he became a member of the executive committee. He even took $65,000 in donations to the students in Beijing before the crackdown. Now, he was considered "a deviant" within leftist circles. Beijing had branded the Hong Kong Alliance a counterrevolutionary organization. He had to proceed cautiously. Any overt attempts to unify political groups in Hong Kong would anger Beijing.

Cheng pulled his Federation of Education Workers out of the Alliance and adopted a more conciliatory stance towards the Chinese government. It was the only way he would be able to play a role in breaking the deadlock over the future political system. Then he called Vincent Lo.

"The three major political groups in Hong Kong must reach a consensus," he said. "That is the only way we can help to restore people's confidence in Hong Kong. Are you interested in holding a dialogue with us and the liberals?"

Lo said he was. He was deeply disturbed by the massacre of innocent students. He realized that Chinese leaders really were *Communists*, that they were more concerned about maintaining their hold on power than in doing what was best for the country. Hong Kong needed to be protected from these people.* Lo was also greatly impressed by the peaceful and orderly demonstrations in Hong Kong. If people here were willing to become so active in politics, maybe the time was right to speed up the pace of democratization. He told Cheng that he would approach members of his group to see if they were ready to resume the dialogue.

Cheng and Lo met privately at Lo's office several times in late July and early August to work out a compromise proposal. The press was kept in the dark because if it knew the two were talking, their ability to compromise would be restricted. They came up with a model that called for forty percent of the legislature to be returned by universal suffrage in 1997, forty percent by functional groups, and twenty percent by an electoral college. This was eventually dubbed the 4-4-2 model. Each thought they could sell it to their own group. The problem was how to approach the pro-democracy camp. Lee and Szeto were under heavy pressure because of their activities during the crisis in Beijing. A *People's Daily* editorial accused them, without naming them directly, of being counter-revolutionaries. (Lee, in particular, had infuriated Beijing by appearing before a U.S. Congressional committee to request that America impose sanctions on China. He equated handing over Hong Kong people to China to handing over six million Jews to Hitler during World War II.) China would never accept a model drafted with the help of counterrevolutionaries. Moreover, the crackdown in Beijing and the massive demonstrations in Hong Kong might have made the liberals even more determined to fight for the most democratic political model possible.

One of Cheng's colleagues approached a friend who was among the more moderate members of the Joint Committee to see if he wanted to resume the dialogue. He did, and he met secretly with Cheng and Lo several times. It was imperative that his colleagues not find out since he was acting without permission from the Joint Committee. He liked the 4-4-2 model and thought the Joint Committee might accept it. "You should test the water step by step," he said.

In mid-August, Cheng contacted the Joint Committee directly to see if it wanted to resume the dialogue. Lee was strongly opposed to compromising with the other groups. Omelco had already reached an acceptable consensus. The Foreign Affairs Select Committee had put pressure on the British government to speed up the pace of reform. It was stupid to compromise now. At

* I interviewed Lo at this time and pointed out to him that this is what Martin Lee had been saying all along. "That's true," he said sheepishly, "but we didn't like the way he was saying it."

one point, he even threatened to pull out of the Joint Committee if it did compromise. (Lee was not above throwing his weight around in private if he thought it was in the best interests of Hong Kong.) Some of the younger liberals disagreed. They felt that they had to try to reach a compromise. Otherwise, Beijing would draft its own conservative model and justify forcing it on Hong Kong since local factions could not reach a consensus. They did not want to go down in history as the people who had prevented Hong Kong from having a more democratic government. Eventually, they prevailed. Several secret meetings were held at Lo's office to work out the details of the 4-4-2 model.

Everything was going well until August 29. On that day, T.S. Lo threatened to undermine the chance of reaching a consensus when his New Hong Kong Alliance proposed a novel political blueprint featuring a bicameral legislature. Lo probably knew that the three main political groups were meeting secretly (he was also a member of the Group of 89).

Lo was concerned about the situation in Hong Kong in the wake of the Beijing massacre. If there were democratic elections, the pro-democracy camp would likely sweep most of the seats. There was a possibility that they might pass anti-China legislation, or even promote independence. Since Beijing would step in to prevent this, such a scenario had to be avoided. For this reason (and perhaps to undermine any consensus), Lo devised a clever scheme to check the power of the liberals. The Legislative Council would be replaced by a two-house Legislative Assembly (a name with no colonial overtones, which would appeal to the Chinese government). The Functional House would be composed of representatives from business and professional groups. Half of the Elected House would be returned indirectly by members of the District Boards and the two municipal councils, the other half by universal suffrage. Lo figured that the Elected House would likely be dominated by the liberals and the Functional House by conservatives. Each would have to pass a bill separately before it could become law. Thus, the conservatives could block any radical proposal introduced by the liberals and vice versa.

Under Lo's scheme, the governor would be returned by an electoral college until at least 2003. He offered no timetable for when more legislators might be chosen by universal suffrage. Rather, he suggested that this be left for Hong Kong people to decide at a later date. Obviously, the conservatives could block any legislation aimed at making the political system more democratic.

Lo showed his proposal to Xu Jiatun. Xu liked it and arranged for Lo to see Ji Pengfei and key mainland Basic Law drafters in Beijing. Ji said it was worth considering.

The bicameral proposal was rejected by all of the major political groups. Vincent Lo felt T.S. Lo was setting himself up as Beijing's man in Hong Kong and proposing the model to further his own political ambitions. Martin Lee claimed the proposal was divisive, elitist, and undemocratic. Legislative Councilors called it clumsy and alien to Hong Kong. The press heaped scorn on it, pointing out that a few thousand lawyers would have the same representation as 400,000 residents of the New Territories. Even organizations with functional representatives in the Legislative Council, the bodies who would benefit most from the system, opposed it because it was not democratic enough.

Lo's proposal put a great deal of pressure on the three main political factions. If they did not reach a compromise, Beijing would almost certainly force the bicameral model on Hong Kong. To counter T.S. Lo, leaders of the three political factions leaked word that they were about to reach a compromise on the future political system. In mid-September, representatives met openly for the first time on neutral ground—the World Trade Center, a skyscraper in the Causeway Bay shopping district. Szeto Wah joined three younger liberals for the first meeting. "Don't come here," Vincent Lo told him. "You'll ruin everything."

Lo argued that Szeto should not be there to meet the press at the end of the meeting. If Chinese officials saw that he was involved, they would never accept the consensus. He left early and did not return for any more meetings. (Szeto and Martin Lee remained part of the negotiating team and were involved with deciding positions and tactics before each meeting.)

The three groups were very close to reaching a consensus. They held several more meetings to put the finishing touches on the model. The moderates wanted to build in a level of flexibility so that Lu Ping could accept the proposal without appearing to be caving in to pressure from Hong Kong. When that was settled in an annex, the representatives went back to their groups to lobby support for the proposal. The liberal camp was split. Lee was against it, and Szeto was unenthusiastic. Several groups in the Joint Committee agreed that the proposal was too conservative. The three liberals who had negotiated with the other factions argued that there had to be a consensus, that the people of Hong Kong had to be united or all would be lost. Some accused them of being soft. In the end, the Joint Committee backed the 4-4-2 model. Lee and Szeto agreed to support either the 4-4-2 or the Omelco consensus, whichever the people of Hong Kong preferred.

BEIJING had become the pariah of the international community after the June 4 crackdown. The U.S. and most European countries suspended high level contacts. The British government was pushing for improvements to the Basic Law. Chinese leaders were backed into a corner, and they responded to the diplomatic pressure the same way they had to the pressure from students in Tiananmen Square: with aggression. Xu Jiatun was summoned to the capital, and in a meeting marked by anti-Western rhetoric, he was told that the Chinese government would not compromise with London or the Hong Kong Basic Law drafters because of the June 4 incident. Any changes in policy had to be based on China's long-term strategic interests. Beijing knew it had lost all credibility with Hong Kong residents. Short of sacrificing Li Peng and bringing back Zhao Ziyang, there was nothing it could do to regain support. There was nothing left to lose by playing hardball.

When Xu returned to Hong Kong, he adopted a hard line on the pace of democratization. His future was under a cloud for allowing leftists to join the demonstrations in Hong Kong. He worked zealously, as though trying to hang on to his job. He went against the advice of his subordinates and threw his weight behind T.S. Lo's bicameral model. In early September, before the three factions went public, Xu invited Cheng Kai-nam and other leading moderates to Xinhua to push the bicameral model. Cheng rejected it and pointed out that no other political group supported it.

"I am not afraid," Xu said. "No matter how many people come out against this proposal, I will insist on it being adopted."

Cheng took out a slip of paper from his pocket. It contained the essential elements of the 4-4-2 proposal. Xu removed his spectacles and read it carefully.

"Forget it," he said. "It cannot be accepted."

"Why not?"

"I will push for the bicameral model," Xu said. "I don't care about the cost."

"Okay," Cheng said. "You do what you have to do, and we will do what we have to do."

Xu was worried that China would be forced to accept the 4-4-2 model. Li Hou and Lu Ping had promised repeatedly that they would accept any consensus reached in Hong Kong. Now, the three main groups were close to reaching a consensus, one Xu could not accept. He dispatched his deputies to lean on Cheng.

"If you insist on the 4-4-2 model, then you are organizing all the forces in Hong Kong, including the British, to oppose the Chinese government," one warned him.

When Hong Kong government officials leaked word that they intended to introduce twenty democratically elected seats in 1991 in accordance with the Omelco consensus, they gave Xu added ammunition. China had rejected the Omelco proposal. The 4-4-2 model would strengthen Britain's hand. Xu pressured Vincent Lo, Cheng Kai-nam, and members of their groups to drop the 4-4-2 proposal on patriotic grounds. "This is between Britain and China," he told them. "If you present this model, you will be helping Britain."

Lo and the others said they did not want to help Britain, but they refused to abandon the proposal. The consultation period was almost over. There would be no other opportunity to fight for Hong Kong's interests. Xu was able to persuade the pro-Beijing Federation of Trade Unions and two other groups to pull out of the moderate alliance. But he failed to split the consensus.

By late September, members of the three main political factions had approved the 4-4-2 model. Leaders of the groups planned to hold a press conference on September 30 to unveil their compromise proposal. A few days beforehand, one of Cheng Kai-nam's friends at Xinhua told him that if he attended, he should sit off to one side so that he would not appear on television. If he was seen to be publicly opposing Xu, it would destroy Cheng's career. After talking to a friend, Cheng decided that most of the work was done. There was no point risking his future. He did not attend the last three meetings to finalize the 4-4-2 proposal, or the press conference.

Having failed to prevent the 4-4-2 model from being made public, Xu floated the idea that it was another, more surreptitious attempt by the British to put forward a model and pressure China into accepting a faster pace of democratization.

Xu Jiatun was well aware that the moderates were the driving force behind the proposal and that work on it had started before T.S. Lo introduced his bicameral model. He hid these facts from Li Hou and Lu Ping because he wanted to push through the bicameral model. Lu was not unaware of what Xu was doing. He contacted the moderates directly, and let them know that he was sympathetic to their efforts. From then on, the moderates tried to work with Lu to give him a way out without supporting the bicameral model.

THE BASIC LAW Consultative Committee received only 6,522 submissions before the October 30 deadline. One did not have to look hard to find the reason for the apathy. A professional opinion poll conducted in late October found that seven out of ten people had no confidence that China would stick to the Basic Law, uphold the rights of individuals, or protect Hong Kong's separate economic system for fifty years after 1997.

On the day the public consultation ended, Martin Lee and Szeto Wah were expelled from the Basic Law Drafting Committee because, a Chinese government spokesperson said, their words and deeds contradicted their roles as drafters. The future of democracy in Hong Kong was looking truly bleak.

As the Basic Law drafters prepared for subgroup meetings in Guangzhou in December, Hong Kong was on edge. The crackdown was still fresh in people's minds. They were waiting for Britain to announce details of the nationality package, and the five-year battle over the shape of the future government was coming to a head. Political groups lobbied intensely for their respective models.

Behind the scenes, Lydia Dunn pushed the Hong Kong government to introduce the Omelco consensus. The Foreign Office in London was resisting because Beijing would simply scrap the political set-up after 1997 and institute something of its own design. Suddenly, the issue of convergence leapt back into the headlines. In 1988, Britain had played the liberals against the "unholy alliance" to avoid a confrontation with Beijing. Now, conservatives, moderates, and liberals were united in their demand for a faster pace of democratization. If London did not bow to the will of the people, it would look bad at home and abroad.

Percy Cradock did not believe that a fully democratic government would solve Hong Kong's problems, and he knew that Beijing would be in no mood to tolerate further democratic reforms. Implementing the Omelco consensus would end any chance of a smooth transition. With another major diplomatic storm looming on the horizon, he convinced Prime Minister Thatcher to allow him to make a secret trip to Beijing to reestablish contacts with the Chinese government and to try to avoid a confrontation over the pace of democratization. He arrived in Beijing in early December. (A few days later, President Bush sent his national security adviser, Brent Scowcroft, to Beijing, which caused an uproar in Congress when it was revealed.) During his three-day mission, Cradock pushed for concessions that would satisfy the people of Hong Kong.

Zhou Nan stuck to China's original position that reform should not be speeded up because of the June 4 incident. "You will have trouble if you go down this road," he said.

Cradock made no headway. Zhou agreed that the two sides should continue to discuss the issue. Cradock hoped that the pace of reform could be increased, and that a compromise could be struck, so that there would be no jolt when Hong Kong crossed the 1997 threshold.

THE WEATHER WAS unseasonably fine as the Hong Kong Basic Law drafters in the relationship subgroup arrived in Guangzhou on December 10 for their last meeting. The mood at the posh Garden Hotel was decidedly tense. Guards were stationed on their floor and outside the conference room while meetings were being held. Without Martin Lee at the table, debate was less strident, but mainland drafters were more rigid. The Hong Kong members once won concessions by arguing that a provision would damage confidence in the colony. Now there was no confidence left, so Beijing had nothing to lose. Chinese drafters intended to introduce clauses in the Basic Law to protect Beijing from outside interference and to counter confidence-boosting measures proposed by Britain.

Li Hou and Lu Ping used their ten-to-six majority to push through a new clause requiring the Hong Kong legislature to pass laws prohibiting acts of subversion against the central government. After 1997, there would be no demonstrations in Hong Kong calling for the ouster of the Communist Party. The mainland drafters also added a clause prohibiting "political activities of foreign political organizations and groups in Hong Kong, or local political groups from establishing links with foreign political organizations or groups." The dissidents who fled China had set up an organization aimed at eventually establishing a more liberal regime in Beijing. This clause would prevent them from using Hong Kong as a base after the exchange of sovereignty. The Hong Kong drafters were helpless to prevent these measures from being introduced.

The political subgroup met at the same hotel under similar conditions on December 14. Members were not expecting to finalize a political blueprint, but were hoping to lay the ground work for a consensus at the following meeting scheduled for mid-January. The first order of business, however, was to elect a new Hong Kong convener to replace Louis Cha. The Chinese officials on the Drafting Committee had learned not to make unilateral decisions. They informed Dr. Raymond Wu, representative of the medical community and member of the Group of 89, that he was being considered for the position and consulted other Hong Kong drafters and even Consultative Committee members. On the first morning, a mainland drafter formally recommended Wu for the position, and he was elected by a show of hands.

Wu was not sure that he would be voted in, but prepared material for the meeting just in case. He knew that the mainland drafters would refuse to discuss the Omelco consensus or the 4-2-2 model. He tried to get around the problem by drawing up a chart, which listed the essential elements of a political model across the top and the details of each of the major proposals without naming them down the side. He hoped the drafters could discuss the pros and cons of each element and come to a successful conclusion. (By not having his name attached to a proposal, he also hoped to avoid the problems Louis Cha encountered.)

The drafters quickly agreed that the legislature would consist of sixty seats and that its members would initially be returned by universal suffrage, functional constituencies, and an electoral college. They could not agree on percentages. Executive Councilor Maria Tam raised the 4-4-2 model. The mainlanders refused to discuss it. Li Hou and Lu Ping had always refrained from forcing Beijing's views on the committee, but now they wanted to block the Hong Kong government's attempt to introduce twenty democratically elected seats in 1991. They suggested that only thirty percent of the legislature, or eighteen seats, be returned by universal suffrage in 1997. This set up the confrontation that Percy Cradock had feared.

Li and Lu also scrapped the referendum. Instead, they took a page out of Britain's book and said a review would be held in 2007 to determine any future changes to the composition of the legislature and the method of selecting the governor. Any changes to the system would have to be approved by two-thirds of the legislature, the governor, and the Standing Committee of China's National People's Congress. If this proposal was adopted, it was likely that Hong Kong would never have a fully elected government. People were already afraid to oppose China on elections when Britain was running the colony. Who was going to do so after 1997?

Later in the week, the rights and obligations subgroup adopted a clause that said no law could be given status above other laws in Hong Kong, effectively castrating the bill of rights proposed by Geoffrey Howe. China was playing hardball, and she was winning.

AT MIDNIGHT ON December 20, British officials in London unveiled a nationality package that would grant passports to 50,000 heads of households in Hong Kong and their dependents. They said that a total of up to 225,000 Hong Kong people would get the right to live in the U.K. under the scheme. Because of persistent rumors that Thatcher had put a ceiling of 150,000 on immigrants from Hong Kong, the press in the colony described the package as "unexpectedly generous." (About a year later, a Hong Kong academic figured out that 50,000 households would probably include no more than 160,000 people, close to Thatcher's original limit. Hong Kong and British government sources admitted that the 225,000 figure was exaggerated.)

Announcing the package, Foreign Secretary Douglas Hurd explained that it would be based on a point system and be administered in Hong Kong. It would favor the private sector over civil servants (no doubt to ease China's concerns that Britain would use nationality to manipulate the future government), but special consideration would be given to those who worked in sensitive government positions, which would make them vulnerable after 1997.

"It's not just our duty to look after Hong Kong—it's a matter of honor," Hurd told the Commons. "It is also in our national interest." He added that Hong Kong was "the last main chapter of the country's empire" and it "should not end in a shabby way."

Although Zhou Nan had told members of the British Foreign Affairs Select Committee that China would not oppose a nationality package, the Chinese Foreign Ministry released a statement on December 30, condemning the scheme. It said that the proposal was "a gross violation of [Britain's] own solemn commitment" made under the Joint Declaration and called on London to "change its mistaken practice. Otherwise, it will have to bear a series of consequences arising therefrom."

British officials insisted that the package would be implemented despite objections from Beijing. Equally encouraging were reports in British newspapers that Foreign Secretary Hurd was going to stand tough and dramatically increase the pace of democratization in Hong Kong. It seemed that Britain had finally found the courage to stand up to China.

Chapter 23

"A Shameful Act of Surrender"

O N NEW YEAR'S Day, 1990, people began congregating at 1:30 P.M. in Chater Garden in Central District for a protest march organized by the Hong Kong Alliance. The demonstrators were buoyed by the collapse of the Berlin Wall and the fall of Communism in eastern Europe. The small park became festooned with colorful homemade banners declaring: Today's Romania, Tomorrow's China and We love China, Not Communism. More than 10,000 people marched for ninety minutes to the Xinhua building in Happy Valley, chanting: "Down with the Deng-Li-Yang clique," "Put an end to one-party totalitarian rule," and "Release all pro-democracy activists." Some protesters called for the downfall of the Communist Party, though Alliance leaders avoided such statements. Outside Xinhua, Alliance spokesperson Cheung Man-kwong told the crowd: "We will come back again and again until the Deng-Li-Yang clique steps down. There will be the day when we will come back to Tiananmen Square. There will be the day when we will no longer hoist the black flag, but the red one."

Vincent Lo and other businesspeople worried that such demonstrations would only worsen relations with China and cause more instability. When asked about this, Szeto Wah responded: "If it's a tiger, it will eat men regardless of whether or not you irritate it." (Lo was later subjected to a torrent of abuse when he suggested that the Alliance should disband to help to restore good relations with China.)

CRADOCK'S TRIP to Beijing in December paved the way for Governor Wilson to hold further talks with Chinese officials in mid-January 1990. The Hong Kong press reported that Xu Jiatun flew to Beijing to brief Chinese officials personally before the visit. Xu was, in fact, called to Beijing to be informed that he was being replaced as China's chief representative in Hong Kong. He was now over seventy years old, and there had long been speculation that Beijing was looking for a successor, but no one of suitable stature and finesse had been found. Events in Hong Kong in May and June 1989 had changed the situation dramatically. Out of favor, Xu was now held responsible for the maladministration of and corruption within hundreds of mainland-owned companies in the colony. He owed his allegiance to the reformist faction within the leadership and had personally given the okay for leftists to join the marches in Hong Kong.

On January 11, 1990, Hong Kong newspapers reported that Vice-Foreign Minister Zhou Nan would replace Xu as director of Xinhua in Hong Kong. The news was greeted with dismay, particularly by the British diplomats who had sat opposite Zhou at the negotiating table. Zhou would vigorously defend China's interests in Hong Kong.

As Wilson prepared for his trip, his aides leaked word that he planned to adopt a tough stance and tell the Chinese government that if the pace of reform was not speeded up, it could lead to unrest in Hong Kong. Martin Lee was encouraged.

During a photo call before a meeting with officials from the Hong Kong and Macao Affairs Office, Li Hou set the tone when he rebuked Wilson indirectly for allowing anti-China demonstrations on New Year's Day. "Last month, I told a delegation of journalists that the rain has stopped, but the sky has yet to become clear," Li said, returning to the weather analogies of the Sino-British negotiations. "But recently some people were creating wind and rain."

The governor responded that Li needed to "distinguish between a small shower of rain and a typhoon."

During the three-hour meeting, Wilson emphasized that Britain was committed to the Lo Wu solution. Legislators elected before 1997 had to continue serving after the exchange of sovereignty to ensure a smooth transition. But the situation in Hong Kong had changed. People were pressing for a faster pace of political reform. Executive and Legislative Councilors had reached a consensus and so had the three largest political factions within the colony. He said the Hong Kong government wanted to introduce twenty democratically elected seats in 1991 and thirty in 1995 in accordance with the Omelco consensus.

Li Hou insisted that the pace was far too fast and that the Chinese government could not even consider the Omelco model. China was prepared to accept twenty legislators returned by universal suffrage in 1997, thirty by functional groups, and ten by an electoral college. This was a slight concession on the eighteen democratically elected seats proposed by the political subgroup. Wilson did not reject the offer. He said he would discuss it with his superiors.

FOREIGN SECRETARY Douglas Hurd arrived in Hong Kong on Saturday, January 13, promising that a decision on the number of democratically elected seats to be introduced in 1991 would be made "within weeks." Some observers were surprised. The statement seemed to indicate that an announcement would be made before the promulgation of the Basic Law in March.

"We are not going to sit back passively as the British government and let the clock tick on until 1997," Hurd declared.

Over the weekend, he met Governor Wilson, Alan Donald, who had finally been made British ambassador to China, and other senior Hong Kong and Foreign Office officials at Wilson's sprawling country house in the New Territories. The atmosphere was supposed to be less formal than at Government House, but everyone there knew it was a crucial meeting. Wilson and Donald briefed Hurd on the situation in Hong Kong and China respectively. They said that the Chinese government was paranoid about subversive elements in Hong Kong and deeply suspicious of recent political developments. Wilson raised China's offer of twenty elected seats in 1997. Accepting it would enable the Hong Kong government to implement Omelco's proposal for 1991, but would not allow further increase until after the exchange of sovereignty. This was deemed unacceptable. There had to be a steady increase in democracy in the run-up to 1997. They decided to make a counter-offer based on the 4-4-2 model, which called for twenty-four seats to be returned by universal suffrage in 1997.

During the political review in 1987, the British and Hong Kong governments repeatedly assured Hong Kong people that Britain was acting independently, that China had no say in constitutional reform before 1997. This time, Hurd did not hide that Britain was negotiating with China over the number of seats. (Nor did China hide that it was giving Britain a direct say in drafting the Basic Law.)

"The first prize is to achieve a system of convergence, of continuity, so that people who want to stand for election for the Legislative Council know that it is not just 1991, 1995, but a continuous upward movement towards democracy," Hurd told members of the District Board in the industrial area of Kwun Tong. "If that prize is not attainable, then we have to make our own decision, the British government and the government of Hong Kong."

At a press conference before leaving for London, Hurd made it clear that Britain had not decided on a course of action. He encouraged local residents to make their feelings known to China on the future political structure. Critics said British officials wanted the Hong Kong people to speak up only when it helped Britain's bargaining position.

FIVE YEARS OF work and it came down to one last meeting of the political subgroup. The Hong Kong drafters arrived at the Guangzhou Hotel, a ponderous U-shaped building across from the famous Guangzhou fair grounds, on January 16, just as a cold front from the north was driving temperatures down. They had to agree on a political model that would be presented to the final plenum in Beijing in February. They were not alone. T.S. Lo checked in before the first session and quietly met drafters in their rooms on the VIP floor. Two days later, Vincent Lo and core members of the Group of 89 flew in from Beijing, where they had met Li Peng. Then Cheng Kai-nam and three other leaders of the moderate coalition were spotted dining with Li Hou and Lu Ping.

Just before the meeting started, Ambassador Donald called on the Foreign Ministry in Beijing and made the counteroffer of twenty-four democratically elected seats in 1997 in accordance with the 4-4-2 model. The Chinese side rejected it. They would not go beyond the twenty seats offered to Wilson. As the negotiations continued in the Chinese capital, the mainland Basic Law drafters stalled by refusing to discuss the two most important issues: the composition of the legislature and the method of selecting the governor. Instead, they continued to counter Britain's confidence-boosting measures. To prevent London from using offers of residency to manipulate individuals in the post-1997 administration, one mainland member proposed that the governor and senior officials should not have the right to live in another country.

The next day, Lu Ping proposed an amendment that would bar foreign nationals and those with the right to live in a foreign country from holding two more key posts, the commissioner of immigration and the inspector-general of customs and excise. A Hong Kong drafter reminded Lu that the Joint Declaration stated that only secretary-grade civil servants had to be Chinese nationals.

"After 1997, we will make these posts secretary grade," Lu replied. "Then, it will be in line with the Joint Declaration."

Dorothy Liu proposed that the number of foreign nationals allowed to sit on the sixty-member legislature be limited to nine, or fifteen percent. This was also aimed at limiting Britain's power to manipulate the government after 1997. Though many of the Hong Kong drafters were opposed to the idea, they saw little harm in it because so few foreigners were currently on the legislature. Her motion was passed fourteen to two with one abstention.

Several Hong Kong drafters had been informed privately that Britain and China were negotiating over the political blueprint. Others guessed it. Every time a Hong Kong drafter raised a suggestion on the political structure, Lu responded: "Yes, that is interesting. But we'll have to wait."

On the third day of the meeting, the subgroup discussed whether the legislature should be bicameral. Lu knew there were problems with T.S. Lo's proposal. The liberals could check the conservatives as easily as the conservatives could check the liberals. The government would find it difficult to pass legislation without support from both groups, and the efficiency of the administration would be severely hampered. To correct the problem, Lo had proposed a split voting system: Bills introduced by legislators would have to be passed by the Functional and Elected Houses separately; those proposed by the government would have to be passed by only a simple majority of all members. This made the model even more repulsive to pro-democracy activists.

Lu was in a difficult position. He understood that Hong Kong was totally opposed to the bicameral system. But Xu Jiatun had pushed very hard for it in Beijing. He tried to strike a compromise. Split voting could be used for both types of bills. If the government could not obtain a majority in each of the two houses for its bills, then the total votes would be counted and the legislation would be passed by a simple majority.

Dr. Raymond Wu was furious. He had helped to negotiate the 4-4-2 model, and he wanted it to be accepted intact. He felt that Lu was retaining a bicameral facade so that T.S. Lo would not lose face. Angry that Chinese officials could behave so foolishly about something that was so important, he delivered a tirade against the proposal, then broke down and cried.

Finally, Lu proposed that split voting be used for both government bills and those proposed by legislators. If a bill was not passed separately by a majority of each house, it would be returned for amendment. The amended bill would be passed by a simple majority of all legislators. His motion passed eleven to four. Cheng Kai-nam and some of the moderates felt they had achieved something by encouraging Lu not to adopt the bicameral model intact. Vincent Lo, Martin Lee, and Szeto Wah were all bitter. After all the fighting they had done over the political system, the Chinese adopted the one Beijing wanted.

On the last day of the meeting, China and Britain were still deadlocked over the number of democratically elected seats. The political subgroup had to come to a decision on the composition of the legislature. Maria Tam raised the 4-4-2 model, and again, Li and Lu refused to discuss it. Mainland drafter Xu Chongde proposed a political model that called for thirty seats to be returned by functional groups, eighteen by universal suffrage, and twelve by a grand electoral college. This was a step backward from the twenty democratically elected seats Li had offered Governor Wilson.

The meeting soon resembled a commodities trading pit, with members shouting out numbers and bargaining over the percentage of democratically elected seats in a desperate attempt to reach a compromise. Three Hong Kong drafters proposed models similar to Xu Chongde's, but slightly more conservative. The other three Hong Kong drafters backed these proposals so they could be considered by the final plenum.

Some of the Hong Kong drafters were furious at the way the mainland officials conducted the meeting. Several times when mainland members expressed sympathy towards a Hong Kong drafter's proposal, they were interrupted by either Xiao Weiyun or Lu Ping. Hong Kong convener Dr. Wu was so angry he refused to attend the standard press briefing after the morning session, despite repeated requests made by his mainland counterpart. Instead, he and three other local drafters gave an informal press conference to report on the meeting.

Pro-democracy activists were angry that the Hong Kong drafters supported such conservative models. That evening, a group of students carrying placards waited at the Kowloon railway stations for the drafters to return. When they emerged from the VIP room, the students shouted: "Shame! Shame!"

BRITAIN'S FAILURE to win a significant concession on the number of democratically elected seats in 1997 created a split between London and Hong Kong. Cradock stuck to the line that it was not in Hong Kong's interest to introduce political changes that would be scrapped after 1997. The Executive Council had gone along in 1988, but was standing firm this time. Lydia Dunn and Allen Lee secured Governor Wilson's permission to go to London to ask the British government to accept the Omelco consensus. Dunn tried unsuccessfully to arrange a meeting with Thatcher without Cradock present.

It was an extraordinary mission and showed how much the Beijing massacre had altered the situation in Hong Kong. In 1984, Umelco had gone to London to push for a slow pace of reform. Now, here was Dunn, the senior Executive Councilor, in London pushing for a faster pace of democratization. She and Lee saw the prime minister on January 23, 1990. During the seventy-five-minute session at No. 10 Downing Street, they argued that if British diplomats could not secure an agreement that was acceptable to the people of Hong Kong, the Hong Kong government should introduce democratic reforms unilaterally. This might incite China, they said, but Hong Kong residents were ready to take that risk. Cradock insisted it was useless to introduce the Omelco consensus without Beijing's consent. It would simply write eighteen seats into the Basic Law. That would end convergence, and perhaps none of the legislators sitting in 1997 would be allowed to carry on after the exchange of sovereignty. Thatcher did not commit herself either way.

ON FEBRUARY 12, the Hong Kong vice-chairpersons of the Basic Law Drafting Committee flew to Beijing to prepare the agenda for the final plenum. As usual, they held a meeting that evening with Ji Pengfei and the mainland vice-chairpersons. Ji had some surprising news. "This afternoon, the British ambassador visited the Chinese Foreign Ministry," he said. "He accepted our proposal that twenty seats would be elected by universal suffrage in 1997."

In the end, Thatcher accepted Cradock's view that it was useless to force the pace of reform. Dunn felt Cradock had betrayed Hong Kong in October 1983 when he encouraged Thatcher to concede sovereignty and administration during the negotiations, and now, she believed that he had betrayed the colony a second time. For once, Dunn had stood up to the British government on a matter of principle, and she was bitter about being rebuffed. Though she was reappointed as senior Executive Councilor, she stopped giving interviews to the press. Thatcher tried to make amends by making Dunn a lifetime member of the House of Lords. Dunn was also bitter that Wilson had not fought harder for the Omelco consensus. According to a well-placed source, she came to the conclusion that it would be in Hong Kong's interest if Wilson were replaced and communicated this sentiment to an influential Lord, who passed the message to the prime minister.

When the other Hong Kong drafters arrived, they were put in the new VIP wing of the Beijing Hotel. The Hong Kong vice-chairpersons and Chinese officials spoke to some of them. Word of the Sino-British deal spread quickly, though the details were vague. On the third day of the plenum, Dorothy Liu proposed three amendments to the political model approved at the last political subgroup meeting: the number of seats elected by universal suffrage in 1997 should be raised from eighteen to twenty; the number of foreign nationals allowed to sit on the legislature should be increased from nine to twelve; and split voting should be limited to bills and amendments proposed by legislators.

Some Hong Kong drafters were surprised. At the previous meeting, Liu had been adamant that the number of democratically elected seats should not be increased and had long argued that the political rights of foreign nationals should be restricted. Her complete about-face gave them the impression that she was being used by the Chinese drafters (which would avoid the appearance that diplomats were determining the final shape of the Basic Law) to put forward amendments that were part of the deal between Britain and China.

It is not clear why Liu changed her position. She told the author that she went to Beijing two days earlier than the other drafters, but denied she was acting on behalf of Li and Lu. Whatever her reasons, only the proposal to raise the number of elected members reflected China's deal with Britain.

London was only interested in convergence. As it did not plan to introduce nationality restrictions or a separate voting mechanism before 1997, there was no need to discuss these with China. Ten Hong Kong drafters who had signed a petition against separate voting dropped it because they believed that they could not override an agreement between the two governments. They made a crucial mistake and lost a chance to scrap the separate voting system.

The proposal to limit separate voting to private bills and amendments was clearly in China's interests because it would make it easier for the future Hong Kong government to get its bills passed. The Chinese drafters obviously felt that it was a harmless concession to boost the number of foreign nationals allowed to sit on the legislature because all three of Liu's amendments were endorsed by a majority of the drafters. They also agreed that the future governor would be chosen by an electoral college. Any change in the method of selecting him would be "specified in light of the actual situation in Hong Kong and in accordance with the principle of gradual and orderly progress." The ultimate aim would be to elect the governor by universal suffrage, but no time frame was given.

Liu smiled broadly as she emerged from the conference room and gave the press the thumbs-up sign. In the hotel dining hall that evening, she serenaded senior Chinese officials and other drafters with a song from the hit Broadway musical *Phantom of the Opera*.

On Friday, February 16, the Basic Law drafters convened in the Great Hall of the People to cast their ballots. They filled out a single sheet of paper and voted for, against, or abstain, on each of the 159 articles in the Basic Law and on each amendment. One by one they strode up to a large black box and slipped their voting form into the slot. When the votes were tallied, all of the provisions in the draft were passed by at least forty-one of the fifty-one drafters present.

On the final day of the plenum, Deng Xiaoping, Communist Party chief Jiang Zemin, Premier Li Peng, and President Yang Shangkun congratulated drafters on the completion of their work. It was more than just a public relations gesture. The leaders were taking credit for the successful recovery of Hong Kong. Deng, who had officially retired from all of his posts, shook hands with some of the drafters. The eighty-five-year-old leader looked tired and his hearing had deteriorated. He had to lean close to the drafters to hear what they said, and his voice was unsteady during his brief speech.

"This document has tremendous implications worldwide," he said, "not only for China and Hong Kong, but for all mankind—that is the one country, two systems concept."

WITHIN MINUTES of the announcement that the plenum had passed the draft Basic Law, the Hong Kong government announced that eighteen democratically elected seats would be introduced in 1991 and two more in 1995. In London, Foreign Secretary Hurd addressed the House of Commons to reveal details of the agreement with China. He admitted that the pace of democracy was slower than many people in Hong Kong would have liked, but said: "I would regard the outcome as one which, although not ideal, we could reasonably recommend to the House and to the people of Hong Kong as a basis for the future."

Gerald Kaufman, Labour's shadow foreign secretary, accused Hurd of having "caved in completely" to China's demands.

In Hong Kong, Martin Lee denounced the agreement between Britain and China as "a shameful act of surrender." All along, the two governments had said the future political structure would be based on the will of the Hong Kong people. Now, the people were stuck with a political system that none of them had supported, that was completely alien to Hong Kong, and that was, in fact, designed to thwart their will. A day after the draft was completed, about 1,200 people gathered in Chater Garden, despite a light rain, to denounce the agreement on the political system and to show their disapproval of the final draft of the Basic Law. Lee told the crowd that London and Beijing had breached the Joint Declaration.

"Hong Kong people want to see the Joint Declaration implemented," he said. "We can't accept a Basic Law that can't ensure the basic objectives of allowing Hong Kong people to rule Hong Kong and a high degree of autonomy here after 1997. The final Basic Law draft instead allows the Chinese government to have a high degree of control over Hong Kong through a puppet government."

Szeto Wah, looking angry and defiant, said: "When I was stopped from participating in the Basic Law drafters' activities because of my fight for democracy last summer, I felt honored. Now I am happy that I won't become a culprit of history because I took no part in deciding the final Basic Law draft."

The group marched to the Xinhua headquarters in Happy Valley. The rain came down harder. The demonstrators placed a cardboard mock-up of the Basic Law on top of two oil drums across the street from the building. With several policemen watching, Lee and Szeto set it alight.

This time it was not just the liberals who were angry. All sides felt that Britain had sold out the colony. She had ignored a mandate for greater democracy because of her interest in maintaining cordial relations with China. British and Hong Kong officials denied there had been a sellout. They said that if the 1991 elections were successful, they would encourage the Chinese government to increase the number of democratically elected seats in 1995. Li Hou and other Chinese officials told journalists that the number of elected seats could not be increased. The Basic Law would not come into effect until after 1997, and it could not be amended until that time.

IF THE PEOPLE of Hong Kong thought that the deal between Britain and China on Hong Kong's political structure meant that all differences between the two sides had been resolved and relations could return to normal, they were mistaken. On the day Legislative Councilors were calling for better cooperation with Beijing, a spokesperson for China's Foreign Ministry had some chilling news: The Chinese government might choose not to recognize British passports held by Hong Kong residents. If the threat was carried out, all 160,000 beneficiaries of Britain's nationality scheme would be forced to take up residence in Britain before 1997, thereby exacerbating the brain drain rather than arresting it. The statement did not say if Hong Kong residents who had obtained other foreign passports would be considered Chinese nationals. It left open the possibility that a Chinese-American working in Hong Kong might also not be able to leave after 1997.

The announcement was probably a political move aimed at bolstering opposition to the nationality package within the British Parliament. Norman Tebbit, a tough-talking, right-wing Conservative MP, was threatening to lead a revolt against the package. He claimed that it was a mistake to allow the establishment of a "large, unintegrated community divided from the British people by culture, language, religion, and ethnic origin" and that the plan would cause "division, friction, and at the extreme, violence." He recruited eighty like-minded colleagues in the House of Commons to sign a letter opposing the scheme. Some Labour MPs said they would vote against the package because it was elitist and discriminatory. The possibility that the British government might not get the package through Parliament seemed real. Thatcher was reportedly shaken by the extent of the opposition.

On April 4, London unveiled details of its nationality package. The majority of the 50,000 passports would go to businesspeople, executives, and professionals. Thatcher denied that the package was elitist and said that the aim was to keep people vital to Hong Kong's prosperity from leaving to seek the insurance of residency elsewhere. "That is our undertaking," she said. "To keep it is a matter of solemn duty."

When a vote was taken two weeks later, Tebbit's rebellion fizzled. The package passed 313 to 216. The vote was seen as a major triumph for the Thatcher administration. It had accepted 50,000 of Hong Kong's best and brightest, people other countries were expending great efforts to attract, and made it appear that it was doing something magnanimous for Britain's last important colony. The Chinese government said it would take "correspond-

290 • *The Fall of Hong Kong*

ing measures." But its attacks on the scheme grew less frequent and less virulent until they gradually disappeared.

THE DELEGATES filed slowly into the main theater of the Great Hall of the People on March 28, 1990. Over 2,700 of them had come from as far away as Heilongjiang in the north, Guangxi in the south, and Xinjiang in the west for the third session of the seventh National People's Congress. Below the towering red curtains and the massive national emblem of the People's Republic, a tiny figure stood at the podium. Ji Pengfei was submitting the final version of the Basic Law and a twenty-page report on its drafting, which had taken four years and eight months to complete. He claimed that the process was open and democratic.

"Every article is the product of thorough research and studies and debate," he said. "We have followed the majority views while respecting the opinions of the minority."

On the same day that Parliament was voting on the nationality package, the delegates cast votes on the Basic Law and three resolutions relating to the charter. The first resolution was to establish the Hong Kong Special Administrative Region on July 1, 1997. Another enabled the NPC to set up the Basic Law Committee, which would advise the Standing Committee on the interpretation and amendment of the Basic Law. The most important one dealt with the formation of the first government of the region. The NPC would establish a preparatory committee in 1996, which would be responsible for setting up the first government. At least half of its members would be from Hong Kong and the rest from the mainland. The preparatory committee would determine whether or not sitting Legislative Councilors could carry on after 1997. It would also establish a selection committee, comprised of 400 Hong Kong residents, to choose the first post-1997 governor. He or she would then be appointed by Beijing.

When Li Hou and Lu Ping briefed Deng Xiaoping on the Basic Law before the plenum, the Chinese leader said it was not necessary for him to know the details. China's interests had been protected; he was satisfied. The vote was, therefore, a foregone conclusion. The Basic Law and its "corresponding resolutions" were passed by more than ninety-eight percent of all delegates. When the announcement was made, the Great Hall erupted into perfunctory applause, which lasted almost a minute.

IT WAS OVER. Martin Lee had lost. Still, he refused to give up the fight. Three hours after the promulgation of the Basic Law, he was standing before his colleagues in the Legislative Council to sponsor a motion urging the National People's Congress to amend, at a suitable time, the relevant clauses of the Basic Law according to the Omelco consensus. For once, he was able to gain enough support to get his largely symbolic motion passed.

Lee went on to head the United Democrats, Hong Kong's first major political party, which swept, along with two minor liberal groups, seventeen of the eighteen seats that were filled by democratic election in 1991. Vincent Lo dropped out of the political limelight, though he and other members of the Group of 89 remained active behind the scenes through an economic think tank. Cheng Kai-nam was welcomed back into the pro-China fold because Beijing had few other supporters with any credibility. Cheng ran against Lee in the maiden democratic elections. But despite strong support from all of the left-wing forces in the colony, he was soundly beaten.

The people of Hong Kong knew there was little chance that the Basic Law would be amended. There would be no referendum after 1997, and it was likely that the colony would never enjoy full democracy. Those with money or skills would emigrate. The millions who could not leave could only hope that the forces that had brought down Communism in eastern Europe would do the same in China, or at least that the next generation of leaders would be more enlightened than the current one.

Chapter 24

The Takeover Begins

THE PUBLICATION of the Basic Law marked the end of the first half of the transition period. The legal and constitutional framework for post-1997 Hong Kong was now in place. The Chinese government had successfully negotiated the recovery of Hong Kong while tenuously preserving the confidence of investors. It had safeguarded China's sovereignty and ensured a comfortable degree of control over the future Hong Kong Special Administrative Region while remaining, for the most part, within the letter of the Joint Declaration. But the job was not finished.

Deng wanted China to play a larger role in Hong Kong's affairs during the second half of the transition. This would make for a smooth transfer of power, prevent Britain from pulling any tricks, and keep the Hong Kong people from assuming too much autonomy. The British, of course, rejected the idea of a gradual transfer of power and had it written into the agreement that London alone would be responsible for administering Hong Kong up to June 30, 1997. But what Britain would not give willing, China was prepared to take by coercion.

In October 1989, Governor Wilson had unveiled a bold scheme to build a new airport and expand the colony's container port in the western harbor. With connecting rail links and other infrastructure, the total cost of the Port and Airport Development Strategy (PADS), would be over $16 billion in 1989 dollars. Chinese officials expressed concern about the cost. They saw the project as a plot by Britain to siphon off Hong Kong's financial reserves, estimated at the time to be almost $10 billion. (By 1994, they had ballooned to $43 billion.) Banks and private companies, nervous because the project would not be completed until after 1997, said publicly that they would not help to finance and build PADS unless China supported it. Beijing realized that by withholding its backing, it could demand that it be consulted on other projects, utility franchises, appointments, and other matters that had implications for post-1997 Hong Kong.

In July 1990, the Hong Kong government agreed to hold talks with

China to reassure her that PADS was feasible and would not leave the colony bankrupt. During the negotiations, the most intensive since 1984, the Chinese said they wanted to be consulted on the airport and to be allowed to examine all borrowing by the Hong Kong government. They also demanded that at least $6 billion in fiscal reserves be turned over in 1997 and that they be "consulted on all matters that straddle 1997."

Hong Kong officials were eager to cooperate with Beijing. They offered to set aside almost $2 billion in reserves, to consult China if borrowing exceeded $1.3 billion, and to allow Beijing to nominate representatives in Hong Kong to sit on the Airport Authority. But they refused to give Beijing veto power over decisions and appointments made during the transition period.

The Chinese government stepped up pressure on Britain by refusing to discuss important issues in the Joint Liaison Group, including the formation of the Court of Final Appeal and the stationing of Chinese troops in Hong Kong after 1997. Even a trip to Beijing by Foreign Secretary Hurd in April 1991 failed to break the deadlock.

As the deadline approached for companies to tender for major construction projects related to the airport, the Hong Kong government threatened to scrap or shelve the project. This was a negotiating ploy rather than a serious option. Shelving PADS could not prevent Beijing from having a say during the transition period. It could object to other projects or franchises approved by the government. It could throw the financial markets into chaos with public threats, as it did in 1983. It could bring Hong Kong to its knees simply by no longer acquiescing to daily administrative decisions.

As with the controversy over the Joint Liaison Group during the Sino-British negotiations in 1984, it was Percy Cradock who made the breakthrough. In June 1991, Prime Minister John Major, who had taken over from Margaret Thatcher in November 1990 after an internal party challenge, sent Cradock on a highly secretive mission to Beijing in a last-ditch attempt to resolve the crisis. During four days of intensive negotiations, he and Lu Ping hammered out a "Memorandum of Understanding" on the airport and "related questions."

In the memorandum, the Hong Kong government agreed to satisfy all of China's concerns about the airport. It would consult the Chinese government on major projects, franchises, and government-secured loans related to the airport and on appointments to the Airport Authority. It would try to complete most of the airport by 1997, and it would bequeath to the future Hong Kong government at least $3 billion in financial reserves. In exchange, China agreed to support PADS and to convey this support to potential investors.

On the sticky question of China's role in other issues that extended beyond 1997, the memorandum was left deliberately vague, just as the Joint Declaration had been left vague in areas where the two sides could not agree.

It said that both sides wished to "intensify consultation over Hong Kong in the approach to June 30, 1997." As part of this consultation, the British and Chinese foreign ministers would meet twice a year "to discuss matters of mutual concern." The governor of Hong Kong and the head of the Hong Kong and Macao Affairs Office would also hold regular meetings.

To get the Chinese to agree to these terms, Cradock had to promise that Prime Minister Major would fly to Beijing to sign it. Foreign leaders had stopped visiting the Chinese capital after the crackdown in Beijing and Chinese leaders were eager to break the isolation. When Major arrived in Beijing in September, he was told, apparently at the last minute, that the Chinese had arranged for him to review an honor guard of the same People's Liberation Army that had fired on innocent protesters on June 4, 1989. He was publicly humiliated and only managed to save some credibility back home by briefing the press on the human rights issues that he had raised with Chinese leaders.

With the signing of the memorandum, relations between Britain and China returned to normal. It appeared that Major, like Thatcher, was willing to give China a voice in the administration of Hong Kong for the sake of achieving a smooth transition. Then in April 1992, Major suddenly reversed his position. That month, he led the Conservative Party to a stunning—if narrow—come-from-behind victory. With a mandate from the people, he felt confident enough to chart a bold new course in Hong Kong policy, one not totally dependent on cooperation.

Major replaced Governor David Wilson with Chris Patten, a close friend and the man who had engineered the political victory. When Major took over as prime minister in November 1990, he chose Patten to be the chairperson of the Conservative Party. Patten worked so diligently that he neglected his own reelection bid and lost his seat in Parliament. Rather than take a seat in the House of Lords or wait for a seat to open in the Commons, he decided to accept the post in Hong Kong. He was told he would be given a free hand to establish Britain's policies during the final five years of its rule.

Patten was born in Blackpool, England, in 1944. His grandparents had left Ireland during the famine of the 1800s. His parents, both teachers in Catholic schools, were "low to lower middle class," he told one interviewer. Always an overachiever, young Chris was an altar boy, the captain of the cricket team, and a better than average student. He received a scholarship to a good university and upon graduating won a traveling fellowship to the United States. It was there that he got his first taste of politics, when he landed a job as a researcher working on John Lindsay's campaign to be New York's mayor.

Patten returned to London in 1966. He dropped all of his previous career plans and took a job in the Conservative Party's research department. His ability did not escape notice and he rose to become director of the research department in 1974. He was elected to the House of Commons in 1979 by the middle-class constituency of Bath, a popular tourist site about 150 miles outside of London. Patten was widely regarded as the most gifted Conservative politician of his generation. But under Thatcher, who became prime minister that same year, his career slowed. Although he wrote many of her speeches, she did not reward him with a Cabinet post until July 1989. He was one of two ministers who informed her that her time was up during the Tory revolt in November 1990 that brought Major to power.

Patten had little experience in foreign affairs and almost no knowledge of China or the Chinese. Nevertheless, he believed that his leadership could win concessions for Hong Kong, and he was determined to try. He clearly intended to take back some of the control Britain had ceded during the past few years. He immediately announced that after he arrived in the colony, he would examine ways to expand democratic representation there. China promptly reneged on the Memorandum of Understanding and withdrew her support for the airport project.

Patten landed in Hong Kong in July 1992. As if to emphasize that he was a new breed of governor, he dispensed with the plumed hat, epaulets, and sword worn by Youde and Wilson and arrived in a business suit. He immediately took to the streets, shaking hands and chatting with local residents. They dubbed him, affectionately, Fei Pang (Fat Patten). He gave interviews to journalists and dispensed with some of the secrecy that had always surrounded the Hong Kong government. His approval rating soared. Beijing, however, treated him with total suspicion as it waited to see what reforms he would propose.

In October, Patten gave his first address to the Legislative Council and unveiled his reform plans. He was bound by the Basic Law, which said that thirty of the sixty seats in the Legislative Council would be returned by functional constituency elections, twenty by democratic elections, and ten by an electoral college. Just as China had exploited the vagueness of the Joint Declaration to limit democracy, he exploited the lack of precision in the Basic Law to expand it. He proposed lowering the voting age from twenty-one to eighteen and defining the existing functional constituencies and nine new ones so broadly as to give almost anyone with a job a vote. He also proposed that all District Board members be elected and that they make up the electoral college that would choose ten legislators.

China vehemently opposed the scheme. She could not tolerate Britain determining Hong Kong's post-1997 political structure. Beijing threatened to overturn the plans if they were introduced. The pro-China newspapers in Hong Kong denounced the proposals and attacked Patten personally, calling him a "clown," a "strutting prostitute," a "serpent," and sarcastically referring to him as "the god of democracy." Lu Ping said "in the history of Hong Kong, [Patten] should be regarded as the criminal of all time." Chinese Premier Li Peng declared in his opening speech to the National People's Congress on

March 15, 1993, that Patten's proposals were a "perfidious" attempt "to create disorder [in Hong Kong] and to impede the smooth transfer of power."

The governor's initial reaction was to thumb his nose at the Chinese. He called the insults "background noise." His attitude seemed to be that Britain would not allow China to control Hong Kong before 1997, and if that meant an open dispute, so be it. But Beijing had worked hard to gain a say in Hong Kong affairs, and it was not prepared to relinquish it to a lowly, failed politician. In November 1992, it announced that "contracts, leases, and agreements signed by the Hong Kong government which are not approved by the Chinese side will be invalid after June 30, 1997." The statement threw into doubt not just the airport, but other major projects, utility franchises, and the future of some businesses. Investors shuddered, and the Hang Seng Index plunged more than 1,000 points to below 5,000.

In December, Chinese officials kept up the campaign to undermine business confidence in Hong Kong. They questioned the legal status of Terminal Nine, a much needed extension to Hong Kong's congested port facilities. The project was held hostage to the Sino-British battle over political reform, and the construction delays that resulted meant that Hong Kong was unlikely to keep pace with the projected growth in container traffic. Shipping companies began looking at alternatives, even within China.

Later that month, Beijing denounced Jardine Matheson, the British trading company, for supporting Patten's plans. A commentary released by the Xinhua News Agency said the company, which was not named directly, had made its money from selling opium in China in the nineteenth century and had switched its domicile to Bermuda in 1984. "It adopts an anti-China attitude to undermine the smooth transition in Hong Kong," it said. Though no one took seriously the charge that Jardines was trying to undermine the transition, the company's share price plummeted because the outburst raised doubts about the "princely hong's" ability to do business in Hong Kong after 1997. The message to the rest of the business community was clear: Don't oppose Beijing.*

The Chinese took their opposition a step further that month when a senior official visiting London hinted that if Patten insisted on having his way the Joint Declaration might be scrapped. Although the statement was seen as a negotiating ploy, China's willingness to make such threats worried many people.

---

* One of Jardines' China subsidiaries was later forced to close, and in March 1994, Jardine Matheson Holdings, parent company for the group, announced that it would delist its shares from the Hong Kong Stock Exchange because it was not granted an exemption from the colony's takeover regulations. Jardine executives reportedly encouraged the government of Bermuda, where the company was incorporated, to enact legislation protecting corporations from a hostile takeover because they feared mainland companies would try to seize control of Jardines for political reasons.

Patten insisted that his reforms were only proposals. He expressed a willingness to negotiate with the Chinese and called on them to make counterproposals. The Chinese refused and continued to attack both Patten and his ideas. In early February 1993, as Patten was recovering from an operation to relieve a heart condition, Chinese officials responsible for Hong Kong affairs met in Guangzhou and decided to set up a shadow government to handle the transition to Chinese sovereignty. Press reports in Hong Kong said that Deng Xiaoping himself had proposed the idea.

On February 6, Robin McLaren, the former political adviser who had taken over as British ambassador to China from Alan Donald, passed a copy of Patten's reform bill to the Chinese foreign ministry. The Chinese took their time in responding, perhaps reflecting a split within the Chinese government over how to deal with it. When the Chinese did respond, they insisted that no Hong Kong representatives be involved in the negotiations over the bill. Patten insisted that members of the Hong Kong government join the British team. He pointed out that they had been involved in meetings of the Sino-British Joint Liaison Group and other official discussions. That issue was resolved and by March 12 the two sides were about to issue a joint communiqué stating that London and Beijing would enter negotiations to resolve their differences over political reform. Suddenly, the Chinese refused to include even a rough date for when the talks should begin. A few hours later, Patten published his proposals in the government gazette.

By publishing his bill instead of submitting it to the legislature for approval, Patten left the door to negotiations with the Chinese open a crack. The chances that China would agree to talk seemed slim. A few days later, Lu Ping, who had taken over as director of the Hong Kong and Macao Affairs Office, announced that China was making preparations to create a shadow government, which would assume control of Hong Kong on July 1, 1997. Beijing then appointed forty-nine prominent Hong Kong people as advisers for that purpose. The through train, it appeared, had been derailed again.

As suddenly as the Chinese had backed out of the talks, they reversed their position and on April 13, the two sides agreed to begin negotiations nine days later. The Hang Seng Index jumped almost five percent to a record high of 6,740.

Some observers felt that Patten's tough stand in publishing his proposals had brought China to the negotiating table. In fact, it was simply the most intelligent move on China's part. By agreeing to talks, Beijing could control the outcome of the dispute. If it did not, and the Hong Kong legislature passed Patten's proposals, China would be in the awkward position of having to carry out her threat to scrap the Hong Kong political setup and hold fresh elections in 1997. Moreover, China was looking to improve her international reputation because she wanted the U.S. government to renew her most favored nation status on June 3 and because Beijing was bidding to host the 2000 Olympic Games.

If the British thought there was a breakthrough, they were mistaken. The Chinese dragged their feet through seven rounds of talks, all the while preventing Patten from introducing his bill. Patten insisted that the two sides had to reach a decision by July so the Legislative Council could vote on the bill before its summer recess. But July came and went without any positive results. Another visit to Beijing by British Foreign Secretary Hurd did not produce a breakthrough. Meanwhile, the Chinese confirmed that Hurd's counterpart, Qian Qichen, would head a formal transition committee made up of Chinese officials and pro-China residents in Hong Kong.

Senior Hong Kong officials claimed that an agreement had to be reached with China by October to give them time to prepare for the 1995 elections. Two more rounds were held in the summer. During the next eight rounds, held between September and November 1993, Patten agreed to drastically scale back his proposal to expand the franchise of the functional constituencies if China would spell out the criteria under which legislators would be allowed to continue to serve after 1997. His aim was to prevent China from unseating Martin Lee and Szeto Wah and anyone else who expressed opinions contrary to the Chinese government. China refused because any rules strict enough to keep Lee and Szeto off the body were likely to contravene the terms of the Joint Declaration and the Basic Law.

By December, Patten had had enough of China's delaying tactics. He submitted to the Legislative Council draft legislation on the voting age, on the voting method for seats returned by universal suffrage (double seat constituencies would be replaced with single seat ones), and on the abolition of appointed members to the District Boards and Municipal Councils. These were the least controversial of Patten's proposals, and he hoped that they would be passed by the legislature while Britain and China continued to discuss the more controversial ones. China, however, broke off the talks.

In February 1994, the Council passed Patten's reforms. China's response was muted in comparison with the diatribe that greeted the governor's proposals when they were unveiled in October 1992. But the passage of the bill probably spelled the end of cooperation between Britain and China in the years remaining until 1997.

China is not prepared to accept true democracy in Hong Kong because it will undermine one-party rule in Beijing. She will continue to oppose political reforms in Hong Kong and antagonize the Hong Kong government over issues related to the transition. However, Beijing is unlikely to do anything that will severely disrupt Hong Kong's economy. When it takes over, it might scrap political changes introduced by Patten. Clearly, it intends to exert a high degree of control over the Special Administrative Region.

Britain does not have the power to force China to accept even a small measure of real democracy in Hong Kong. Patten knows that there is nothing Britain can do now to keep China from overturning his reforms. Had he truly been concerned about the interests of the Hong Kong people, he would have recommended to his friend the prime minister that Britain give everyone in the colony a British passport.

No BRITISH OFFICIAL explained the government's change of policy on Hong Kong. To do so would have been to admit that the previous policy of cooperation had failed to safeguard Hong Kong's interests. London abandoned its strategy of cooperating with China and seeking a smooth transfer of sovereignty because Prime Minister Major and Foreign Secretary Hurd felt it had to be seen by history as having done—or having tried to do—right by Hong Kong. No matter how genuine Patten's concern for Hong Kong was and no matter how admirable his zeal was in trying to implement his reforms, the policy change had more to do with British honor than with helping the people of Hong Kong.

Major had little to lose. Getting tough with China was popular with voters in Britain, who were disgusted by the massacre in Beijing. With the collapse of the Soviet Union, China was no longer strategically important in Cold War geopolitics. British companies were hardly getting rich in the China market, and by increasing democratic reform, Britain silenced demands for more Hong Kong Chinese to be allowed into Britain.

Patten himself told an interviewer: "I freely confess that my proposals are not a great step forward towards democracy for Hong Kong. They aren't even a small step." He claimed they were "an attempt to secure a Legislative Council which is broadly based, which is credible, which isn't simply a rubber stamp." The Foreign Office undermined that goal in the summer of 1993, when it secretly amended the Letters Patent, apparently with the governor's knowledge, to limit the number of democratically elected seats that could be introduced because it feared that liberals on the Legislative Council would amend Patten's proposals to make them more democratic. The governor was pushing for reforms that would make the Legislative Council more independent under Chinese rule, while Her Majesty's Government was limiting its ability to act independently while Hong Kong was still administered by Britain.

The truth is that Patten's proposals for political reform were a smokescreen put up so the British could avoid feeling guilty about turning six million people over to a brutal regime. No matter how representative the reforms made the legislature, the Basic Law gave it little authority to check the power of the governor and senior civil servants, who would be appointed by Beijing. London had given away the store and decided at the last minute to ask for a nominal fee so it could claim it got a good deal.

Throughout the remaining years of the transition, China will continue to use threats, coercion, and intimidation until she is given a say in the administration of Hong Kong. Britain may refuse to give in in order to appear to have done right by Hong Kong, but in the end it will matter little. After 1997, the Hong Kong government will answer to Beijing, not to the people of Hong Kong.

HISTORY WILL RECORD that throughout the period covered in this book, Britain put her own interests above those of her colony and failed to get adequate safeguards for the Hong Kong people. In 1971, when the Heath Cabinet decided that the colony would be returned to China, the Hong Kong government should have begun to introduce democratic reforms. The argument that it would have stirred up the old Communist-Nationalist rivalry is weak. The Nationalists had been all but vanquished in Hong Kong. Had the Communists run openly for office, they would have been defeated because they had lost support during the riots in 1967.

In 1978, Governor MacLehose was concerned only with maintaining a British presence in Hong Kong after 1997. If he had begun introducing meaningful democracy during his tenure, Hong Kong would have had a much better system of government in place by 1997. It was not until Britain had formally agreed to return Hong Kong to China that the Hong Kong government began introducing democratic reforms. China had every right to feel tricked. Democracy, it seemed, was good for Hong Kong only when the British were no longer running it.

The role of the Old China Hands in determining Hong Kong's future has been the subject of much controversy and speculation. MacLehose and Cradock have been accused of bungling the initial attempt to resolve the question of the New Territories lease during the meeting with Deng Xiaoping in 1979. Some colonial officials in Hong Kong even believe that these two diplomats deliberately provoked China into taking back Hong Kong to rid themselves of an obstacle to better Sino-British relations. This is ridiculous. They made a legitimate effort to keep Hong Kong British. Their mistake was in overestimating Deng's grasp of the subtleties of the issues involved. Even if they had raised the matter with lower-level cadres more familiar with Hong Kong, as Executive Councilor Y.K. Kan suggested, Deng would never have accepted a British presence in Hong Kong after 1997. He had decided in 1978 that Hong Kong and Macao would be recovered under the formula being worked out for reunification with Taiwan.

In recent years, the Foreign Office has tried to make it appear that Britain had to enter talks with China because businesspeople in Hong Kong were getting nervous about the expiration of the New Territories lease. This is nonsense. None of the dozens of business leaders interviewed for this book were concerned about the lease at that time because they usually made a return on their investment in five years and the lease would not run out for almost twenty. The Foreign Office diplomats pushed China to enter negotiations because they felt Hong Kong would be better able to handle the situation in 1982 than 1992. They were right. The panic in Hong Kong during the talks would have been magnified tenfold if the termination of the lease were only a few years away.

Cradock and the Old China hands have consistently been accused of kowtowing to China. There were, indeed, times during the negotiations when Cradock was too soft with China. He was incorrect to advise Geoffrey Howe that Beijing would never accept the Joint Liaison Group continuing its work after 1997. There were also times when the Executive Councilors felt Cradock was being soft when, in fact, he was being clever. His decision to accept China's two-year deadline for the negotiations clearly worked to Hong Kong's advantage, as he predicted it would.

Blaming Cradock and the Old China Hands for not being tough enough with China obscures the crucial role of Thatcher's government and the British Parliament, which decided that the land taken from China would be returned and that the people of Hong Kong would not be given the option of living in the United Kingdom. Cradock and his team were given the task of negotiating an agreement that would enable the Hong Kong people to remain in the colony after 1997 and enjoy the same rights and freedoms that they had under the British. This was nearly impossible because China was not prepared to accept an independent, or even semi-independent, Hong Kong.

During the negotiations, British diplomats worked hard to get a good agreement because only a good agreement would enable London to withdraw from Hong Kong without having to take in tens of thousands of Chinese refugees from the colony. They failed, however, to get an accord that would safeguard the rights and livelihoods of the people of Hong Kong. Without some form of elected government that is beholden to no one but the people of Hong Kong, the rights and freedoms contained in the Joint Declaration and the Basic Law are just words. Patten himself has said as much.

The critical point in the negotiations came at the very end, in September 1984, when Britain was insisting that the term "elections" be defined as democratic elections and China was holding out. Governor Youde and his advisers in Hong Kong believed that democracy was crucial to protecting Hong Kong's interests after 1997, that only an elected government could resist interference from Beijing and safeguard human rights. The British should have made an elected government a precondition for signing the agreement. Only this would have given the Hong Kong people a measure of self-determination, a right supposedly guaranteed to all people under colonial domination by the United Nations.

Even if the British had held out, it is unlikely that Beijing would have given in. The British did not try harder because they knew the Chinese leadership saw a truly democratic government in Hong Kong as a threat, because they were not prepared to offer the people of Hong Kong a safe haven in the U.K., and because they felt they had something that they could sell to Parliament, Hong Kong, and the world. They were not prepared to risk seeing it unravel at the last minute—even if it meant they would abandon Hong Kong without adequate safeguards.

The gap between what the Hong Kong people needed to continue living in freedom and what China was willing to give could not be bridged, so the Foreign Office and Thatcher's government simply covered it up. Having gotten some general, undefined terms, they encouraged Hong Kong people, Parliament, and the world to believe that the colony would have a democratic system after 1997, even though they knew China was staunchly opposed to that. At a press conference on the day after the Joint Declaration was unveiled, Governor Youde said: "What China has undertaken to do is to respect certain principles, which are that there will be an elected legislature, that there will be an executive accountable to that legislature, and that the executive will be bound by the law."

The Chinese government had not committed itself to these principles, at least not as Youde knew his audience would interpret them. The British government never told the people of Hong Kong, or Parliament, that China had made it clear during the negotiations that she was not in favor of democratic elections and that she did not want the legislature to have any real power to call the executive authorities to account.*

Had Margaret Thatcher and Geoffrey Howe told Parliament and Hong Kong that Britain had made a big push to include democratic elections in the Joint Declaration and China rejected it, they would have had a realistic basis for accepting or rejecting the accord.

---

* One of the most senior Foreign Office officials involved in the negotiations with China told me that "a gloss" was put on the constitutional provisions. "Not by the government," he added quickly. Clearly a gloss was put on by Youde in Hong Kong and some ministers in Parliament.

By her duplicity, Britain created an atmosphere of fear and distrust in Hong Kong and complicated the chances for a successful transfer of power. Even before the June 4 massacre, Martin Lee and his followers felt China was reneging on promises she had never made. They blamed Beijing for forcing London to backtrack on its pledge to introduce democratic elections in 1988. In fact, the British government had put itself in the impossible position of trying to live up to the expectations it had created in Hong Kong and implementing the vague agreement it had negotiated with China.

During the transition period, Foreign Office diplomats were clearly working to avoid a confrontation with China, even if it meant sacrificing Hong Kong's interests. Lee felt it was imperative that Britain fulfill Howe's 1984 promise to introduce a representative government "in the years immediately ahead" despite China's objections. Cradock believed that this would be ruinous because Beijing would simply scrap the existing system in 1997 and implement something even less democratic. Thatcher was prepared to risk upsetting China by introducing democratic elections in 1988 if that was what Hong Kong people wanted. But the Hong Kong government produced a flawed survey of public opinion, and David Wilson, perhaps unintentionally, undermined Thatcher's determination to do right by the Hong Kong people by asking the Executive Council to vote on putting off elections until 1991 even before they saw the highly disputed Survey Office report. His actions avoided a showdown with China and enabled the British government to back down on its pledge without losing face.

Having failed to provide the Hong Kong people with either a truly representative government to protect them after 1997 or a place of refuge, Britain has left her colonial subjects to the mercy and whims of China's leaders. The Basic Law gives Beijing the means to control every facet of Hong Kong's administration through its hand-picked governor.

Britain's claim to have provided guarantees that Hong Kong people will enjoy the same fundamental rights under Chinese rule as under British rule has already been exposed as a lie. Hong Kong people are already being denied basic human rights. One of the most fundamental freedoms is the freedom from fear. Under British rule, no one in Hong Kong worried about being arrested for expressing a point of view. But student activists who organized protest marches in June 1989, brought money to comrades in Tiananmen Square, or helped to spirit dissidents out of China after the bloody crackdown are worried that their names may be on a blacklist of people to be rounded up on July 1, 1997. Journalists are toning down their criticism of China and newspapers practice self-censorship because they fear reprisals after 1997. A climate of fear has already begun to set in.

The British government's decision to hand over the people of Hong Kong along with the territory it took in the nineteenth century is unprecedented in modern times. In defending her actions, Britain claims to have consulted the Hong Kong people regarding their future. This is a fraud. The people of Hong Kong were given no choice but to accept the Joint Declaration. Regarding the future political system they would live under, the Hong Kong government asked for opinions—then ignored them. In 1984 and 1987, the appointed Executive Council made decisions based on its own opinion of what was best for the colony. There were no elected representatives on the Basic Law Drafting Committee, and although China held extensive consultations on the Basic Law, in the end, she negotiated a political system that was only superficially democratic. Without an adequately representative government, iron-clad protection against human rights abuses, and the guarantee of an independent judiciary, the people of Hong Kong have been consigned to an uncertain future. They have every right to feel that Britain has betrayed them.

Conclusion

The New Power Elite

I T IS COMMONLY said in Hong Kong that the Joint Declaration is a good agreement and that everything will be fine after 1997 if Britain and China just implement it faithfully. This view is based on highly subjective readings of the document. When Martin Lee reads "the legislature shall be constituted by elections," he interprets that to mean the legislature will be returned by universal suffrage in free and fair elections. When some of Hong Kong's most powerful businesspeople read that phrase, they interpret it to mean something much less broad, something that will guarantee their control over the government and economic policy.

New evidence presented in this book shows that the Joint Declaration was not a good agreement, that it was only a partial agreement. Britain and China agreed that Hong Kong should remain a prosperous international financial and commercial center. This would enable Britain to leave her colony without taking responsibility for its people and China to achieve her economic modernization goals more quickly. The two sides could not agree, however, on a system of government that would enable Hong Kong to continue to prosper. It was as if two companies decided to start a joint venture and agreed on where it would be based and what and how much it would produce, but could not agree on who would run the enterprise and how.

This is a critical flaw in the Joint Declaration that threatens Hong Kong's future success. The system of government is the foundation on which everything else in a given society rests. There can be no guarantee of human rights, no protection of private property, no stability, and no prosperity without a government that can uphold the rule of law. Governor Chris Patten himself warned that without "a credible legislature, fairly and openly elected," the rule of law would be undermined and this in turn would put at risk "the maintenance of Hong Kong's prosperity and freedom."

Britain and China's failure to agree to a form of government that could uphold the rule of law and act independently of China and in the best interests of Hong Kong does not mean that the colony will founder after it returns to Chinese rule in 1997. But it does mean that there will be major changes in the business landscape that will affect all foreign and local companies operating there. It also means that Hong Kong's role as an international center is likely to diminish and that it will become primarily a commercial and financial center for South China.

When the British grabbed Hong Kong from China, they installed an all-powerful governor to run the new colony and sent out a team of professional administrators to execute his policy. But the raison d'être of Hong Kong was business, and the governor needed the cooperation of the merchant class for the colony to succeed. He appointed the most influential businesspeople in the colony to the Executive and Legislative Councils. Initially only British businesspeople were appointed, but as the Chinese prospered, they were admitted to the inner circle. The administrators and this small group of wealthy businesspeople formed a powerful elite that ran the colony with the primary aim of maintaining the best possible climate for doing business.

The British administration's role can be best described as the referee in a free-for-all. The governor and his civil servants sat down with all of the major players and devised rules that would enable everyone to prosper. Since the professional administrators had no financial interests in Hong Kong, they could set policies fairly and objectively for all. They enforced the rules to allow everyone an equal chance for success. When disputes arose, they were settled without fear or favor in British-style courts, which acted independently of the administration.

This system succeeded spectacularly. Hong Kong grew to become the tenth largest trading power in the world, even though it ranks eighty-ninth in terms of population. It built up a critical mass of merchant and commercial banks, investment companies, accounting and advertising firms, business consultants, and other specialty firms, which made it the logical location for new companies looking to set up regional headquarters in Asia. Over seventy percent of American companies with regional operations in Asia were based there in 1993. By that year, the standard of living of the local people was equal to that in Britain and was forecast to rival that of Canada by the end of 1994.

To satisfy the Hong Kong people, bolster world opinion, and assuage its own guilt about handing over six million freedom-loving people to a brutal communist regime, the British government wanted to devolve power from the elite to the people of Hong Kong, or at least to disperse it among representatives of major sectors of the society through the functional constituencies. By preventing power from being concentrated in the hands of a few people, Britain hoped to protect the people from human rights abuses, and to protect the government from administrative abuses.

By replacing Hong Kong's antiquated system of government with one that would be self-perpetuating and broadly based through some form of elections, Britain hoped to enhance Hong Kong's chances of remaining successful after the transition to Chinese rule. Diffusing power that had been in the hands of the elite would prevent a small group of individuals from using it to benefit themselves at the expense of the rest of the society, or from making serious policy mistakes. An elected government would respect the rights of individuals, uphold the independence of the courts, and formulate economic policies—after vigorous public debate—that were in the interests of the whole society.

But Chinese leaders could not accept the people of Hong Kong running their own affairs through a democratically elected government because, if they were successful, it would undermine centralized, one-party rule on the mainland. Chinese citizens would point to Hong Kong and say, if they can run their own affairs so well under a democracy, maybe we can do better than the Communist Party. Beijing wanted to control the government, the legal system, and the bureaucracy to prevent Hong Kong from becoming a model for change in China. It believed that the best strategy would be simply to replace the British-appointed governor with a Chinese-appointed one—that is, replace the British power elite with a pro-China one.

These two visions of how Hong Kong should be run after 1997 were not reconciled by the Joint Declaration. The two sides could not agree on a form of government, so they papered over the chasm with vague wording. The British believed they had gotten enough key terms into the agreement— elections, accountability—to build a democratic system after it was signed. But the minute the Hong Kong government tried to turn those vague provisions into real democracy for Hong Kong, China stepped in to stop it. All of the bitter disputes between London and Beijing since the accord was signed in 1984 were an extension of the fundamental disagreement that was never resolved by the Joint Declaration.

The Basic Law contains a partially elected legislature. However, China largely succeeded in preventing Britain from dismantling the colonial system. After 1997, China will be able to virtually handpick the governor and his senior civil servants, and they will be able to govern the colony almost completely unchecked by the legislature, which has been given little power. Governor Patten tried to expand the elected element in the legislature with the hope that legitimacy in the eyes of the people would bring its own form of power. The future governor and his backers in Beijing would not be able to ignore the clamoring of legislators who truly represented the people. It was a noble gesture, but it was too little, too late.

On July 1, 1997, the pro-British power elite will be replaced. Beijing will select a governor whom it can control. It will send a senior cadre to Hong Kong, ostensibly to handle foreign affairs, who is likely to be consulted by the governor on all major decisions. The governor will appoint pro-China figures from all sectors of the society to sit on the Executive Council, and he will probably try to marginalize the role of the Legislative Council by encouraging the election of "patriots"—ie, people who will do and say whatever the leadership in Beijing wishes.

Chinese leaders believe that switching from a pro-Britain elite to a pro-China one will have little or no impact on Hong Kong's economic success. After all, they want to maintain that success as much as Britain did, perhaps more so since Hong Kong is driving the economic modernization of South China. The truth is, however, that there are fundamental differences between a pro-Britain and a pro-China elite, and they have wide ranging and serious implications for Hong Kong.

The biggest difference is that the pro-China elite will be much more unified. Hong Kong was not a democracy, but the governors sent out by Britain were men brought up in a democratic society, where the rights of individuals are respected. They accepted dissent, so businesspeople in the colony had no compunction about disagreeing with them. Moreover, the British administrators did not simply attend to the interests of a few British companies because wide-spread discontent among the predominantly Chinese population would make governing difficult. The government had to balance the needs of special interest groups and carry out extensive consultations to enable it to devise policies that had broad support. The pro-British power elite was thus somewhat fractious and divided, reflecting the nature of a democratic society.

In China, however, administrators, law enforcement officials, the courts, and the people all obey the Communist Party, which has always been dominated by one man or a small group of men. Since the Communist Revolution in 1949, some pro-Beijing groups in Hong Kong have acted on the instructions of the Communist Party—even to their own detriment. When Deng Xiaoping launched his modernization program in 1978, Chinese officials envisioned Hong Kong playing a major role. They instructed the pro-China trade unions not to agitate for higher pay and better working conditions. Since that time, union leaders have been acquiescent. Some rank-and-file members have complained publicly at times that union leaders have ignored the problems of workers for political reasons.

Beijing knows that the majority of Hong Kong people would prefer to remain under British rule. It therefore has to court support and rely on the few people who favor the Chinese takeover. The way Chinese officials see it, community leaders in Hong Kong must accept that the Communist Party has the right to run Hong Kong as it sees fit. Those that do not are labeled "unpatriotic" and are ostracized. Those that conform are hailed as "patriots" and rewarded with all the benefits that being part of the power elite confers.

After 1997, individuals who aspire to positions of wealth and power will necessarily do and say whatever Beijing commands to gain entry into the inner circle. Along with mainland companies in Hong Kong, pro-China businesses, and trade unions, they will form a unified bloc that will take orders from Chinese officials. If they are told not to advertise in a newspaper that has been particularly critical of China's policies, they will obey. If they are told not to do business with someone who has been outspoken against the party, they will obey. If they are told to support a major change in the Hong Kong government's policies, or to make donations to mainland charities, or to ignore a flagrant abuse of human rights, they will obey. If they do not, they will lose their influence and be booted out of the elite.

The size of this new power elite is enormous and still growing. China is the single largest foreign investor in Hong Kong. The Hong Kong government does not keep statistics on mainland investments, but analysts conservatively estimate them to be $10 billion, or forty percent more than the 900 American firms registered in Hong Kong have invested there. Some put the figure at closer to $20 billion. Add to that the clout of pro-China businesspeople, the power of major pro-China trade unions, and the influence of grassroots groups—from the rural welfare associations to the triad gangs—and it becomes clear that this is a force that will shape every aspect of business in Hong Kong.

The unity of this new power elite, which has been coalescing since the early 1980s, means that fair competition will be replaced by unfair competition. By simply threatening to withdraw the patronage of hundreds of pro-China firms from any company that opposes it, Beijing will be able to influence any business decision made in Hong Kong. It could silence foreign firms who criticize mainland-backed companies for illegal practices. It could pressure foreign companies to withdraw from a public tender, or it could encourage them to favor one bank or trading partner over another.

Beijing will also be able to influence political decisions and court cases where politicians and judges are susceptible to economic coercion. It could threaten to blacklist companies owned by elected politicians if they do not vote Beijing's way, or boycott companies owned by the families of judges if they do not decide a case the way Chinese officials want. If the U.S. government withdraws China's most favored nation trading status, as it has threatened to do every year since 1989, Chinese officials could withdraw business from American companies in Hong Kong.

Beijing is unlikely to be too heavy-handed in wielding this power because it does not want to damage confidence in Hong Kong or disrupt relations with important trading partners. But it does not have to be. Just the knowledge that the threat exists has changed and will continue to change the political-economic picture in Hong Kong.

In the summer of 1993, Simon Li, the former appeals court judge and Basic Law drafter, was appointed to cochair a Chinese government committee responsible for handling legal issues during the transition period. Shortly after accepting the appointment, Li said publicly that Martin Lee and Szeto Wah were unfit to serve as legislators beyond 1997 because they had engaged in unpatriotic activities. Giving an example, he said they had called on the people of Hong Kong to withdraw money from the Bank of China in the wake of the massacre in Beijing. Lee and Szeto denied they had encouraged people to withdraw their money and claimed they had, in fact, urged people *not* to because the government said the banking system could be adversely affected. But when the two decided to bring a defamation suit against Li, eighteen law firms, including some of Hong Kong's most prestigious, refused to take their case. And Lee and Szeto approached only firms they thought might be willing to accept it.

The two did find a law firm after their problem was publicized, but the incident raised questions about the chance local and foreign businesspeople would have of ever winning a case against a Chinese company that had connections in the Hong Kong and Chinese governments.* As the *Far Eastern Economic Review* said in an editorial: "We also wonder about 'one country, two systems' pledges to protect private property, contracts, and free speech in Hong Kong. Other aspects of the rule of law—clearly stated rights, sensible rules, and independent judges—count for nothing if litigants cannot find lawyers willing to go to court."

The pro-China bloc is so powerful that people in Hong Kong quake at the possibility of being blacklisted because any company isolated by Beijing will suffer considerable financial loss. "The specter of China's withdrawal of business or connections," said Martin Lee, "is enough to have many businessmen and lawyers in town toeing an invisible line."

MAINLAND AND pro-China companies in Hong Kong will enjoy far greater advantages after 1997 than British companies ever did. Having the right connections in China is considered to be crucial for doing business there. The right partner can eliminate labor problems and bureaucratic red tape or provide materials that are in short supply. Business will flow to the compa-

---

* At the time this book went to press, the case was still pending.

nies in Hong Kong that can provide those connections. An American manufacturer that wants to raise funds to set up a factory in Guangzhou could go to an American merchant bank in Hong Kong to arrange financing. But using a merchant bank partially owned by a provincial government body might help it to obtain the necessary permits.

In 1979, a mainland businessman named Rong Yiren set up China International Trust & Investment Corporation (CITIC) as the Chinese government's overseas investing arm. Rong enjoyed a close relationship with Zhao Ziyang and other Chinese leaders and answered directly to the State Council, China's cabinet. After starting off cautiously, CITIC began investing heavily in Hong Kong. Major Hong Kong companies offered the firm shares (often at below-market prices) as political insurance. The theory was that Beijing would not crack down on a company it owned. Among CITIC's investments were twenty percent of Hong Kong Telecom, which had the telephone franchise; twelve and a half percent of Cathay Pacific Airways, Hong Kong's leading airline; twenty-five percent of the second cross harbor tunnel; thirty-three percent of Asia Satellite, a firm providing satellite television and communications; and thirty-three percent of Hong Kong Petrochemical, a major plastics producer. The company prospered on the strength of politically inspired deals and by 1990 was already being hailed as the first Chinese *hong*.

After 1997, pro-China companies will continue to enjoy an unfair advantage. One area where that might be particularly obvious is government tenders. When the Hong Kong government put out tenders for public works projects, it tended to look more favorably on British bids. But contracts were often awarded to American and Japanese companies when their bids were substantially lower than, or technically superior to, British ones. It was, in fact, an American company that won the first major contract for the new airport at Chek Lap Kok. After 1997, tenders are less likely to be open and fair.

Beijing sees Hong Kong as a resource to be exploited much more than London ever did. China needs foreign exchange, and Hong Kong is one of the best places to earn it. Beijing, therefore, will look favorably upon the Hong Kong government if it awards contracts to mainland companies. It is no surprise that Chinese officials have become increasingly vocal in the last few years about the Hong Kong government's awarding franchises that extend beyond 1997. Beijing does not want to see all the most lucrative opportunities going to British firms. After 1997, the Hong Kong governor is likely to award more contracts to mainland companies to please his masters in Beijing.

Many foreign and local companies have already sensed the shifting landscape, and for the past few years, leaders of consortia bidding for major infrastructure projects, such as the second and third cross harbor tunnels and the airport, have teamed up with mainland companies to try to gain access to the emerging power elite. This will become increasingly common. Foreign businesses in Hong Kong will have to spend more time developing connections with Chinese companies, Chinese officials, and senior members of the Hong Kong government.

This, however, will present new challenges and new problems for foreign businesses. New challenges, because they are unlikely to be as trusted as Chinese businesspeople (such as Robert Kuok, developer Gordon Wu, and billionaire Li Ka-shing), which means they might be shut out of the most important deals. New problems, because a political element is injected into their business. Foreign investors who team up with a company that has close ties to Li Peng, or with a pro-China company close to the premier, may find themselves in a strong position today and completely out of the loop tomorrow if Li is purged. Thus, businesspeople will have to be keenly aware of where their connections lead, and they will have to keep a sharp eye on the machiavellian politics in Beijing and in Hong Kong.

UNDER THE COLONIAL system, the British tried to maintain a wall between government and business. Civil servants who made policy decisions were rotated every few years to prevent them from developing too close a relationship with key people in their area of responsibility. This was an old colonial practice introduced to discourage corruption. When the Executive Council had to make a decision that would affect the companies of one of its members, he or she was asked to leave the chamber. All of the Executive Councilors were privy to secret information that could affect their businesses, but if the governor perceived that one member was using the inside information for personal gain, that member would likely have been dropped from the council when his or her term expired.

After 1997, the wall between government and business might be torn down, or at least have large holes punched in it. Most of those China is said to be considering for the position of governor after 1997 are businesspeople. They will have a financial stake in Hong Kong and will be less objective than British governors when formulating policy. Future governors may appoint friends, associates, and even relatives to run departments, rather than rely on career civil servants, whom Beijing will have much less influence over. This will exacerbate the problem of unfair competition and perhaps lead to the kind of official corruption that is so prevalent on the mainland.

In China, there is little or no distinction between government and business. Most ministries and government departments have set up companies, including the State Council, the Ministry of Justice, the Ministry of Communications, and the Hong Kong and Macao Affairs Office. Stockbrokers have grumbled privately about what they perceive to be insider trading in Hong Kong by mainland companies. During the numerous disputes between China and Britain, brokers noticed Chinese companies buying stocks right before a positive announcement by the two governments. The creation of a company in Hong Kong linking pro-China businesspeople, powerful mainland companies, and Chinese government bodies has deepened their concerns.

In 1993, a pro-China businessman named T.T. Tsui got permission from Premier Li Peng to set up a fund in Hong Kong that would invest in China. It was originally designed to be a $25 million fund with twenty Hong Kong and ten mainland shareholders. But when word got out that the project had been sanctioned at the highest levels of the Chinese government, everyone wanted in. The fund swelled to $65 million with fifty-four shareholders.

A new company, New China Hong Kong, was formed. Thirteen Chinese government companies took 32.5 percent, thirty-nine Hong Kong investors took 55 percent, and two Singapore firms controlled the remaining 12.5 percent. The Hong Kong investors included some of the biggest names in the colony, including Li Ka-shing. Eleven of the Chinese-backed companies belonged to Chinese national government bodies or ministries, including the State Council. The group was supposed to include a company called Beijing Hong Kong Development, which happened to be owned by the Hong Kong and Macao Affairs Office. Many businesspeople were unhappy that the Chinese government body charged with overseeing Hong Kong policy would be competing with them in the marketplace. They feared that Beijing Hong Kong Development's participation would give New China Hong Kong's merchant banking arm a profound edge in the stock market. Lu Ping, director of the Hong Kong and Macao Affairs Office, could move the market just by issuing statements. After 1997, the company would also have an unfair advantage if it bid for public works contracts in Hong Kong.

Although many businesspeople were concerned, none spoke out. Instead, it was Martin Lee who publicly opposed Beijing Hong Kong Development's participation in New China Hong Kong. The Hong Kong and Macao Affairs Office subsequently heeded the public outcry and withdrew its plans to participate in the fund. But the fact that Lu Ping failed to see anything wrong with its participation and that the business community was unwilling to speak out against it are worrying.

UNFAIR COMPETITION is just one of the major changes the new power elite will bring. Another is less competition.

Throughout most of Hong Kong's history, the government adopted a strict laissez-faire economic policy. Unlike the governments of Singapore, Taiwan, and South Korea—the other "Little Dragons"—the colonial administration did not micro-manage the economy. It did not subsidize key industries or provide incentives to certain sectors. It did not block imports and stress exports to make itself wealthy. The Hong Kong government kept taxes low and regulation to a minimum to encourage the creation of jobs to provide opportunities for the local people. The Chinese who fled the communist system were eager to take advantage of those opportunities. Their hard work, talent, and drive fueled the colony's incredible growth.

Chinese officials, however, have studied the economies of the other Little Dragons and believe that their model of authoritarian capitalism is suitable for Hong Kong. After 1997, they might abandon Hong Kong's formula for success and offer incentives to high-tech industries, such as software development, computer manufacturing, and telecommunications, which Beijing deems vital to its modernization drive. They might place greater emphasis on port development and other infrastructure projects that benefit China, such as roads connecting Hong Kong and Guangdong. The question is: Can communist officials run an economy as sophisticated as Hong Kong's? The answer is almost certainly: No.

Moves towards a more centralized economy with less competition are already under way. Since the Joint Declaration was signed in 1984, Chinese state-owned firms have been investing heavily in the colony. Much of the investment has been aimed simply at making money, but some of it is politically motivated. Beijing has targeted key industries, such as transportation, telecommunications, communications, and finance. Given that many mainland companies are owned and controlled by Chinese government bodies, Beijing will limit competition to protect its investments.

In 1985, pro-China investors from Hong Kong and Macao started a second airline in Hong Kong—dubbed Hong Kong Dragon Airlines and later Dragonair—to challenge British-owned Cathay Pacific Airways, particularly on China routes. They obtained some financial backing from a mainland company, which would be helpful in gaining approval from the Chinese government to fly to major cities, specifically Shanghai and Beijing. The Hong Kong government protected the interests of the British carrier by declaring a "one airline, one route" policy, which meant Cathay alone could serve Beijing and Shanghai, while Dragonair could serve smaller cities.

Had Britain and China agreed on a formula for an elected government, the future administration, no doubt, would have changed the policy to allow direct competition, which would benefit the average Hong Kong consumer by bringing down ticket prices and improving service. But they did not agree, so Cathay Pacific executives began to fear that after 1997 a new pro-China administration in Hong Kong might make China-backed Dragonair the designated carrier on the important China routes. They apparently approached CITIC about taking a stake in Cathay.* CITIC happily agreed, as the airline was extremely profitable. Cathay also floated shares on the stock exchange and began a major publicity campaign to promote itself as "Hong Kong's airline."

In 1989 and 1990, competition between the carriers was eliminated when CITIC bought a twenty percent stake in Dragonair (later increased to forty-six percent) and encouraged Cathay to take thirty percent of its erstwhile competitor. As part of the deal, Cathay signed a fifteen-year management contract under which it seconded senior staff to Dragonair. The two airlines became partners, with Dragonair taking over all of the China routes. Although Hong Kong consumers never benefitted from price competition, China benefitted from enhanced profits, which she now earns from two carriers acting as a monopoly.

It is virtually inconceivable that a new airline could be launched to challenge Cathay and Dragonair, and it is likely that foreign companies will have difficulty breaking into other sectors dominated by companies owned or partially owned by Chinese state firms or major pro-China figures in Hong Kong. Companies may shy away from going head to head with mainland-backed companies for fear of antagonizing Beijing, which will hurt competition and could, in the long term, erode Hong Kong's celebrated efficiency.

UNDER BRITISH RULE, the people of Hong Kong shared most of the rights and freedoms enjoyed by people in Britain (two exceptions were the right of assembly and the right to elect their own leaders). They could come and go as they pleased, criticize the government, join trade unions, and strike. The colony boasted the freest press in Asia, which enticed many international publications to base their Asia operations there. This atmosphere of freedom contributed to the free-wheeling nature of Hong Kong's economy.

China has promised to allow the people of Hong Kong to continue enjoying all of these freedoms after 1997. But few believe that promise will be kept. Observers point to Beijing's attitude towards the press in Hong Kong as a sign that other freedoms will also be curtailed after 1997. Both the Joint Declaration and the Basic Law guarantee freedom of the press. Since the Beijing massacre in June 1989, however, Beijing has declared war on the

---

* Cathay never revealed who made the initial approach, but most analysts in Hong Kong believed it was the airline.

Hong Kong media. Some journalists have been banned from covering major events in China. When a Chinese speech writer leaked to a Hong Kong newspaper a copy of Jiang Zemin's address to the fourteenth National Party Congress in October 1992, he received a ten-year sentence for "selling state secrets overseas." At Jiang's insistence, the courts increased his term to life in prison. A mainland-born journalist working for Louis Cha's *Ming Pao* daily was arrested in Beijing shortly thereafter on charges of spying. Beijing is clearly trying to intimidate Hong Kong reporters and their sources.

China also launched a campaign to have friendly Hong Kongers take over publications critical of Beijing. A prime target was the English-language *South China Morning Post*, which Chinese officials felt was too pro-British. This disturbed them not just because the *Post* was influential in Hong Kong, but because it was the West's window on the colony. Xu Jiatun, the former director of the Xinhua News Agency, revealed in his memoirs that in the mid-1980s his agency considered buying the *Post* or starting its own English-language newspaper. Neither idea ever got off the ground because of a lack of coordination and financing. During the drafting of the Basic Law, Chinese officials approached billionaires Li Ka-shing and Y.K. Pao about the possibility of starting an English-language newspaper. Apparently, neither wanted to get involved in a turf war between Britain and China. A source familiar with China's proposal says neither saw it as a money-making proposition and both declined.

In the early 1990s, T.S. Lo sunk a considerable amount of his family's fortune in *Window*, an English-language weekly that covered Hong Kong and China. It was widely seen as a mouthpiece for Beijing and had little influence. Then, in August 1993, Beijing got what it wanted—someone more friendly to China at the helm of the *Post*. Robert Kuok, a Malaysian Chinese billionaire who owns, among other things, the Shangri-La Hotel Group, and who has substantial investments in China, purchased a 34.9 percent stake in the *Post* from Rupert Murdoch for $349 million. Earlier, Kuok had taken a major stake in Hong Kong's English-language television station. Kuok insists that he is not fronting for the Chinese and that he will maintain the paper's editorial integrity, but that has failed to allay fears in Hong Kong. Even if Kuok has the best intentions, with millions of dollars invested in China, he could easily be pressured by Beijing.

In the first six months under Kuok, there have been no signs that the *Post* is taking a softer line on its China coverage. But should a more hostile regime in Beijing hold Kuok's investments in China hostage and force him to adopt more positive coverage in China, the business community would lose one of its best sources of information on political maneuvering within the Communist Party and the senior levels of Hong Kong government. Other sources may spring up outside of Hong Kong, but it is not clear if the post-1997 regime will allow them to circulate in the Special Administrative Region.

The *Post* is not the only paper to change hands. In 1992, the *Hong Kong Daily News* was taken over by Emperor International Holdings, a major property developer in China. And T.T. Tsui, founder of New China Hong Kong, bought *Pai Shing*, a weekly once known for its fearless criticisms of China. Tsui turned *Pai Shing* into a glossy, general interest magazine. Other media companies have been expanding aggressively in China and will have to practice self-censorship in Hong Kong to remain viable in China. In 1993, Television Broadcasts Ltd., the leading station in Hong Kong, set up a Chinese-language satellite channel, which it hoped to beam into China. In early 1994, it refused to air in Hong Kong a BBC documentary that sharply criticized Mao Zedong and angered China. And media mogul Rupert Murdoch threatened to drop the BBC's twenty-four-hour television news channel from his Star TV in Asia over the same documentary.

China is likely to exert control over the population in Hong Kong the same way she keeps a billion people on the mainland in line—with threats or implied threats. Liberal laws granting freedoms will remain on the statute books and in the Basic Law, but Beijing will likely use the economic clout of its power elite in Hong Kong to intimidate people into sacrificing those freedoms. Many journalists are already practicing self-censorship. Newspapers are deeply concerned about losing advertising from mainland and pro-China companies. Many lawyers and small businesspeople refuse to speak out for fear of reprisals.

Taking away freedoms in Hong Kong might suppress local residents' entrepreneurial zeal. Even if this psychological impact is discounted or dismissed, the lack of freedoms will have real consequences. If people feel they cannot criticize the Hong Kong government openly, there is likely to be less debate over economic policies, which will drastically increase chances that the government will make major mistakes.

Chinese officials and many Hong Kong and Western businesspeople believe that the Hong Kong people will not mind losing certain freedoms as long as they can still make money. The truth is revealed by the thousands of people who are leaving each month to take lower paying jobs in the United States, Canada, and Australia. That trend will be exacerbated if the future government is repressive.

The exodus of professionals and skilled laborers continues at a rate of about 60,000 people a year, according to the Hong Kong government's conservative figures. Some people dismiss the significance of the brain drain, saying that Hong Kong has an almost miraculous ability to bounce back from adversity. They point out that after each crisis in the past—the civil war on the mainland, the riots in 1967, the oil shocks of the 1970s—thousands left, but they were replaced by new and seemingly harder working immigrants. These individuals do not realize that this time is different. After 1997, Hong Kong will no longer hold the same attraction for people on the mainland. It may still enjoy a higher standard of living and more freedom than the rest of the country, but peasants will not risk their lives to reach Hong Kong knowing the People's Liberation Army is also on the other side of the border. Those allowed in legally—or because they bribed someone or had connections—will not share the same work ethic as those who risked their lives to come in the 1950s and 1960s.

The brain drain has already driven up labor costs appreciably. Companies have adapted by bringing in Chinese from Singapore and Malaysia and by hiring Hong Kong people who have returned after obtaining residency abroad. But this raises new concerns. If there is a crisis in China after 1997 similar to the one in Tiananmen Square in 1989, Hong Kong could see tens of thousands of its most skilled workers heading for the exits. The result of losing all those people with foreign passports could be devastating to the economy.

Companies have also been trying to compensate for the brain drain by shifting some functions overseas and by employing people in China to do some white collar jobs, such as bookkeeping and software development. These strategies have kept costs down, but in the long term, they could erode Hong Kong's position as an international center. Companies might find that they cannot hire skilled workers to handle regional responsibilities and shift those functions to other Asian capitals, such as Singapore, which is eager to welcome them.

THROUGHOUT HONG KONG'S history, the British administration provided a buffer that insulated the colony from the effects of turmoil on the mainland. Hong Kong's economy tooled along through China's civil war in the 1940s, through the Great Leap Forward in the 1950s, through the Cultural Revolution in the 1960s, and through the power struggles of the 1970s. One of the colony's great advantages in attracting foreign businesses was that it was an island of stability in a region that had communist insurgencies in Malaysia, Thailand, Indonesia, and the Philippines. The creation of a democratic government in Hong Kong would have created a new (albeit weaker) buffer. An elected administration would be able to make decisions despite confusion in Beijing. Britain and China's failure to introduce such a government means that while the rest of the region is becoming more stable, Hong Kong is becoming less so.

Hong Kong's economic integration with South China has only accelerated in recent years. Hong Kong manufacturers largely avoided the negative effects of the worldwide economic slowdown of the early 1990s by shifting production to China where land and labor were cheap, while maintaining their management and marketing headquarters in Hong Kong. From 1987 to 1992, the colony's exports grew a respectable twenty percent, from $25 billion to $30.2 billion. Over the same period, reexports—that is, goods brought in from China or elsewhere, packaged, and shipped out—skyrocketed by 281 percent, from $23.4 billion to $89.2 billion. Despite greater investments in China by Japanese and American firms, Hong Kong still accounts for two-thirds of the foreign investment there and one-third of the country's total foreign exchange earnings.

Integration with South China, however, is a double-edged sword because it makes Hong Kong more vulnerable to unrest on the mainland. When Chinese troops cracked down on student protestors in Beijing in June 1989, there were reports of fighting between military divisions from different regions. Although the reports were later discredited, they sent shock waves through Hong Kong's economy. U.S. buyers were unsure if Hong Kong companies with factories in Guangdong would be able to fulfill Christmas orders. Had the uncertainty lasted for several months, they would have made purchases elsewhere. The damage to Hong Kong's economy would have been extensive.

The lack of a democratic government in Hong Kong after 1997 compounds the problem because it makes Hong Kong vulnerable politically as well as economically. During the Tiananmen crisis, people in Hong Kong knew that they would be unaffected by the power struggle in China. After 1997, Beijing will exert direct control over Hong Kong. Local residents will fear that if a hard-liner takes over the Chinese government, he might crack down on them. Those with passports might leave. Companies with contracts or partnerships with firms associated with one faction in Beijing could find themselves the victims of retaliation from another group. At the very least, a protracted power struggle in Beijing could leave the local government paralyzed, unable to make important decisions because it cannot get approval from a divided party leadership or because members of the pro-China elite are afraid to make a move that might bring about their own downfall.

So far, Hong Kong has played only a minor role in China's domestic politics. But given its wealth, talent, and organizational abilities, it could find itself being drawn into power struggles in Beijing. Chinese companies in Hong Kong could be the victims of purges launched by one faction against the other. Pretenders to the throne in Beijing might use Hong Kong as a place to raise money and organize campaigns to assume power in China, which could lead to heavy-handed—perhaps even bloody—reprisals.

THE EXTENT TO which Beijing uses the new power elite in Hong Kong to silence its opponents, to obtain an edge in competition, to influence court cases, and to establish centralized control over the economy will depend heavily on the political situation in China itself. The country has gone through dramatic economic changes in the last fifteen years. In 1992 and 1993 the economy grew more than ten percent a year, faster than that of any other country in the world. Foreign businesspeople and economists who visited China during those heady days believed that Communism was all but dead there.

If Communism is swept away and China becomes a democratic capitalist country, Hong Kong would enjoy the biggest boom in its history. It would be to China what New York was to the United States in the late 1800s, the leading commercial and financial center for an economy on the cusp of extraordinary growth. However, the prospects of Communism being replaced by a capitalist democracy are remote.

Since 1949, the Communist Party has succeeded in improving the standard of living of the vast majority of China's one billion people, and it still enjoys considerable support in the countryside, where agricultural reforms have benefitted China's 800 million peasants. The demonstration in Tiananmen Square was a result of rising prices, which hurt urban intellectuals who live on fixed salaries. They directed their anger over their declining standard of living at the party because corrupt cadres were getting rich by buying goods at state-set prices and selling them on the free market for a huge profit, thus helping to push up prices. Inflation has been brought down, and salaries have risen in urban areas. The party also launched an anticorruption campaign in 1993 to help assuage the people's anger.

Having witnessed the collapse of the Communist Party in the Soviet Union, Chinese leaders are trying to avoid a similar fate by working harder to boost the standard of living of the Chinese people. Stock markets have been introduced in Shanghai and Shenzhen to enable them to invest. Labor restrictions have been relaxed to allow people to switch from one job to another more freely. New reforms are continually being tested.

The recurring battles between the reformers and conservatives in Beijing have not been over whether or not there should be changes to the economic system, but rather over the pace and extent of those changes. Deng encouraged a faster pace of economic growth and of reform in 1992 to bolster his political power so that he could stack the upper echelon of the party with his supporters. The conservatives believed that faster growth would create problems, such as infrastructure bottlenecks and inflation. They wanted to proceed at a more measured pace, to test the results of reforms in one area before extending them to the rest of the country.

According to academics, economists, and journalists with good contacts in Beijing, the vast majority of middle-ranking party members are technocrats, the sons and daughters of the first generation of party leaders. Because of the privileged position of their parents, they went to the best universities in China and received further training in the Soviet Union in the 1950s. They became scientists and engineers. Many worked in China's nuclear weapons and space programs in the 1960s. They were put into positions of power in the government and party in the mid-1980s by Deng, who wanted to replace the aging conservatives who were blocking his reforms. This new generation of potential leaders was less ideological and more open to reform, but they were scientists by temperament and training. They favored a steady, cautious approach to reform with experimentation to prove a thesis before it was introduced nationwide. Moreover, they opposed radical reform because if things went wrong it would threaten their own privileged positions.

These technocrats will likely assume full control of the party, the government, and the economy as the last of China's aging leaders die off. They will likely rule as an oligarchy to compensate for their lack of legitimacy. They will maintain the open-door policy and continue to reform the economy, albeit at a more measured pace than under Deng.

Such a scenario bodes well for Hong Kong. If China proceeds too rapidly down the road to reform there will be endless cycles of overheating and retrenchment, which affect Hong Kong's economy. In the worst case scenario, rapid reform could undermine the control of the central government, and China could split apart and degenerate into a civil war that would cripple Hong Kong. A moderate government in China will maintain the stability Hong Kong needs to thrive. The technocrats will still want to exercise control over Hong Kong through the power elite, and they are more likely to centralize control over its economy. But they may be less likely to engage in unfair government policies and interfere in court cases than either a conservative regime, which would want to maximize control over Hong Kong, or a liberal regime, which would want to maximize the economic benefits of Hong Kong.

Even if there is a dramatic upheaval in China and the communist system is swept away, there is no guarantee that the new government will be any less totalitarian than the current regime. China has never had a democratic system. It is a large, fractious country. Any new leader will need to maintain control over the provinces to prevent the country from splitting up. Thus, he will likely maintain the communist systems of control. He will pay particularly close attention to Hong Kong—the richest, best-organized, and most Westernized city in the country—since it will be potentially the biggest threat to him. The power elite under such a regime would not be any less unified or control-oriented than under a communist system.

Whoever emerges as Deng's successor will have serious problems to deal with. China must increase energy production, free the labor market, relax price control, boost efficiency, develop a financial sector, and introduce a legal system that will protect businesses operating there. Beijing is likely to have successes and failures as the country moves down the road to modernization. Economic growth is likely to continue to be erratic and geographically uneven. This will present constant challenges for foreign businesses operating in Hong Kong, as well as in China.

EVEN WITH A slower rate of economic growth and a more moderate pace of reform, China will still be a magnet for companies around the world looking to benefit from the country's economic development, or seeking to sell products to the growing middle class (estimated in 1993 to be about 200 million strong). Hong Kong's well-developed physical infrastructure, highly trained work force, communication and transportation links to the outside world, and cultural affinity to China make it the obvious base for foreign companies doing business in China for years to come.

It will also serve as a commercial and financial center for South China. In 1992 and 1993, several mainland companies were listed on the Hong Kong Stock Exchange, and a number of Chinese banks and investment companies issued Eurobonds in Hong Kong. Foreign investors and fund managers were eager to cash in on the booming economy in China. The only way to do that was to invest in the Hong Kong market. The flood of foreign money pushed the Hang Seng Index from 5,512 at the start of the year to almost 12,000 by late December, making it the world's best performing market in 1993.

The negative factors that the transition to Chinese rule will have on Hong Kong are unlikely to deter companies from setting up in Hong Kong to do business in China. Companies will go anywhere money can be made and will endure difficult conditions—corruption, inefficiency, biased courts, unfair competition—for the sake of earning big profits. These conditions will still be far worse on the mainland, so Hong Kong will have an advantage over other Chinese cities.

However, it is unlikely that international companies will expose their regional operations to the risks of a legal system that cannot protect their assets, to a government that could blacklist them and force them to lose business, to competitive disadvantages in getting information, to political uncertainty, and perhaps to social turmoil. Virtually all major regional operations in Hong Kong have looked at, or are beginning to look at, moving out of Hong Kong. Most have found it better in the short term to remain there, but after 1997, there is likely to be a slow but steady—and quiet—exodus of regional operations to other cities within the Asia-Pacific region. Within twenty years of 1997, Hong Kong could well be almost exclusively a Chinese financial and commercial center.

Glossary of Names

Akers-Jones, David Hong Kong civil servant; chief secretary from 1985 to 1987.

Ann, T.K. Industrialist; former member of Hong Kong's Executive and Legislative Councils; vice-chairperson of the Basic Law Drafting Committee; chairperson of the Basic Law Consultative Committee.

Boyd, John British diplomat; political adviser to Hong Kong's governor from 1985 to 1987.

Bramall, Edwin British field marshal; commander of British forces in Hong Kong from 1973 to 1976; chief of Britain's defense staffs from 1982 to 1985.

Bryan, Paul British member of Parliament; chairperson of the All Party Hong Kong Parliamentary Group from 1974 to 1987.

Burrows, Fred British Foreign Office legal adviser.

Carrington, Lord British foreign secretary from 1979 to 1982.

Cater, Jack Hong Kong civil servant; chief secretary from 1978 to 1981; Hong Kong's commissioner in London from 1982 to 1984.

Cha Chi-ming Conservative Hong Kong businessman; appointed by China in 1985 to the Basic Law Drafting Committee; member of the political and relationship subgroups.

Cha, Louis Publisher of the independent *Ming Pao* daily; appointed by China in 1985 to be a member of the Basic Law Drafting Committee; coconvener of the political subgroup.

Cheng Kai-nam Hong Kong teacher; member of the pro-China Federation of Education Workers; a moderate elected in 1985 to the Basic Law Consultative Committee.

Chung, S.Y. Hong Kong businessman; appointed to the Legislative Council in 1965 and to the Executive Council in 1972; senior member of the Executive Council from 1980 to 1988.

Clift, Richard (Dick) British diplomat; head of the Hong Kong and General Department of the Foreign Office from 1979 to 1984; political adviser to the Hong Kong governor from 1987 to 1989.

Cradock, Percy British diplomat; ambassador to Beijing from 1978 to 1983; head of the British team that negotiated the settlement of Hong Kong's future from 1982 to 1984; adviser to the prime minister on foreign affairs from 1984 to 1992.

Donald, Alan British diplomat; ambassador to China from 1988 to 1991.

Dunn, Lydia Hong Kong businesswoman; member of the Legislative Council from 1976 to 1988 and senior member from 1985 to 1988; appointed to the Executive Council in 1982 and senior member since 1988.

Ehrman, William British diplomat; member of the British team that negotiated the settlement of Hong Kong's future from 1983 to 1984; became political adviser to the Hong Kong governor in 1989.

Evans, Richard British diplomat; ambassador to Beijing from 1984 to 1988; member of the British team that negotiated the settlement of Hong Kong's future in 1984.

Ford, David Hong Kong civil servant; chief secretary from 1987 to 1993.

Galsworthy, Anthony British diplomat; member of the British team that negotiated the settlement of Hong Kong's future from 1982 to 1984; became the chief British representative to the Sino-British Joint Liaison Group in 1989.

Glenarthur, Simon (Lord) British Member of Parliament; minister of state at the Foreign Office responsible for overseeing Hong Kong affairs from 1987 to 1989.

Haddon-Cave, Philip Hong Kong civil servant; chief secretary from 1981 to 1985.

Heath, Edward British prime minister from 1970 to 1974.

Howe, Geoffrey British foreign secretary from 1983 to 1989.

Hu Yaobang General secretary of the Chinese Communist Party from 1982 to January 1987. Died April 15, 1989.

Hua Guofeng Chinese premier from 1976 to 1981.

Huang Hua China's permanent representative to the United Nations from 1971 to 1976; foreign minister from 1976 to 1982.

Huang, Rayson Former vice-chancellor of Hong Kong University; former Legislative Councilor; appointed by China in 1985 to be a member of the Basic Law Drafting Committee; coconvener of the relationship subgroup.

Hurd, Douglas British foreign secretary since 1989.

Ji Pengfei Director of China's Hong Kong and Macao Affairs Office from 1983 to 1991.

Kan, Y.K. Hong Kong businessman; member of the Executive Council from 1966 to 1980 and senior member from 1974 to 1980; a close adviser to Governor Murray MacLehose.

Ke Zaishuo Chinese diplomat; member of the Chinese team that negotiated the settlement of Hong Kong's future from 1982 to 1984; appointed senior Chinese representative to the Joint Liaison Group in 1985; member of the Basic Law Drafting Committee's relationship subgroup.

Lee, Allen Hong Kong businessman; appointed to the Legislative Council in 1978 and senior member from 1988 to 1993; appointed to the Executive Council in 1985.

Lee, Martin Hong Kong lawyer; elected member of the Legislative Council since 1985; appointed by China in 1985 to be a member of the Basic Law Drafting Committee; the leader of the crusade for greater democracy in Hong Kong both before and after 1997.

Lee, Q.W. Hong Kong banker; member of Hong Kong's Executive Council from 1972 to 1978 and 1983 to 1988.

Li Hou Deputy director of China's Hong Kong and Macao Affairs Office; member of the Basic Law Drafting Committee; a key functionary in executing Beijing's Hong Kong policies.

Li Ka-shing Hong Kong property developer; the richest man in the colony; appointed by China in 1985 to be a member of the Basic Law Drafting Committee.

Li, Simon Former Hong Kong judge; appointed by China in 1985 to be a member of the Basic Law Drafting Committee; coconvener of the subgroup dealing with the rights and obligations of Hong Kong residents after 1997; member of the political subgroup.

Liu, Dorothy Outspoken pro-China lawyer in Hong Kong; appointed by China in 1985 to be a member of the Basic Law Drafting Committee; member of the political and relationship subgroups.

Lo, T.S. Hong Kong lawyer; appointed to the Legislative Council in 1974 and to the Executive Council in 1980; resigned from both councils in early 1985 and sought closer ties with Beijing; appointed by China in 1985 to the Basic Law Consultative Committee.

Lo, Vincent Hong Kong businessman; member of the Basic Law Consultative Committee from 1985 to 1990; leader of the conservative Group of 89.

Luce, Richard British Member of Parliament; minister of state at the Foreign Office responsible for overseeing Hong Kong affairs from 1983 to 1985.

Lu Ping Deputy director and later director of China's Hong Kong and Macao Affairs Office; member of the Basic Law Drafting Committee; a key functionary in executing Beijing's Hong Kong policies.

MacLehose, Murray British diplomat; Hong Kong governor from 1971 to 1982.

Maude, Francis British Member of Parliament; minister of state at the Foreign Office responsible for overseeing Hong Kong affairs from 1989 to 1990.

McLaren, Robin British diplomat; member of the British team that negotiated the settlement of Hong Kong's future from 1982 to 1984; political adviser to the Hong Kong governor from 1981 to 1984; senior British representative to the Joint Liaison Group from 1987 to 1989; appointed British ambassador to China in 1991.

Owen, David British foreign secretary from 1977 to 1979.

Pao, Y.K. Hong Kong shipping tycoon; among the richest men in the colony; appointed by China in 1985 to be a vice-chairperson of the Basic Law Drafting Committee.

Patten, Chris British politician; appointed governor of Hong Kong in 1992.

Renton, Timothy British Member of Parliament; minister of state at the Foreign Office responsible for overseeing Hong Kong affairs from 1985 to 1987.

Shao Tianren Chinese legal expert on foreign affairs; member of the Chinese team that negotiated the Joint Declaration from 1982 to 1984; member of the Basic Law Drafting Committee; coconvener of its relationship subgroup.

Szeto Wah Elected member of the Legislative Council since 1985; appointed by China in 1985 to be a member of the Basic Law Drafting Committee; a close associate of Martin Lee.

Tam, Maria Hong Kong lawyer; appointed to the Legislative Council in 1981 and to the Executive Council in 1983; only member of the Executive

Council to be appointed by China in 1985 to sit on the Basic Law Drafting Committee; member of the political subgroup.

Wilson, David British diplomat; political adviser to Governor MacLehose from 1977 to 1981; member of the British team that negotiated the settlement of Hong Kong's future in 1984; senior British representative to the Joint Liaison Group from 1985 to 1987; governor of Hong Kong from 1987 to 1992.

Wu Jianfan Chinese legal expert; member of the Basic Law Drafting Committee; member of the relationship subgroup.

Wu, Dr. Raymond Hong Kong medical practitioner; appointed by China in 1985 to sit on the Basic Law Drafting Committee; appointed coconvener of the political subgroup when Louis Cha resigned from the body; a founding member of the conservative Group of 89.

Wu Xueqian China's foreign minister from 1982 to 1988.

Xiao Weiyun Chinese legal expert; member of the Basic Law Drafting Committee; coconvener of the political subgroup; played a key role in the formation of Hong Kong's future political system.

Xu Chongde Chinese legal expert; a member of the Basic Law Drafting Committee; member of the political subgroup.

Xu Jiatun Director of the Xinhua News Agency in Hong Kong and China's most senior representative in the colony from 1983 to 1990; member of the Basic Law Drafting Committee.

Yang Shangkun Chinese president from 1988 to 1992.

Yao Guang Chinese vice-foreign minister from 1982 to 1986 and chief negotiator on Hong Kong from January 1983 until January 1984.

Youde, Edward British diplomat; Hong Kong governor from 1982 until he died in December 1986; Hong Kong's representative in the Sino-British negotiations from 1982 to 1984.

Zhang Wenjin Chinese vice-foreign minister from 1978 to December 1982.

Zhao Ziyang Chinese premier from 1980 to 1987; Chinese Communist Party general secretary from 1987 to 1989.

Zhou Nan Chinese diplomat; member of the Chinese team that negotiated the Joint Declaration; head of the Chinese team in 1984; member of the Basic Law Drafting Committee and a key player in executing China's Hong Kong policy; appointed director of the Xinhua News Agency in Hong Kong in 1990.

Index